AFTER OUR LIKENESS

*The Church as the Image
of the Trinity*

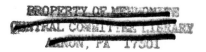

SACRA DOCTRINA

Christian Theology for a Postmodern Age

AFTER
OUR LIKENESS

The Church as the Image of the Trinity

Miroslav Volf

WILLIAM B. EERDMANS PUBLISHING COMPANY
GRAND RAPIDS, MICHIGAN / CAMBRIDGE, U.K.

© 1998 Wm. B. Eerdmans Publishing Co.
255 Jefferson Ave. S.E., Grand Rapids, Michigan 49503 /
P.O. Box 163, Cambridge CB3 9PU U.K.

Printed in the United States of America

03 02 01 00 99 98   7 6 5 4 3 2 1

Library of Congress Cataloging-in-Publication Data

Volf, Miroslav.
After our likeness: The church as the image of the trinity/
Miroslav Volf.
p.   cm.
Includes bibliographical references.
ISBN 0-8028-4440-5 (pbk.: alk. paper)
1. Christian communities. 2. Religions — Relations. 3. Church —
History of doctrines. 4. Trinity. 5. Catholic Church — Relations —
Orthodox Eastern Church. 6. Orthodox Eastern Church — Relations —
Catholic Church. I. Title.
BV4405.V65   1998
262 — dc21   97-39593
CIP

Contents

CONTENTS

Contents

To my parents, Dragutin and Mira

Preface

All the attempts to trace the origins of this book take me back into the foggy regions of my earliest childhood memories. I was born while my father was a student of theology, and I grew up in a parsonage in the city of Novi Sad (Yugoslavia) at the time when Marshall Tito and his communists exercised their uncontested rule. It would not be quite accurate to say that my parents *worked* for the church; they *lived* for that small community of believers entrusted to their care. As children, my sister and I were, so to speak, sucked into the orbit of that community's life. Our home was in the church, and the church had insinuated itself into our home. We were part of it because it had become part of us.

As a child, I resented both the expectations of sainthood placed on me by the church folk (for whom I was the pastor's mischievous son who ought to know better) and the blatant discrimination I encountered in school (where I was a gifted but despised son of "the enemy of the people"). Though such resentments were at one time so real that I vowed never to follow in my father's footsteps, I have since cheerfully broken that vow and the resentments have faded away. What remains indelibly inscribed not so much in my memory as in my very soul is the deep and unwavering commitment — love, I think, is the right word — that my parents had for that community. It was a strange group of people living in difficult times. So many bizarre characters, whose petty battles had much more to do with their own personal frustrations than with the Gospel of Jesus Christ! And then the repeated visits to our home by apparatchiks who, I suppose, wanted to underline in person what the inconspicuous presence of informers in the church communicated clearly enough, namely, that the state had drawn lines that could not be transgressed with impunity. Yet despite the petty conflicts within and persistent pressures from without, for

ix

over thirty years my parents kept giving that community much of their time and energy and a good deal of their very selves. Now as I look back from a distance I see what I failed to recognize clearly at the time but what nevertheless shaped me profoundly: their commitments mirrored the commitment of Christ, who "loved the church and gave himself up for her" (Eph. 5:25). Without that love — a love which was both Christ's and theirs — I would never have become a Christian and never gone to be a student of theology. And I would certainly never have written a book in which I join the chorus of the tradition that in all seriousness claims that in some real sense these fragile and frustrating communities called churches are images of the triune God. It is therefore appropriate that I dedicate this book to them.

Life in the small Christian community in Novi Sad taught me two basic ecclesiological lessons even before I possessed theological language to express them. The first lesson: *no church without the reign of God.* The church lives from something and toward something that is greater than the church itself. When the windows facing toward the reign of God get closed, darkness descends upon the churches and the air becomes heavy. When the windows facing toward the reign of God are opened, the life-giving breath and light of God give the churches fresh hope. The second lesson: *no reign of God without the church.* Just as the life of the churches depends on the reign of God, so also does the vitality of the *hope* for the reign of God depend on the communities of faith. We come to recognize the fresh breath of God and the light of God that renew the creation only because there are communities called churches — communities that keep alive the memory of the crucified Messiah and the hope for the Coming One. Without communities born and sustained by the Spirit, the hope for the reign of God would die out. Would the Christian community in Novi Sad have survived let alone thrived if it had not directed its gaze beyond itself to that city whose architect and builder is God? Would the hope for that city have survived in a hostile and indifferent environment without this community and many other communities who witnessed to it in word and deed? The same holds true for the churches in Berlin and Los Angeles, in Madras and Nairobi, and for the hope in the reign of God in Africa, the Americas, Asia, Australia, and Europe. These two lessons about the relation between the reign of God and the church form the theological framework of the book.

My interest in the topic and the theological framework of the book stem from my early ecclesial experiences. The content of the book — its themes, accents, perspectives, and arguments — stem mainly from my ecumenical engagement. When I entered the world of ecumenism in the mid eighties, *communio* was just emerging as the central ecumenical idea. From the outset, and above all under the influence of Catholic and Orthodox theologians, the ecclesiological use of *communio* was placed in the larger framework of trinitarian *communio.* The present volume, whose theme is the relation between the Trinity and community, is both the fruit of ecumenical dialogues and my own contribution to them. In the most general way, I am trying to show that the typically Protestant — above all "Free Church" — form of ecclesial individualism and the classical Catholic and Orthodox forms of ecclesiological holism are not the only adequate ecclesiological alternatives, but that an appropriate understanding of the Trinity suggests a more nuanced and promising model of the relationship between person and community in the church. The goal of my efforts is an ecumenical ecclesiology — not in the sense of a construct that draws on all traditions but is rooted in none, but in the sense that all the great themes of this unmistakably Protestant ecclesiological melody are enriched by Catholic and Orthodox voices.

In the process of writing the book, I have incurred many debts, most of them so large that I can repay them only with a word of sincere thanks. Originally, the manuscript was submitted as a *Habilitationsschrift* — a dissertation required for a postdoctoral degree — at the Evangelical Theological Faculty of the University of Tübingen. I have revised it for publication and made it a bit more user friendly. Professor Jürgen Moltmann, who served as the supervisor, not only was a ready source of theological wisdom but gave me as much space as I needed in my research. Professor Oswald Bayer was a careful second reader. In the context of official ecumenical dialogues and in private conversations Professor Hervé-Marie Legrand of the Institut Catholique, Paris, made extraordinarily informed and nuanced comments. He was also my host during the memorable month and a half that my wife and I spent in Paris — researching, writing, and enjoying a Parisian spring. The library Saulchoir provided the workspace, and Marie-Thérèse Denzer kindly let us use her apartment. My colleague at Fuller Theological Seminary, Professor Robert Banks, read a good deal of the manuscript with the competent eye of both a New Testament scholar and a practical theologian. My students at Fuller Theological Seminary, Pasadena, California, and at Evangelical Theological Faculty, Osijek, Croatia, heard most of the material as lectures; their frowns, yawns, wide-open eyes, and smiles, and not just their many good comments, shaped its contents.

An earlier version of the last chapter was delivered as a lecture at the University of Salamanca (Spain) in April 1991 at a conference on the catholicity of the local church and then published in Spanish and English.[1] Portions of an earlier version of the third chapter were delivered as a lecture at the Institute

---

1. "Aportaciones ecumenicas al tema del coloquio: causa nostra agitur? Iglesias liberes," in *Iglesias Locales y Catolicidad: Actas del Coloquio International celebrado en Salamanca, 2-7 de abril de 1991*, ed. H. Legrand et al., 701-731 (Salamanca: Universidad Pontificia de Salamanca, 1992); "Catholicity of 'Two and Three': A Free Church Reflection on the Catholicity of the Local Church," *The Jurist* 52 (1992): 525-546.

for Ecumenical Research in Strasbourg (France). Discussions at both institutions sharpened my understanding of the issues and contributed to the clarity of my thinking.

Most of the book was written during a year and a half that I was a fellow of the Alexander von Humboldt Foundation (1989-1991), which also supported its publication with a generous grant. Fuller Theological Seminary awarded me a sabbatical to work on the project. Bruno Kern of Matthias Grünewald Press showed enough interest in the manuscript to help make a book out of it. Neukirchener Press agreed to function as a copublisher, thereby making the book more accessible to a Protestant public. Marianne Bröckel, who does such a marvelous job of being my German mother, spent many hours pondering difficult sentences in order to help me, a nonnative speaker, express my thoughts in proper German. She also did the tedious work of correcting the proofs and making the indexes. Finally, Judy, my wife, knows best how grateful I am for all she does and, above all, for the wonderful human being that she is. She also knows that without her advice and support I would never even have started, let alone finished, the book.

Tübingen, May 1996

Introduction to the
American Edition

A book is always written for a given context — for a linguistic community living at a particular time and place with particular shared beliefs, institutions, and practices.[1] From an author's perspective, it is unfortunate that a translator can translate only the book but not its context. But then, an author can often help the imagination of the readers by situating the book in its context. That is what I propose to do here: I will indicate how this book relates to some of the important American ecclesiological developments.

I will begin by briefly stating what I am after and conclude by naming some issues that I consider of immense importance but could not address within the confines of the book. In the middle sections I will first place my argument in the context of some developments in feminist and "believers' church" ecclesiologies. Though the two are by no means all that is happening on the North American academic scene with regard to ecclesiology, in many respects they represent the most significant trends (most significant, that is, if one excepts Catholic, Orthodox, and ecumenical ecclesiological efforts with which the book deals directly). Second, I will touch briefly on my background interest in what Andrew F. Walls calls "the transmission of faith"[2] and on how it relates to recent sociological studies of American congregations and to some practical experiments with alternative forms of ecclesiality.

Put most broadly, my topic is the relation between persons and community in Christian theology. The focus is the community of grace, the Christian

1. MacIntyre, *Whose Justice?* 373-88.
2. Walls, *Missionary Movement.*

1

church. The point of departure is the thought of the first Baptist, John Smyth, and the notion of church as "gathered community" that he shared with Radical Reformers. The purpose of the book is to counter the tendencies toward individualism in Protestant ecclesiology and to suggest a viable understanding of the church in which both person and community are given their proper due. The ultimate goal is to spell out a vision of the church as an image of the triune God. The road I have taken is that of a sustained and critical ecumenical dialogue with Catholic and Orthodox ecclesiology in the persons of their more or less official representatives.

Though feminist theology is complex and multifaceted, the major thrust of *feminist ecclesiology* can be fairly summarized by naming titles by two of feminist theology's most prominent proponents, Elisabeth Schüssler Fiorenza's *Discipleship of Equals* and Letty M. Russell's *Church in the Round*. In Russell's terminology, the main task of a feminist ecclesiology is to dismantle the model of the church as a "household ruled by a patriarch" and replace it with the model of "a household where everyone gathers around the common table to break bread and share table talk and hospitality."[3]

A major strand of my argument stands in close affinity with this egalitarian agenda of feminist ecclesiology. I argue that the presence of Christ, which constitutes the church, is mediated not simply through the ordained ministers but through the whole congregation, that the whole congregation functions as *mater ecclesia* to the children engendered by the Holy Spirit, and that the whole congregation is called to engage in ministry and make decisions about leadership roles. I do not specifically address the ordination of women; I simply assume it. Everything in my ecclesiology speaks in its favor, and I find none of the biblical, anthropological, christological, and theological arguments against it persuasive — neither those propounded by fundamentalist Protestant groups nor those proffered by the teaching office of the Roman Catholic Church.

Another strand of my argument is closely related to a widely shared feminist critique of individualism. A rejection of the "separative self" and a conceptualization of a self situated in a web of relationships, so prominent both in feminist philosophy and theological anthropology,[4] has so far, however, not been a major theme in feminist ecclesiology. But it is prominent in recent developments in "believers' church" ecclesiology.[5] Traditionally, believers' church ecclesiology has championed both voluntarism and egalitarianism — voluntarism in the sense that the incorporative act is "deliberate on the part of the candidate and the community alike"[6] and egalitarianism in the sense that the responsibility for the

---

3. Russell, *Church in the Round*, 42.
4. See Keller, *Broken Web*; Weir, *Sacrificial Logics*.
5. For the term, see Williams, "Believer's Church."
6. McClendon, "Believer's Church," 5.

2

corporate life of the church ultimately rests on the broad shoulders of the whole local community. Especially under the conditions of advanced modernity (or postmodernity), the two emphases have often conspired to lead down the paths either of rugged individualism or of its obverse, coercive authoritarianism.

An important and widespread movement has emerged, however, seeking to reclaim the communal dimensions of the believers' church heritage. It is associated with names such as John Howard Yoder, James W. McClendon Jr., and others. In "Re-Envisioning Baptist Identity," for instance, a group of Baptist theologians seeks to find a way between two well-trodden paths, the one taken by those "who would shackle God's freedom to a narrow biblical interpretation and a coercive hierarchy of authority" and the other followed by those "who would, in the name of freedom, sever freedom from our membership in the body of Christ and the community's legitimate authority, confusing the gift of God with notions of autonomy or libertarian theories."[7]

A critique of ecclesial individualism and a proposal of an alternative that avoids a retreat into old-style hierarchical holism are at the very center of my interest here. Voluntarism and egalitarianism are goods that must be preserved, but they must be redeemed from their own dark shadows — from the false autonomy of self-enclosed individuals whose relationships are at bottom contractual and whose attachment lasts only "until better return is available elsewhere."[8] For such redemption to take place, we must learn to think of free and equal persons as communal beings from the outset, rather than construing their belonging as a result simply of their "free" decisions. Hence a dual emphasis in the book on community and on persons, on belonging and on choice (which itself must be properly understood as a response to a divine summons). The two are separable only for analytic and strategic purposes. When we examine the nature of ecclesial sociality, we look at it either from the angle of community or from the angle of persons; when we seek to correct the ills of individualism and authoritarianism, we emphasize either belonging or choice. But whatever we do, we must hold in view both together.

The consequences of the dual emphasis on person and community for the construction of the ecclesial self are significant: it is a self that is always "inhabited" or "indwelled" by others. In suggesting this complex notion of the self as inhabited by others toward the end of the book — "catholic personality" is the term I use — I go a step beyond both feminist and believers' church ecclesiologies. Newer feminist reflection on the doctrine of God and anthropology has already moved in this direction.[9] Except for process thought[10],

---

7. "Re-Envisioning Baptist Identity," 8.
8. Luntley, *Reason, Truth and Self*, 190.
9. See Jones, "This God."
10. See Suchocki, *God, Christ, Church*, 129-98.

however, ecclesiology remains so far innocent of these developments. On this matter, as on many others in this book, I take my lead from the notion of identity inscribed in the doctrine of the Trinity and, in dialogue with a Catholic notion of an *anima ecclesiastica* (Ratzinger) and an Orthodox notion of a "catholic person" (Zizioulas), try to make fruitful the idea of the internality of others in the self for Protestant ecclesiology.[11]

On the whole, neither feminist nor believers' church ecclesiological thought seeks to root itself in the *doctrine of the Trinity*. The believers' church ecclesiology echoes in this respect a long tradition in Protestant theology in general.[12] Only recently, in *The Trinity and the Kingdom of God*, Jürgen Moltmann has led the way in connecting the divine and ecclesial communities. He has, however, offered no more than a brief sketch of a trinitarian ecclesiology, sharply focused on the issue of "hierarchy" vs. "equality."[13] In *God for Us*, feminist theologian Catherine LaCugna has made significant programmatic remarks about the relation between the Trinity and the church.[14] It is no accident that LaCugna is a Catholic theologian, and that Moltmann's trinitarian reflections owe much to impulses from Orthodox theology. For a consistent connecting of ecclesial community with the divine community we need to turn toward mainstream Catholic and Orthodox thought. Except for the more recent theologians, however, even there the relation is more affirmed than carefully reflected on. Moreover, as I have tried to show, in Catholic and Orthodox thought earthly hierarchies tend to mirror the heavenly one. Given the conflictual nature of all social realities, the church not excepted, a hierarchical notion of the Trinity ends up underwriting an authoritarian practice in the church. In contrast, I have tried to develop a nonhierarchical but truly communal ecclesiology based on a nonhierarchical doctrine of the Trinity.[15]

More than either of the two traditions of ecclesiological thought mentioned, I am interested in the *transmission of faith*. Feminist theologians fear that if one concentrates too much on the transmission, what will end up passed on is oppressive faith — beliefs and practices that perpetuate sexist ideology and systematically exclude more than half of their members from even the possibility of holding an office. Some believers' church theologians, on the other hand, fear that concern for transmission entails acculturation, which in turn spells betrayal in the very act of transmission — churches stripped of crosses and of anything else that offends shallow suburban sensibilities. I share both concerns. Yet if the Christian faith is worth believing, it must be worth passing

---

11. See Volf, *Exclusion and Embrace*.
12. See Gunton, "Church on Earth."
13. Moltmann, *Trinity and Kingdom*, 200-202.
14. LaCugna, *God for Us*, 401-403.
15. See also Volf, "Trinity Is Social Program."

4

on. And if it is worth passing on, then it is mandatory to reflect on how this is most responsibly and effectively done, above all, to forestall passing on a faith that is either loaded with oppressive baggage or emptied of its proper content. My concern is, however, not that of a pragmatic missiologist, who tends to concentrate on the technique because the primary goal is to increase either the number of converts or the utility of social effects. My concern is rather that of a constructive theologian, who seeks to develop an ecclesiology that will facilitate culturally appropriate — which is to say, both culturally *sensitive* and culturally *critical* — social embodiments of the Gospel.

Combined interest in the relation between person and community and social embodiment of the Gospel has led me to enter occasionally the world of sociology. Not that I am joining sociologists as they spread their wings at dusk and, like Hegel's philosophers, with an eye of an owl gaze upon life grown old. I am a theologian, and my task is not mainly to gaze upon withering life, but to help infuse it with new vibrancy and vision. It would be presumptuous and wrong-headed, however, to imagine that a theologian can, by a few strokes of the pen, undo history and return the church to its youth. To put it differently, a theologian comes to the subject neither at the end nor at the beginning, but in the middle — to a pilgrim church in the midst of its own history that is lived in a culture with its own past and its own future. A theologian must always start with what is already there. And this is where sociology, together with other related disciplines, comes in. Theology needs help in understanding the social shapes of a pilgrim church in changing cultural contexts.

Help, I said, not orders. A theologian should be ready to learn, even to be told what to learn, but should never give up the prerogative of ultimately deciding when and from whom help is needed and how best to use it. So I make no apologies for a piecemeal and occasional appeal to social scientists — Max Weber, Ferdinand Tönnies, Talcott Parsons, Niklas Luhmann, Peter L. Berger, and Robert Wuthnow, to name just a few. From my perspective, this is what I *ought* to be doing. Had I written the book in the United States, I would have paid closer attention, among other things, to recent studies of American congregations[16] — and treated them in the same ad hoc fashion as I treat the thinkers mentioned earlier. Had I done so, my sense is that I would have found many of my assumptions confirmed.

An interest in the transmission of faith has led me to write with a side glance at today's *thriving churches* — thriving at least on the surface and if one is to judge by the level of commitment and enthusiasm of their members. Most of them are in the Third World, and their vibrancy has transformed Christian faith from a predominantly Western to a "predominantly non-Western reli-

---

16. See Ammerman, *Congregation and Community;* Wind and Lewis, *American Congregations.*

5

gion."[17] Constructive theologians in the West, and not just missiologists, are well advised to attend to the practice of these churches in order to learn from their explicit and implicit ecclesiologies and theologies.

It is also high time for constructive theologians, and not just practical theologians, to take seriously the vast experiment in ecclesial practice taking place in this country. Had I written the book here, I would have attended carefully to this experiment, including the so-called megachurches. True, some of these churches are best described with a term meant as a compliment but that in fact comes dangerously close to being an insult — successfully "marketed churches."[18] To the extent that the description fits, these churches are a case in point of how pervasive in American culture is the transformation of everything and everyone into "manageable objects and marketable commodities."[19] When the Big Three supplant the Holy Three as the model of the church, prophetic rage is in order, not congratulation — sackcloth and ashes, not celebration.

Others will have to judge how widespread is the selling out of the church in the marketplace of desire.[20] At least some megachurches are, however, making a good effort to resist the seduction of the market — at least as good an effort as most other churches. Take the most celebrated of the megachurches, Willow Creek Community Church. It can be faulted for many things, including its inability to reach beyond its own suburban cultural boundaries. But if one is to judge by what Gilbert Bilezikian, its "resident theologian," writes about the church and by what John Ortberg, its teaching pastor, endorses enthusiastically, Willow Creek's vision of church as community is in many respects impressive. In *Community 101,* a text clearly written for lay people and at points theologically deficient, Bilezikian grounds the identity of the church firmly in the Trinity, combines a strong emphasis on community with an equally strong emphasis on the nonhierarchical character of the church; he passionately argues in favor of the ministry of women and resists strenuously dividing the church into interest groups along lines of race and gender. He is as concerned about social involvement as he is about evangelism, and is committed to the pattern of life modeled on the crucified Messiah.[21] All this is exactly right. Even more, all this is extraordinary for the simple reason that it is a vision for a church that is extraordinarily successful in passing on the Christian faith. When it comes to such communities, before theologians critique — and critique we must! — we should observe the vision, consider the practice, and learn from both — unless

---

17. Walls, *Missionary Movement,* xix.

18. Barna, *Marketing the Church.*

19. Kenneson, "Selling [Out] the Church," 319.

20. For a pessimistic reading, see Guinness, *Dining with the Devil;* Wells, *God in the Wasteland.*

21. Bilezikian, *Community 101.*

we want to be guilty of that sophisticated kind of obtuseness so characteristic of second-rate intellectuals.

Finally, some of my readers will miss *important ecclesiological themes* in the book. I look mainly inside, at the inner nature of the church; the outside world and the church's mission are only in my peripheral vision. Moreover, even as I look inside, I concentrate on the formal features of the relation between persons and community, rather than on their material character. What does it mean for the church to embody and pass on the love of Christ and "the righteousness and peace and joy in the Holy Spirit" (Rom. 14:17)? How should it fulfill its most proper calling to participate in God's mission in the world? What is the nature of the relation between the churches and the societies they inhabit? How is participation in the life of the church — how is *being* a church — related to the plausibility of the Christian way of life? I do not address these questions directly, not, however, because I find them unimportant, but because one cannot say everything at once; working through the issues takes time and space, and requires patience of both the writer and the reader. The best I can do here is to point the reader to some of my articles[22] and especially to my book *Exclusion and Embrace: A Theological Exploration of Identity, Otherness, and Reconciliation.*[23] I consider this book a necessary companion to the present volume. The vision of the triune God provides the foundation there as here. But there I pursue a different question; instead of asking what the doctrine of the Trinity implies for the formal relations between person and community, I ask how the vision of the triune God's coming into the world of sin ought to inform the way in which we live in a world suffused with deception, injustice, and violence.[24]

Alan Padgett and the editorial board of *Sacra Doctrina* do their work in style. Double thanks are in order if you first get the world's best barbecued shrimp served in New Orleans and are then invited to submit your manuscript. Jon Pott of Eerdmans, whose inimitable dry humor more than matched all the delicacies to which he treated me in New Orleans and elsewhere, is an editor *extraordinaire*. It is above all to his generosity that I owe the translation of the book. Doug Stott, who translated the book (except for the Preface and this Introduction), and Daniel Harlow, who edited it, both deserve my gratitude. Finally, John Ortberg and Telford Work have read a version of this Introduction and offered valuable comments, and in the process of its writing Medi Sorterup, my research assistant, has been her usual self — perceptive and helpful.

22. See Volf, "Church as Prophetic Community"; "Worship as Adoration and Action"; "Soft Difference"; "Christliche Identität und Differenz"; "When Gospel and Culture Intersect."

23. Nashville: Abingdon, 1996.

24. See also Volf, "Trinity Is Social Program."

Introduction

1. A Cry of Protest and Its Fate

"We are the people!" was the cry with which the wall between East and West was stormed in November 1989, the people's cry of protest against patronization by the Communist Party and by its appointed government; it was a resounding "no" to the self-appointed avant-garde of the people that was repressing this very people. Although hardly anyone will argue the necessity of the Eastern European velvet revolution, its ultimate success will likely depend on just what becomes of this "we" in its cry of protest. Will this "we" split up into individuals and individual groups concerned only with their own interests? Will it melt into a mass, relinquishing its autonomy to new (nationalistic?) "Führer" who manipulate through old memories and new insecurities?[1]

To my knowledge, no one has tried to storm the ecclesial walls with the cry "We are the church!" (though a broad movement has indeed tried with this slogan to change certain things in the German-speaking Catholic Church). This particular slogan does nonetheless express the protest out of which the Free Churches emerged historically.[2] Although it would doubtless be an oversimplification to understand the early English Separatist movement with Peter Lake

---

1. In this regard, cf. Volf, "Unclean Spirit," 88f.

2. The expression "Free Churches" involves two primary meanings: It designates first those churches with a congregationalist church constitution, and second those churches affirming a consistent separation of church and state (see Mead, *Experiment*, 103). I use the term primarily in the first sense, though this meaning also implies the second and is inseparable from it.

9

merely as a "populist revolt against any sort of ministerial élite,"[3] the dominance of the problem of power in the polemical writings of its main representatives clearly attests the populist protest against the hierarchical structure of the church. The ecclesiological principle of the first Baptist, John Smyth, was: "We say the Church or two or three faithful people Separated from the world & joyned together in a true covenant, have both Christ, the covenant, & promises, & the ministerial powre of Christ given to them. . . ."[4] It is the "faithful people" who have Christ and his power; it is *they* who have the covenant and the promises. As Henry Ainsworth formulated it, the Separatists' criticism of the church of their time was not directed "against any personal, or accidentary profanation of the temple, but against the faulty frame of it."[5] The structures of that particular ecclesial power would have to be changed in which "two or three faithful people" remain powerless against the powerful hierarchy. The positive background to this criticism was the idea that the church is actually the people of God itself assembling in various places. "*We* are the church, and for that reason, it is also *we* who are the subjects of the government of Christ in the church" — this is the red thread running through all their writings. The antimonarchical and generally antihierarchical political implications of this basic, anticlerical ecclesiological decision are unmistakable.[6] The expression "We are the people!" could clearly be heard in the "We are the church!" of the Free Churches.

In the meantime, the cry of protest "We are the church!" seems to have become redundant. No one contests it today, and it thus shares the fate of many cries of protest that not only derive from empty discontent, but rather denounce genuine social grievances: They are often incorporated into the self-understanding of the group against which they are directed, and thereby domesticated. Thus, for example, the notion "We are the church!" is integrated into "The church is a 'we.'" Although this formulation is unobjectionable in and of itself, concern arises whenever the singularization of the plural ("are" being transformed to "is") signals a reduction of the complexity of that "we" to the simplicity of a quasi-"I"; a populist cry of protest becomes an integralistic formula of palliation! By contrast, the slogan "We are the church!" quite correctly expresses the notion that "church" is a collective noun. The church *is* not a "we"; the church *are* we. On the other hand, this plural does not express merely a relationless multiplicity. The ecclesial plural is not to be confused with the grammatical plural. While several "I's" together do constitute a grammatical plural, they do not yet constitute an ecclesial "we." "We are the

---

3. So Lake, *Puritans,* 89. For a critical view, see Brachlow, *Communion,* 175.

4. Smyth, *Works,* 403.

5. Cited in Collinson, "Early Dissenting Tradition," 544.

6. Historical scholarship seems to agree on this point. See, e.g., Förster, *Thomas Hobbes,* 116, 174; Zaret, *Contract,* 94; Collinson, "Early Dissenting Tradition," 548.

church!" does not mean "We meet occasionally," nor "We cooperate in a common project"; rather, it means basically, "Each of us in his or her own being is qualified by others." Whoever says less than this in saying "We are the church!" is saying too little, and the cry of protest "We are the church!" has degenerated into an ideological slogan.

The following study is concerned *with placing this cry of protest of the Free Churches — "We are the church" — into a trinitarian framework and with elevating it to the status of an ecclesiological program, and with doing so in dialogue with Catholic and Orthodox ecclesiologies.* I am hopeful that this will also indirectly provide a modest theological contribution to clarifying the problem the political protest "We are the people!" presents to social philosophy. My primary objective, however, is to contribute to the rediscovery of the church.

As a cry of protest, "We are the church!" presupposes that someone does want together to be the church. In many churches, especially those of the non-Western world, this desire is quite robust. I would like to provide these churches with the ecclesiological categories through which they might better understand themselves as and live better as a community.[7] In modern societies, however, the worm of modernity is slowly eating away at the root of this will to ecclesial community; faith lived ecclesially is being replaced by faith lived individualistically, a diffuse faith that includes within itself the elements of multiple forms of religiosity and is continually changing.[8] Those whose yearning for community is undiminished must first learn to say "We are the church!"; the church must first awaken in their souls, as Romano Guardini put it in a well-known expression.[9] The ecclesiological dispute concerning the church as community is therefore simultaneously a missiological dispute concerning the correct way in which the communal form of Christian faith today is to be lived authentically and transmitted effectively.

2. Free Churches: The Churches of the Future?

1. A global ecclesial transformation has been under way during the second half of this century; from the religion of the so-called First World, Christianity has become a religion of the so-called "Two-Thirds World." In the process, it is slowly

---

7. In this study, I do *not* use the term "community" in the sense of Ferdinand Tönnies' distinction between "community" and "society" (see Tönnies, *Gemeinschaft*). The term "community" for me refers quite generally to the concrete relationships within the social edifice that is the church. I do admittedly inquire theologically concerning just how the relationships within the church as a community ought to look if they are to correspond to the community or fellowship of the triune God.

8. See Marty, *Church*, 45ff.

9. See Guardini, *Kirche*, 19.

(and laboriously) shedding its European forms of enculturation and is becoming a genuine global religion with its own varied forms of enculturation. Despite the culturally determined pluriformity of the churches emerging thus worldwide, however, a general ecclesiological shift is discernible. The understanding of the church seems to be moving away from the traditional hierarchical model to the (no longer quite so new) participative models of church configuration.[10]

The various Free Churches are growing most rapidly among Protestants, particularly among the Pentecostals and the charismatic groups, who are characterized not only by the notion of religious immediacy, but also by a high degree of participation and flexibility with respect to filling leadership roles (but which at the same time are often populist-authoritarian).[11] Just as significant as the rapid growth of these Free Churches, however, are the incipient structural transformations within the traditional Protestant and Catholic churches, which are undergoing a process of growing "congregationalization," even where this process has not yet been accommodated ecclesiologically. The life of the church is becoming increasingly less the exclusive prerogative of pastors and priests. The increasing professionalization of church activities in the Western world only seemingly contradicts this trend.[12] This "process of congregationalization" is clearly evident even in the Catholic Church, which is (still?) committed to a hierarchical structure.[13] The well-known interview of Joseph Cardinal Ratzinger, *Zur Lage des Glaubens*, confirms that this observation is not merely an outsider's misinterpretation of the situation. There we read:

> My impression is that the authentically Catholic meaning of the reality "Church" is tacitly disappearing, without being expressly rejected. . . . In other words, in many ways a conception of Church is spreading in Catholic thought, and even in Catholic theology, that cannot even be called Protestant in a "classic" sense. Many current ecclesiological ideas, rather, correspond more to the model of certain North American "Free Churches."[14]

It seems Ratzinger does not sufficiently consider the fact that those Catholic theologians representing an ecclesiology moving toward congregationalism[15]

---

10. Regarding Latin America, see the statistics in Stoll, *Latin America*, 333ff.

11. In this regard, see Martin, *Tongues*; Wilson, "Evangelization"; Hocken, "The Challenge."

12. See the discussions concerning "inclusion" below in section 2.2 of the present chapter.

13. In an essay written within the framework of the "Congregational History Projects," the sociologist R. Stephen Warner emphasizes that one can observe a "convergence across religious traditions toward de facto congregationalism" in the U.S.A. ("The Place," 54).

14. Ratzinger, *Report*, 45f.

15. Cf., e.g., Boff, *Die Neuentdeckung*, and idem, *Kirche*.

are less the actual motor driving these transformations than the seismograph registering and expressing theologically the grassroots movements prompted by social developments.

Today's global developments seem to imply that Protestant Christendom of the future will exhibit largely a Free Christian form. Although the episcopal churches[16] will probably not surrender their own hierarchical structures, they, too, will increasingly have to integrate these Free Church elements into the mainstream of their own lives both theologically and practically.[17] Although restorative efforts will slow the appropriation of these elements, they will be unable to obstruct them entirely. It seems to me that we are standing in the middle of a clear and irreversible "process of congregationalization" of all Christianity.[18] In his book *The Silencing of Leonardo Boff*, Harvey Cox correctly formulated one of the crucial ecclesiological and ecclesial-political questions as follows: "How will the church leaders deal with a restless spiritual energy splashing up from the underside of society and threatening to erode traditional modes of ecclesiastical governance?"[19]

2. Various reactions are possible to the slow disappearance of the traditional form of church life, which was nourished in part by an extensive identification between church and society in a premodern social context. One might, for example, lament it as an evil temptation of the church by modernity itself, or greet it as an example of what Paul Tillich called "reverse prophetism," "an unconsciously prophetic criticism directed toward the church from outside."[20] However one reacts to it, the continuing global expansion of the Free Church model is without a doubt being borne by irreversible social changes of global proportions.[21] Modern societies have long ceased to be more or less self-enclosed social systems, and have become parts of an economic-technological world system. An in-depth analysis of this system is not necessary here; for our purposes, it will suffice to emphasize briefly those particular features promoting the expansion of the Free Church model. These include the differentiation of societies, the privatization of decision, the generalization of values, and inclusion.[22]

---

16. By this I mean those churches in which the office of the episcopate is affirmed for strictly dogmatic rather than practical reasons.

17. See Whitehead, *Emerging*.

18. See Chandler, *Racing*, 210ff.

19. Cox, *Silencing*, 17.

20. Concerning "reverse prophetism," see Tillich, *Theology*, 3.214.

21. Admittedly, the same social changes pose a threat with the horrific vision of an electronic church in which the individual Christians are utterly isolated from one another and obey only the voice of the one shepherd delivered by the media. The actualization of this horrific vision would constitute the radical privatization of salvation and the dissolution of the church.

22. My own presentation of these characteristics of modern societies follows especially Luhmann, *Religion*.

Modern societies are characterized by progressive *differentiation* into various interdependent and yet autodynamic subsystems. These subsystems then become specialized with regard to certain spheres of social life; altogether, they represent "the inner-societal environment for one another" and attain stability through complex interdependence.[23] The position of the church in modern societies must be determined from the perspective of this particular social development. Whereas in premodern European societies the church still represented "a kind of basic element of security and limit to variation for all functional and media spheres,"[24] today it has become a specialized institution for religious questions. "Today, religion survives as a functional subsystem of a functionally differentiated society."[25]

As such a subsystem of society, the church itself is subject to the vortex of progressive differentiation. Accordingly, various Christian traditions and churches emerged in the differentiation following the Protestant Reformation. Even if from a theological perspective one cannot simply affirm sociological developments but must carefully evaluate them, it is clear that churches in modern societies represent sociologically the different religious institutions that have become specialized in satisfying the religious needs of various social and cultural groups, a situation applying both to the larger, more comprehensive ecclesial communities and to individual local churches within these communities. It is no accident that sociological studies employ market terminology in describing the social position and function of the church.[26] Just as a consumer is able to choose between the offerings of various merchants, so also can one choose between the religious offerings of the various churches (even when churches justifiably neither understand themselves nor want to be understood merely as "merchants"). In a culture resembling a warehouse, where a person can take whatever he or she wants, religion too must become a "commodity," "a social possibility one can use or not use."[27]

That religion has become a "commodity" is not just a result of social differentiation; it is also connected with yet another important structural feature of modern societies: The latter are characterized by a low degree of social *ascriptivism* and by the corresponding *privatization of decision*. In traditional societies, people are directed toward certain subsystems largely by circumstances beyond their control (such as the class into which a person is born). By contrast, modern, differentiated societies must relinquish this ascriptive directing of

---

23. Luhmann, *Religion*, 243.

24. Ibid., 102. See also Kaufmann, "Kirche," 6.

25. Luhmann, "Society," 14.

26. Concerning such market terminology, cf. Berger, "Market," 77-93; Berger and Luckmann, "Secularization," 76ff.

27. Kaufmann, *Religion*, 143, 223.

individuals into specific social roles and institutions.[28] Individuals now largely determine their own social roles. These societies are thus characterized by a high degree of *associationism*; membership in institutions and organizations is determined by the private decisions of the affected individuals.[29] For church life, the privatization of decision means

> that both participation in spiritual communication (church) and that part of faith involving the act of believing become a matter of individual decision; it means that religiosity is expected only on the basis of individual decision, and that this is now becoming consciously so. Whereas unbelief was a private matter earlier, now belief is such.[30]

The self-evident nature of membership in a religious community is thus largely disappearing, and the question of truth and salvation is becoming a matter for the individual to decide.

The privatization of decision goes hand in hand with a *generalization of values*. Freedom and equality are welcomed as universal values regulating social behavior without recourse to particularistic prohibitions.[31] What follows from this is "the full inclusion of all persons as possible participants in all functional areas."[32] The specific differences between people may not function as the basis on which to exclude anyone in principle from access to certain functions; every person must be able to get an education, vote, satisfy needs through work, and so on. The generalization of values implies not only that "access to religion is not restricted by other roles, nor may access to other roles be restricted by religion"; it simultaneously shatters "the distinction between clergy and laity, and requires a purely organizational (religiously irrelevant) reconstruction of this distinction."[33]

3. Only a poor ecclesiology would simply chase after the developmental tendencies of modern societies. Although history does indeed teach that with regard to the development of its own order the church is to a large extent dependent on developments within society itself,[34] the social form of the church must find its basis in its own faith rather than in its social environment. Only thus can churches function effectively as prophetic signs in their environment.

---

28. Luhmann, *Religion*, 236.
29. Concerning the implications of this social development for religion, see Berger, *Imperative*.
30. Luhmann, *Religion*, 238f. Empirical research in Germany also confirms this; see Kaufmann, *Religion*, 142.
31. Parsons, *System*, 13ff.
32. Luhmann, *Religion*, 234.
33. Ibid.
34. See Kottje and Risse, *Wahlrecht*, 44.

The entire present study is concerned with finding a theologically appropriate ecclesiological response to the challenge of modern societies. Here I wish only to point out how the structural elements of modern societies affect ecclesial self-understanding and the success of the transmission of faith.

Opinion polls in the United States (although the North American situation cannot really be universalized, it does reveal some of the general tendencies within modern societies) clearly attest people's conviction that their faith should reflect the values of freedom and equality which they themselves presuppose as self-evident within their own social and political lives.[35] They view their faith as something taking place between themselves and God. Church membership is important to them not so much for determining their faith as for supporting it. "They see religious institutions as serving the people, not the people serving the institutions."[36] Americans quite clearly expect one thing from their churches, namely, more lay participation in church life. To the question, "Who do you think should have greater influence in determining the future of religion in America: the clergy, or the people who attend the services?" sixty-one percent responded: "Laity, the people who attend religious services, should have greater influence."[37] Among young adults (ages 18-29), seventy percent gave this answer, while only nine percent favored greater influence on the part of the clergy.

As for any religion, so for Christianity the transmission of faith is a question of survival. Such transmission, however, becomes a serious question only in a situation in which decisions have been privatized. In a pluralistic situation, several factors favor or hinder the transmission of faith. Here I will address only those particular factors involved with the social form of the church. Church historians, recently especially Nathan O. Hatch in his widely respected book *The Democratization of American Christianity,* have traced the rapid spread of various Christian movements back to their "populism."[38] The religious sociologists Roger Finke and Rodney Stark confirm this; it was precisely the democratic-populist and congregationalist character of the Baptists and early Methodists that enabled them to "conquer" North America between 1776 and 1850. They write:

> Perhaps "congregationalism" was not a sufficient basis for meeting these [evangelistic] demands, but it appears to have been necessary. This suggestion is further supported by the fact that the "Methodist miracle" of growth which occurred during this period, when local congregations were pretty much

35. See Gallup and Castelli, *Religion,* 90.
36. Ibid., 252.
37. Ibid., 252f. Similarly also Dudley and Laurens, "Alienation."
38. See esp. Hatch, *Democratization.*

self-governing, was followed by the "Methodist collapse" which began after the clergy had assumed full control.[39]

The experiences of various churches worldwide, especially of Baptist and Pentecostal-charismatic churches, confirm this sociological observation.[40]

It is not my intention here to recommend certain methods of evangelization, nor to affirm in an undifferentiated fashion ecclesial populism. On the other hand, given the experiences of the growing Free Churches, though also of the "mainline" Protestant churches, which are increasingly becoming "sideline" churches throughout the world,[41] one must reflect on "the social factors affecting the possibility of transmitting Christianity" within modern societies.[42] Apart from the actual content of faith,[43] it seems to me that the successful transmission of the Christian faith presupposes a twofold identification with the churches: that of outsiders and that of church members themselves. If it is through conscious decision that faith is taken up — faith no longer belonging to the self-evident features of a given social milieu — then the mediation of faith can succeed only *if those standing outside that faith are able to identify with the church communities embodying and transmitting it.* Such identification presupposes a certain degree of sympathy. People in modern societies, however, have little sympathy for top-down organizations, including for churches structured top-down. The search of contemporary human beings for community is a search for those particular forms of socialization in which they themselves are taken seriously with their various religious and social needs, in which their personal engagement is valued, and in which they can participate formatively. If, as Franz-Xaver Kaufmann has emphasized,[44] the appropriation of values indeed can take place only in "sympathetically structured" circumstances, then

39. Finke and Stark, "Upstart Sects," 34.

40. See Martin, *Tongues*.

41. See Roof and McKinney, *Mainline Religion*.

42. Kaufmann, "Kirche," 7.

43. Roger Finke and Rodney Stark suggest that "secularization" is one of the most important factors relating to the content of faith that affect the success of transmitting such faith. They define "secularization" as follows: "By 'secularize' we mean to move from other-worldiness to worldliness, to present a more distant and indistinct conception of the supernatural, to relax the moral restrictions on members, and to surrender claims to an exclusive and superior truth" (Finke and Stark, "Upstart Sects," 28). With regard to the transmission of faith, they then draw the following conclusion: "As groups secularize they will proselytize less vigorously. It is hard to witness for a faith with nothing special to offer in the religious message" (ibid.). One might question whether this analysis draws sufficiently precise distinctions. One would have to conclude from it that only the fundamentalists are in a position to transmit their faith effectively. For a brief theological reflection concerning this problem, see Volf, "Herausforderung."

44. Kaufmann, "Kirche," 7. See also Kaufmann, *Religion*, 268, 275.

in addition to the family, one will be able to transmit faith effectively today only in social groups with a participative structure.

As the history of the early church, and indeed the entirety of church history, attests, faith is not transmitted primarily by priests or pastors and academics,[45] but rather by the loyal and inspired people of God. The interest the people of God have in transmitting their faith, however, will not be much greater than their interest in the Christian congregation in which they actually live that faith. Thus the transmission of faith also presupposes *the identification of a church's members with that church.* Such identification, however, will take place only to the extent individual Christians are permitted to understand and affirm themselves as fully entitled, formative coparticipants in church life. Although the guarantee of inclusion does not yet suffice to create the "sympathetic social relationships" within the church, without such inclusion such relationships become increasingly more improbable, since "social dissonance" becomes too great between what one endorses in society at large and what one experiences in the church.

This participative character of Christian communities, or the capacity for all believers to become subjects,[46] to express the same thing from the perspective of the individual, is an important presupposition for both outsiders and members in identifying with the church. Without this twofold identification with the church, the transmission crisis experienced by the Christian faith, discernible especially in Europe, will be extremely difficult to overcome.

Is then the salvation of worldwide Christendom to be expected from the Free Churches? By no means. Too often, the latter merely reflect the cultural worlds surrounding them along with the serious illnesses attaching to those worlds. Let me mention but one example. Whether they want to or not, Free Churches often function as "homogeneous units" specializing in the specific needs of specific social classes and cultural circles, and then in mutual competition try to sell their commodity at dumping prices to the religious consumer in the supermarket of life projects; the customer is king and the one best suited to evaluate his or her own religious needs and from whom nothing more is required than a bit of loyalty and as much money as possible. If the Free Churches want to contribute to the salvation of Christendom, they themselves must first be healed.

---

45. So, correctly, Kaufmann, *Religion,* 222; Kaufmann, *Zukunft,* 19.
46. So Metz, "Das Konzil," 250.

3. An Ecumenical Study

1. Today, a reevaluation of the church is meaningful only as an ecumenical project. Four decades ago, Karl Barth wrote:

> If a man can acquiesce in divisions, if he can even take pleasure in them, if he can be complacent in relation to the obvious faults and errors of others and therefore his own responsibility for them, then that man may be a good and loyal confessor in the sense of his own particular denomination, he may be a good Roman Catholic or Reformed or Orthodox or Baptist, but he must not imagine that he is a good Christian.[47]

Today Barth's warning seems almost superfluous. It has in the meantime become quite self-evident that *all* of us are poor Christians if we live divided, and that no ecclesiology can proceed in self-satisfied isolation.

Although ecumenical values have generally prevailed, the ecumenical movement as such finds itself in a profound crisis today. A precise analysis of the causes of this crisis, particularly of the causes associated with inner-Catholic and inner-Orthodox developments, is not necessary in this context. Let me draw attention only to two complementary factors relevant for my purposes. The first is the current decline of rigid denominationalism. Although people do indeed still identify with a particular denomination, they feel free to attend the local church of a different denomination or even to change denominations.[48] A postconfessional Christianity is emerging.[49] The great ecumenical project that was oriented toward relations among the various confessions is having a great deal of difficulty accommodating itself to these new developments.[50] Old-style ecumenicists find the ecumenical idea itself endangered. The second factor in the ecumenical crisis of relevance for this study is the diminution of the societal and ecclesial significance of the old Protestant denominations (what are known as the "mainline denominations"). This is in part a result of the inner dynamic of modern societies at large, though no less of the inability of these denominations themselves to transmit the Christian faith effectively. In any case, one

---

47. Barth, *Church Dogmatics*, IV/1.676.

48. In this regard, see Wuthnow, *Restructuring*, 71-99; Barna and McKay, *Vital Signs*, 124.

49. So also Raiser, "Ökumene," 413.

50. George A. Lindbeck's remarks concerning the reconceptualization of the ecumenical project are accurate: "Unitive ecumenism . . . needs to be reconceived. It can no longer be thought of, as I have done most of my life, as a matter of reconciling relatively intact and structurally still-Constantinian communions from the top down. Rather, it must be thought of as reconstituting Christian community and unity from, so to speak, the bottom up" (Lindbeck, "Confession," 496).

of the three pillars of the ecumenical movement, in addition to the Catholic and Orthodox churches, is supporting increasingly less weight.

Parallel with these developments, Free Churches, which emphasize the relative independence of local churches, are acquiring ever greater significance through their rapid worldwide growth. They continue, however, to be the step-children of the ecumenical movement if they are reckoned as family at all. In many respects, this is no doubt their own fault. I do not, however, want to engage in the unfruitful business of appropriate assignment of blame. I merely note that many ecumenical discussions of recent decades have been conducted with the unspoken assumption that the Free Churches as well as congrega-tionalist ecclesiology can be ignored with impunity. The report of the Lausanne Conference (1927) still viewed Free Churches as equal partners with the epis-copal and presbyterial churches. It demands that

> these several elements [i.e., episcopal, presbyterial and congregational systems — M.V.] must all, under conditions which require further study, have an appropriate place in the order of life of a reunited Church. . . . each separate communion . . . should gladly bring to the common life of the united Church its own spiritual treasures.[51]

From the perspective of the Free Churches, the "Baptism, Eucharist, and Ministry" (BEM) Document (1982) did not fulfill this demand; Free Churches are wholly dissatisfied with the BEM Document because they feel left out.[52] As a matter of fact, they were indeed expressly left out of the ecumenical proposal of Heinrich Fries and Karl Rahner, to mention another example, since "smaller church associa-tions or sects (!), even those basically expressing an interest in unity," are not considered for the union proposed by Fries and Rahner.[53] People seem to forget in this context that for simple "numerical" reasons there can be no unity in the church that bypasses these Free Churches, since they represent worldwide the largest Protestant grouping. Furthermore, from the evangelical perspective and against this proposal one must question along with Eberhard Jüngel whether "the Lutheran and Reformed churches [can] unite with Rome if in return they have to renounce their previous proximity, for example, to the Baptists."[54]

One of the intentions of this study is to contribute toward making the Free Churches and their ecclesiology (or ecclesiologies) presentable, Free Churches that are dogmatically fully orthodox (though too often simul-taneously expressly fundamentalist) and that are numerically becoming increas-

---

51. *Faith*, 469.

52. See, e.g., "Evangelical."

53. Fries and Rahner, *Einigung*, 64.

54. Jüngel, "Einheit," 341. See also the criticism directed at Fries and Rahner's sugges-tion by Joseph Cardinal Ratzinger (*Church*, 132f.).

ingly significant. (At the same time, however, I will try to teach them something in the way of good theological and ecumenical manners.) Insofar as the ecclesiology of the Free Churches becomes ecumenically plausible, it can perhaps also function as a catalyst in the search for a postconfessional ecumenical conceptual framework.

2. Good manners do not include showing up at the party and then immediately beginning an argument. I will observe proper etiquette, and not merely for ceremonial purposes. Although this study is not concerned with controversial theology, I will not shy away from clearly delineating relevant differences and from inquiring concerning their consequences. This is admittedly not the only legitimate form in which one can participate in ecumenical dialogue. Although one can very well engage in theological ecumenism without addressing ecclesiastical-confessional differences, one should not forget that these differences do nonetheless color the entire undertaking at least latently.[55] If such differences are brought fully into the open, the possibility exists that they can contribute to mutual enlightenment; if they are avoided, the false impression can arise that one has already learned from them everything there is to learn. The informed reader will easily discern where I have learned from my dialogue partners and thereby enhanced (I hope) the Free Church model.

In one point, however, I still remain unconvinced. Both the episcopal and the original Free Church ecclesiological models proceed on the assumption that there is but one correct ecclesiology; God has revealed a certain structure for the church, and this one structure must accordingly be maintained for all time. By contrast, exegetes speak of the several ecclesial models one can find in the New Testament. I proceed on the simple systematic assumption that what was legitimate during the New Testament period cannot be illegitimate today. Furthermore, I consider the plurality of models to be not only legitimate, but indeed desirable. The differentiation of various Christian traditions is not simply to be lamented as a scandal, but rather welcomed as a sign of the vitality of the Christian faith within multicultural, rapidly changing societies demanding diversification and flexibility. Franz-Xaver Kaufmann sees in this differentiation "the real chance for Christianity on the threshold of the emerging world society." He goes on:

> In my opinion, one can show not only that the various traditions of Christianity posit different emphases in their religious experience, but also that beyond this they have developed different social forms and different forms of community configuration, and that in the kind of situation in which we find ourselves today, namely, one difficult to assess as a whole, it is precisely these differences that offer the best chances of survival.[56]

55. See Schillebeeckx, *Menschen*, 241.
56. Kaufmann, *Zukunft*, 23.

One must admittedly also inquire concerning and grapple with the unity of these different traditions.

One might reject the legitimacy of several ecclesial models with the following argument: Anyone who does not wish to accept the one institutional church willed by Christ will necessarily create one's own church modeled according to one's own needs.[57] Yet whoever argues in this way (contrary to the New Testament witness, I believe) will also have to face the question whether this appeal to the unchangeable will of God is not serving rather to veil ideologically one's own interest in maintaining certain ecclesial structures. I doubt, though, whether such an exchange of arguments concerning needs and interests would make us any wiser. The dispute concerning the plurality of ecclesial models would have to be carried on with somewhat better arguments. Within the framework of the present study, however, I do not need to address this dispute any further. Here I acknowledge my commitment to the plurality of ecclesial models merely for the sake of drawing attention to the limits of my own objectives. I do not intend to advocate the extreme thesis that one specific Free Church ecclesiology is the only correct one, nor that such an ecclesiology is the best one for all times and all places. I wish to demonstrate in a much more modest fashion that a Free Church ecclesiology can be dogmatically legitimate, can be commensurate with contemporary societies, and, for that reason and under certain conditions, can prove to be superior to other ecclesiologies. This argument presupposes a rejection both of a "progressivist" understanding of history ("what comes later is better than what is there now or what came earlier") and of a "primitivist" understanding of history ("what came earlier is better than what is there now or what will come later"). I am advocating what I have elsewhere called a "kaleidoscopic" understanding of history, namely, the view that "social arrangements shift in various ways under various influences . . . without necessarily following an evolutionist or involutionist pattern."[58] I am not, however, suggesting that we accept an anarchy of ecclesial models. An ecclesial model acquires theological legitimacy through an appeal to the New Testament witness concerning the church, and through reflection on how faith in the triune God and in salvation in Jesus Christ is to intersect with the cultural locations in which churches live.

3. I will conduct my ecumenical dialogue here with the two great traditions

---

57. So Ratzinger, who disqualifies ecclesiologically the North American Free Churches with the following argument: Those who fled to North America "took refuge from the oppressive model of the 'State Church' produced by the Reformation . . . created *their own* church, an organization structured according to their needs," since they "no longer believed in an institutional Church willed by Christ, and wanted at the same time to escape the State Church" (*Report*, 46).

58. Volf, *Work*, 84.

of ecclesiological thinking, namely, the Catholic and the Orthodox. The two dialogue partners I have chosen are Joseph Cardinal Ratzinger[59] and the Metropolitan John Zizioulas.[60] These two have one thing in common: They are not prophets standing on the periphery of their own tradition (otherwise they would not have received the high episcopal honors of their churches). Although Ratzinger has already long been a figure of considerable dispute not only as the Prefect of the Congregation for the Doctrine of the Faith, but in part for that reason also as a theologian, these two are exceptional contemporary theologians consciously trying to give contemporary expression to their respective traditions. Those among my readers who are prophetically inclined might think that for just this reason they do not qualify as dialogue partners, and that one ought simply to leave them to the business of stabilizing their own communities. I do not need to determine here whether as theologians they occupy merely a conservative stabilizing function without making any constructive contributions. Because I am looking for the so-called postmodern forms of ecclesial relationships, however, it seems to me that dialogue with contemporary reformulations of *premodern* traditions is extraordinarily important. Moreover, the wisdom inhering in a long tradition should not be underestimated even if one feels compelled to reject that tradition.

In the broad dialogue I carry on with Ratzinger and Zizioulas, I am often inclined to lend an ear to the voice of the first Baptist — "Se-Baptists" — John Smyth (1554-1612), "one of the most gifted, and, with all his faults, one of the best of the great company who have borne that name."[61] He is the voice of the Free Church tradition to whose theological maturation and ecumenical presentability I hope to contribute here. I am, however, audacious enough not simply

59. Relatively much has been published on Ratzinger's theology, especially since his controversial interview, *The Ratzinger Report* (see, e.g., Rollet, *Le cardinal*; Thils, *En dialogue*). There has, however, still been no thorough study of his ecclesiology, the area in which he probably has made his greatest theological contribution. Aidan Nichols's *Theology of Joseph Ratzinger* is a portrayal of Ratzinger's theological development, a portrayal with no claims to being a critical analysis. The penetrating study by Gerhard Nachtwei (*Unsterblichkeit*), though analytical, nevertheless seeks through dialogue with Ratzinger's own dialogue partners to present and defend his eschatology within the framework of his overall theology.

60. Two dissertations have dealt with Zizioulas's thought. Gaëtan Baillargeon (*Communion*) analyzes in particular Zizioulas's express ecclesiological proposals but does not deal in any detail with the ontology of person and community constituting the background to these proposals. Paul Gerard McPartlan's study, which pursues a critical comparison between the eucharistic ecclesiology of Henri de Lubac and Zizioulas (*Eucharist*), delves more deeply in investigating Zizioulas not only as an ecclesiologist, but also as a thinker who fathoms ecclesial existence as such. McPartlan, however, only touches peripherally on the themes of particular interest to me (e.g., the structure of the communion at the trinitarian and ecclesial levels).

61. Dexter, *Congregationalism*, 323.

to repeat with new words and new arguments that which he whispers into my ear. John Smyth began a tradition; I would like to enrich that tradition in an ecumenical dialogue with other traditions.

No great reflection is needed to discover that ecclesial life and ecclesial theory do not always or fully coincide. Recognition of this may be understood not only as an indictment of ecclesial reality, but also as a criticism of ecclesial theory. In this study, I am interested less in the misuse of the theory justifying the authoritarian structures of social unity than in the conscious or unconscious misuse of such theory for the sake of delimiting one's own social sphere from other social spheres; certain interpretations of ecclesial reality are advocated in order to maintain the wall between the churches. This is why I have attempted not only to discuss various ecclesial models, but also to pay attention to the ecclesial reality these bring to expression. Only thus can the models be effectively enriched.

Admittedly, I will allow ecclesial reality to function as a corrective only for the Free Church model; my concern with Catholic and Orthodox ecclesiology remains at the level of the models proposed by Ratzinger and Zizioulas. In so doing, I expose myself to the suspicion of wanting to present my own Protestant tradition in the best possible light. The schema according to which my thinking proceeds in several of the following discussions goes something like this: although traditional Free Church ecclesiology is individualistic, in reality the community plays an important role in the ecclesial life of the Free Church; in dialogue with other ecclesial models, I try theoretically to retrieve ecclesial life. This schema, however, evokes the impression that Free Church ecclesiology is flexible and capable of improvement, while the Catholic and Orthodox models are by contrast immobile. I am well aware that both these traditions have a *history* of ecclesiology; Ratzinger and Zizioulas are part of that history. It would be presumptuous, however, for a Protestant theologian to try to improve Catholic or Orthodox ecclesiology. Hence my own modus operandi is also intended as an offer to Catholic and Orthodox theologians through which they might, in dialogue with the Free Church model, examine ecclesiological reality at large and thereby keep their own models in motion.

4. "Not only does the question of the church constitute the determinative background to any unresolved points pertaining to the question of office, it also basically constitutes the background to all questions."[62] One can probably argue how strictly "all" is to be taken in Walter Kasper's assertion here. There is probably no disagreement, however, that all decisive theological questions are reflected more or less clearly in the question of the social form of the Christian faith. This is also why critical analysis of Ratzinger's and Zizioulas's theology of the *communio* in part I (chapters I and II) is not restricted merely to the strictly

62. Kasper, "Grundkonsens," 178.

ecclesiological level; in the course of this analysis, I will also examine questions regarding the doctrine of the Trinity, anthropology, Christology, soteriology, and the theology of revelation. In this part, I inquire concerning the structure of the *communio* in Catholic and Orthodox theology. The criticism directed at Ratzinger and Zizioulas here remains focused on the system as such. Criticism involving considerations external to the systems then follows in the second part.

The primary goal of the second part, however, is not criticism but rather construction. I inquire first of all concerning just what makes the church the church (chapter III). Since I localize this in the communal confession of faith, in the next chapter I address the question of the mediation of faith. A specific character of faith and of its mediation always presupposes a specific anthropology. Hence at the end of chapter IV, I attempt to sketch a communal view of personhood. This in turn leads to the ecclesiologically foundational study of the relationship between church and Trinity (chapter V). I then examine the problem of the structures of the church from the perspective of these ecclesiological, soteriological, anthropological, and trinitarian views (chapter VI). The final chapter then attempts to summarize the entirety from the perspective of the problem of catholicity.

The central focus of my constructive interest is the local church, and only on the periphery do I address the theme of the relationships obtaining between various local churches[63] and between these and their surrounding social reality.[64] By focusing on the local church, however, I am by no means suggesting indirectly that one should simply settle for the many local churches that are concerned exclusively with their own affairs. I feel obligated to the great ecumenical task of witnessing to the one faith with contextual sensibility, of proclaiming publicly and living responsibly the one, world-altering gospel, and of building up the *communio*-structures between the churches dispersed throughout the entire ecumene. This task cannot, however, be fulfilled without local churches; as a matter of fact, it must be addressed primarily by way of those local churches, for the people of God gathering at one place constitute the primary subject of ecclesiality. From the perspective of this basic ecclesiological conviction, one which although often forgotten does not represent a view specific to the Free Churches, I focus on the local church itself in this ecumenical study of the ecclesial community as an icon of the trinitarian community.

63. See below III.3; VII.3.1.3.
64. See below VII.3.2.

PART I

Chapter I

Ratzinger:
Communion and the Whole

The church occupies the center of the theology of Joseph (Cardinal) Ratzinger.[1] What the young Ratzinger maintained about Cyprian applies with virtually no restrictions to Ratzinger himself: "Regardless of where one begins, one always gets back to the church."[2] From his dissertation on Augustine's ecclesiology to his most recent theological publications as Prefect of the Congregation for the Doctrine of the Faith,[3] he has always tried to uncover and elucidate the inner logic of the Catholic form of ecclesiality, albeit from the perspective of this ecclesiality itself rather than from any neutral perspective.[4] Ratzinger's attempt to ground the requisite structure of the church from the inside, however, is not a purely ecclesiological undertaking; ultimately, he is concerned with the "communal shape of the Christian faith."[5] This is anchored in his basic conviction

---

1. For Ratzinger's theology in general, see Fahey, "Ratzinger"; Häring, "Nightmare Theology"; Nachtwei, *Unsterblichkeit*; Nichols, *Theology*.

2. Ratzinger, *Volk*, 99; see Ratzinger, *Eschatologie*, 14. Concerning the centrality of the church in Ratzinger's thinking, see Eyt, "Überlegungen," 40.

3. See Ratzinger, *Gemeinschaft*.

4. See Ratzinger, *Volk*, 57. The young Ratzinger believed that Augustine's attempt to appeal to scripture as an impartial authority within ecclesiological disputes — i.e., to demonstrate the church outside the church itself — resembles the attempt to "demonstrate faith outside faith" (Ratzinger, *Volk*, 131). According to his view, both attempts are doomed to failure because — as he explains later — "all reason is determined by a historical location, and hence pure reason does not really exist" (Ratzinger, "Kirche in der Welt," 317). Concerning Ratzinger's theological method, see Nachtwei, *Unsterblichkeit*, 226ff.

5. Ratzinger, *Prinzipienlehre*, 50.

that "only the whole sustains"[6] — more precisely, the whole in the most comprehensive sense of a great unity of "love" that overcomes not only the isolation of the individual self from the entirety of humankind, but also the isolation of humankind itself from God.[7] Ratzinger locates the essence of the church in the arc between the self and the whole; it is the communion between the human "I" and the divine "Thou" in a universally communal "We."

To protect the community of human beings with their fellow human beings and with God from the individualism of modern pluralistic societies, Ratzinger polemicizes against two mutually determinative aberrations of the Christian faith and of its ecclesial practice. The first is found in the formula of the early Augustine, *deus et anima — nihil aliud, nihil,* and its Reformational, liberal, personalistic, or existentialist variations. The second consists in delimiting the local church from the larger church, and in reducing it to group-dynamic interaction. These two aberrations allegedly coincide in Free Church ecclesial theory and practice. The impression is that Ratzinger considers Free Church ecclesiology to be the paradigmatic model of an *individualistic* view of what is Christian. Since the Christian faith obviously can be lived in a nonindividualistic fashion only if ecclesial life is communal, from the very beginning of his theological work Ratzinger either explicitly or implicitly polemicizes against Free Church ecclesiology, albeit less in its classical Protestant form than in that of the increasingly widespread, postconciliar Catholic "flight to the 'congregation.'"[8]

Pierre Eyt has rightly emphasized that few Catholic theologians have explicated more urgently than Ratzinger the intertwining of human "I," divine "Thou," and ecclesial "We."[9] Even fewer have debated with so much theological acumen the basic assumptions of Free Church ecclesiology by articulating the communal structure of the Christian faith that sustains Catholic ecclesiology. These are two important reasons why Ratzinger seems to be an appropriate primary Catholic dialogue partner in the search for a communal Free Church ecclesiology.[10] My interest is in Ratzinger as theologian rather than as Prefect of the Congregation for the Doctrine of the Faith (though it would doubtless be instructive to examine how his understanding of *communio* is translated into ecclesiastical practice in his own function as bishop and prefect).[11] And I will

6. Ratzinger, "Buchstabe," 254.

7. See Ratzinger, *Introduction,* 204; idem, *Fest,* 129.

8. Ratzinger, *Prinzipienlehre,* 6. Cf., e.g., idem, *Volk,* 90, note 7; "Liturgie," 244; *Church,* 9f.

9. Eyt, "Überlegungen," 45.

10. For additional reasons why I have chosen Ratzinger as the Catholic dialogue partner, see section 3.3 of the Introduction above.

11. I do not intend to pursue the theologically, ecclesiastically, and politically charged question whether Ratzinger does indeed distinguish sufficiently "within himself between the

not enter the inner-Catholic dispute concerning whether Ratzinger does indeed authentically express the spirit and letter of the Second Vatican Council. Because my own investigation aims not immediately at establishing an ecumenical consensus or ecumenical convergence, but rather at reformulating Free Church ecclesiology, I need not deal with *the* definitive Catholic ecclesiology, if such exists in the first place even in the Catholic sphere; it will suffice to examine *one* incontestably "not un-Catholic" ecclesiology. The ecclesiology of a peritus at the Second Vatican Council and of a Prefect of the Congregation for the Doctrine of the Faith should fulfill this requirement.[12]

Ratzinger has not published a comprehensive ecclesiology. Apart from his investigations into Augustine's doctrine of the church, his own ecclesiological explications are dispersed among various essays and lectures appearing within a span of forty years and quite often exhibiting the character of occasional writings; of occasional character is also the book *Zur Gemeinschaft gerufen,* which appeared in 1991 and tries to offer "an initial guide for Catholic ecclesiology."[13] One is confronted with an ecclesiological puzzle whose various parts do, however, fit more easily into an overall picture than one might expect at first. Over the years, and from the very outset up to his most recent publications, Ratzinger's ecclesiological thinking has remained remarkably consistent.[14]

---

theologian and the leader of the Congregation for the Doctrine of the Faith," as Henri de Lubac asserts (de Lubac, *Zwanzig Jahre,* 113), or whether one is rather justified in charging him with a "confusion between the magisterial function and the theological function" (Pelchat, "Ratzinger," 323). It is hard to deny, however, that the theological content of his promulgations as Prefect of the Congregation for the Doctrine of the Faith follow the line of his own theological convictions over many years. On the other hand, in his function as theologian as well, as Walter Kasper remarks in a review of Ratzinger's book, "It was not always clear just what constituted a sound thesis and what a mere hypothesis, what constituted common ecclesiastical and theological doctrine and what the author's own personal theology" (Kasper, "Einführung," 184).

12. At the end of his discussion of Ratzinger's controversial interview, *The Ratzinger Report,* J. K. S. Reid writes: "Without doubt this figure is representative of the Church of which he is so distinguished a servant. But it is not totally representative" (Reid, "Report," 132).

13. Ratzinger, *Gemeinschaft,* 9.

14. See Fahey, "Ratzinger," 79. There is no question that Ratzinger's theological development took a significant turn a few years after the Second Vatican Council. Some of his colleagues from that period (such as Hans Küng) claim hardly to know him any longer (see Cox, *Silencing,* 75). It seems to me, however, that this turn did not involve fundamental theological positions. Discounting the changes in emphases, his positions have not only remained constant, but were relatively unaffected by the great turn in the Catholic Church itself introduced by the Second Vatican Council. What Ratzinger as the Prefect of the Congregation for the Doctrine of the Faith so vigorously defends now largely coincides either with what he wrote as a young theologian or with what was already implied in his statements. But his theology, which before and during the Council gave the impression of being pro-

By taking *communio* as the central concept of Ratzinger's ecclesiology, I am directing my interest to Ratzinger the systematician; I will try to get at the inner logic of his ecclesiology and to present it critically. I will address first the church's mediation of faith and thus also of Christian existence, and then the larger church's mediation of ecclesiality itself. In a further step, I will examine the ecclesiastical form of the word of God underlying the communality of the individual Christian and of the local church. This in turn will lead to an examination of the communal form of office, the presupposition of the communality of the sacraments and of the word. The critical reconstruction of the inner logic of Ratzinger's *communio*-concept will conclude with an identification of the communally determined individual within the church. In a final step I will then question Ratzinger's understanding of the relationship between the trinitarian and ecclesial community.

1. Faith, Sacrament, and Communion

Providing an "inner grounding of the requisite disposition of the church" means showing that the church belongs not only to the necessary external presuppositions of the Christian initiation, but to its internal structure itself, since becoming a Christian, and quite generally the "fundamental form of the reception of the word in history," must be communal if Christian life itself is to be communal.[15] I will first examine the communality of the act of faith and then deal with the sacramental structure accompanying this communality.[16]

------

gressive, appeared conservative after the Council, particularly if one interprets the new elements in the conciliar texts as the as yet incomplete expression of the Council's actual intention. It was not Ratzinger's theology that changed, but rather his focus and function. From a balanced, albeit always personally engaged, thinker who was thoroughly capable of self-criticism, there emerged an apologete seemingly incapable of compromise, one on whom in addition the power of the highest church service was bestowed. Before the Council, he still wanted to trust the "victorious power of the truth . . . that lives in freedom" and had no need of sheltering through promulgation and normative decree (Ratzinger, *Das neue Volk*, 265); after the Council, he adopted the "call for a clear delineation of boundaries" and found it regrettable that the Pope and bishops "were as yet unable to decide in favor of this" (Ratzinger, *Prinzipienlehre*, 241).

15. Ratzinger, *Prinzipienlehre*, 204.

16. In this chapter, I am not making any terminological distinction between church and community (as a translation of *communio*), and I am thus following Ratzinger's own practice, who uses the two terms synonymously. Later, when I distinguish between the ecclesial communion in a local and universal sense, I use the expressions "local church" (*ecclesia localis*) or "congregation" on the one hand, and "church" (*ecclesia universalis/universa*) on the other. Concerning the (ambivalent) terminology of the Second Vatican Council, see Legrand, *Réalisation*, 145f.

32

1.1. Faith and Communion

According to Ratzinger, the goal and process of the act of faith are inextricably connected with the church community. On the one hand, the act of faith incorporates human beings into the community; on the other, it is simultaneously sustained by that community.

1. Because the "object" of faith itself is the triune God or Jesus Christ, faith always actually means co-faith; indeed, communion with other Christians is not merely an "external circumstance of salvation, but virtually enters into its metaphysical essence."[17] The God in whom one believes is the triune God, and thus not a self-enclosed unity, but rather a community of the three divine persons. Believing in this God — surrendering one's existence to this God — necessarily means entering into the divine community. Because the triune God is not a private deity, one cannot create a private fellowship with this God. Fellowship with the triune God *is* therefore at once also fellowship with all other human beings who in faith have surrendered their existence to the same God. Trinitarian faith accordingly means becoming community.[18] Hence the church community is a necessary consequence "of the counterpart who is confessed in faith, and who thereby ceases to be merely a counterpart."[19]

One enters into the trinitarian community through communion with Jesus Christ in faith. One can construct a private relationship with Christ as little as one can create a private relationship with the triune God. For Christ is not at all an individual, self-enclosed person. As the new "Adam," he is a corporate personality embodying within himself "the unity of the whole creature 'man.' "[20] To believe in Christ accordingly means to "enter" into this corporate personality and for that reason also into communion with others.

Ratzinger explicates this christological grounding of the essential ecclesiality of salvation with a theological exegesis of Gal. 2:20. When Paul writes that "now it is no longer I who live, but it is Christ who lives in me," he means that the self of the believer ceases to be a "self-contained subject," and is "inserted into a new subject."[21] Yet this new subject is not simply Christ, as one might expect at first on the basis of Gal. 2:20. Ratzinger interprets Gal. 2:20 from the perspective of his favorite ecclesiological passages, namely, Gal. 3:16 and 3:28, which speak of "the seed" and "the one," and from which he alleges that the "one" is "a new, *single* subject with Christ."[22] This new subject into which one

---

17. Ratzinger, *Volk*, 245, note 21.
18. See Ratzinger, *Prinzipienlehre*, 23, 51; cf. Ratzinger, *Church*, 29ff.
19. Ratzinger, *Prinzipienlehre*, 23.
20. Ratzinger, *Introduction*, 176; cf. Ratzinger, *Dogma*, 221f.
21. Ratzinger, "Theologie," 519.
22. Ibid. My emphasis. Cf. Ratzinger, *Brüderlichkeit*, 69f.; Ratzinger, *Introduction*, 179.

is "inserted" arises insofar as all who have united with Christ in faith become "*one* in Christ." The church itself acquires its character as a subject — in the sense of being an acting agent — in this unity with Christ. The head (Christ) and the body (church) constitute the "whole Christ," the only place where "human existence fully attains the goal of itself,"[23] and does so in such a way that within the church human beings "coalesce indissolubly into a single existence" with Christ, as Ratzinger believes he can conclude on the basis of Eph. 5:32.[24] "The deepest essence of the church" consists in being "together with Christ the *Christus totus, caput et membra.*"[25]

The Pauline statement that all Christians are "*one* in Christ," however, does not quite suffice to ascribe subjectivity to the church, that is, social subjectivity constituted through the subjectivity of Christ. A *theological interpretation* going beyond Paul himself is needed to transform the Pauline "one *in* Christ" into Ratzinger's "a single subject *with* Christ," or certainly into "a single . . . Jesus Christ."[26] The intention of such theological reinterpretation is clear. The subjectivity of the church implies an entire soteriology and ecclesiology; in fact, it implies a clearly Catholic soteriology and ecclesiology in which the church acts *with* Christ in bishops and priests. What remains unclear are the exegetical and theological grounds for this reinterpretation. In any event, Ratzinger does not provide any.

It is also questionable just how the church can be a single subject with Christ and yet can be distinguished from Christ. Ratzinger expressly asserts that this identification of Christ and church is not to be understood as "distinctionless identity," but rather as "dynamic union," as a "pneumatic-actual act of matrimonial love."[27] Through the Holy Spirit, the Lord who "departed" on the cross has "returned" and is now engaged in affectionate dialogue with his "bride," the church.[28] Yet even recourse to the representational work of the Holy Spirit cannot free the idea of dialogue within the *one, single* subject of the suspicion of being mere conversation with oneself. It does not seem possible to conceive the juxtaposition of church and Christ without giving up the notion of the one subject that includes both bridegroom and bride.

2. Faith does not just lead into communion; according to Ratzinger, faith

23. Ratzinger, "Identifikation," 28; cf. Ratzinger, *Introduction,* 178f.

24. Ratzinger, *Sakrament,* 10.

25. Ratzinger, "Kirche," 180. This perspective reveals why, according to Ratzinger, the expression "people of God" is an inadequate designation for the church. The *corpus Christi* provides "the *differentia specifica* through which the communal being of the 'new people' is fundamentally different from that of the nations of the world and of Israel" (Ratzinger, "Kirche," 176; cf. Ratzinger, *Gemeinschaft,* 25f.).

26. Ratzinger, "Theologie," 519; Ratzinger, *Prinzipienlehre,* 51.

27. Ratzinger, *Gemeinschaft,* 36; Ratzinger, *Das neue Volk,* 239.

28. Ratzinger, "Offenbarung," 522.

is also sustained by the church and is in actuality *a gift of the church*. This notion does not deny that faith is "a profoundly personal act anchored in the innermost depths of the human self"[29] and that it is a gift of the Lord. As a personal act, however, faith does not take place in solitude between the individual and God. Believing in a personal fashion means essentially "coming to participate in the already existing decision of the believing community."[30]

Such participation is first of all an individual appropriation of the collective faith of the church. An individual does not invent faith in solitary reflection, but rather receives from the communion of faith itself the "language and form of the experience of faith."[31] Since certain "language games" become meaningful only after one has entered into the language community sustaining such games, faith further presupposes that an individual has "become acclimatized to the community of the church," the "locus of the common experience of the Spirit."[32] It is this common life that first makes possible an individual understanding of the communal symbols of faith.

Yet if this communally transpiring process of coming to understand the church's "language games" constituted the entire breadth of the community's own participation in the emergence of personal faith, then the act of faith itself, although indeed shaped by the community, would nonetheless remain a fundamentally individual act. Every human being would, so to speak, control his or her own ecclesial socialization. For Ratzinger, however, faith is essentially communal, not only in its emergence, but in its very *structure*. By believing, one *allows oneself to be taken up* "into the decision already there [in the believing community]."[33] This *allowing* oneself to be taken up, whose subject is the believer, corresponds to *being* taken up, whose subject is the church. Of decisive significance here is that being taken up is "not . . . a subsequent legal act" following faith, but rather "*part of faith itself*."[34] Hence at baptism, "that particular faith" is given "which one receives from the church."[35] Accordingly, faith — that faith "which is at once both hope and love" and which represents "the total form of the preparation for justification," as Ratzinger puts it in an unequivocally un-Protestant formulation[36] — is both a personal act of the believing human being and a collective act of the church.

---

29. Ratzinger, *Auf Christus Schauen*, 39; cf. Ratzinger, *Prinzipienlehre*, 116.

30. Ratzinger, *Prinzipienlehre*, 38.

31. Ratzinger, "Dogmatische Formeln," 37; cf. Ratzinger, *Prinzipienlehre*, 346.

32. Ratzinger, *Prinzipienlehre*, 26, 130. Here Ratzinger is probably appropriating elements of the philosophy of language of the later Ludwig Wittgenstein (*Philosophische Untersuchungen*), albeit without referring expressly to him.

33. Ratzinger, *Prinzipienlehre*, 38.

34. Ibid., 42 (my emphasis); cf. ibid., 346.

35. Ibid., 109, note 8.

36. Ibid., 108f.

The participation of the ecclesial community in the personal act of faith is grounded in the nature of conversion and of the church. According to Ratzinger, conversion is not simply a turn that a human being executes, but rather in an even more fundamental fashion a change of the self enabling the converted person to say "I now live, but it is no longer I who live" (see Gal. 2:20). This change of the self presupposes complete passivity on the part of the self; activity would merely confirm the old self and in this way fail precisely in precipitating the *change* of the self.[37] "Because Christian conversion sunders the boundary between self and non-self, it can be given to someone only from the perspective of the non-self," from which Ratzinger concludes that conversion can "never be realized fully in the mere inwardness of personal decision."[38] One premise with which he consistently operates, however, remains unspoken in this line of argumentation, namely, that what occurs only in inwardness always derives from the human being rather than from God. Only this particular assumption (one implying far more than merely that genuine faith is always mediated socially) illuminates Ratzinger's peculiar grounding of the thesis that faith cannot be given directly from the Lord, and must essentially come simultaneously from the church. His reasoning is that because no one can execute this change of the self alone, the *church* must participate in the process. The change of the self comes about when one is presented with the gift of faith from the church, albeit a church that must receive both this gift and itself from the Lord.[39]

Although probably no one will deny that the experience of God is always mediated socially, the question arises whether one can correctly describe this as an ecclesial bestowal of faith, and just how one is to understand the church that participates in this mediation. Ratzinger's understanding of the mediation of faith and of its ecclesial bearer is sustained by the idea of the subjective unity of Christ and church. If the church is a single subject with Christ, then the faith coming from Christ must simultaneously be the gift of the church acting with Christ. When the church acts, Christ is acting; where Christ acts, the church is acting. And the church that as a single subject with Christ can give faith must

---

37. See Ratzinger, *Introduction*, 201ff., where Ratzinger emphasizes the primacy of reception and then concludes from this the necessity of "Christian positivity" — not only historical positivity, but also *ecclesial* positivity.

38. Ratzinger, "Theologie," 520. The same grounding of the essential ecclesial nature of faith, formulated now more from the horizontal perspective, is that one cannot give oneself faith because in its very nature such faith "is precisely the establishment of communication with all brethren of Jesus in the Holy Church" (Ratzinger, *Prinzipienlehre*, 35). This communication must be established from both sides — from that of the believing individuals *and* from that of the community accepting them.

39. From this perspective it would also be impossible for someone to decree on his or her own initiative to be a believer (see Ratzinger, *Prinzipienlehre*, 42).

be the entire *communio sanctorum* (which does, however, acquire the capacity for action in specific human beings). From this it follows that the ecclesial character of the mediation of faith, which takes place through the sacramental reception of faith from the entire church, is the sign and guarantee of its divine origin and thus also of its quality of not being at our disposal.

The church's participation in personal human faith does not, of course, end with initiation. After receiving the gift of faith from the one divine-human subject, one does not simply believe by oneself that which the church believes, but rather basically believes along with the entire church. The believing self is the self of the *anima ecclesiastica,* that is, "the 'I' of the human being in whom the entire community of the Church expresses itself, with which he lives, which lives in him, and from which he lives."[40] Accordingly, the self of the creed, according to studies of Henri de Lubac, whom Ratzinger follows, is a collective rather than an individual self, the self of the believing *Mater Ecclesiae* "to which the individual self belongs insofar as it believes."[41] Ratzinger even elucidates this notion of cobelief with the church with the expression "surrender one's act [of faith] to it [the church]."[42]

The exact character of this collective self, however, as well as its relationship to the individual self, remains obscure. Although the notion that a person lives "with" and "from " the church is comprehensible enough, how is one to understand the idea that the community lives *in* the self of the individual or "expresses" itself *in* that person? The implication is that a human community can inhere and act within an individual human being as *subject;* when that individual believes, *this community* believes *in that same individual.* Furthermore, how are we to understand the assertion that I can surrender my personal act of faith to the church? The implication here is that I as subject can inhere within the subject of the church, which is itself capable of action; when the church believes, then *I* believe *in it.* This accordingly insinuates a mutual "personal interiority" between the individual human being and the church conceived as subject. Although the New Testament does indeed attest the phenomenon of personal interiority,[43] it is no accident that *only the divine persons* dwell in human beings, or human beings in the divine persons (e.g., the Pauline "Christ in you" [see Rom. 8:10]; "we in Christ" [see Rom. 8:1]), never human beings — neither as individuals nor as community — in other human beings.

The notion of the church as one subject with Christ makes it difficult for Ratzinger to conceive not only the relational juxtaposition of the church with Christ, but also that of the individual human being with the church and Christ.

40. Ratzinger, *Church,* 127.
41. Ratzinger, *Prinzipienlehre,* 23; cf. idem, "Dogmatische Formeln," 36.
42. Ratzinger, "Dogmatische Formeln," 44.
43. See IV.3.2.1 below.

He does assure us that the believing self is "not simply" submerged in the collective subject, but rather must allow itself to fall completely "in order then to receive itself anew in and together with a greater self."[44] Similarly, the "personal dialogue of love" between Christ and the individual remains possible.[45] What remains obscure is how the subjectivity of individuals, which is, after all, the presupposition of this dialogue of love, is to be conceived positively within the framework of a comprehensive subject that the church with Christ represents. It is probably no accident that Ratzinger speaks of the "coalescence of existences," of "assimilation," and of an increasing sundering of dividing lines.[46]

Even the notion of a collective subject, a notion underlying all of Ratzinger's soteriological and ecclesiological thinking, is simply postulated. With great leaps, Ratzinger draws a line from the Hebrew notion of Adam to the Greek idea that "the human existence of all human beings . . . is one"[47] and then tries to express both ideas in the categories of modern personalism. He notes that the modern concept of subject is gradually loosening today, revealing "that no securely self-enclosed self really exists at all, but rather that many different kinds of forces go in and out of us."[48] Although this reference certainly prompts us to reconsider the relationship between person and community, it does not suffice to render plausible the idea of a "comprehensive personality"[49] or of a (divine-human) "super-I," as Ratzinger formulates this elsewhere.[50]

3. Although it would be appropriate at this point to query soteriologically the motives behind Ratzinger's notion of the mediation of faith, such inquiry would exceed the scope of the present internal critique to which I am limiting myself.[51] Hence I will only briefly address the anthropological presuppositions of the mediation of faith, undertaking then only at the end of the chapter and within the framework of a discussion of trinitarian personhood a more precise analysis of Ratzinger's understanding of personhood.

According to Ratzinger, the ecclesiality of the act of faith is grounded in the essential sociality of human beings.[52] The identity of the individual cannot consist in a self-enclosed personality, however articulated. "For man is the more himself the more he is with 'the other.' . . . Only through 'the other' and through

44. Ratzinger, "Theologie," 519.
45. Ratzinger, "Kirche in der Welt," 351.
46. Ratzinger, *Gemeinschaft*, 34.
47. Ratzinger, "Kirche in der Welt," 350. Cf. idem, "Wurzel," 223.
48. Ratzinger, *Gemeinschaft*, 33.
49. Ibid.
50. Ratzinger, *Introduction*, 178.
51. See IV.1.1.1 below.
52. Ratzinger repeatedly illustrates the essentially social nature of human beings by using the example of language (see Ratzinger, *Introduction*, 185f.; *Die sakramentale Begründung*, 23; *Prinzipienlehre*, 91f.).

'being' with 'the other' does he come to himself."[53] Ratzinger understands "being with others" as being *for others*. The being of the paradigmatic human being, Christ, is "pure *actualitas* of 'from' and 'for.'"[54] This double relation of human beings to others, namely, "being from" and "being toward," corresponds to the character of faith as a gift of the church incorporating believers into the church. The individual is integrated into the comprehensive ecclesial communion from and for which the individual lives. Like true human beings themselves, so also according to Ratzinger is faith essentially communal, coming as it does from and leading to others. It is both anthropologically and ecclesiologically consistent when Ratzinger defines sin as the "mystery of separation" and when, it seems, he interprets Genesis 3 from the perspective of Genesis 11. Babylon, the locus of language confusion, is a "mysterious sign" of the disintegration constituting the essence of sin.[55] This "sign" functions as the negative foil for his ecclesiology and for his view of what is Christian.

Our analysis of Ratzinger's theology of the local church and of the collegiality of bishops will confirm that *"being from" and "being toward" constitute the fundamental structure of communality.* Moreover, as the figure of Christ shows, who "receives himself from the Father and perpetually gives himself back to the Father,"[56] the basic structure of communality and fellowship is simultaneously the basic structure of what is Christian in the larger sense.[57] This not only reveals clearly the identity between what is truly Christian and what is truly ecclesial, but at the same time underscores the notion that communal Christian existence must be conceived in correspondence to trinitarian communion.[58]

1.2. Sacrament and Communion

Humans are corporeal as well as communal beings. If a person's relation to God is to be a human relation to God, then it must also be a *corporeal* and, precisely in its corporeal quality, a social relation to God.[59] It is here that the sacramental mediation of faith finds its anthropological grounding. The sacraments express and guarantee all three essential features of faith, namely, faith as personal act and as ecclesial and divine gift.

The communality of Christian life is expressed in the appropriation and reception of faith in the sacraments. The sacraments, which one cannot give to

---

53. Ratzinger, *Introduction*, 175.
54. Ibid., 170. Cf. in this regard Nachtwei, *Unsterblichkeit*, 27-30.
55. Ratzinger, *Das neue Volk*, 104.
56. Ratzinger, *Prinzipienlehre*, 97.
57. See Ratzinger, *Das neue Volk*, 213.
58. See 6.1 below; Ratzinger, *Prinzipienlehre*, 23.
59. See Ratzinger, *Introduction*, 184; *Die sakramentale Begründung*, 23f.

oneself, but must receive exclusively from others, attest that a person does not believe as an isolated self, but rather receives faith from the community of those "who have believed before him and who bring to him God as a given reality of their history."[60] As already emphasized, faith has in addition also an indispensable personal dimension. The simple act of dispensing the sacraments does not suffice, since conversion cannot simply "be decreed from above; one must appropriate it oneself."[61] Hence without personal response, the sacraments are "meaningless."[62]

Sacraments, however, at least according to Ratzinger and to general Catholic sacramental theology, are more than a sign of the communal mediation of personal faith. They simultaneously qualify this mediation in a certain way by making it possible to understand the gift of faith from the church as a *divine gift*. Precisely in the case of the decisive actions of the church grounding Christian existence as such (actions from which the church also lives as the church), God does not simply *use* human actions without being bound to them.[63] A person does not simply always come to faith through the witness of another person. Ratzinger distinguishes being led to faith by "private teachers" and the participation of the *church* in this same process[64] (albeit without wanting thereby to exclude these "private teachers" from the concept of church, since "church" refers not only to an "institution" preceding the individual, but also to a "community consisting of individuals").[65] If the witness of others were the only issue, then although the divine action would indeed be mediated through human beings, it would not be taking place *in* human action, and the sociality of the mediation of faith would be weakened. By contrast, sacramental mediation of faith means that "divine action *is* always divine-*human* action." Just as in Christ as the origin of the church God has acted through the God-*man*, so also in the present does God link "his quality of not being at our disposal . . . with the body of Christ."[66] Accordingly, the sacraments presuppose a community in which the historical continuity of divine action is realized;[67] Christ acts concretely through his body. However, this very community presupposes the sacraments as the medium of historical divine action; the church as the body

---

60. Ratzinger, *Prinzipienlehre*, 30.

61. Ibid., 35. Ratzinger finds the personal and communal pole of conversion expressed in the interrogatory, dialogical form of baptismal administration in the early church (Ratzinger, *Prinzipienlehre*, 34ff.).

62. Ratzinger, *Das neue Volk*, 330. Ratzinger speaks in the same context about a "primacy of conviction, of faith before mere sacramentalism" (ibid., 330).

63. This does not imply, of course, that God does not act outside the church.

64. See Ratzinger, *Prinzipienlehre*, 115.

65. Ratzinger, *Das neue Volk*, 149.

66. Ratzinger, *Church*, 126 (first emphasis mine).

67. See Ratzinger, *Sakrament*, 17.

of Christ is constituted through the sacraments. Because the subject of the sacramental action is the Lord — the church is the subject only insofar as it constitutes the one subject with Christ — the church cannot produce the sacraments from within itself. It must receive the authority to administer the sacraments. The sacramentality of the mediation of faith accordingly also attests that the acceptance of the individual by the church, which is constitutive for the faith of the individual, "is in its own turn encompassed by its [the church's] own situation of both allowing itself to be accepted and actually being accepted." Thus do the sacraments clearly reveal not only the "ecclesial dimension" of faith, but also the "theological dimension of the ecclesial being."[68]

The fundamentally communal nature of faith is the sign that faith is not at our arbitrary disposal. Both features, namely, faith's communal nature and its inaccessibility to arbitrary control, are secured by the sacraments. The character of faith as a gift (or the primacy of reception) cannot be secured by simply understanding personal faith theologically as a gift of God; one must also liturgically "practice" this faith as a gift of the church in the dispensing of the sacraments. According to Ratzinger, faith not sacramentally mediated is "self-invented faith."[69] The sacraments show that a "double transcendence" inheres in the act of faith, namely, an ecclesiastical and a divine.[70] The sacramentally anchored ecclesiastical transcendence of the act of faith both corresponds to and secures its divine transcendence. The sacramental mediation of faith guarantees that faith as a gift of God does not degenerate into a human product theologically stylized into a gift of God.

Substantively, inclusion in the ecclesial communion is a result of inclusion in the trinitarian communion. Through faith in the triune God, one becomes a member of the church. From a temporal perspective, however, inclusion in the trinitarian communion proceeds by way of inclusion in the ecclesial communion, since faith presupposes a process of acclimation to the already extant life form of the church community, as well as acceptance into this community. Thus is ecclesial unity bound to the unity of human beings with the triune God and realized through it.[71] Acceptance into the ecclesial communion and entrance into the trinitarian communion coincide temporally in the sacrament of baptism.

68. Ratzinger, *Prinzipienlehre,* 116.
69. Ratzinger, "Warum," 70.
70. Ratzinger, *Prinzipienlehre,* 42.
71. Ibid., 51; cf. *Volk,* 210.

2. Eucharist and Communion

Through baptism, human beings step out of isolation and into the trinitarian communion, and thus also into the communion of the church, thereby becoming ecclesial beings. *As* ecclesial beings, however, they live from the *Eucharist.* The church itself, which participates sacramentally in making individuals into Christians, realizes its own being as church in the Eucharist.[72] This is the fundamental thesis of eucharistic ecclesiology. In what follows, I will examine the specific form of Ratzinger's eucharistic ecclesiology and in the process also address the question of how consistently he represents it.

1. Although Ratzinger calls eucharistic ecclesiology "the real core of Vatican II's teaching on the church,"[73] he did not have to wait until Vatican II to execute this turn to eucharistic ecclesiology. He was already advocating eucharistic ecclesiology in his first ecclesiological works (1954) and was doing so in express delimitation over against both a "hierarchical-institutional" ecclesiology (shaped partly by anti-Reformation polemic) and an "organic-mystical" ecclesiology.[74] Both these ecclesiologies are one-sided, the first because it brackets out the decisive pneumatological dimension of the church, the second because it is unable to ground sufficiently the visibility of the church. According to Ratzinger, the strength of correctly understood eucharistic ecclesiology is that it eliminates both defects.

The church emerged from Jesus' Passover meal with his disciples and found its "vital center" in the Lord's Supper. "The church is celebration of the Eucharist; the Eucharist is the church. These two do not stand next to one another, but rather are the same."[75] Regular celebration of the Eucharist realizes ever anew the ecclesially mediated union with Christ that makes human beings into Christians through incorporation into the trinitarian and ecclesial communion; "through his sacramental body, Christ draws Christians into himself." They become the "whole Christ," head and body, and bear his existence through the ages.[76] In this eucharistic view of the church, ecclesiology and soteriology move into intimate proximity, making comprehensible Ratzinger's reference to the "necessity of the Eucharist," which is nothing other than the necessity of the church itself.[77]

---

72. Ratzinger, *Das neue Volk*, 82.

73. Ratzinger, *Church*, 7.

74. See Ratzinger, *Volk*, 211; *Das neue Volk*, 90ff.

75. Ratzinger, *Prinzipienlehre*, 55; cf. Ratzinger, *Volk*, 93ff. Although in *Gemeinschaft*, 70ff., Ratzinger does distinguish between Eucharist and assembly, he finds both concepts expressed in the designation of the church as *communio.*

76. Ratzinger, *Das neue Volk*, 83.

77. Ratzinger, *Schauen*, 79. "The necessity of the Eucharist is identical with the necessity of the church, and vice versa."

Union with Christ realized concretely through the sacramental body of Christ shows that referring to the church as the body of Christ is alluding not merely to the "mysterious interior" of the church, but rather to the visible "communion of those who celebrate the Lord's Supper together."[78] Whoever participates in the celebration of the Eucharist not only stands through Christ in communion with the triune God and with all other participants, but is also *visibly identified* as such. Insofar as the church is conceived from the perspective of the Eucharist as the body of Christ, the body of Christ itself acquires "a concretely tangible, virtually legally identifiable point of departure."[79] The Eucharist makes the church into the church by making it into the *visible* communion with the triune God.

2. Eucharistic ecclesiology makes it possible to ascribe full ecclesiality to the local church rather than demoting it to the lowest degree or to an administrative district of the larger church (as was the tendency in the theology of the Latin church, especially in the second millennium). Every local assembly in which the Eucharist is celebrated is an "immediate and actual realization of the church itself," for it has the Lord totally.[80] Hence the ecclesiality of a eucharistic communion cannot be increased. "There is nothing more than the eucharistic communion. The unity of the larger church is in such a view a pleromatic enhancement, but not a completion or increase of ecclesiality."[81] The one church of God exists in no other way than "in the various individual local congregations, and is realized there in the cultic assembly."[82]

Wherever the Eucharist is celebrated, there, too, is a church in the full sense of the word. If this is the case, then the question concerning the ecclesiality of a congregation changes into the question concerning the conditions that congregation must fulfill in order to celebrate the Eucharist. Ratzinger mentions two, deriving both from the character of Christ's presence in the Eucharist. First, the Lord does not emerge from the assembly itself, but rather is only able "to come to it from the outside, as the one who gives himself."[83] This is why no community can celebrate the Eucharist and make itself into a church simply of its own accord. To become a church, it must receive itself, and must do so "from where it already is and where it really is: from the sacramental community of his [Christ's] body that progresses through history."[84] Second, the Lord present in the Eucharist is "always only one, undivided not only at the particular place itself, but in the whole world."[85]

---

78. Ratzinger, *Das neue Volk,* 98.
79. Ibid., 84.
80. Ratzinger, *Prinzipienlehre,* 315; cf. p. 308; also *Church,* 7.
81. Ratzinger, *Prinzipienlehre,* 308.
82. Ratzinger, *Das neue Volk,* 97; cf. pp. 107f.
83. Ratzinger, *Prinzipienlehre,* 308.
84. Ratzinger, *Church,* 10; cf. *Fest,* 59.
85. Ratzinger, *Prinzipienlehre,* 308.

One can have the Lord in the Eucharist only if one stands in unity with other congregations celebrating the Eucharist. This is why there can be no church that separates itself from other churches of God. "The unity among themselves of the communities that celebrate the Eucharist is not an external accessory for eucharistic ecclesiology but its inmost condition."[86]

Ratzinger sets this *communio*-ecclesiology up against congregationalist ecclesiology, whose basic idea is allegedly that "assembling in the name of Jesus itself produces the church."[87] From the Free Church perspective, of course, this is certainly a caricature that ignores the work of the Holy Spirit to which Free Church ecclesiology refers in this context.[88] From Ratzinger's perspective, however, this is an adequate description, deriving as it does from one (not quite plausible) basic principle of his own ecclesiology, namely, that the Holy Spirit who makes Christ present can be had only with his *whole* body. Given this principle, one can understand why Ratzinger believes he must criticize the thesis, one explicitly rejected by Free Church ecclesiology itself, that the church is constituted through the interaction of its members. According to his own principle, the church can be constituted only by "receiving itself from the whole and giving itself back to the whole."[89] Because Christ himself is only with the whole, so also must the local church derive from the whole and be for the whole. The correct "translation" of the expression "the church is the Eucharist" is accordingly "the church is communion, and is such with the whole body of Christ."[90] For in the Eucharist, which is only one just as the Lord is one,[91] one enjoys communion with the whole body of Christ.

Here we encounter the same basic structure of communion, which, as we have seen, underlies Ratzinger's understanding of faith. Just as a human being cannot make himself into a Christian, but rather must receive Christian existence from the church, so also a congregation cannot make itself into a church, but rather must receive its being as church from the whole church. Moreover, just as a Christian cannot isolate herself from the church if she is to live as a Christian, but rather must live for the church, so also can a congregation not isolate itself from the whole church, but rather derives its being as a church only through abiding "in the whole" and in life for the whole. In this double fashion — being from and being toward — the individual needs the church congregation in order to be a Christian just as a congregation needs the larger church in order to be a church. For both the individual Christian

---

86. Ratzinger, *Church*, 11; cf. *Prinzipienlehre*, 308.
87. Ratzinger, *Gemeinschaft*, 76.
88. See chapter III below.
89. Ratzinger, *Fest*, 59; cf. p. 128; *Prinzipienlehre*, 309.
90. Ratzinger, *Gemeinschaft*, 77.
91. See "Kirche," note 5.

and the local church can exist as such only within the comprehensive communion.

What, however, does this thesis, implied in the notion of *Christus totus*, concerning the constitution of local churches and individual Christians mean for the ecclesiality of non-Catholic churches and for church membership of non-Catholic Christians? Shortly after Vatican II, Ratzinger wrote, doubtless not just as an interpretation of the Council, that the Council "with full consciousness designated as churches not only the churches of the East, but also communities deriving from the Reformation."[92] A few years later, however, he suggested that using the term *ecclesia* for "the separated Oriental churches, that separation notwithstanding," represented an "as yet unresolved systematic-theological situation."[93] This statement is followed, however, only by reference to the replacement of *est* by *subsistit* in *Lumen gentium* 8 *("corpus Christi* est *ecclesia Romana"* was replaced by *"haec ecclesia . . .* subsistit *in ecclesia catholica"*), though with no attempt to clarify theologically this decision not to identify straightaway the Catholic Church with the church of Christ. Nor is this an accident. It seems that Ratzinger's ecclesiological premise offers no real possibilities for such theological clarification. One might have predicted his later insistence that certain life forms of universal church unity do not merely have the character of manifestation, but rather are constitutive for the being of individual churches as churches.[94] A local church exists in communion with the entire church; that is, "it is Catholic, or it does not exist at all."[95]

The inner logic of his ecclesiology must also lead to the assertion that whoever "does not take communion (or does so outside the one *communio*) . . . is not in the body of Christ, in the church," since the church as the body of Christ is the "communion of those who together receive the body of the Lord."[96] The ancient tradition according to which baptism "is the sacrament through which one becomes a Christian and thus is to be understood as constitutive for membership" functions as a disruptive factor in eucharistic ecclesiology. This

92. Ratzinger, *Das neue Volk*, 319.

93. Ibid., 235f.

94. Ratzinger suggested as much in his polemic against the Anglican-Catholic Consensus Documents, according to which "a Church out of communion with the Roman See may lack nothing from the viewpoint of the Roman Catholic Church except that it does not belong to the visible manifestation of full Christian communion" (Ratzinger, *Church*, 74). I do not wish to enter into the inner-Catholic, though ecumenically extremely significant, dispute concerning how Vatican II is to be interpreted on this point. For an interpretation corresponding more to Ratzinger's own interpretation in *Das neue Volk* (p. 319) than *Church* (p. 74, note 15), see Sullivan, *Church*, 63ff.

95. Ratzinger, *Gemeinschaft*, 77.

96. Ratzinger, "Kirche," 179.

tradition can be accommodated only through the paradoxical assertion that "the *excommunicatus* belongs to the communion in the negative form of *excommunicatio*."[97] Insofar as Ratzinger's ecclesiological premise holds that those who do not commune in the one communion are excommunicated, his ecclesiological thought is exclusive.

3. Notwithstanding the eucharistic basis of ecclesiology according to which the Eucharist is always celebrated in a local church,[98] Ratzinger still believes that the *priority of the larger church* is implied in the two ways the local church is related to the larger church, namely, in its being "from the church" and "toward the church." Because the one Lord is present in all eucharistic communions, the one larger church comes about not through addition of these self-enclosed and fully developed eucharistic communions, but rather antecedes and sustains them; the church derives its unity "in correspondence to the singularity of the body of Jesus Christ."[99] Furthermore, the congregation receives itself from the larger church together with the Lord, who comes to it from the larger church and precisely thereby "from outside." A "double transcendence" attaches to ecclesiality just as it does to faith, namely, a derivation from the larger church and from the divine, whereby the derivation from the larger church is not only an expression, but also the guarantee of the divine transcendence. For if a congregation lacks derivation from the larger church, then according to Ratzinger it becomes a human work, and is demoted from the communal locus of communion with the triune God to a mere framework for self-realization, however articulated, or for social engagement.[100]

If one associates eucharistic ecclesiology with the notion of the universal unity of the church as a subject, then the priority of the church is unavoidable. Because the "whole Christ," *caput et membra,* is present in every Eucharist, the "church of Christ" is simultaneously present in every local church, as stated in *Lumen gentium.*[101] Each local church is nothing other than a concrete realization of the universal church, which "is truly active and present" within it.[102] The universal church can be understood here only in the sense of the entire *communio sanctorum* transcending but also encompassing the overall earthly church; the whole Christ expressly includes the sojourning church. Under the — false, as I will try to show[103] — assumption that the church is one subject

97. Ibid.

98. There can be no Eucharist of the universal church in the sense of a *statio orbis* (see Afanassief, "Statio orbis"; Legrand, *Réalisation,* 166, note 23.

99. Ratzinger, *Schauen,* 79.

100. See Ratzinger, *Church,* 194f.; *Fest,* 128.

101. *Lumen Gentium* 26.

102. See *Christus Dominus* 11. Cf. Ratzinger, *Gemeinschaft,* 41.

103. See III.2.1.3 below.

with Christ, it is impossible to argue against the "temporal and ontological priority" of the universal church.[104] It is doubtful, however, whether this can also be demonstrated in the actual development of the early church and of Lukan ecclesiology, as Ratzinger believes. Calling the first church in Jerusalem (Acts 2) an *ecclesia universalis* "speaking all languages," which then begets "a church at the most varied locales" as its own "realizations," corresponds more to universalistic Catholic ecclesiology than to the New Testament text.

If one begins with a nonmetaphorical notion of the body of Christ, interprets this notion as implying the subjectivity of the whole church, and at the same time asserts the precedence of the universal church, then one must ask how every individual local church (even if it is standing in communion with the larger church) can also be conceived as the body of Christ. One possibility is to understand each local church as a concretization of the universal church, which does not exist visibly outside these local concretizations. As we will see, this is Zizioulas's proposal.[105] In this case, however, the *visible* universal church enjoys no precedence over local churches and cannot be conceived as a subject; the subjects are the local churches alone. If, by contrast, one thinks of the one visible universal church as a subject, as does Ratzinger, and if this universal church is conceived in a primary sense as the body of Christ, then the local churches become organically connected *parts* of the universal church. The question then becomes whether the eucharistic character of Ratzinger's ecclesiology does not thereby crumble from the inside. In any case, in the context of Ratzinger's ecclesiology, it is unclear why the larger church should not represent an increase of ecclesiality over against the eucharistic assembly (something Ratzinger expressly denies).[106]

The priority of the larger church, understood both diachronically and synchronically, over the local church is underscored yet again by Ratzinger's understanding of the relation between God's word and the communion, which I will examine in the next section. In the preceding discussion, we have moved from the ecclesiality of the act of faith to the priority of the larger church over the local church and *a fortiori* also over the individual Christian. Ratzinger's communal view of what is Christian is a view conceived from the perspective of the whole. This accommodates ecclesiologically the fact that biblical thinking, so Ratzinger, "seeks first the whole, and then the individual within the whole."[107]

---

104. Ratzinger, *Gemeinschaft*, 41. So also the document of the Congregation of Faith concerning the church as *communio* ("Kirche," note 9).

105. See II.3.2.3 below.

106. See 2.2 above.

107. Ratzinger, *Das neue Volk*, 95.

3. The Word of God and Communion

The sacrament of baptism makes the communality of the individual Christian visible, and the sacrament of the Eucharist makes the broader ecclesiastical communality of the local church visible. The communal form of Christian life and of ecclesiality presupposes communal mediation of the word of God, and the communality of all three — of both sacraments and of the word of God — is sustained by the universal church's sacramental role of constituting the office. In this section, I will analyze the relation between God's word and communion, and in the following section that between office and communion.

1. The relation of the word of God and communion is directly connected with the understanding of faith as a fruit of the word of God. As we have already seen, faith is for Ratzinger essentially a gift of the church. Yet if the faith of a person is a gift of the church, then the content of faith must also be a gift of the church. The cognitive content of the Christian faith is constitutive for that faith, so that without this content, it is utterly incapable of transmission. From the character of faith as a gift, it follows that if one believes correctly, then in decisive matters one can basically only believe that which the church itself believes. The community through whose sacramentally mediated gift of faith a person becomes a Christian obviously also determines the content of that faith. This is why "given the inner disposition of faith, the church has a primary claim to understanding the word."[108]

Here, the term "church" means first of all the *whole* church, including lay people. The knowledge of faith it has to give, which is subject to no higher interpretation but is rather "the measure of every interpretation," is nothing other than the "common knowledge coming from baptism."[109] This already implies that the church cannot give this knowledge of faith to itself, but rather can only receive it "from the outside." According to Ratzinger, this can happen only through revelation.

Yet how does the church come to such revelation, and how can it authoritatively transmit revelation today? Ratzinger's answer is: through tradition. He develops his initially quite general understanding of tradition from the perspective of the Augustinian concept of *memoria*. Memory is the "context creating unity in a fashion transcending the limits of the moment,"[110] thereby making

---

108. Ratzinger, *Prinzipienlehre*, 347.

109. Ibid., 347f.; cf. "Glaubensvermittlung," 23f.; "Theologie," 527, 531. Here it again becomes clear that Ratzinger, commensurate with the notion of *Christus totus,* does not wish to separate the *ecclesia congregans* from the *ecclesia congregata*, even though he by no means identifies the *ecclesia congregans* with the *ecclesia congregata* (see Ratzinger, *Das neue Volk,* 149; cf. also Eyt, "Überlegungen," 40).

110. Ratzinger, *Prinzipienlehre*, 90.

possible the mediation of the past into the present, mediation that can, however, take place only through communication, through "externalization," in language, "of memory to others."[111] Next to transtemporality, communicability is the most important characteristic of tradition as collective memory. From this it follows, Ratzinger claims, that tradition cannot live without the bearer of tradition; the latter can only be a certain community of discourse.

Ratzinger is not satisfied, however, with merely establishing the connection between tradition and community of discourse. His ecclesiology, whose foundation is the subjectivity of the church with Christ, requires that this community of discourse be understood in a particular way. Tradition is possible, Ratzinger writes, only "because many subjects become something like a single subject in the context of the common transmission of tradition."[112] Ratzinger does not, however, derive the claim that the bearer of tradition is a subject from any consideration of the conditions of tradition, but rather insinuates an understanding of the community of discourse as a feature of tradition, albeit an understanding shaped from the perspective of a certain ecclesiology. It seems obvious enough that a community of discourse is more than merely a sum of speaking human beings; it should be equally obvious, however, that from this it does not follow that a community of discourse is "one subject." (Of course, this is not to deny that social units do exhibit certain behavioral modes *similar to those of a subject.*)

The church is the bearer of the tradition of Jesus Christ. It is not, however, an "amorphous mass," but rather a subject. That the communion is a subject is, according to Ratzinger, first of all an empirical reality; the church is the language bearer of the symbol of faith. Learning to understand the language of faith means learning to understand the *church's* language of faith. The fact that the church acts as a subject of the language of faith, however, is merely a sign that it *is* a subject and a medium through which it expresses itself as a subject.[113] Without assuming that the church is ontologically a subject, it would also be impossible to interpret the empirical linguistic community of the church as a subject; "the experiential sphere transcending time" does not yet constitute a "subject unity."[114] By speaking the common language of faith, however, the church stands in the Holy Spirit opposite Christ and is thereby constituted by

111. Ibid., 91.

112. Ibid., 92.

113. Ratzinger has a tendency to search for something more profound or real behind the historical, and to view concrete reality merely as a sign for spiritual, transcendent content. Hence the earthly Jesus is portrayed less as a concrete human being than as "merely an *exemplum* of human beings" (so Kasper, "Einführung," 186; similarly also Krieg, "Ratzinger," 119). This is a result of Ratzinger's Platonizing "commitment to the primacy of the invisible as that which is genuinely real" (Ratzinger, *Einführung*, 48).

114. Ratzinger, "Dogmatische Formeln," 37.

him as subject, that is, as a subject not separated from Christ or existing in and of itself, but rather as "a new, single subject *with* Christ."[115] The process by which the church becomes a subject through the language of faith and through Christ's presence within it is not to be understood as two separate processes, but rather as two levels of the same process; the language of faith is the form of Christ's presence, and Christ's presence is the content of the language of faith.

The church is a single subject with Christ not only synchronically, at every temporal point, but also in its totality diachronically through the entirety of history. According to Ratzinger, it has always remained a subject identical with itself, a statement which is, of course, theological rather than historical. This is why the church not only spiritually but also historically bridges the hermeneutical chasm separating today from yesterday. In the church, the "pluralism of history is held together in the unity of a single *memoria*."[116] This *memoria Ecclesiae* — of the whole church — is the key that opens the door to revelation for the present.[117] The one transtemporal *memoria Ecclesiae* grounds with regard to the documents of the transmission of tradition the hermeneutics of unity, which itself consists in "reading the individual statements in the context of the whole tradition and with a deeper understanding of scripture."[118]

That the church is one subject with Christ means that it has the authority to interpret "Christ yesterday with respect to Christ today."[119] The subject of revelation is and remains the living Christ, though he is such in unity with the church as his body, a unity deriving from him.[120] This is why the church is also able to mediate between the binding then and the now, and to proclaim in a binding fashion the Christ of then as one who is living now as well. Through the voice of the one and whole church, Christ himself speaks today.

2. The ecclesial subject bridging time is for Ratzinger the fundamental solution to the hermeneutical question. Scripture, which the church received rather than invented and which it thus is to serve, can only be understood from within the faith of the church itself.[121] In his commentary to *Dei Verbum*,

115. Ratzinger, "Theologie," 519 (my emphasis). Cf. Ratzinger, *Prinzipienlehre,* 138; "Dogmatische Formeln," 37.

116. Ratzinger, "Dogmatische Formeln," 34.

117. In Ratzinger's own opinion, his hemeneutic differs from South American liberation theology only insofar as he prefers to understand the "*entire* people of God in its synchronic and diachronic extension," rather than merely a specific people, as the point of mediation between then and today (Ratzinger, "Vorwort," 9).

118. Ratzinger, *Church,* 82.

119. Ratzinger, "Traditionsbegriff," 45.

120. See Ratzinger, "Buchstabe," 257.

121. Concerning Ratzinger's understanding of the relation between scripture and the faith of the church, see Ratzinger, *Das neue Volk,* 118f.; "Traditionsbegriff," 25-49; "Dogmatische Formeln," 40ff.; *Church,* 70ff.

Ratzinger did indeed dare to say that the "Holy Scriptures stand at our disposal as a standard" for the "indispensable criticism of tradition."[122] The critical function of scripture over against tradition presupposes hermeneutically that scripture "*first* must be seen, considered, and queried from within itself, and that *only then* can the development of the transmission of tradition and dogmatic analysis commence."[123] Ratzinger quickly abandoned the sequence of scripture and transmission of tradition, which already seemed like a foreign body in his commentary to *Dei Verbum,* because it could not be reconciled with the notion of the one living "whole Christ" that remains self-identical through the ages. He now resolutely took as his point of departure a reciprocity between scripture and church within the framework of the priority of the church. "The last word belongs to the church," Ratzinger said at a conference on Bible and church, "but the church must give the last word to the Bible."[124] He does not seem to consider the dangerous possibility that the church might not in fact give the last word to the Bible. The Antichrist, so Ratzinger in discussion, is lurking wherever "the Christonomy [!] of the *totus Christus*" is not taken seriously.[125]

If receptivity is to be maintained as a basic feature of faith, if faith itself is not to degenerate into a human intellectual or religious construction, the only alternative to ecclesial understanding is that each individual come directly to God's word in scripture. For both hermeneutical and theological reasons, Ratzinger considers this alternative to be mistaken. Referring to the more recent history of exegesis, he maintains that all attempts at engaging directly in dialogue with God merely end in fruitless dialogue with oneself,[126] or at best in hypotheses "about which one can certainly argue, but not on which one can depend with one's life."[127] Moreover, such an undertaking misses the character of the biblical writings themselves, since the unity and canonicity of scripture derive exclusively "from its historical bearer, the one people of God."[128] Without the faith of the church, scripture dissociates into a multiplicity of unrelated voices from the past out of which each person must distill his or her own philosophy of life. If, however, one grants to the church, to the *Christus totus,* the last word in the interpretation of scripture, then scripture ceases to be "a dead witness of past things, and becomes instead the sustaining element of common life."[129]

An analysis of the relation of unity obtaining between scripture and

---

122. Ratzinger, "Offenbarung," 519.
123. Ibid., 577 (my emphasis).
124. Stallsworth, "Story," 118. Similarly already Ratzinger, *Geschichtstheologie,* 69, 83.
125. Stallsworth, "Story," 167.
126. See Ratzinger, "Buchstabe," 257.
127. Ratzinger, "Theologie," 516; cf. "Schriftauslegung," 21.
128. Ratzinger, "Schriftauslegung," 21.
129. See Ratzinger, "Glaubensvermittlung," 31.

church would take us far beyond the goal of the present critical analysis of Ratzinger's ecclesiology. I will limit myself to a brief examination of his critique with regard to the hypothetical character of exegetical results. Now, *every* interpretation is hypothetical, even that of church documents (as the dispute surrounding Vatican II clearly shows). The temptation here is to take refuge in the doctrine of infallibility. From the fact "that God's revelatory word exists in no other fashion than through the living and witnessing mediation of the church, and that it does exist in this world in actuality through that mediation," Ratzinger concludes that "its fundamental infallibility emerges quite of itself"; that is, the conviction emerges that the church could not possibly "through that which it declares to be indispensable lead human beings away from Christ instead of to him."[130] Different interpretations are possible, however, with regard to what the church declares to be indispensable. But to free ourselves from the hypothetical, the doctrine of infallibility would have to be conceived so broadly that it would affect not only the decisive truths of faith, but their concrete *interpretation* as well. This, however, would be an utterly fundamentalist alternative to the Protestant notion of *sola scriptura*.

3. The turn to faith is fundamentally an issue of turning to truth. Because one can come to faith only through the church, however, access to truth is necessarily ecclesial. Finding truth comes about through learning the language and life forms of ecclesial communion.[131] As already explicated, this cannot be a separate community, but rather only the larger church. Christian truth discloses itself only to the *whole* church.[132]

This does not, however, mean that truth is identical with that which is believed *semper ubique ab omnibus* understood in static terms. Commensurate with the basic ecclesiological conviction of the historically transpiring and living subjectivity of the church, the disclosure of truth from the perspective of the whole church introduces rather a historical dynamic into the understanding of truth. That is, at no one point in history does truth exist absolutely, nor will it be able to do so until the end of time.[133] Every "today" is relativized both through the memory of the entirety of "yesterday" and through anticipation of the final "tomorrow." From this it follows that the sojourning church's understanding of truth can never be perfect, even though it is better and deeper today than yesterday.[134] But is this progressivist view of our access to truth plausible? J. K. S. Reid rightly asks, "Do 20th century Roman bishops really have a 'deeper'

---

130. Ratzinger, *Das neue Volk*, 148.

131. See Ratzinger, *Prinzipienlehre*, 130.

132. Ratzinger, "Dogmatische Formeln," 32f.

133. See ibid., 33. In this sense, one can speak of a "history of the Christian faith" (see in this regard Ratzinger, *Dogmengeschichte*).

134. See Ratzinger, *Report*, 76.

and 'better' understanding than St. Paul, than the Apostles? Or is the difference not better described as 'other'?"[135]

Communal access to truth does not, according to Ratzinger, imply that truth is constituted by the church. Rather, truth precedes the church. Christ as the abiding origin of the church is truth, which is why one cannot *invent* truth; one can only *find* it, and can do so only in the church as the body of Christ.[136] As in the case of Christian existence in the larger sense, one can have Christian truth only by becoming an *anima ecclesiastica*. Like faith, Christian truth is characterized by "double transcendence"; divine truth can be received only as the truth proclaimed by the larger church. Here again, the sacramentally anchored transcendence of the church is the sign and guarantee of divine transcendence.

4. Office and Communion

1. It is only here, in the middle of my analysis of Ratzinger's ecclesiology, that I come to his understanding of office. This may surprise those who know him only as the Prefect of the Congregation for the Doctrine of the Faith who insists that the hierarchical order of the church is willed by God. His own ecclesiology, however, is so little a case of hierarchology that one could state its essentials without mentioning office even once. On the other hand, the concept of office is already contained in Ratzinger's understanding of the act of faith that makes a person into a Christian, and it is most certainly contained in his understanding of the Eucharist as that which makes the church into a communion and in his understanding of the word of God.

Ratzinger is a Catholic theologian, and accordingly he defines the concept of church not only through the sacraments and the word, but essentially also through the concept of office.[137] Office, however, is subordinated to sacraments and the word. The church is constituted in the Holy Spirit through the power of the sacraments (above all the Eucharist and baptism as initiatory sacraments) and the word. Office is not constitutive for the church in the same sense. It is merely the indispensable condition for the sacraments and the word, the sign and guarantee of their communality and thus also of their divine origin. Through the sacraments and the word, there occurs that unique interweaving of human "I" and divine "Thou" in the ecclesial "We" that actually

---

135. Reid, "Report," 131.

136. Neither, of course, can the resolutions of councils create truth. The unanimity of the council fathers does not invent new truth, but rather witnesses to truth that is already present and is now found (see Ratzinger, *Church*, 57ff., 129f.; *Report*, 61).

137. See Ratzinger, "Traditionsbegriff," 27; *Das neue Volk*, 119.

constitutes the essence of the church. Only insofar as office is necessary for the sacraments and for the word does it belong to the *esse* of the church. In any case, the purpose of office is to be a "means," albeit an indispensable means, for the sacrament and the word and only as such then for the being of the church as church.[138]

In this section, I will first try to show how with regard to the word of God Ratzinger considers the concept of office to be an inner requirement of the communality of Christian existence as implied in the act of faith. In a second step, I will examine the necessity of office for the eucharistically grounded understanding of the church as *communio ecclesiarum*. I will then examine Ratzinger's grounding of the sacramentality of office in the specific character of the church as communion. The section will conclude with a presentation of Ratzinger's understanding of the relation between the one and the many and of his understanding of an ecclesial spirituality illustrating the most significant dimension of the church reform he demands.

2. As we have already seen, the "primary claim of the church to understanding the word" follows from Ratzinger's analysis of the structure of the act of faith.[139] Although the church making this claim is indeed always more than merely an institution, it is also "not an intangible spiritual sphere in which every person might choose what he or she likes."[140] If it were such, then every person would have to "distill out" his or her own life philosophy alone, though now no longer from scripture, but rather from the wisdom of faith of the entire church. This in its own turn would mean for Ratzinger that Christian truth ultimately is a product of the reflection of the individual rather than a gift. One receives truth only if access to it is communal, only if one does not select it oneself (as in modern supermarkets), that is, only if it is given to one by the church (as in old stores). This, however, presupposes that the church itself has a voice speaking both concretely and authoritatively and attesting the truth authentically. Ratzinger's argumentation here is persuasive, however, only if one decisive but not explicitly expressed premise is persuasive, namely, that whatever is not offered and given to the individual by the whole church, speaking "in the organs of faith,"[141] is actually produced by the individual.

---

138. Ratzinger, *Das neue Volk*, 244. Prior to the Second Vatican Council, Ratzinger wrote that "the most important task of ecclesiology today will be to show how all the essential elements of the visible form of the church are anchored in its being as the body of Christ, and thus are not part of any self-sufficient visibility in which the usurpatory will of human beings opposes the event of God's free love, but rather represents part of that comprehensive reference from the visible to the invisible, the establishment of which was the meaning of the sending of Jesus Christ" (Ratzinger, "Leib," 912).

139. Ratzinger, *Prinzipienlehre*, 347; cf. 3.1 above.

140. Ratzinger, "Theologie," 526.

141. Ibid.

If with Ratzinger one accepts the necessity of a binding, authoritative voice, who can then have this voice? It cannot be a local church, since that church can only proclaim authoritatively what it has received rather than "produced" itself. Truth and the whole are indissolubly connected with one another, since Christ, who is the truth, is accessible only together with his whole body. The truth can be proclaimed authoritatively only by the concretely existing, active *universal church*. The "Church, living in the form of the apostolic succssion with the Petrine office as its centre," is the place at which the revelation given once for all is interpreted in an ongoing, authoritative, and binding fashion.[142]

These reflections on the relationship between the word of God and office reveal why, according to Ratzinger, it is precisely in one's position regarding *sola scriptura* that the difference between Protestant and Catholic ecclesiology manifests itself most clearly. Positing the principle of *sola scriptura* means committing the two greatest ecclesiological-soteriological sins. Since, according to this principle, every individual allegedly has direct access to the word of God, it confirms ecclesiological individualism; but since every attempt at conducting direct dialogue with the word of God ends basically in a dialogue with oneself, the freedom of the individual intended by the principle of *sola scriptura* leads to covert soteriological high-handedness.

Drawing on church tradition in the interpretation of scripture offers little help. Because the individual is still the subject of interpretation, the two problems with *sola scriptura* simply appear at a new level. Only if one has the authoritative and fundamentally unrevisable ecclesiastical decisions of persons holding office in the church can faith be lived communally and thereby also as a gift of God. Hence for Ratzinger, the "real antithesis in the concept of church between Catholics and Protestants"[143] resides less in making the word independent of tradition than in making it independent of *office*. For without authoritative office, tradition and scripture are taken rather than given.

3. According to Ratzinger's eucharistic ecclesiology, communion with all churches is the essential condition for the full ecclesiality of a local church.[144] The necessity of episcopally and collegially structured office derives from his specific understanding of this communion. The ability to stand in the *communio ecclesiarum* as *ecclesia* requires that every local church have at its head a bishop as its reference person to the larger church. The bishop has two intertwining

---

142. Ratzinger, *Church*, 79f. This ongoing official interpretive process is to be understood as the representational safekeeping of simple faith and of its original insights, a safekeeping, however, that simultaneously discloses the new possibilities of this faith (see Ratzinger, "Theologie," 531; *Church*, 82).

143. Ratzinger, "Traditionsbegriff," 28; cf. *Das neue Volk*, 106; *Report*, 160.

144. See 2.2 above.

functions. As the head of a local church, he ensures its ecclesiality, and as a member of the *ordo episcoporum*, he ties it into the communion of the larger church. On the basis of the bishop's dual function here, one deriving from the requirements of the communion itself,[145] the church is organized vertically (local church), and then within this vertical structure is arranged horizontally into a network through the *ordo episcoporum* (larger church).[146]

Every local congregation is organized internally in a vertical fashion, since it is led by a bishop (together with presbyters and deacons). The bishop gathers together all the believers at a specific locale into a church. From this follows the singularity of the episcopal office at a specific locale and the binding of church membership to communion with the bishop. "One cannot enjoy the 'blood shed for many' by withdrawing to the 'few.' "[147] This is one of the main reasons why the "monarchical episcopate" represents "an irrevocable essential form of the church." "The one bishop at a single locale stands for the church being one for all, since God is one for all."[148] Furthermore, the bishop represents the thus assembled congregation to the whole church and to the one Christ; in this way, he ensures the unity of the congregation and makes it into a self-contained (not isolated!) totality in which the one church of God is realized. If through the bishop this vertically organized local church is indeed to be bound into the *communio ecclesiarum*, however, then the bishop must also be a representative of his congregation to the larger church. A bishop can correctly discharge his task within the *ordo episcoporum*, which is itself indispensable for the *communio ecclesiarum*, only by standing in "a sibling relationship with those who believe with him."[149]

Every bishop simultaneously stands within the horizontal structure of the

---

145. See Ratzinger, *Das neue Volk*, 178.

146. See ibid., 205. According to Ratzinger, the idea of collegiality involves the "reestablishment of the organism of individual churches in the unity of the larger church," and not "the *plena et suprema potestas* of the *collegium* over the larger church and its counterbalancing with the *plena et suprema potestas* of the Pope" (ibid., 186, polemicizing explicitly against Rahner).

147. Ratzinger, *Gemeinschaft*, 73.

148. Ibid., 73f.

149. Ratzinger, *Das neue Volk*, 215. This representative function of the bishop is not to be confused with parliamentary representation. The bishop does not represent the members of the congregation as individuals, but rather the congregation as such in the sense of a "personification and summary of the body" whose head he is (ibid., 162). Neither, however, can the body thus represented by a bishop be an internally closed-off local church, but rather only a local church that is what it is precisely because in it the entire church is actualized. Hence the task of the bishop as representative is not "to determine the statistical mean value of the opinions of those whom he represents and then to bring these to bear in a form as chemically free as possible of his own additions"; his task is rather to represent "the *common elements of the church*" (Ratzinger, *Das neue Volk*, 162, my emphasis; cf. Ratzinger, *Church*, 57ff.).

one *ordo episcoporum*. The bishop's membership in this *ordo* is not something that may or may not be added as a supplement to his status as bishop, but rather is itself constitutive for that status. Just as a Christian is a Christian only by standing in communion with other Christians, and just as a congregation is a church only by standing in communion with other congregations, so also is a bishop a bishop only by "standing in communion with other bishops."[150] One is a bishop only if one is accepted by the communion of bishops as a bishop and then remains in that communion, a communion to be understood both synchronically (catholicity) and diachronically (apostolicity).[151] The status of bishop is accordingly shaped by the same basic structure of communality as is the status of the Christian; a person is a bishop from and toward others. Nor should this come as a surprise, since the communality of office is but an expression of the general Christian communion at the level of office, just as this communion itself is an expression of the trinitarian communion.[152]

At the anthropological, soteriological, and ecclesiological level, one encounters in Ratzinger the same double definition of the basic structure of communality derived from the Trinity, namely, *being from* and *being toward.* Closer examination, however, reveals that the occurrence of this basic structure is the *maximal form* of ecclesial communion rather than its indispensable condition. Ratzinger resolutely maintains the first member of this basic structure; only that which comes from others, and that means from the whole, can be communal. By contrast, the second member is often reduced from "toward" to "with," and the indispensable content of this "with" is then sometimes understood as "not against." If this is the case, then the ecclesial communion, although indeed oriented toward love, is not constituted by love, at least not by the love exhibiting the basic structure derived from the Trinity. As underscored by the indispensability of "being from others," communion is constituted by *standing* in a relation of sacramental and for that reason also office-bound reception. Although this indeed can, following Augustine, be *interpreted* as love,[153] it is another question entirely whether doing so illuminates or veils ecclesial reality.

4. The communality of office deriving from the whole church is both expressed and secured through the sacramentality of episcopal consecration. It is in the nature of this sacrament that it does not involve the individual as individual, but rather incorporates him into a new communion and obligates

---

150. Ratzinger, *Das neue Volk,* 116; cf. pp. 164, 204, 206.

151. See Ratzinger, *Prinzipienlehre,* 256.

152. See Ratzinger, *Das neue Volk,* 214, 220.

153. According to Augustine, *caritas* is not "a subjective disposition," but rather "attachment to the church, specifically and necessarily to that particular church which itself stands in *caritate,* i.e., in the eucharistic love relationship with the entire planet" (Ratzinger, *Volk,* 138).

him to service in it.[154] Because one can receive consecration only from bishops standing both synchronically and diachronically in communion with other bishops *(ordo episcoporum in successio apostolica)*, this consecration binds the new bishop into the entire *ordo episcoporum*. The consecratory sacrament is thus "the expression and simultaneously also the guarantee of standing together within tradition from the beginning on."[155]

The sacrament of consecration qualifies the status of bishop as derived from the whole. This is why consecration vouches for the divine origin of episcopal authority. One cannot receive this authority from the Lord in the solitude of a private relationship with God, nor through the mediation of one or even several congregations. It can be grounded only in "the 'sacramental' empowerment of Jesus Christ himself as given to the whole church."[156] The sacrament of consecration at once grounds not only this episcopal authority, but also the universal communality of the Christian faith and thus also its quality of not being at our arbitrary disposal.[157] The transmission of faith is bound to episcopal authority. Through the actions of the universally and communally constituted bishop, the person comes into contact with the entire communion of the church and thus also into contact with Christ, who binds both the person and the entire church into the trinitarian communion; for Christ has bound himself to his whole body, since the body is indeed one subject with him.

5. Ratzinger's understanding of the episcopal structure of the church is based on a certain understanding of the relation between the one and the whole. At the local level, as we have already seen, the multiplicity of church members is brought together into a totality by the one bishop. A similar relation between the individual and the whole also obtains at the level of the larger church. The horizontal network of bishops and their congregations is dependent on its vertical connection with the bishop of Rome. Although "the unity of the larger church is indeed based on the cross-connections of bishops to one another," it must orient itself toward the *sedes Romana.*[158] For the Pope is "placed in direct responsibility to the Lord . . . to embody and secure the *unity* of Christ's word and work."[159] The structure of the universal church corresponds to the structure of the local church (more precisely, the reverse is the case; the local churches, which are secondary with regard to the universal church, are shaped "after the model of the universal Church"[160]).

---

154. See Ratzinger, *Das neue Volk*, 219.
155. Ratzinger, *Prinzipienlehre*, 256.
156. Ratzinger, *Fest*, 84.
157. See Ratzinger, *Prinzipienlehre*, 309.
158. Ratzinger, *Das neue Volk*, 206, 211.
159. Ibid., 169 (my emphasis).
160. *Lumen Gentium* 23; cf. *Ad Gentes* 20.

Over against every individual or communal particularism, Ratzinger underscores the totality; a Christian, a local church, and a bishop always derive from and orient themselves toward the whole. Nor can this be otherwise if the primary category of his ecclesiology is *Christus totus*. From this it also follows that the totality is to be conceived from the principle "single individual," a principle grounded both soteriologically and christologically. Because Christianity is concerned with the salvation of the whole, it subscribes to the principle "single individual." There can be but one redeemer for the whole world;[161] any plurality of redeemers would necessarily involve their respective particularity. Christ's singularity follows from his universality, and this singularity then constitutes the foundation of the unity of the church as his body. Since the earthly church is the visible side of the one body of Christ, bearing through the ages the work of its head, which is itself directed toward the whole, the principle "single individual" applies within the church as well; at its head it must always have the one who is responsible for it and for its unity and who thus guarantees its totality; otherwise, the visible church would not correspond to the invisible.[162] An ecclesiology of universal communion thus requires an ecclesiology of individual responsibility, not least at the level of the single individual who vouches for totality.[163]

If the relation to all other churches is essential for the ecclesiality of the local church, and if the bishop of Rome is essential for the unity of the church, then the bishop of Rome is also essential for the ecclesiality of individual local churches. Loss of this element of unity with the successors of Peter wounds the church "in the essence of its being as church."[164] That this ecumenically so offensive thesis could come from Ratzinger's pen can surprise only those unfamiliar with his theology. The systematic vortex of his eucharistic ecclesiology

161. See Ratzinger, *Introduction*, 187f.

162. The principle of "individuals" must apply at the local level no less than at the universal level, since it is in the local church that the entire being of the church as church is actualized. For the fact that the church "as a *whole* is only one manifests itself concretely insofar as at a given *place* it is only one." And the fact that at that given place it is only one also entails the principle "only one bishop in a congregation"; a local congregation can have but *one* leader — even if this leadership could "at first be collegial" (Ratzinger, *Das neue Volk*, 123).

163. See Ratzinger, *Church*, 32ff., where "personal responsibility" is viewed as the "core of the doctrine of primacy" (p. 43). Concerning the personal reponsibility of the laity, see section 5, *"Communio Fidelium,"* below.

164. Ratzinger, *Gemeinschaft*, 88. Cf. also "Kirche," note 13. It is revealing that in his book *Zur Gemeinschaft gerufen*, which seeks to offer "something like an initial guide for Catholic ecclesiology" (p. 9), the chapter on "Origin and Nature of the Church" is followed immediately by the transition to a discussion of the primacy of Peter and the unity of the church. Only then come the chapters concerning the commission of the bishop and the nature of priesthood.

takes him precisely to the (un)ecumenical position he held before Vatican II, namely, that the unity of the church consists

> in the *communio* of the individual congregations with one another. The characteristic sign of the true *communio* over against the false *communiones* of heretics is *communio* with the *sedes apostolicae*. The *sedes apostolica* as such is Rome, so that one can say that *communio catholica* = *communio Romana*; only those who commune with Rome are standing in the true, that is, catholic *communio;* whomever Rome excommunicates is no longer in the *communio catholica,* that is, in the unity of the church.[165]

Ratzinger's understanding of the relation between the one and the whole, grounded as it is in the notion of *Christus totus,* has important consequences for access to pneumatic authority within the church. The one Christ acts through the one and whole church that is his body. Because the latter exists visibly and is capable of action *as a totality* only through the one, all of Christ's activity must proceed through the narrow portals of the office of Peter. Of course, Ratzinger stipulates that this one must be completely transparent for Christ.[166] His authority is "vicarial" power, power that is not his own, but rather of the one whom he visibly represents; it is the *living Christ* who acts through him. Nevertheless, it is only by way of him that Christ acts even in his whole body. Here, direct papal authority over every individual local church moves into the foreground at the cost of the autonomous and immediate responsibility of every bishop for his local church. This seems to me to be the consequence of Ratzinger's understanding of the relation between the one and the whole within the framework of the notion of *Christus totus.* Hence here, too, we see that in his ecclesiology the notion of *Christus totus* stands in tension with his own intention of presenting a eucharistic ecclesiology, since a consistent eucharistic ecclesiology would have to preserve the independence of every bishop.

    6. The sacramental authority deriving from Christ — "I give what I myself cannot give; I do what does not come from me"[167] — corresponds to a spirituality of divestment consisting in perpetual renunciation of what is one's own. Such divestment should characterize the entire church, from the Pope to simple believers. In such "self-divestment and selflessness," all the members of the church are then "assimilated to the trinitarian mystery," living thus according to the basic pattern according to which they themselves have been created.[168] No one should live for himself or herself; every person should divest himself or herself and live in the relation of pure "being from" and "being toward."

165. Ratzinger, "Kirche," 178f.
166. See ibid., 41ff.
167. Ratzinger, *Gemeinschaft,* 108.
168. Ibid.

Thus does spirituality correspond to the basic structure of communality. Rather than being a pious supplement to ecclesiology, it is grounded in its very premise; the church is a communion of love of human beings among one another and with the triune God.[169] Before examining the relation between the trinitarian and ecclesial communion, I must address Ratzinger's understanding of the position of believers within the church; first, however, a comment about reform in the church.

Spirituality is Ratzinger's answer to the desire for reform in the church. Vicarial authority deriving only from the whole, from *Christus totus,* basically determines the structure of the church. Once the structure of the church is established, a structure willed by the Lord and which alone allows Christ to act within the church, then reforms affecting essentials can only involve either the correct ecclesiastical "functioning" of this same structure or spirituality. Efforts at other reforms merely distract from the essentials. "Because of so much talk about 'reforming,' we end up speaking only about ourselves, and the gospel is hardly even mentioned."[170] This is why the sloughing of what is one's own occupies far more space in Ratzinger's writings than does, for example, the securing of rights within the church.[171]

This position is based on the conviction that no "reform of human beings and of humankind [is possible] without moral renewal."[172] There are no optimal (so to speak, "foolproof") structures needing no spirituality; if such were to exist, they would be merely the structures of slavery.[173] If the church is to continue to be concerned with encountering the triune God, then, in Ratzinger's view, any structural elements not involving the mediation of this encounter can only be secondary.[174] It is hard to dispute Ratzinger's main point, though what is secondary can either facilitate or hinder access to what is primary, can correspond to or contradict it. Moreover, structures could be created that are not foolproof but whose functioning must not necessarily presuppose unrealistic ethical maturity. In this sense, neglect of institutional reality and concentration on spirituality and morality risk passing by the important problems of church life.[175]

---

169. Concerning the significance of spirituality in Ratzinger's ecclesiology, see Fahey, "Ratzinger," 82.

170. Ratzinger, "Glaube," 538.

171. Ratzinger also speaks about the rights of individual Christians and about those of the community (see Ratzinger, "Demokratisierung," 38f.), and he does mention the necessity of the practical "modes of mutual exchange and of mutual care" (Ratzinger, *Das neue Volk,* 216); the center of gravity, however, resides in spirituality and service.

172. Ratzinger, *Gemeinschaft,* 140.

173. See Ratzinger, *Das neue Volk,* 142, 189.

174. See Ratzinger, "Warum," 60.

175. See Legrand, *Réalisation,* 216.

5. *Communio Fidelium*

1. Commensurate with his eucharistic premise, Ratzinger examines the position of the laity within the church from the perspective of the liturgical "We" bound into the "I" of the larger church. In worship, laypersons are not the passive objects of the priest's activity of making Christ present; rather, the subject of the liturgical event is "precisely the assembled congregation as a whole; the priest is the subject only insofar as he co-embodies this subject and is its interpreter."[176] To be sure, the individual congregation possesses this subjectivity only insofar as it is the locus of realization of the whole church, which is the real subject of the liturgical event. From Augustine, Ratzinger learned not to ascribe one-sidedly to priests what actually attaches to the church as such. Augustine ascribed to the entire holy people of God "the entire salvific action of the church," since the subject of priestly action is not Christ directly, but rather "along with Christ the entire *ecclesia sancta.*"[177]

The priest stands not opposite the church, but rather fundamentally "*in* the entire living church" acting in him.[178] In this limited sense, there is in the church "no laity that is merely the recipient of the word and not also the word's active bearer."[179] Like Augustine, however, Ratzinger understands the salvific acts of the church acting with Christ as proceeding "through the visible instrumental acts of the official hierarchy."[180] Nor can it be otherwise if in the liturgy Christ is to act with the *whole* church, since a concrete congregation can act liturgically as a whole only through the one, namely, the bishop or the priest who makes it into a unity; and the *Christus totus* can act in this one only if the latter possesses authority coming from the entire church. The exclusivity of priestly activity is thus the indispensable presupposition of the comprehensive inclusivity of liturgical action.

In what follows, I will analyze Ratzinger's understanding of democratization in the church, of the liturgical form of worship, and of ecclesial spirituality, all of which derive from the above understanding of the position of the *communio fidelium* in liturgy.

2. Because the church is a eucharistic assembly (and does not simply assemble, among other things, to celebrate the Eucharist), church leadership cannot be a "purely political-administrative matter," but rather must take place "in the authority of sacramental proclamation."[181] This is why laypersons can-

---

176. Ratzinger, "Demokratisierung," 39.
177. Ratzinger, *Volk*, 149.
178. Ratzinger, *Das neue Volk*, 151 (my emphasis).
179. Ibid.
180. Ratzinger, *Volk*, 149.
181. Ratzinger, "Demokratisierung," 32.

not lead the church; they do not possess this authority coming from the whole,[182] though this does not mean that the laity is to be excluded completely from church leadership. Because every assembled congregation as a whole is the subject of liturgical celebration, Ratzinger concludes that as a congregation it is also a legal subject within the church. This subjectivity of the congregation should be concretely appropriated "through the empowering of its own congregational ('democratic') activity."[183] From this it then follows that appointment to office is "never to come about *only* from above."[184]

The individual congregation, however, is not the subject of liturgical activity as a self-enclosed entity. Because the *one* church is realized in the worship service of the individual congregation, the real subject of the liturgy is the "*communio sanctorum* of all places and all times" realizing itself in the assembled congregation.[185] This expresses liturgically the fact that the assembled congregation is a church only from and toward the larger church. Thus the individual congregation can act as a subject "correctly only if it stands in unity with the larger church." From this it follows that appointment to office can never come about "only from below," but rather must "always *also* include within itself a consideration of the larger church."[186]

Quite independent of how appointment to office is to occur, one must certainly ask how compatible is the claim that a local church is a legal subject with the ontological and temporal priority of the larger church. If the local church is only a local church insofar as the larger church, both the invisible *and* the visible, is realized and active within it, how can it then have rights *over against* the larger church? For the local church to be a legal subject seems to require (at least) an ecclesiology acknowledging a relation of mutual indwelling and inclusion between the larger church and the local church rather than a relation of one-sided realization.

3. Although all the members of a congregation are coparticipants in the liturgical *actio*,[187] no individual congregation is permitted to "fashion" its own liturgy. Precisely as participants in liturgy, the members of a congregation do not stand as a self-contained entity, but rather are integrated into the liturgical activity of the whole church, of the entire *communio sanctorum*, and realize it

---

182. According to Ratzinger, democracy in the church cannot be grounded charismatically, since charisma is a pneumatic rather than a democratic principle: charisma is the "expression of an inaccessible empowerment from above, not of commonly accessible empowerment from below." Hence according to Ratzinger, "the concept of charisma should disappear from the debate concerning democratization" (Ratzinger, "Demokratisierung," 26f.).

183. Ratzinger, "Demokratisierung," 41; cf. *Das neue Volk*, 221.

184. Ratzinger, "Demokratisierung," 41.

185. Ratzinger, "Liturgie," 249; cf. Ratzinger, *Das neue Volk*, 219.

186. Ratzinger, "Demokratisierung," 41.

at a concrete locale. This is why the liturgy must be protected against "the arbitrariness of the group (including clerics and specialists)."[188] One cannot design the liturgy oneself; one must receive it from the whole church in which it lives and organically grows. This universally and communally secured, dynamic, nonarbitrary character of the liturgy "guarantees and demonstrates that something more and greater is taking place here . . . than human beings could ever do on their own; as such, it expresses the objective empowerment for joy and participation in the cosmic drama of Christ's resurrection, with which the status of the liturgy stands or falls."[189] Wherever the individual person or group "acts liturgically" in an independent fashion, the common liturgical subject that is the church is pushed aside, and with it also Christ as "the real actant in the liturgy." This is why the arbitrarily independent group remains alone with itself, and rather than celebrating the liturgy, it merely celebrates "itself" and thus "nothing at all."[190] This demand for a universally communal activity of liturgy reflects Ratzinger's basic conviction that the salvific encounter between a person and the triune God is always realized by way of universal communion.

What Ratzinger calls the "primacy of reception" is encountered at every level of his ecclesiology. The liturgy, Christian existence, the being of the church and of the bishop — all these are always received from the whole. Reception is a basic form of ecclesial existence and of human existence as such. Protestant Christianity emphasized the primacy of reception over the "justification by works" of Catholic soteriology and ecclesiology. Ratzinger gives to this charge of "justification by works" an anti-Protestant, and especially an anti-Free Church twist. The activity of the larger church is indispensable for securing the primacy of reception; the activity of the Gospel or of scripture (or even of tradition) does not suffice. A faith, a church, the word of God, a liturgy not received from the larger church is "self-invented faith," a "self-constructed congregation,"[191] a word one speaks to oneself, or a liturgy in which people merely celebrate themselves. Commensurate with the notion of *Christus totus,* there seems to be only one alternative for Ratzinger: either "from the larger church and thus from the Lord," or "self-constructed." The Protestant charge that the church has usurped for itself what God alone can do, and in the process shown itself to be a purely human organization, Ratzinger now directs against an individual Christian or an ecclesial community separated from the whole church.

187. See Ratzinger, *Fest,* 79.
188. Ratzinger, "Liturgie," 249.
189. Ratzinger, *Fest,* 60.
190. Ratzinger, "Liturgie," 247f.
191. Ratzinger, "Warum," 70.

But is it plausible to disqualify as "self-constructed" anything not received sacramentally from the larger church through the institution of hierarchical office? Does secularity really follow from equality?[192] Could one not with equal justification (for example, following the religious sociology of Emil Durkheim[193]) dare to suggest that the church identifies itself with God here precisely in order to force itself onto human beings all the more easily as a purely human organization? Ratzinger's reductive hermeneutic of the religious and ecclesial experiences of Protestant (especially Free Church) Christians is of little ecumenical promise. The implicit and explicit assertion is that those Christians living outside the sacramental framework of the larger church (or certainly those living outside communion with the bishop of Rome) merely interact with themselves, for example, in worship. Is this assertion not in fact implying that these Christians are not standing in any communion at all with the triune God? Although one is tempted to interpret Ratzinger's exclusivity merely as situationally determined polemical exaggeration, it seems rather to be a necessary consequence of his ecclesiological premise.

The exclusivity of Ratzinger's ecclesiological thinking can be seen in his use of the term "guarantee." The sacramental communality of the mediation of faith, of the way the word of God comes to bear, of the constituting of a local church and of a bishop, or the communality of the liturgy are all viewed as "guaranteeing" that in each case one is dealing with divine rather than human activity. Ratzinger's premise does not allow that there may be other guarantors of the same reality, and that one can have access to this reality even without these "guarantors."[194] For only what derives from the ecclesial whole, which can be only one, can function as a guarantor of divine actions. The exclusivity of these guarantors is corroborated by Ratzinger's frequent use of exclusive and reductionist adjectives and adverbs (such as "only," "alone," "nothing other"); these are applied not only to the being of the church and of bishops, but also to being a Christian as such and to access to revelation.[195]

4. The communal form of Christian liturgy corresponds to a fundamentally communal spirituality, since communal liturgical expression requires that it be individually internalized. Without such internalization, a person plays

192. So Ratzinger expressly in *Prinzipienlehre*, 260.
193. See Durkheim, *Elementary Forms*, 205ff.
194. Avery Dulles expresses his preference for the Catholic sacramental and official structures with the conceptual pair "likely/unlikely" (see Dulles, *Catholicity*, 165). Ratzinger's own ecclesiological point of departure does not allow this.
195. With reference to faith, see Ratzinger, *Prinzipienlehre*, 35 (though he later takes a more differentiated position: faith cannot reach *its full articulation* in a private decision of conversion" [p. 116, my emphasis, but who would argue with this anyway?]) and Ratzinger, "Theologie," 520; with reference to the status or being of the church and bishop, see Ratzinger, *Prinzipienlehre*, 266; with reference to the word of God, see Ratzinger, *Das neue Volk*, 148.

merely a communal "role" at the celebration of the liturgy, which can only mean that this person's communion with others and so also with the triune God is merely "pretended communion."[196] The reality of the communion depends in a decisive fashion on the process of internalizing the liturgical event and liturgical reality. Only where such internalization occurs "are people no longer merely juxtaposed in role-playing but actually touch one another at the level of being. *Only in this way can 'community' come about.*"[197] This *actuosa participatio* — albeit not in the sense of external activity, but rather in the sense of profound personal participation — is thus the presupposition of the communion.

Communality not only characterizes liturgical spirituality, but is a common feature of all Christian spirituality. Nor can this be otherwise, since spirituality consists in internalizing the salvific grace adopted and appropriated in faith, grace which is itself communally structured. Hence according to Ratzinger, praying is not the wrestling of a soul with its God. Here, too, one cannot "start a conversation with Christ alone, cutting out the church."[198] Learning to pray means learning the language of prayer of the mother church in order then, through appropriation of its language, to come into contact with the reality coming to expression in this very language.

The communal process of praying corresponds to the "aim of prayer (and the movement of being in which it consists)," namely, to become an *anima ecclesiastica.*[199] *Anima ecclesiastica* — this is a person who has come to herself and who at the same time stands as a free being in communion with fellow human beings and with the triune God. It does not, of course, come about simply through psychological identification with the sociological entity "church." Here the church is understood as a pneumatic organism of the body of Christ which transcends the institutional and visible but which cannot be separated from them. This is why authentic ecclesial spirituality is identical with Christ-devotion, and wherever the latter can indeed be found, there one also finds "the inner apex of the church."[200] Given this situation, one can understand how Ratzinger can describe the all-decisive ecclesiological event as well as "the deepest desire of the Council" with Romano Guardini's expression concerning the awakening of the church in our souls.[201]

---

196. Ratzinger, *Feast*, 68.
197. Ibid., 70 (my emphasis).
198. Ibid., 30.
199. Ibid, 29.
200. Ratzinger, *Das neue Volk*, 243; cf. Ratzinger, *Volk*, 146.
201. Ratzinger, *Church*, 20.

6. Trinitarian and Ecclesial Communion

Ratzinger has written little about the Trinity, though key passages in his argumentation do regularly contain brief references to the relations between the triune God and human beings. These references, however, reflect what closer examination confirms, namely, that *all* the crucial elements in his ecclesiology and entire theology are rooted in the doctrine of the Trinity. The entire life of the church, including its spirituality and structures, is shaped in correspondence to a certain understanding of the Trinity. "The church's action and behaviour must correspond to the 'we' of God by following the pattern of this relationship."[202] Nor would we expect anything different in an ecclesiology whose basic category is *Christus totus,* since *Christus totus* implies that the church, constituting one subject with Christ, is integrated into the trinitarian life of God.

1. Ratzinger's basic ecclesiological and soteriological conviction concerning the relation of the individual Christian to the collective subject of the church presupposes a certain understanding of personhood, one Ratzinger develops in analogy to trinitarian personhood. In the Trinity, "person" consists in *pure relationality; persona est relatio.*[203] Thus the Father as person is not the one begetting, but rather the "act of begetting."[204] Similarly, the Son "really loses his own identity in the role of ambassador";[205] he is the activity of being sent. Ratzinger tries to anchor this view of trinitarian personhood in the New Testament witness to Jesus Christ. According to his interpretation of Phil. 2:5-11, Jesus Christ is a person who has "emptied" himself, and, "surrendering existence-for-himself, entered into the pure movement of the 'for.' "[206] Divestment is *"pure* movement," a process of "consisting *completely"* in being sent. This movement does not take place *on* the person of Christ; rather, Christ's personhood itself consists in divestment. To arrive at this understanding of personhood, however, Ratzinger must withdraw the subject from this activity of self-divestment and then condense the activity itself into a person. As in Nietzsche's anthropology, so also here: the agent is nothing; the activity is everything.[207] Nor does Ratzinger shy away from expressly drawing this conclusion; there is no "I" remaining behind the deeds and actions of the divine persons; their actions *are* their "I."[208]

---

202. Ibid., 31 (with reference to Mühlen, *Entsakralisierung,* that is complementary [the explications are allegedly impressive and certainly take us further] though also critical [the ecclesiological applicability of the trinitarian statement is allegedly overextended]).

203. See Thomas Aquinas, *Summa Theologiae* i.40.2.

204. Ratzinger, *Introduction,* 132; *Dogma,* 211.

205. Ratzinger, *Introduction,* 135.

206. *Ibid.,* 164.

207. See Nietzsche, *Moral,* 293.

208. See Ratzinger, *Introduction,* 149.

According to Ratzinger, it would be a "great misunderstanding" to believe that Jesus Christ is an ontological anomaly. In Christ, "whom faith with certainty conceives as the one who is unique and nonrecurring, it is not merely a speculative exception that is being disclosed; rather, we find here revealed for the first time in truth what is meant by the puzzle 'human being.'"[209] The trinitarian-christological concept of person is the model for how the human personality is to be understood.[210] The meaning of this anthropological thesis for Ratzinger's ecclesiology is obvious. Only if human personhood consists in its relationality can human beings become a single subject with Christ, participate in the trinitarian communion of God, and in this way fulfill their true being. Being one subject with Christ presupposes more than that "a human being . . . does not attempt to constitute the substance of the self-enclosed self."[211] Like the persons of the Trinity, so also is the human being not permitted to have an "I" behind its relations. A purely relational understanding of human and divine personhood is the presupposition for Ratzinger's communal ecclesiology and soteriology.

Robert Krieg has rightly pointed out that the notion of person as relation evades clear understanding.[212] Quite apart from Ratzinger having to reinterpret radically the biblical story of the Son — the *Son* does not divest *himself*, but rather is the activity of divestment — he still has difficulty conceiving Christ's being as pure relation, something already evident in the inconsistency of his formulations. Next to his references to total relationality, one also finds statements such as "if there is nothing in which he [the Son] is just he, no kind of fenced-off private ground, then he coincides with the Father, is 'one' with him."[213] Ratzinger's conclusion does not follow. That there is nothing wherein the Son is just himself means that the Son is determined in everything *also* by the Father, and this in its own turn means that the Son is determined *also* by

---

209. Ratzinger, *Dogma*, 217.

210. Robert A. Krieg interprets Ratzinger's understanding of the person of Christ from the perspective of the phenomenology of love and of human personality. "Being a person means being a human being committed to other human beings in giving and taking" (Krieg, "Ratzinger," 109). This leads him to reconstruct Ratzinger's Christ as the merely "exemplary human being" whom Christians are to imitate. Ratzinger himself, however, takes the methodologically and substantively opposite path: the trinitarian concept of person is the key to the anthropological and ecclesial concept of person (see in this regard Nachtwei, *Unsterblichkeit*, 46, and esp. 262f.). This is why human beings cannot become persons simply by imitating Christ, but rather by dying and becoming new selves. This can come about only by means of an external act — according to Ratzinger, by means of a divine gift from the church.

211. Ratzinger, *Dogma*, 212.

212. Krieg, "Ratzinger," 121.

213. Ratzinger, *Introduction*, 134 (my emphasis).

himself. If this is the case, then neither *is* he *pure* relation, but rather is determined in every aspect of his being *by* the relation to his Father. Moreover, Ratzinger's understanding of the trinitarian persons as pure relations does not reconcile with his assumed biblical basis of trinitarian personhood in the "phenomenon of God who is *in* dialogue,"[214] unless one were to seek behind this divine dialogue something more profound or more real. Pure relations can neither speak nor hear.

Assuming for a moment that this purely relational understanding of the trinitarian persons is plausible,[215] one must still ask whether it can be applied to human persons. Ratzinger himself first distinguishes between divine and human personhood. In the case of human beings, the relation is added to the person; in the case of God, the person *is* simply "relationality."[216] Divine personhood as total relationality, however, provides the "guide for all personal being." Human personhood must develop toward this goal, attaining it only in the eschaton.[217] "*Pure* relation" as the fullness of human existence will then replace "*standing* in relation" as not-quite-full human existence. This movement from partial to total relationality presupposes a *quantitative* difference between "standing in relation" and "pure relation." Otherwise, radical discontinuity would obtain between protological and eschatological anthropology. Only a quantitative difference makes the gradual transition from the one to the other possible. Ratzinger seems to be convinced of such quantitative difference, as suggested by his quantitative formulations. The human being, he writes, "is all the more himself the more he is with the completely other, with God."[218] The bridge between "standing in relation" and "pure relation," however, cannot be built with quantitative categories. If relationality is total, then personhood is "pure relation"; if it is partial, then personhood is "standing in relation." The person who *is* relation (the eschatological person) cannot be the same person who *stands* in relation or has stood in relation (protological person). Put differently, the person who stands in the process of self-divestment — who is divested of self, since in Ratzinger's anthropology *self*-divestment is, strictly speaking, a self-contradiction — cannot be the same person who arises only through this process itself. Ratzinger seems to sense this as well, since even his understanding of eschatological personhood vacillates between "standing in relation" and "relation."[219]

214. Ratzinger, *Dogma*, 210.
215. For criticism, see V.3.1 below.
216. Ratzinger, *Introduction*, 132f.
217. Ratzinger, *Dogma*, 213, 221.
218. Ibid., 220.
219. When Ratzinger defines the human person as "pure relation" and then consistently describes this as the "phenomenon of total relationality," he finds himself forced to add immediately that "ultimately, of course, this can occur in fullness only in the one who

The thesis that Christ does not represent an ontological exception becomes comprehensible given the qualitative understanding of the difference between protological human personhood and eschatological human personhood, conceived in strict correspondence to the trinitarian persons. Ratzinger does not understand Christ as a "highly extraordinary human being" whom one should imitate,[220] but rather as the Son of God who at the same time is the paradigmatic human being, so that in him human beings become that which he himself is. His goal is to integrate human beings into the trinitarian life of God. Given the inner logic of Ratzinger's thinking, one must say that if anything comes up short, it is not the divinity of Christ (which according to Ratzinger consists in total relationality with regard to the Father, a relationality which, although not completely thought through, is nonetheless vigorously postulated), but rather his humanity and the humanity of human beings themselves (which Ratzinger does not even feel in a position to postulate resolutely as total relationality).

2. This understanding of person as pure relation yields a certain view of trinitarian unity. Because all persons are total relationality, their unity cannot come about by way of their specific personal selfhood. For this reason, trinitarian unity is also not a differentiated unity of persons standing in these relations, but rather a unity in which the Father, Son, and Holy Spirit "coincide" and in this way are "*pure* unity."[221] From this perspective, it is consistent when Ratzinger locates the unity of the triune God not at the level of persons, but rather together with the whole tradition of Western trinitarian thought at the level of substance. The result, however, is that the one substance gains the upper hand over the three relations. Ratzinger does maintain that the relations represent a form of being equiprimal with that of substance.[222] Reference to this equiprimacy "of the element of the one" and "of that of the triad" suggests a reciprocity in the relation between the two. Yet he expressly asserts that this equiprimacy of substance and persons can obtain only under the presupposition of an "all-embracing dominance of oneness" of substance.[223] This priority of substance becomes evident in yet another way as well. If persons are *pure*

---

is God" (*Dogma*, 213). However, the idea of "total relationality" that as a matter of fact cannot occur in fullness is obviously a contradiction. Despite Ratzinger's own intentions, the eschatological human person also seems to be a case of "standing in relation" rather than "pure relation."

220. So Krieg, "Ratzinger," 113.

221. See Ratzinger, *Introduction*, 135 (my emphasis).

222. Ibid., 131.

223. Ratzinger, *Introduction*, 129. Gerhard Nachtwei suggests that, according to Ratzinger, the basic categorical form is relation (Nachtwei, *Unsterblichkeit*, 196). Although this thesis does correspond to the demands of relational ontology, there is no real evidence for it in Ratzinger's own writings.

relations, if *no* person possesses anything of its own (and according to Ratzinger, the Father apparently constitutes no exception), then they can hardly be distinguished from one another and from the divine substance sustaining them.[224] Although Ratzinger criticizes Augustine's doctrine of the Trinity insofar as in it "the persons of God are enclosed completely in God's interior, and that externally God becomes a pure I,"[225] nonetheless, if all persons are total relationality with regard to one another, then the agent in the deity can only be the one substance, both externally and internally.

The dominance of the one in the doctrine of the Trinity has important ecclesiological correspondences. With reference to Erik Peterson's well-known essay "Monotheism as Political Problem," Ratzinger does maintain that the "indivisible unity of the church" is better illustrated in the perichoresis of the three divine persons, in this "perpetual, dynamic intertwining and mutual interpenetration of spirit to spirit, love to love," than in the image of the one divine monarchy.[226] I will leave in abeyance the question of how such mutual interpenetration can be conceived under the assumption of personhood as *pure* relationality. According to Ratzinger, the divine perichoresis is to function as a model for relations between churches, bishops, and believers. The relations between the divine persons, however, are able to shape ecclesial spirituality only, not ecclesial structures. Since each divine "I" in the Trinity exists "completely from the Thou,"[227] the relations between the persons *cannot be structured at all,* since every person is utterly transparent for the others. The relations between the trinitarian persons have no structural consequences.[228]

This notion of "existing completely from the Thou," however, actually refers to Ratzinger's understanding of the self of the Son. If the Father were to constitute an exception (which does not seem to be the case with Ratzinger), one would return to the one monarchy of God, which functioned as a model for hierarchical relations in the church. It is more consistent with Ratzinger's own (sketchy) trinitarian thinking *to conceive ecclesial structures by way of the one substance of God.* The one, externally acting divine substance corresponds to the one church that, together with Christ, constitutes one subject and in that way becomes capable of action. A *monistic structure* for the church emerges from this. The one Christ acting as subject in the church is represented by the

---

224. Admittedly, this is not only Ratzinger's problem, but that of the tradition that identifies persons with relations. This tradition has never succeeded in demonstrating persuasively how these relations can become concentrated in persons. Concerning the difficulties in conceiving the persons as "subsistent relations," see Pannenberg, *Theology,* 1:288.

225. Ratzinger, *Dogma,* 223.

226. Ratzinger, *Das neue Volk,* 214.

227. Ratzinger, *Dogma,* 214.

228. Ratzinger does not claim that the structures of the church correspond to the "We" of God, but rather that the *actions* of the church do (Ratzinger, *Church,* 31).

one visible head of the church, namely, by the Pope as head of the universal church, and by the bishop as head of the local church. Thus only the one Pope and the one bishop, and not the college of bishops, can be grounded as structural elements through the doctrine of God.

Because Ratzinger understands the church from the perspective of the whole, that is, from that of the one subject of the church, relations between Pope and bishops as well as between the individual bishops and congregation members (or priests) must necessarily be structured *hierarchically*. Just as the one substance of God (or the Father) is over Christ, so also must the one who is to vouch for the totality of the church, namely, the Pope as *vicarius Christi*, be over the bishops, and the bishops over congregation members (or priests). Because these relations are conceived as pure, one ideally has a linear series of selfless hierarchs. Just as the Son is pure relation with regard to the Father, so also are the Pope and bishops to possess pure "power as vicars."[229] Pure trinitarian relationality seems to relativize the power of the hierarchs, even though (also according to Ratzinger) this hierarchical power does in its concrete realization always also appear as personal power.[230] If one conceives ecclesial relations in analogy to pure trinitarian relations, then there is nothing with which to counter this hierarchical personal power other than the goodwill of the hierarchs themselves, since by understanding persons as pure relations one never gets to the notion of the *rights of persons*. Since the person "nowhere stands on its own,"[231] as pure relation it cannot have any rights over against the others. Whereas it initially seemed as if pure relationality would relativize the hierarchical structure of relationships, in reality it merely gives free hand to the power of the hierarchs.

John Zizioulas, to whom I will turn my attention in the next chapter, tries to give priority not to the one substance of God, but rather to the person of the Father, and at the same time to understand the Father as conditioned by the Son and Spirit. This yields not only a different doctrine of the Trinity, but also a different, albeit equally eucharistic, ecclesiology.

229. Ratzinger, *Church*, 44.
230. See ibid.
231. Ratzinger, *Introduction*, 134.

Chapter II

Zizioulas:
Communion, One and Many

The metropolitan John D. Zizioulas (titular bishop of Pergamon) is considered one of the most influential Orthodox theologians of the present.[1] This reputation is not undeserved; in a review of his collection *L'être ecclésial*,[2] no less a theologian than Yves Congar called Zizioulas "one of the most original and profound theologians of our age," one who has presented a "penetrating and coherent reading of the tradition of the Greek fathers on that living reality that is the church."[3]

Zizioulas's thinking focuses on the church. At the center of his ecclesiology stands the Eucharist "as the sacrament of unity par excellence, and therefore, the expression of the mystery of the Church itself."[4] With this fundamental ecclesiological premise, he consciously locates himself in the tradition of the eucharistic ecclesiology of Nicolas Afanassieff. Not only has he appropriated this ecclesiology creatively (albeit also in part quite critically, especially with regard to Afanassieff's understanding of the parish and of the relationship between the local and universal church),[5] he has also tried to place this eucharistic ecclesiology within a comprehensive theological framework and to

1. See Meyendorff, "Foreword," 12. Concerning the theological development and ecumenical activity of Zizioulas, see Baillargeon, *Communion*, 27-58, 326-79; cf. also Legrand, "Zizioulas."

2. Except for two essays, *L'être ecclésial* is identical with *Communion*.

3. Congar, "Bulletin," 88; cf. also de Halleux, "Personalisme," 132f.; Williams, "Being," 102, 105.

4. Zizioulas, "Bishop," 25.

5. See Zizioulas, *Communion*, 24f.; Ἡ ἑνότης, 197ff.; see 3.1 below.

work out its theological and anthropological presuppositions in the form of an ontology of person.[6] Zizioulas is more than a theologian interested in ecclesiology; he is a thinker who seeks to understand ecclesial *being* as such.

Like Joseph Cardinal Ratzinger,[7] Zizioulas has not presented a systematic ecclesiology.[8] Apart from his dissertation, published only in Greek (Ἡ ἑνότης τῆς Ἐκκλησίας ἐν τῇ Θεῖα Ἐυχαριστία καὶ τῷ Ἐπισκόπῳ κατὰ τοὺς τρεῖς πτώτους αἰῶνας [Athens, 1965]), he has written only essays on various ecclesiological problems and ecclesiologically related themes.[9] From these, however, the clear contours of an intended "neopatristic synthesis" become discernible — Rowan Williams speaks of "powerful imaginative consistency"[10] — which are worthy of closer examination. Even though his investigations regarding the relations between the life of the triune God, the ontology of the human person, and the essence of the church have not yet been explicated in full,[11] they nonetheless are some of the most penetrating studies in contemporary Orthodox theology.

Zizioulas's most important publications have originated within the framework of his ecumenical activity, or his "principal vocation";[12] their goal is to provide new impulses for the ecumenical dialogue between East and West. In addition to these ecumenical endeavors, he is interested in mediating the "neopatristic synthesis" to the larger world, for he is convinced that the "ecclesial way of being" offered by this synthesis is the only correct response to contemporary questions.[13] The ecclesial way of being in which the eschatological communion of human beings with the triune God, with one another, and with the world is anticipated, he conceives emphatically in contrast to both ecclesiastical and secular individualism, an individualism which must be understood as a genuine "anticipation" of nonbeing in being.

According to Zizioulas, in the *ordo cognoscendi* one moves from the experience of the ecclesial communion to the correct understanding of the divine communion.[14] In the *ordo essendi*, however, ecclesial communion pre-

---

6. See Zizioulas, *Communion*, 23.

7. See chapter I above.

8. Orthodox theology has not yet developed a systematic theology of the church (so Afanassieff, "Church," 58).

9. I am basing my own analysis on the essays as they appear in *Being as Communion*, since before their publication in that book the texts underwent "special revision" (see Zizioulas, *Communion*, 13).

10. Williams, "Being," 105.

11. Even as well disposed an interpreter of Zizioulas as Paul G. McPartlan, e.g., asks for clarification of the concept of the corporate personality (see McPartlan, *Eucharist*, 303).

12. Baillargeon, *Communion*, 33, 56f.

13. See Zizioulas, *Communion*, 26.

14. See ibid., 16ff.

supposes the trinitarian communion, since the church is *imago trinitatis.* In my presentation of Zizioulas's understanding of the ecclesial interweaving of human and divine communion, I will follow the *ordo essendi.*[15] I will begin with an examination of the ontology of person at the trinitarian and anthropological levels, and will conclude with an examination of the essence and structure of the ecclesial communion. The bridge between trinitarian and anthropological reflection and strictly ecclesiological reflection is provided by an analysis of the communal nature of the Christ event and of truth.

Commensurate with his intention of presenting a neopatristic synthesis, Zizioulas's thinking as a rule consists in an interpretation of the Greek fathers. His interpretation of the patristic texts, especially his construal of the personalism of the Cappadocians, has recently been sharply criticized.[16] I will not enter into this patristic dispute, however, since my own interest is in Zizioulas as a systematic theologian rather than as a historian. The same applies with regard to his explications concerning the history of philosophical ideas. This methodology accords well with his own self-understanding; his interest has always been directed to "the *issues* lying behind historical developments."[17] The critical inquiries which I do introduce during the course of my presentation refer exclusively to the theological plausibility of *his* thinking. In the discussion of Zizioulas's ecclesiology to which I limit myself in this chapter, I assume that individual ecclesiological theses can very well be acceptable and ecumenically fruitful even if their theological grounding remains questionable.

1. The Ontology of Person

Zizioulas's *communio*-ecclesiology is based on an ontology of person acquired from a consideration of the nature of the triune God. This ontology in its own turn is conceived in contrast to any individualism destructive to community

---

15. According to Gaëtan Baillargeon, the methodology I am choosing here is not commensurate with Zizioulas's work, since "the heart" of his thinking resides in the Eucharist (Baillargeon, *Communion,* 61). As soon as one inquires what it is that actually gives his eucharistic thinking its particular character, however, one must go back to his ontology of person as acquired from the perspective of trinitarian reflection. It is thus advisable to follow the inner logic of Zizioulas's thinking and to begin with the Trinity itself, and then to make the transition to the eucharistic community. This is precisely how Zizioulas himself proceeds (see Zizioulas, *Communion,* 27-65); it is probably no accident that his widely published and widely translated essay "Eucharist and Catholicity" stands in the middle rather than at the beginning of his volume of essays (see Zizioulas, *Communion,* 143-69).

16. See Halleux, "Personalisme"; cf. also Bori, "L'unité," 65ff.; Baillargeon, *Communion,* 232-53.

17. See Zizioulas, "Holy Spirit," 29.

(and thus to life itself) as well as to any monistic, isolated ontology that necessarily excludes freedom and in which for that very reason personhood must
lack any "ontological content."[18]

1.1. Trinitarian Personhood

1. According to Zizioulas, it was the Greek fathers, especially the Cappadocians,
whose efforts to formulate trinitarian theology laid the groundwork for an
ontology of person. They effected what amounts to a "revolution" within monistic Greek philosophical thinking by identifying "hypostasis" (ὑπόστασις, *sub-
stantia*) with "person" (πρόσωπον, *persona*), that is, with a concept to which no
ontological content could be attributed within the framework of this particular
thinking.[19] This identification entailed two weighty consequences:

> (a) The person is no longer an adjunct to a being, a category we *add* to a
> concrete entity once we have first verified its ontological hypostasis. *It is itself
> the hypostasis of the being.* (b) Entities no longer trace their being to being
> itself — that is, being is not an absolute category in itself — but to the person,
> to precisely that which *constitutes* being, that is, enables entities to be enti-
> ties.[20]

In what follows, I will examine more closely these two consequences of the
patristic theological and philosophical revolution, consequences which together
constitute the two cornerstones of the ontology of person represented by Zizioulas.

If one understands the trinitarian postulate μία οὐσία, τρία πρόσωπα
("one substance, three persons") to mean that God at first (in the ontological
sense) *is* the one God, and only then exists as three persons, then "the ontological
principle" of the deity is lodged at the level of substance, and one still remains
entangled in monistic ontology. The trinitarian identification of "hypostasis"
and "person" effected by the Cappadocians breaks through this ontology. This
identification asserts that *God's being coincides with God's personhood.* This is
precisely the sense of the statement that God the Father is not only the πηγή
("source"), but also the personal αἰτία ("cause") of the Son and Spirit.[21] The
being of the triune God is a result of God's personal freedom. "God does not

---

18. See Zizioulas, *Communion,* 27-35. Concerning the Christian overcoming of the
ontological monism of Greek philosophy, cf. also Zizioulas, "Christologie," 155-61; "Relation,"
60ff.; "Contribution."

19. See Zizioulas, *Communion,* 36f.

20. Ibid., 39.

21. See Zizioulas, "Holy Spirit," 37.

exist because He cannot but exist";[22] quite the contrary: God the Father perpetually confirms — constitutes! — his own existence in the free personal activity of the divine life.[23]

This free confirmation of the divine being on the side of God, however, does not occur in self-isolation, but rather through constitutive relationships with the Son and Spirit: "it is precisely His trinitarian existence that constitutes this confirmation."[24] The person of the Father is equiprimally the αἰτία of the divine being and trinitarian unity. From this perspective, it is inconceivable to speak of the one God independent of the communion that God is. "The Holy Trinity is a *primordial* ontological concept and not a notion which is added to the divine substance or rather that follows it."[25] This is why one must also say that the personal existence of God (the Father) *constitutes the divine substance.*[26] The one God has his being in a personal confirmation of this being, a confirmation coming about, however, as the constituting of the divine communion. This demonstrates both that the person represents the ultimate ontological reality and that personhood is fundamentally relational and accordingly can exist only as communion.[27] The following basic principle emerges from this regarding the relationship between person and communion: "The person cannot exist without communion; but every form of communion which denies or suppresses the person, is inadmissible."[28]

If the divine substance is constituted through the divine person, then divinity must be contained in the idea of the person, argues Zizioulas; all of God's characteristics must be derivable from his personhood. For in God,

22. Zizioulas, *Communion,* 18.

23. "God, as Father and not as substance, perpetually confirms through 'being' His *free* will to exist" (Zizioulas, *Communion,* 41).

24. Zizioulas, *Communion,* 41.

25. Ibid., 17.

26. See Zizioulas, *Communion,* 41; apparently Zizioulas takes a different view in *Communion,* 134. Even if one can imagine how personalism and essentialism might be understood in a complementary fashion (see de Halleux, "Personalisme," 130f.), one should not try to combine in peaceful complementarity the trinitarian personalism Zizioulas advocates with the essentialism he rejects (so Baillargeon, *Communion,* 252). For the question is not whether Zizioulas can accept "a certain 'well-understood essentialism'" (Baillargeon, *Communion,* 251), but rather whether in Zizioulas's thinking the person is "the 'ecstasy' of the substance" or "a *hypostasis* of the substance" (Zizioulas, *Communion,* 46f.), or expressed differently, *whether substance or person represents the ultimate ontological reality.* Since obviously both cannot do so simultaneously, these represent mutually exclusive alternatives. Zizioulas's entire ontology of person — and thus also the foundation of his understanding of salvation and of the church — stands or falls with the claim of ontologically grounding substance through person.

27. See Zizioulas, "Holy Spirit," 36.

28. Zizioulas, *Communion,* 18.

characteristics are not something qualifying God's being, but rather are identical with it. Personhood is God's essence and logically precedes God's characteristics; that *God's essence is person* means nothing other than that God *is* love. This is why the statement "God is person" acquires its full significance only if it is also reversible: "person is God." Strictly speaking, personhood is something attributable only to God. That is, God is an entity "whose particularity is established in full ontological freedom, i.e., not by virtue of its boundaries (he is 'incomprehensible,' 'indivisible,' etc.) but by its ekstasis of communion (he is eternally Trinity and love)."[29] Human beings can become persons only by participating in God's personhood.

2. Zizioulas insists on the monarchy of the Father. The trinitarian communion is "hypostasized" through the ecstatic character of the Father, who is the αἰτία of the Son and Spirit and so also of the trinitarian communion.[30] Without the monarchy of the Father, the unity of the trinitarian communion would be lost (unless one took recourse in the one divine substance, thereby surrendering, however, the priority of the person). The *communio*-unity of God presupposes the one.[31] Because the person can exist only in communion, and communion can never exist without the one, the "concept of hierarchy . . . inheres in the idea of person."[32]

The following structure of the trinitarian communion emerges from these trinitarian reflections, a structure that will be of decisive significance at the christological, anthropological, and ecclesiological levels. On the one hand, the Father never exists alone, but rather only in communion with the Son and Spirit; the other two persons are the presupposition of his identity,[33] indeed, of his very existence.[34] On the other hand, the Son and the Spirit exist only through the Father, who is their cause, and in "a kind of subordination" to him.[35] The communion is always *constituted and internally structured by an asymmetrical-reciprocal relationship between the one and the many.* The reciprocity consists in the many being unable to live as communion without the one,

29. Zizioulas, "Human Capacity," 410.

30. See Zizioulas, *Communion*, 44-46.

31. See Zizioulas, "Holy Spirit," 45.

32. Zizioulas, "Die pneumatologische Dimension," 141.

33. ". . . the identity even of God depends on the relation of the Father with the persons other than himself. There is no 'one' whose identity is not conditioned by the 'many'" (Zizioulas, "Mystère," 330).

34. "The 'one' . . . requires the many from the very start in order to exist" (Zizioulas, "Contribution," 29).

35. Zizioulas, *Communion*, 89 (a different sentence is found in the German version [Zizioulas, "Wahrheit," 20], which, as a comparison with the French original shows [Zizioulas, *L'être ecclésial*, 77], must be false); cf. also Zizioulas, "Die pneumatologische Dimension," 141. For a nonsubordinationist understanding of the Trinity, see Zizioulas, "Holy Spirit," 38-40.

and in the one being unable to exist without the many. The asymmetry, however, consists in the many being constituted by the one, whereas the one is only conditioned on the many; although he cannot exist without them, they are not his cause, but rather he theirs.

By emphasizing that the Father is the personal αἰτία of the Son and Spirit, Zizioulas has underscored the asymmetry within the trinitarian communion (despite his preference for the doxological point of departure of trinitarian reflection, according to which "the three persons of the Trinity appear to be equal in honour and [are] placed one next to the other without hierarchical distinction"[36]). It is easy to understand why the Father alone is called the origin of the Son and Spirit. Their origin must be a *person* to preserve the precedence of person over substance; however, not *all* the persons can exhibit mutually reciprocal causality, for then it would be impossible to distinguish them from one another (unless one were to identify the immanent and economical Trinity).[37] The monarchy of the Father is the presupposition of the distinction between the persons. What remains obscure, however, is why the monarchy of the Father should be necessary for preserving the unity of God, who is, after all, love, or why the only alternative for securing the unity of God is by way of recourse to "the ultimacy of substance in ontology."[38] This remains merely a postulate for Zizioulas that does not correspond to the attempt at providing a personal grounding for the unity of God, for it presupposes that the unity of God cannot be conceived without numerical oneness and accordingly without something apersonal. This arouses the suspicion that he is not actually grounding the necessity of the one for the unity of the church by way of the Trinity, but rather quite the reverse is projecting the hierarchical grounding of unity into the doctrine of the Trinity from the perspective of a particular ecclesiology.

Another question is whether the notion that the Father confirms his relational being through the begetting of the Son and the emergence of the Spirit does not already contain the logical priority of person over communion. A human being who begets is constituted as such only through the actual process of begetting; in this case, however, being as begetter is added to being as person; a person who has begotten becomes one who begets. God the Father, however, is identical with the one begetting and thus also with himself as God. This is why God cannot become Father only through begetting, but rather must already have been Father and thus person even before this begetting — before, that is, in the ontological, not the temporal sense. The begetting can then only *confirm* his being as Father. The Father is not constituted relationally; rather, his fatherhood is necessarily expressed and confirmed relationally. This seems to me to

36. Zizioulas, "Holy Spirit," 39.
37. See Zizioulas, *Communion*, 45, note 40.
38. Zizioulas, "Holy Spirit," 45, note 18.

be the implication of Zizioulas's assertion that the being of the *Father* is "a result of the 'willing one' — the Father Himself."[39]

Zizioulas distinguishes between *being constituted* (the Son and Spirit through the Father) and *being conditioned* (the Father by the Son and Spirit). If one presumes that the Father alone is the constitutive entity within God, then, as we have already seen, it is difficult not to ascribe priority to the person before the communion. If, on the other hand, one takes seriously the notion that the Father is conditioned, then the differences between the persons risk being leveled. If the Father is conditioned by the Son and Spirit, then he is constituted by them. That is, he is God *only as Father*. As soon as one allows innertrinitarian reciprocity, the innertrinitarian asymmetry seems to vanish, unless one distinguishes between the level of constitution at which the Father as cause is first, and the level of relations at which all three are equal and mutually conditioned by one another.[40] In any case, Zizioulas's distinction between the Son and Spirit being constituted through the Father, and the Father being conditioned by the Son and Spirit, would have to be explicated more precisely to be persuasive. And only such explication would sufficiently ground the notion of God as a hierarchical-relational entity.

3. As we will see,[41] Zizioulas considers the trinitarian personal communion to be the paradigm for the human communion. The Trinity can be the paradigm for the human communion, however, because the Trinity represents the human communion's ground of possibility. The Trinity is such, first, because the personal triune God created the world *ex nihilo*. The second condition of personhood that makes it possible not only to *conceive* of personhood in a consistent fashion, but also to become a genuine person, is the identity between Christ and the church. Here I will briefly address the first condition and will analyze the second only after having determined more precisely the structure of human personhood.

In Zizioulas's reflection on the ground of possibility of personhood, his negative point of departure is again the monistic ontology of Greek philosophy. Since the latter is governed by the law of necessity, it is impossible within its framework to present an ontological grounding of person.[42] By contrast, according to Christian belief the world was created *ex nihilo*. This overcomes a closed ontology, since the world is created as something opposite God, and is created as such out of God's own free will; God is not integrated into the world itself, as it were, and dependent on it, but rather as a free person bequeaths "being to that which is."[43] If, however, everything that is created is a product

39. Zizioulas, "Persons," 42.
40. See V.4.2 below.
41. See 1.2 below.
42. See Zizioulas, *Communion*, 35.
43. See Zizioulas, "Christologie," 161.

of freedom, then the self-enclosure of the creation governed by necessity is suspended; it *can* be free. It is only this particular freedom of created being, grounded in the creative freedom of a personal God, that makes creaturely personhood possible. This grounding of personhood is the fruit of the identification of hypostasis and person by the Greek fathers. Only an absolute person could have created the world in freedom and in this way rendered human personhood possible.

1.2. Human Personhood

Just as at the divine level, so also at the human level person enjoys precedence over substance. The human person is not an *ecstasis*, but rather a *hypostasis* of substance.[44] Put differently, the person cannot be equated with body or consciousness, and it does not grow out of these two; rather, the person *has* a body and consciousness. After the Fall, however, human personhood is perverted, so that it exists only as "individuals." This distinction between person and individual is the foundation not only of Zizioulas's anthropology, but also of his Christology and ecclesiology. I will attempt first to illuminate this distinction itself, and then to explain how in Christ and the church this being as individual is overcome. In the process, we will find that according to Zizioulas one can understand anthropology, Christology, and ecclesiology only as a unity.

1. Conceiving human beings as individuals means conceiving them so that substance, or their biological nature, has precedence. The individual is a "personality" understood as "a complex of natural, psychological or moral qualities . . . centered on the axis of consciousness."[45] Human beings as individuals are part of the creaturely world; they stand in the cause-effect nexus and accordingly under the law of necessity. At the same time, however, they affirm themselves in contrast to others (other human beings, other creatures, and God), necessarily creating distance between themselves and all other beings. The ultimate consequence of this distance is death.[46] This already shows that the basic problem of human beings resides not at the moral, but rather at the ontological level. Necessity and separation emerge because the individual is substance (however articulated) existing in time and space and is set over against other objects; these qualities inhere in protological creaturely existence itself.

Creation and Fall coalesce into a single entity in Zizioulas's thinking. The Fall consists merely in the revelation and actualization of the limitations and

---

44. See Zizioulas, *Communion,* 46f.
45. Zizioulas, "Human Capacity," 407, 406.
46. Zizioulas, *Communion,* 50ff.

potential dangers inherent in creaturely existence.[47] When elsewhere Zizioulas defines sin as human beings turning away from communion with the personal God and turning to communion only with the creaturely world,[48] this is to be understood not in any psychological-moral sense, but rather in an ontological sense, that is, as *being* in a condition — one determined by protological creaturely existence (biological procreation[49]) — of having turned away or toward. The consequence of this seems to be the "unfree will." Indeed, it is under precisely this assumption that Zizioulas will later conceive the appropriation of salvation. However Zizioulas may understand the capacity of human freedom to influence the all-decisive *how* of human existence,[50] this freedom cannot include any possibility of choosing between being a person and being an individual.[51]

In contrast to the individual, the person is not a self-enclosed substantial entity, but rather an open relational entity. First, the person is *ecstatic,* is "a movement toward communion."[52] This movement itself attests the person's freedom. The person is free because it transcends the boundaries of the self and because it is not determined causally by the given natural or historical reality. Second, within this ecstatic movement the person is a catholic reality: it is *hypostatic;* it bears within itself human nature in its entirety, which within the framework of Zizioulas's thinking means that it includes all other persons within itself and is thus a unique reflection of them all.[53] Thus *ecstasis* (free communality) and *hypostasis* (catholic uniqueness) are the two fundamental aspects of personhood. Personhood is "the mode in which nature exists in its ekstatic movement of communion in which it is hypostasised in its catholicity."[54] As such, the person is essentially relational; it is itself only when it stands in a relation.[55]

2. To become an individual, a human being must merely be born. By contrast, becoming a person exceeds the possibilities of creaturely existence. For even though becoming a person is something that happens to an individual, it is *not merely a matter of an individual opening up relationally.*[56] First, the person

47. See ibid., 102.
48. See Zizioulas, "Human Capacity," 424.
49. See Zizioulas, *Communion,* 52.
50. See Zizioulas, "Contribution," 33.
51. See 2.3 below.
52. Zizioulas, "Human Capacity," 408.
53. Ibid., 408, 418; *Communion,* 106. See McPartlan, *Eucharist,* 139f.
54. Zizioulas, "Human Capacity," 442.
55. See Zizioulas, *Communion,* 236.
56. Despite his assertion that "the Spirit as 'power' or 'giver of life' opens up our existence to become relational" (Zizioulas, *Communion,* 112), the person is according to Zizioulas not merely an ecstatic individual.

is free of the regnant necessity within creaturely existence, and is characterized by "absolute ontological freedom."[57] Thus does the person exist *in* this world, but is not *of* this world.[58] Second, a person is "a particularity which is not determined by space and time, i.e., by circumscribability,"[59] as is the case with an individual. A person's particularity is constituted by its being irreplaceable within the community rather than by being delimited as an individual opposite other individuals. Third, a human being cannot be a person as a mere "biological hypostasis," since no entity whose particularity is grounded in natural birth can be the bearer of the entirety of human nature.[60] For these reasons, human beings can become persons only in communion with the personal God, who alone merits being called a person in the original sense.

According to Zizioulas, human personhood, a person's being as *imago dei,* is present both in a disrupted fashion and as an unfulfilled *tendency.*[61] This is the tragedy of human beings, namely, that as biological hypostases they tend toward personhood while necessarily remaining caught in their individuality as a result of their specific creaturely constitution. Hence salvation must *consist in an ontological deindividualization that actualizes their personhood.* Although the individuality of human beings is conditioned by their biological constitution, salvific grace, which fashions them into persons, does not suspend their creaturely existence as such, since this is the necessary means through which the human person expresses itself in both its ecstatic and its hypostatic dimensions. The biological hypostasis is not simply identical with creaturely nature, but rather is merely its protological/postlapsarian mode of existence.[62] This is why salvific grace can consist only in transforming perverted creaturely existence — perverted insofar as it individualizes human beings — into creaturely existence expressing their being as persons and their communal nature. This transpired paradigmatically in the incarnation.[63]

2. Ecclesial Personhood

The concrete locus of deindividualization and personalization is the church. The church can be so, however, only because it is the pneumatologically constituted body of Christ. For this reason, it is in the church that human beings

57. Zizioulas, *Communion,* 43; cf. also pp. 19, 36, 50.
58. See Zizioulas, "Human Capacity," 420.
59. Ibid., 415, note 1.
60. See ibid., 441, note 3.
61. See Zizioulas, *Communion,* 52.
62. See ibid., 50ff.; "Human Capacity," 417, 423, 439.
63. See Zizioulas, "Human Capacity," 438f.

can become persons through baptism and can live as persons through the Eucharist. I will analyze first how this personalization of human beings in Christ and in baptism occurs and which understanding of truth this personalization process presupposes. Then I will ask how participation in the Eucharist should shape the life human beings live in the church.

2.1. Christ: Person and Community

The soteriological (and thus also anthropological and ontological-existential) significance of the doctrine of the "two natures of Christ" is that in Christ, human personhood became historical reality.[64] As such, Christ is the opposite of an individual; he is the person *par excellence,* since his identity is constituted by a twofold relation, namely, through his relationship as Son to the Father and as head to his body.

1. Consideration of the divine *nature* of Christ should not mislead us into conceiving Christ's deity as a divine substance. His deity is that of the Son as the second *person* of the Trinity, itself constituted by personal begetting. "The filial relationship between the Father and the Son in the Holy Spirit in the Trinity" also constitutes the incarnate word as a "divine person."[65] It is here that, according to Zizioulas, one finds the theological meaning of the virgin birth of Christ; personhood cannot be derived from nature through biological procreation.[66] The soteriological intention behind the identification of Christ's personhood with the Son's personhood is that it renders human personhood possible. As we have already seen, only the uncreated God is a person in the full sense of the word, and only in communion with the triune God can human beings become free, "catholic" persons living in communion. Otherwise, they remain alone with themselves and the world, and for that reason also ensnared in their own individuality and thus ultimately given over to death.

Just as the Son does not stand alone, but rather exists in his relationship with the Father, so also does Jesus Christ, the incarnate Son, not stand merely by himself; he is not an individual. Both in Jesus' own self-understanding and in the Christology of the early church, Christ is a corporate personality who incorporates the many into himself.[67] Here it is important to emphasize that he does not first exist as the one, and then become the many; he is the one

64. See Zizioulas, *Communion,* 54f.
65. Zizioulas, "Human Capacity," 436.
66. See Zizioulas, *Communion,* 55; "Human Capacity," 436.
67. See Zizioulas, *Communion,* 145ff.; "L'eucharistie," 31ff.; "Groupes," 253f.; "Mystère," 330.

"who *at the same time* represents a multiplicity."[68] This deindividualization of Christ comes about through the eschatological Spirit of communion in which Christ's entire existence transpires, from birth to resurrection and headship in the church.[69] "In the Spirit [he] contains by definition . . . ourselves as we shall be."[70] As such, Christ is the true person, the new Adam who in his particularity bears human nature in its catholicity.[71]

From this pneumatic deindividualization of Christ, there follows not only a christological grounding of ecclesiology, but also *the ecclesial character of the identity of Christ*. One can speak of Christ meaningfully only in relation to the church. Although the "I" of Christ does remain the eternal "I" deriving from the relationship between the Son and the Father, "as Christ incarnate *he introduced into this eternal relation yet another element: we ourselves as the other, the many, the church*."[72] Without the church, one only has the eternal Son, not the incarnate Christ.

At the christological and ecclesiological level, one finds a comparable asymmetrical reciprocity of the sort already encountered in Zizioulas's trinitarian reflections. The one Christ constitutes the church (in the Spirit he incorporates the many into himself), but the church conditions the Christ (without the many, he is not the Christ).[73] Reciprocity is to be expected in the Trinity, since the latter involves an inner-divine relation. By contrast, the reciprocity in the relation between Christ and the church is surprising, since this is actually a relationship between uncreated and created reality. This, however, expresses Zizioulas's basic conviction that human personhood is not of this world, but rather is divine, as well as the identity he emphasizes between Christ and the church. The two are inextricably bound together and are underscored by the manner in which he understands the relationship between individual human beings and Christ.

2. The peculiar nature of the relation between Christ and the individual is decisive for determining the relation between person and community at the

---

68. Zizioulas, "Die pneumatologische Dimension," 136 (my emphasis).

69. Zizioulas emphasizes this communal function of the Spirit at the christological and ecclesiological levels (see Zizioulas, *Communion*, 110ff. [esp. pp. 113f., note 116]; "Die pneumatologische Dimension," 135ff.; "Ordination," 6). He speaks of a relational ontology "conditioned by pneumatology" (Zizioulas, "Implications," 151). He never anchors this communally-generative function of the Spirit in the Trinity. At the level of the immanent Trinity, it seems to be the Father who, as the one, establishes unity within multiplicity and thus community: The being of the *Father* is identical with community (see Zizioulas, *Communion*, 44).

70. Zizioulas, *Community*, 183.

71. See Zizioulas, "Human Capacity," 438.

72. Zizioulas, "Mystère," 331 (my emphasis).

73. See Zizioulas, "Mystère," 330.

ecclesial level. Zizioulas's understanding of this relation emerges when one takes Christ's own being as person to be that of the eternal Son, and at the same time understands Christ with respect to his human nature as a corporate personality. Through the one relation between Christ as the Son with the Father, both his divine and his human nature are constituted as such.[74] The many who are incorporated into Christ are accordingly constituted not only in their unity, *but also each in his own personhood* by the same relationship between the Son and the Father, just as is Christ himself. Christ *is* the many. "The same 'schesis' [i.e., the Son's eternal relation to the Father] becomes now the constitutive element — the *hypostases* — of all those whose particularity and uniqueness and therefore ultimate being are constituted through the same filial relationship that constitutes Christ's being."[75] This notion of the one (Christ) and the many (Christians) does not involve an equivalent, but rather a numerically identical relation to the Father, a relation constituting them as persons. *Every person* who is in Christ acquires his particular personhood through the *one relationship* of Christ as the Son to the Father. Human personhood is identical ("exactly the same") with divine personhood, albeit not in and of itself, but rather through unity with the Son.

Every human being is accordingly constituted in Christ into a person, and is such in no other way than by becoming "Christ" on the basis of the same filial relationship constituting Christ himself, that is, by becoming a person who exists in the mode of being of God.[76] Because in Christ a human being is united with God ἀδιαιρέτως ("indivisibly"),[77] that human being is freed from the bondage to necessity and death inherent in creaturely existence. At the same time, the individuality isolating human beings from each other has given way to catholic personhood, since in Christ, in communion with the many (ecstatic dimension), the human being has become the bearer of the catholicity of human nature (hypostatic dimension).

According to Zizioulas, salvific grace consists in a transformation of the individual into a "catholic" person who is at the same time unique in his own catholicity, a person constituted through the relationship between Christ and the Father. At the anthropological and ontological level, we encounter here a parallel to the Reformational understanding of justification. Just as every Christian possesses not the same kind of righteousness as Christ, but rather Christ's righteousness itself, so according to Zizioulas every human being is constituted into a person not in the same way as Christ, but rather precisely

74. Zizioulas, "Human Capacity," 436.

75. Ibid., 438.

76. See ibid., 441, note 3; *Communion*, 19.

77. Concerning the anthropological meaning of the Chalcedonian ἀδιαιρέτως, see Zizioulas, "Christologie," 166f.

in Christ himself. But how can *every* person standing in Christ be constituted in his or her particularity by *the same* relation of the Son to the Father? *Different* persons cannot really be constituted through the relation of the Son to the Father, which is common to all persons. Zizioulas is forced, however, to conceive human personhood by way of the relation of the Son to the Father, for if freedom characterizes the person as such, and if necessity allegedly inheres in nature — a conviction underlying Zizioulas's entire system — then the principle of interpersonal differentiation cannot be found in *nature,* which is to become personalized in Christ, in the biological hypostasis. For in this case one would have to presuppose a common, undifferentiated personhood constituted by God that is then differentiated through the specific nature of every human being. But would this not be equivalent to a personalization of individuals without their deindividualization?[78] Hence it is understandable that Zizioulas insists that the particularity and uniqueness of every person is indeed grounded in the relation of the Son to the Father.[79] In order to remain consistent, however, he would have to surrender the particularity of persons.[80] In that case, however, the result would be precisely what Zizioulas is trying to avoid: Persons would disappear in "one vast ocean of being," namely, in the divine person.[81]

Another possibility emerges for grounding the particularity of person, namely, the specific locus of any given person in the church itself. Zizioulas does indeed seem inclined to take this path. "The new identity given 'in the Spirit' was constituted through . . . a new set of relationships."[82] These relations, however, must be conceived as "*identical* to the relationship of Christ to the Father,"[83] since the human person can arise only through participating in God's own personhood. However, Zizioulas does not explain how the identity of a complex of human relations is to be conceived with the relation of the Son to the Father. One possible answer is that Christ as a corporate personality *is* the community, though in that case it is not clear just how the community can

---

78. If one takes the biological hypostasis as the principle of differentiation, then the identity of every human being would have to come from nature; it could not derive from common personhood, since there can be no nonparticular identity. In that case, however, the person would be nothing more than an open individual — the self-identical self would then enter into relationships and in part reflect these.

79. See Zizioulas, "Person," 45.

80. Perhaps it is because he senses the difficulty of conceiving the particularity and uniqueness of the person that Zizioulas emphasizes several times in his notes (with no apparent explanation) that in working out his understanding of the being of person he is concerned with "beings as *particular living beings*" (Zizioulas, "Human Capacity," 426, note 1; 441, note 2).

81. Zizioulas, *Communion,* 106.

82. Zizioulas, "Community," 28.

contribute to the particularization of a person, since it is itself constituted as an entity identical with Christ through the one relation of the Son to the Father. Yet even apart from this problem, the identity of persons is difficult to conceive if their particularity derives exclusively from the *human* relationships in which they stand. To secure this identity, one would have to presuppose a relatively secure locus for every person within the network of communal relationships, something Zizioulas in fact does by speaking about the *ordo* of the laity or of bishops within the eucharistic synaxis.[84] Yet because *per definitionem* several persons belong to an *ordo,* the particularity of each individual human being cannot be ensured in this way.[85]

2.2. Baptism

How does the personhood actualized historically in Christ become each human being's mode of being? Zizioulas's answer is: in the church. Entry into the ecclesial communion and thus into personhood is baptism.

1. A human being can become a person only if her individualizing "biological hypostasis" is altered in its inner constitution while not really being suspended as such; the change must be ontological and not merely moral. The human being must be born anew, more exactly: from "above," free of the ontological necessity inherent in all creaturely existence. This takes place in baptism; "as the conception and birth of a man constitutes his biological hypostasis, so baptism leads to a new mode of existence, to a regeneration (1 Pet. 1:3, 23), and consequently to a new 'hypostasis.' "[86] In baptism, the individual dies and the person is born.

The new birth mediated in baptism occurs through the union of our created nature with the uncreated God in Christ. According to Zizioulas, the structural identity of the accounts of Christ's baptism with the Christian baptismal liturgy demonstrates that it is in baptism that the personal structure of the Trinity is made into the structure of the human hypostasis.[87] In baptism, human beings are not simply constituted into persons in the same way *as* Christ; rather, baptism is "the *application to humanity of the very filial relationship which*

---

83. Ibid. (my emphasis).

84. See 4.3.1 below.

85. McPartlan writes: "Zizioulas thinks that each is Christ *in a different way* and thus that to say that each is Christ is *not* to say that each is the *same*" (McPartlan, *Eucharist,* 142). To demonstrate the difference between persons asserted by Zizioulas, however, McPartlan can only point to the various ministries within the church. These ministries, however — at least in Zizioulas's ecclesiology — are *common* to several persons.

86. Zizioulas, *Communion,* 53.

87. See ibid., 56, note 50.

exists between the Father and the Son."[88] Thus are human beings personalized through nothing less than their acceptance into the communion of the trinitarian persons, an acceptance taking place in Christ and accorded them in baptism; according to Zizioulas, their true personal life (a life transpiring essentially in an ecclesial fashion) can even be called *"identical* with the eternal life of the triune God."[89] This is what it means to be baptized εἰς Χριστόν ("into Christ"; see Gal. 3:27). Every person *is* the whole Christ, albeit not Christ as an individual, but rather as a corporate personality.[90]

The union of human beings with Christ as an ontological occurrence is according to Zizioulas not to be understood as a union between individuals living today with an individual who lived two thousand years ago in Palestine. Just as the being of Christ takes place in the Spirit, so also can the union of individual human beings with Christ take place only in the Spirit. One is baptized εἰς Χριστόν only ἐν πνεύματι ("by the Spirit"; see 1 Cor. 12:13; Gal. 3:2). Baptism is essentially baptism in the Spirit.[91] Zizioulas follows the New Testament in understanding the Spirit as an eschatological gift (see Acts 2:17). Just as the Spirit constitutes Christ as the "last Adam," the "eschatological human being," so also does the Spirit in baptism constitute the personhood of every human being as an eschatological reality. From this there follows the peculiar,

88. Zizioulas, "Human Capacity," 438 (my emphasis).

89. Zizioulas, *Communion,* 114 (my emphasis).

90. According to McPartlan's interpretation of Zizioulas, each person is "Christ *in a different way"* (McPartlan, *Eucharist,* 142). From this it would then follow that it is not every individual person who is the whole Christ, but rather every differentiated community as a whole. Zizioulas has allegedly encouraged this particular interpretation in private conversations with McPartlan by pointing out that the New Testament does not refer to individual human beings, but rather only to the congregation as the temple of the Spirit. Here Zizioulas has apparently either overlooked or not taken seriously 1 Cor. 6:19, which states that the body of every Christian is a temple of the Holy Spirit. It is even more significant, however, that Zizioulas himself asserts that *"every communicant is the whole Christ* and the whole Church" (Zizioulas, *Communion,* 60f., my emphasis). It is certainly possible that Zizioulas has backed off from this idea because it does not permit him to conceive the particularity of persons. If every person is indeed the whole Christ, then that person cannot differentiate himself from other persons, since he is constituted through the one relation of the Son to the Father. But if the entire community is the whole Christ, then individual persons can be particularized through their respective locus within the community, e.g., person-bishop, person-layperson. As we have already seen, this does not really enable one to conceive the particularity of *every* person. To avoid this difficulty, one would either have to recognize the "substance" of human beings — "a complex of natural, psychological or moral qualities" (Zizioulas, "Human Capacity," 407) — as the principle of differentiation of persons, or have to view personhood as grounded through the individual relation of God to each human being.

91. See Zizioulas, "Baptism," 645ff.; "Human Capacity," 441f.; *Communion,* 113.

and according to Zizioulas also paradoxical, overlapping of the biological and ecclesial hypostasis (individual and person). The human being exists as person "not as that which he is but as that which he *will* be"; personhood "has its roots in the future and its branches in the present."[92]

According to these formulations, Zizioulas understands the entwining of the ages with the aid of "retroactive causality." He tries to clarify this philosophically difficult notion through the equally difficult notion of *pneumatic transtemporality*. That is, it is characteristic of the Spirit not only to permit "reality to become relational," but also to transcend "linear history" and thus also "historical causality."[93] Once this aspect of the Spirit is understood, one can then understand not only how Zizioulas himself can argue that Christology is conditioned by ecclesiology, but also how he can assert that the historical Christ *was* a "corporate personality" *and* that he gives to human beings the *possibility*[94] of being hypostasized in Christ through baptism. This connection between baptism and the Christ event involves a transferal of the Christ event in baptism to those being baptized, and yet simultaneously a conditioning of the Christ by those who are baptized. Such a connection is conceivable only if one can understand both Christ and the church as a communion actualized in the Spirit, a communion in which "past, present, and future are not causally related, but rather are one as the body of Christ in the communion event."[95]

2. Now, one is baptized ἐν πνεύματι not only εἰς Χριστόν, but in one and the same event also εἰς ἓν σῶμα ("into one body"; see 1 Cor. 12:13). If baptismal death is a death of the individual, then the baptismal resurrection is a resurrection of the person, though a resurrection which, given the essential relationality of the person, can be nothing other than incorporation of the baptized person into a network of relationships. The transferal of Christ's existence to human beings in baptism "amounts to nothing other than a realization of the communion of the Church."[96] The communion with Christ, who is himself a corporate personality, can only be an ecclesial event, not an individual one. Here, baptism makes the human being into a "catholic entity"; not only is that person incorporated into the church, he is also himself made into the church. In the Spirit, "the structure of the church becomes the structure of each person's being."[97] Because in baptism a human being puts on Christ as the "catholic human being," Christ's own catholicity and thus also the catholicity of the church become that person's inner

---

92. Zizioulas, *Communion,* 59; cf. also pp. 96, 99.
93. Zizioulas, "Die pneumatologische Dimension," 136, 137.
94. In this regard, see Zizioulas, *Communion,* 56; *Christologie,* 168.
95. Zizioulas, "Die pneumatologische Dimension," 137.
96. Zizioulas, *Communion,* 114; cf. "Christologie," 171.
97. Zizioulas, "Die pneumatologische Dimension," 142.

constitution.[98] Hence in baptism, a human being is constituted into a genuine person with respect to that person's ecstatic and hypostatic dimensions.[99]

The church, however, is not only the body into which one is incorporated and which one then becomes; it is at the same time also the mother who bears these ecclesial persons. The rebirth takes place in the Spirit "from the womb of the Church," in and through the community.[100] Zizioulas seems to be emphasizing the identity of Christ and church to such an extreme that the ecclesial persons who have their own personhood through the one relation of the Son to the Father, in their own turn coconstitute the personhood of those baptized. The church would then participate not only in the being of the Son as determined by the innertrinitarian dynamic, but also in his actions as directed toward the outside. I will leave in abeyance the soteriological implications of such an understanding of the process of becoming a person. The critical question with regard to the social nature of salvation is *how* this constituting of the person takes place within the medium of human communication, and *how* those affected actually participate in this process. In the following discussion of Zizioulas's understanding of truth, I am concerned above all with this issue.

2.3. Truth

According to Zizioulas, truth is intimately connected with salvation and, indeed, is identical with it. Truth is salvation and salvation is truth, and both are the

---

98. Zizioulas, *Communion*, 58.

99. Although Zizioulas understands baptism as the medium through which a human being is constituted as a real person, Baillargeon has justifiably reproached him for *devaluing* baptism in an ecumenically significant fashion at the cost of the Eucharist (see Baillargeon, *Communion*, 254f.). This devaluation manifests itself in the fact that baptism — like "all the fundamental elements which constitute her [the church's] historical existence and structure" — must take place within the eucharistic community in order to be "sure," "valid," or "ecclesiologically *true*" (Zizioulas, *Communion*, 21). Yet another consideration plays a role here as well. As we will see, Zizioulas understands this baptismal process of becoming a person and the realization of personal life in the Eucharist as a *punctiliar* event (see 3.1.3 below). It is difficult to take seriously the notion that the punctiliar salvific experience in baptism — one upon which no other salvific experiences follow (i.e., no repeated participation in the eucharistic celebration) — is the foundation of the unity of Christians. At the same time, it is easy to see why for Zizioulas baptism can have little meaning — or none at all — without the Eucharist. For if one became a Christian through baptism, which takes place but once, then community with other Christians would be something that is added to being a Christian, and Christian life would not from the very outset be communal. Only in the repeated celebration of the Eucharist, which includes the assembly of persons, does one see that being a Christian is essentially a communal affair.

100. Zizioulas, *Communion*, 58, 113.

Son of God and communion with him. One must examine Zizioulas's understanding of truth in order to specify more closely his ecclesial soteriology and also in order better to understand his strictly ecclesiological statements and his statements regarding the theology of office. Since for my own study it will suffice to examine the soteriological and ecclesiological dimensions of this theme, I will omit the creation-theological dimension Zizioulas regularly mentions on the periphery.

1. Zizioulas's understanding of truth is grounded in the ontology of person, which he develops in contrast to the ontology of being. The ontology of being has its correspondence in the "postlapsarian," or simply creaturely, situation in which the status of the biological hypostasis of human beings is higher than that of their personhood, and thus also higher than their communion. By its very constitution, postlapsarian existence is fragmentary existence; every human being encounters every other human being as a self-enclosed entity. Relationships between human beings come about only if mediated through a cognitive act. Hence knowledge acquires (at least) temporal priority over love; "one can love only what one knows, since love comes from knowledge."[101]

Cognitive acts, however, are poorly suited for mediating communion between persons. Cognitive knowledge of necessity begins "with a process of *gathering information* about the other being, i.e., by subjecting it to my observation which will lead to a description (establishing characteristics) and evaluation (establishing qualities and value) of this being."[102] Every cognitive act, precisely as an act of mediation, contains the disconnection of knower and known, since cognition presupposes the otherness of what is known. Communion of persons cannot emerge from cognitive activity, since such communion requires that the relations between persons actually inhere in their identity as persons and are not just added from the outside; an external relation that does not create identity in the ontological sense is, according to Zizioulas, no relation at all, at least not a personal relation.[103] If truth is understood cognitively, that is, as a certain relation of the intellect to being, it cannot lead to personal communion. Quite the contrary, it always entails depersonalization.[104]

Within the framework of the ontology of person, truth is an eminently communal occurrence. If being is ultimately identical with person, then first, love acquires precedence over knowledge. Since the relations in which persons stand inhere in them as persons, a relation of love comes about even before cognitive activity can arise. Rather than coming primarily by way of cognitive activity, this relation follows the occurrence of communion; knowledge is "the

101. Zizioulas, "Human Capacity," 427.
102. Ibid., 426.
103. See Zizioulas, *Communion*, 88.
104. See ibid., 100.

outcome of an event of communion."[105] According to Zizioulas, one can see this expressed paradigmatically in God's relation to the world; God does not love the world because he knows it, but rather knows it because he loves it (and because God has created it out of love).[106] Second, the precedence of person over being, the dependence of being on the loving person of God, fundamentally alters the concept of truth. Truth is no longer a certain cognitive relation between intellect and being, but rather an event of love between persons; being in truth means being in communion. This is also why the question of truth is not about cognitive understanding, but rather about personal life.[107]

From the perspective of this twofold conviction, namely, the precedence of love over knowledge and an understanding of truth as communion, Zizioulas understands Christ as truth. Christ is not truth in the sense of revelation, for in that case he would participate in God's wisdom and thereby represent a rationally comprehensible connection between created and uncreated rationality.[108] Christ is not, however, a rational category, but rather a person, an incarnate person identical with the second person of the Trinity. As such, he is the truth, "for he represents the ultimate, unceasing will of the ecstatic love of God, who intends to lead created being into communion with His own life."[109] To step cognitively into relation with Christ would mean to individualize or objectivize him, and hence actually to block the path to personal communion with him. The truth of Christ, indeed, the truth of every person, surpasses the νοῦς (mind) and is accessible to human beings only as an *event* of communion. Christ is the truth because in the Spirit he exists as the communion embracing human beings.

2. This understanding of truth has important soteriological and ecclesiological consequences. On the basis of a brief analysis of Zizioulas's understanding of God's word, in what follows I will address only those particular consequences affecting the relation of individual human beings to Christ, and I will do so from the perspective of human beings themselves. God's word, Zizioulas suggests, "is truth not in the sense of a series of sentences or kerygmatic statements to be taken in and for themselves, but rather in the sense of life and *communio*."[110] From this it follows that one's disposition toward God's word as truth is not to be one of cognitive understanding or of belief; rather, one should *experience God's word* communally "as the sacramental intimation of God's life."[111]

105. Zizioulas, "Human Capacity," 427.
106. See Zizioulas, *Communion*, 97.
107. Zizioulas sketches out the emergence of this concept of truth in *Communion*, 72-101.
108. Zizioulas, *Communion*, 77.
109. Ibid., 98.
110. Zizioulas, "Die pneumatologische Dimension," 143.
111. Ibid.; *Communion*, 114.

Zizioulas's formulations sometimes seem to imply that a sacramental approach to God's word does not necessarily exclude the cognitive approach. Thus, for example, he writes that "truth is not *just* . . . propositional,"[112] the implication being that truth is *also* propositional. In that case, what is involved would not be an exclusion of the cognitive dimension in the Christian understanding of truth, but rather its subordination to the core personal dimension of truth.[113] Yet given Zizioulas's conviction that cognitive rationality always implies the individualization of the knower and the objectification of the known, this cannot really be what is meant. He is probably closer to his own position when he formulates exclusively: "to know God's word, one may not grasp it."[114] This is why God's word does not stand over against the church, nor even over against the world. The juxtaposition of God's word and God's people corresponds to the Old Testament view of God's word. According to the New Testament, the Logos is not the spoken or even written word, but rather *exclusively* a person.[115] This is why even in the present, God's word only comes to human beings "as the *flesh* or the body of the Logos" and is mediated communally: "It comes as an act of communion created by the Spirit and in which we are implicated, as if in a mystery, at the interior of that network of relations established by the mystery of the ecclesial communion."[116]

This noncognitive interiority of the word in relation to the church can only be secured sacramentally. Deindividualization demands direct or immediate relationships, and these in their turn demand the replacement of language by sacrament. This is why the Eucharist is *the* place where truth occurs. As a communal event *par excellence,* the Eucharist incarnates and actualizes our communion with the life and communion of the Trinity itself.[117] Zizioulas's identification of word and sacrament — "truth as word and truth as sacrament *are one and the same*"[118] — is for that reason equivalent to the absorption of the word into the sacrament: only when the word becomes identical with the eucharistic flesh does the eschatological event come about through the historical forms.[119]

3. Before we can examine the Eucharist and its fundamental ecclesiological (and accordingly also soteriological) function, we must first question critically

112. Zizioulas, *Communion,* 115 (my emphasis).

113. This would be commensurate with his anthropological conviction according to which consciousness is not to be excluded from personhood, but merely understood as one of its dimension (rather than as its content).

114. Zizioulas, "Implications," 152, note 29 (my emphasis).

115. So Zizioulas, *Communion,* 190, note 68.

116. Zizioulas, "Implications," 151, 152, note 29.

117. See Zizioulas, *Communion,* 115.

118. Zizioulas, "Die pneumatologische Dimension," 143 (my emphasis).

119. See Zizioulas, *Communion,* 191.

the presuppositions behind Zizioulas's understanding of God's word and of the noncognitive nature of its appropriation. Pivotal decisions, soteriological as well as ecclesiological, are made at this juncture.

Strikingly, faith plays no role in Zizioulas's soteriology and ecclesiology. It rarely appears in his writings, and in the few places it does, it leads a kind of peripheral soteriological existence, as "faith of man in his capacity to become a person," and not at all as faith in God or in Christ.[120] It is conceivable that Zizioulas is always presupposing faith — following the notion, for example, that the sacraments are after all always sacraments of faith — without mentioning this explicitly or explicating it in any detail. As a matter of fact, however, this is not the case. Faith as the subjective appropriation of salvific grace *is not permitted* to play any role in his soteriology and ecclesiology; at the very least, faith cannot be fitted comfortably into his system without altering systemically important and fundamental positions.[121] Even though the Christian faith cannot be reduced to cognitive content, it is nevertheless inconceivable without this cognitive content; in order to believe, one must at the very least be able to distinguish God, as the person in whom one believes, from idols, something possible only cognitively.[122] Yet if faith is essentially a cognitive act (albeit not only such), then according to Zizioulas it cannot lead to communion, since it must be an individual act. Faith does not appear in Zizioulas's soteriology and ecclesiology, because it would constitute a contradiction within the framework of his system to maintain that person and communion are constituted by way of *individual* activity. Neither would it help here to understand faith as a gift of the church, since faith as such would also have to proceed via the consciousness of the individual human being.

Zizioulas denies that any cognitive dimension attaches to the application of salvific grace, while he still insists that the Eucharist demands a common vision (εἰκών) of Christ protected from heretical distortion by dogmatic formulations.[123] Now, since these formulations are obviously cognitive, how are they then to preserve the authentic experience of Christ in the Eucharist, which is not permitted to be cognitive? Zizioulas believes they are transcended in the Spirit in the direction of a communal event. Yet if there is no *inner connection* between the experience of Christ and the cognitive content of the dogmas preserving that experience — the dogmas "carry *no relationship with truth in*

---

120. See ibid., 58, 114; "Human Capacity," 421f.

121. Zizioulas's christological and ecclesiological concentration on the incarnation and resurrection, and on the Eucharist, confirms that he is indeed involved in screening out faith soteriologically. Congar's lapidary critical remark touches the heart of the problem: "It is true that the word has become flesh, but it has also spoken!" ("Bulletin," 89).

122. See Volf, "Kognitivna dimenzija," 321ff.

123. See Zizioulas, *Communion,* 117; "Die pneumatologische Dimension," 143.

themselves, but only in their being doxological acclamations of the worshiping community"[124] — then the formulations are determined only by cultural and historical circumstances,[125] and for that reason are quite arbitrary from the perspective of the actual issue. The fact that at various councils they have become "elements of communion" changes nothing regarding their arbitrary character. If, by contrast, one associates inwardly the vision of Christ with the cognitive content of the dogmas protecting that vision, then the application of salvific grace necessarily acquires a cognitive dimension.

4. Zizioulas describes the communion between God and human beings as *love.* For Zizioulas, "love" is an *ontological* category; it is "union 'without division' with God."[126] The anthropological locus of this union is "conscience," and the union is to be "free."[127] Zizioulas's description of union with Christ, however, mentions no activity on the side of human beings, not even receptive activity made possible by God. For if human beings were to participate actively in this union, their activity would have to be accompanied by cognition. Zizioulas's soteriology brings the notion of *sola gratia* fully to bear, but in such a way that not only human origination of faith remains excluded (as with the Reformers), but also human experience of faith.[128] This lack of human activity finds its correspondence in Zizioulas's ascribing to *Christ* the freedom attaching to the union of human beings with Christ: this union is not the fruit of a personal necessity, but rather of the personal will of Christ, of his freedom to unite the created with himself as the uncreated. This union is free because it derives from Christ's own personal activity, not because it is freely accepted by every human being.[129] Within the framework of Zizioulas's thinking, salvific grace cannot be received freely in faith, because such reception would always constitute an implicit affirmation of individuality, and one cannot be a communally determined person by affirming one's own individuality. This is also why human beings, once having become persons in Christ, do not have a choice whether to remain such; the possibility of saying "no" would mean that personhood is constituted not through communion, but rather through the individual.

Accordingly, Zizioulas does not understand freedom as a choice between

---

124. Zizioulas, *Communion,* 116f. (my emphasis).

125. So apparently Zizioulas, *Communion,* 117; "Die pneumatologische Dimension," 143.

126. Zizioulas, "Christologie," 167.

127. Ibid.

128. Concerning this distinction, see Joest, *Ontologie,* 234ff.

129. See Zizioulas, "Relation," 70. Baillargeon does not distinguish between these two meanings of freedom, and he asserts (without providing any textual support) that "birth in Christ . . . does not come through a fact independent of a person's will; ecclesial existence is the fruit of freedom" (Baillargeon, *Communion,* 195). Although his second assertion is correct, the first is false.

various possibilities,[130] and he conceives it not "morally," but rather ontologically, in strict correspondence to God's own freedom. God exists "above all affirmation and negation," and yet in such a way that God's divinity is affirmed by God in the *communio*-event by transcending these two possibilities.[131] So also is human freedom to be understood; it consists in "movement toward the *communio*" that neither is nor is able to be conscious of itself as such.[132] For as soon as someone became conscious of this movement, one would be confronted with the possibility of choice. Choice, however, is a characteristic not of the person, but rather of the individual, and derives from the Fall.[133] Is this nonreflected movement toward communion anthropologically plausible? I think not.

3. Ecclesial Communion

To the pneumatic deindividualization of Christ there corresponds ecclesiologically a pneumatically mediated constituting of the church by Christ. The locus of this constituting, of the realization of its life, is the Eucharist. The personalization of human beings that has taken place in Christ and that is transferred to individual human beings in baptism finds its concrete, historical realization in the Eucharist.[134] This is why the Eucharist is the central soteriological and ecclesiological event in which the essence both of salvific grace and of the church manifests itself.

In the preceding analysis of Zizioulas's understanding of salvific grace as a process of personalization, I hardly mentioned the Eucharist. It was, however, consistently presupposed as the locus of realization of personhood and thus as the cognitive basis of soteriology, anthropology, and trinitarian theology. In what follows, I will examine it explicitly and discuss its consequences for the nature and structure of the church.

3.1. Eucharist and Communion

"For Orthodoxy," Zizioulas writes, "the church is in the Eucharist and through the Eucharist."[135] But how, in the specific version of Orthodox theology Zizioulas represents, is the being of the church actually grounded in the Eucharist?

130. See Zizioulas, "Die pneumatologische Dimension," 142.
131. Zizioulas, *Communion*, 121, note 126.
132. Zizioulas, "Die pneumatologische Dimension," 142.
133. See Zizioulas, *Communion*, 121, note 126.
134. See 2.1 and 2.2. above; Zizioulas, *Communion*, 61.
135. Zizioulas, "Welt," 342.

1. As one might expect from a theologian indebted to a specific form of personalism, Zizioulas polemicizes against any objectification of the Eucharist in theology and personal piety. The Eucharist becomes an object when viewed as one sacrament among others. As such, it is an "instrument," the means of grace, equipped with certain characteristics with their corresponding powers. Thus is the theology of the Eucharist dominated by the notion of substance and causality.[136] At the same time, the Eucharist is understood individualistically. It is a means given from one individual to another; priests "administer" it, and believers "use" it to gain access to that particular grace (yet another objectification!) that is to accompany them on their variously individual spiritual paths.[137]

By contrast, Zizioulas understands the Eucharist above all as a *liturgical act*, indeed, as the liturgical mode of life, of the congregation.[138] It is not an isolated means of receiving grace, but rather "an assembly (*synaxis*), a community, a network of relations, in which a man 'subsists.'"[139] The Eucharist and eucharistic communion are identical. Commensurately, what the eucharistic community receives at its celebrations is not simply holy things, nor even the words and deeds of Christ, but rather the *person of Christ in its totality*.[140] Neither can it be otherwise if the Eucharist is to "mediate" salvific grace, since the latter consists in the personalization of human beings through their incorporation into the personal relation of Christ to the Father, a relation constituting the Son into a divine person.

2. But what does it mean to receive the whole person of Christ? The answer leads us to the heart of Zizioulas's ecclesiology. He conceives the eucharistic presence and appropriation of Christ in closest possible correspondence to his pneumatically understood Christology, Christology based, as already shown, on the notion of a "corporate personality." "To eat the body of Christ and to drink his blood means to participate in him who took upon himself the 'multitude' . . . in order to make of them *a single body, his body*."[141] In the eucharistic celebration, the many become one body of Christ, and do so in such a way that Christ takes them up "into himself." This is why in the Eucharist, the body of the one (Christ) and the body of the many (the church) are identical.[142]

From this understanding of the Eucharist follows a particular understanding of the relation between church and Eucharist and between church and

---

136. Zizioulas, "Eucharistie," 166.
137. See Zizioulas, "Presuppositions," 337.
138. See Zizioulas, "Eucharistie," 172; "Presuppositions," 339.
139. Zizioulas, *Communion*, 60.
140. Zizioulas, "L'eucharistie," 55.
141. Ibid., 69.
142. Zizioulas, "Presuppositions," 342.

Christ. The Eucharist is not an act of the ontologically prior church; it is not the church that constitutes the Eucharist, but rather quite the reverse: the Eucharist constitutes the church.[143] Yet even this would be incorrect if understood to mean that the Eucharist *causes* the church, that is, first there is the Eucharist, and then the church emerges from it. Instead of conceiving the relation between church and Eucharist using the categories of causality,[144] Zizioulas views the Eucharist as an "all-inclusive expression of the mystery of the church" that is identical with the church.[145] According to Zizioulas, this is attested by Paul's synonymous use of the expressions ἡ ἐκκλησία ("the church"), συνέρχεσθαι ἐπὶ τὸ αὐτό ("coming together to one place"), and κυριακὸν δεῖπνον ("Lord's Supper") in 1 Corinthians 11.[146]

The ecclesiologically crucial identification of church and Christ manifests itself in the identification of church and Eucharist. The Eucharist is the place where church and Christ become one body, the body *of Christ,* and thus "completely" identical.[147] All distance between Christ and the church is overcome insofar as the Holy Spirit personalizes Christ within the church and "brings him alive, in a concrete state."[148] Commensurate with the notion that the personalization of the many in Christ comes about through the one relation of the Son to the Father constituting Christ as a person, Zizioulas also conceives the identity between Christ and the church in personal categories. The "I" of the church, its "personal identity," is the "I" of Christ. Zizioulas demonstrates the identity between church and Christ using the example of the eucharistic prayer. Although the church prays to the Father through the Son, this "through" is not to be understood in the sense of the Son mediating between the church and the Father. If in the eucharistic *synaxis* a community distinguishing itself from Christ were to pray, then a triadic relationship would emerge between the praying church, the mediating Son, and the listening Father; this triadic relationship would not only distort Christ's role, but would also render the prayer itself meaningless and fruitless. When the church prays, Christ prays for it, and he does so in such a way that *its prayer becomes Christ's prayer,* he prays "instead of [*anti*] us."[150] That "the

---

143. See Zizioulas, *Communion,* 21; "Presuppositions," 335.

144. So correctly Baillargeon, *Communion,* 69.

145. Zizioulas, "Eucharistie," 173; cf. "Presuppositions," 342; "Mystère," 332.

146. Zizioulas, "Presuppositions," 334.

147. Zizioulas, "Mystère," 328.

148. See Zizioulas, "Groupes," 267; *Communion,* 111; "Mystère," 328. Similarly also in his dissertation, where, following Augustine's formulation, he defines the ecclesial union of human beings with Christ as the *Christus totus.* This is why, Zizioulas argues, ecclesiology should cease being a separate chapter of theology and become instead an organic part of Christology (Zizioulas, Ἡ ἑνότης, 14).

149. Zizioulas, "Implications," 144f.

150. Zizioulas, "Community," 26.

prayer of the community is not something different from the prayer of Christ should be understood in no other way than as a *total identification* — at this moment — of Christ with the church."[151]

Just as through baptism human beings are constituted into persons anhypostatically in Christ, so also does the church exist in the Eucharist anhypostatically and acquire its entire identity from the identity of Christ. This paralleling of personhood and ecclesiastical being is not fortuitous. Any distance between Christ and the church would simultaneously mean the individualization of Christ, and the possibility of the deindividualization of human beings would be lost. We accordingly find that the identification of Christ and church in the Eucharist undergirds Zizioulas's entire soteriology and ecclesiology, and it is thus understandable why Zizioulas ignores those particular New Testament metaphors underscoring the difference between Christ and the church (e.g., the church as bride or as flock). I will return to this later.[152] Yet just as in the constituting of a person the particularity of that person is lost and the individual is absorbed into Christ, so also the church itself is threatened with being absorbed into Christ.

3. The eucharistic identification of church and Christ occurs in the Holy Spirit. The latter is the divine person who makes the eschaton historical (so in this way to guide history into the eschaton without destroying it). Here we see why Zizioulas relativizes the identification of church and Eucharist and thus also of church and Christ with the qualification "in some sense."[153] For the historical experience of the Spirit is not straightaway identical with eschatological glory. Commensurate with the dialectic between "already" and "not yet," he wants to understand the Eucharist not only as a realization of the eschaton, but at the same time as a movement toward the eschaton.[154] Yet this movement is not in any sense progressive, nor can it be, "since in every [eucharistic] celebration, the Kingdom *in its entirety* enters into history and is realized *here and now*."[155] While maintaining that the *Eucharist* is "a *movement* of the church toward the *Kingdom*," Zizioulas does not explain how a nonprogressive movement *within the Eucharist itself* is to be conceived, nor is it easy to imagine just

151. Zizioulas, "Mystère," 328 (my emphasis). The question is whether at least the structure of New Testament prayers does not underscore the difference between Christ and church rather than their identity. For although according to the New Testament Christ does indeed pray for us (see Rom. 8:34; Heb. 7:25; 9:24; 1 John 2:1f.), it is not Christ who prays through us; it is *we* who pray *through him* (see Rom. 1:8; 16:27, etc.). And this, our own prayer, takes place *in the Spirit* (Rom. 8:15) and does so in such a way that the *Spirit* — not Christ — prays *in* us (see Gal. 4:6; Rom. 8:26; 1 Cor. 14:15).

152. See III.2.1.3 below.

153. Zizioulas, "Presuppositions," 342.

154. Zizioulas, *Communion,* 61f.

155. Zizioulas, "L'eucharistie," 68, note 52 (Zizioulas's emphasis).

what this might mean.[156] His assertion that the Kingdom is realized in its entirety within the Eucharist excludes not only any historically deterministic, but also any epicletically mediated heightening of this realization of the eschaton. The dialectic "already — not yet" must therefore take place between the eucharistic experience (already) and daily life (not yet).[157] In the Eucharist, the eschaton *is* realized in and through historical reality, while the Eucharist itself remains excluded from the dialectic "already — not yet." It is in this sense that Zizioulas asserts that what actually occurs in the Eucharist "is not to be understood as a reality *parallel* with that of heaven, but rather as *identical* with it."[158] The identification of the church with Christ and the full realization of the eschaton in the Eucharist are intimately connected; the one is possible only through the other. From this it follows that the church is a strictly eschatological reality realized fully in history in every Eucharist.

Zizioulas has been charged — correctly, in my opinion — with having presented "overrealized eschatology."[159] He has no place systemically in the experience of salvific grace for the theologically necessary presence of unredemption. His insistence on the full realization of the Kingdom in the Eucharist is based on his ontology of person and on his understanding of salvific grace as the process of becoming a person. In order to become a person, one must be freed from the restrictions of the biological hypostasis. Hence this process of becoming a person can come about only from the direction of God and as a total eschatological transcending (not annihilation![160]) of biological existence. Furthermore, according to Zizioulas salvation is an *ontological constituting* of the human being into a person. Hence no dialectic of "already — not yet" can attach to the experience of salvific grace. If salvific grace encounters a human being as an already constituted person, then that person can be *simul iustus et peccator* (whether understood from the Catholic or Reformational perspective), since the status of being righteous or sinful becomes the various modes of that individual's being as a person. But if it is salvific grace itself that first constitutes a human being into a person ontologically, then that human being cannot simultaneously be both person and individual, or cannot be the one or the other to a greater or lesser degree; she *is* either the one or the other. Insofar as a human being is an individual at all, insofar as in her own being she is yet

156. Ibid.

157. See Zizioulas, "Groupes," 267.

158. Zizioulas, "L'eucharistie," 40. Cf. Zizioulas, 'Η ἑνότης, 49; in Zizioulas, *Communion*, 233, one reads: ". . . there is no room for the slightest distinction between the worshiping eucharistic community on earth and the actual worship in front of God's throne."

159. See Baillargeon, *Communion*, 256f.

160. Zizioulas is concerned not with negating history, but rather with freeing historical, creaturely reality from the nexus of cause and effect and from transience so that, after being thus transfigured, it can become the bearer of the ultimate (see Zizioulas, *Communion*, 186).

determined by necessity and is characterized by being in and for herself, she cannot at the same time be a person in Zizioulas's sense. To be a person, one must cease to be determined in a historically causal fashion. Thus do Zizioulas's anthropology and soteriology both require that the historical character of the church, if the latter genuinely is to be a church, be transcended eschatologically; it must be identical with Christ and for that reason also be understood as a strictly eschatological reality.[161]

That the eschaton is realized exclusively in the Eucharist means not only that only eucharistic communities constitute the church in the full sense of the word, but also that they are indeed the church *only during the actual eucharistic synaxis*. Zizioulas advocates an *actualistic* ecclesiology; "the church is *an event that takes place unceasingly afresh*, not a community structurally instituted in any permanent manner."[162] Paul McPartlan interprets Zizioulas accurately when he writes that "nothing of Christ is carried into the present from the past, it is only received again in the present from the future."[163] Only insofar as the eucharistic communion repeatedly becomes the realization of the eschaton can it be called "church." Here the dialectic "invisible — visible" acquires a particular shading. The invisible church *is* the church that becomes visible in concrete assemblies. It is not quite clear, however, why the dispersed church is then to be called "church" at all in the proper sense of the term.

Admittedly, Zizioulas's understanding of church and person is actualistic only from the perspective of the ordinary experience of time. Through reference to Spirit-effected transtemporality, Zizioulas believes he is able to emphasize precisely the notion of continuity, namely, the continuity within the life of the person and the continuity of the personal life of the individual with the life of Christ (which is the same thing). For the Spirit frees time from fragmentation; the Spirit bridges the flow of time precisely in the *event* of communion.[164]

---

161. Baillargeon seems to forget this. He suggests that Zizioulas free himself from his "overrealized eschatology" by conceiving eschatological reality as having been realized *in* history (see Baillargeon, *Communion*, 256f.). The question, however, is whether, given his point of departure, Zizioulas is able to conceive eschatological reality as merely partially realized in history, and whether he is able to undersand the dialectic of "already — not yet" in the sense of "both the one — and the other" in every moment of church life. The answer must be negative. Eschatological reality — the ontological realization of personhood — remains what it is only if it is not "tainted" by history — by its necessary causal nexus — i.e., only if it is *fully* eschatological. It is for this reason that the eschaton cannot enter *into* history; "as a state of existence it confronts history .. with *a presence from beyond history*" (Zizioulas, *Communion*, 174).

162. Zizioulas, "Mystère," 333 (my emphasis).

163. McPartlan, *Eucharist*, 192.

164. See Zizioulas, *Communion*, 183; cf. p. 211. The statement, "The people of God is *rhythmically* the Body of Christ" (McPartlan, *Eucharist*, 287), cannot be considered an ade-

3.2. Community and Communities

From this eucharistic grounding of ecclesiology issue important consequences for one's understanding of the local and universal church and for their relationship. The crucial features here are the locality and catholicity of the Eucharist itself.

1. According to Zizioulas, the church can be found in all its fullness wherever the Eucharist is celebrated. This eucharistic synaxis, however, can occur only when people come together at a specific place (συνέρχεσθαι ἐπὶ τὸ αὐτό, 1 Cor. 11:20). A circumscribed geographic *locality* plays a part in defining the church. The church is essentially the church at a specific place, a *local* church.[165] Precisely because every local church is a church in the full sense of the word, all local churches basically enjoy the same status, so that there can be no superior or subordinate churches (expressed through superior or subordinate bishops).

From the eucharistic localization of the church it follows that it is exclusively the local church, necessarily with a bishop at its head, as we will see, that can be viewed as church. The ecclesial status of all other ecclesial structures is derivative rather than inherent:

> A metropolis, an archdiocese or a patriarchate cannot be called a *church* in itself, but only *by extension,* i.e., by virtue of the fact that it is based on one or more episcopal dioceses — local churches which are the only ones on account of the episcopal Eucharist properly called churches.[166]

In addition to locality, *catholicity* is also an essential feature of the Eucharist, and involves the coming together of the *whole* church at a specific place (τῆς ἐκκλησίας ὅλης, 1 Cor. 14:23). The catholicity of the local church, however, does not derive from this assembly of all at a single place; it is not a human work. It is a pneumatically mediated christological reality grounded in the

---

quate interpretation of Zizioulas's ecclesiological actualism. From the perspective of the Spirit insofar as it effects transtemporality, one cannot distinguish in this way between "people of God" and "body of Christ." If, however, one leaves this perspective for a moment and concentrates instead on the time between eucharistic assemblies — a time bridged by this Spirit-effected transtemporality — then there is no reason to interpret human beings during this time theologically as the people of God. Since personhood depends on the Eucharist and for that reason is similarly realized or actualized in this fashion (see 3.2.2 below), the same problem arises at the anthropological level. Neither does the idea of retroactive causality offer any aid here (assuming one were persuaded of its cogency to begin with), since it explains only how the ecclesial assemblies are constituted actualistically as fully eschatological events, and is unable to establish continuity between these assemblies.

165. See Zizioulas, *Communion,* 247.

166. Ibid., 252f., note 7.

eucharistic experience of the presence of the *whole Christ,* who incorporates *all* those many into himself. The larger church is present in the local eucharistic *synaxis;* in a reverse fashion, the eucharistic *synaxis* is an act not only of the concrete eucharistic communion, but also of the larger church.[167] Thus every Eucharist anticipates the eschatological gathering of the *whole* people of God.[168] This eucharistic communion is "the expression *par excellence* of the catholicity of the church, a catholic act of a catholic church."[169]

Although the catholicity of the local church does not really represent a task of the church, being grounded rather in the presence of Christ, it does nonetheless require the catholic composition of the eucharistic communion; it must transcend *all* natural and social divisions at a specific place.[170] According to Zizioulas, this is not merely a moral demand. Any church excluding Christians at a given place is not merely a bad church, but rather is no church at all, since a Eucharist to which not all the Christians at a given place might gather would not be merely a morally deficient Eucharist, but rather no Eucharist at all. That is, it could not be the body of him who encompasses *everyone* into himself.[171] This living and concrete catholicity thus becomes the criterion — "the ultimate criterion," Zizioulas even asserts, albeit not without some measure of exaggeration[172] — of the ecclesiality of the church and of the validity of the Eucharist. This radical conclusion would be incomprehensible if the Eucharist consisted merely in the reception of a means of grace. The conclusion follows of necessity, however, from Zizioulas's understanding of the Eucharist as an eschatological event;[173] if the Eucharist excludes certain baptized persons, it cannot anticipate the eschatological gathering of the people and thus cannot be a Eucharist at all.

Now, Zizioulas does not define catholicity merely in a negative fashion as the absence of any exclusion, but rather also in a positive fashion as the inclusive gathering of all baptized people of a given place. This becomes evident from his understanding of the locality of the church, since he not only localizes the church, but also defines this locality as a *city* and at the same time specifies that only one eucharistic communion can be celebrated in a given city. Only thus can the church include *all* the Christians of a specific geographic locality in its cultural specificity and hence be catholic.[174] The singularity of historical space

167. See Zizioulas, "Welt," 343.

168. See Zizioulas, *Communion,* 144, 158ff., 255.

169. Zizioulas, "Groupes," 255.

170. See Zizioulas, *Communion,* 151; "L'eucharistie," 39f.; "Groupes," 268.

171. See Zizioulas, *Communion,* 255, note 11.

172. Ibid., 257.

173. In his earlier publications, Zizioulas hesitates to draw this systematically necessary conclusion (see Zizioulas, "Groupes," 268).

174. See Zizioulas, Ἡ ἑνότης, 63ff.; "L'eucharistie," 38f.; *Communion,* 247ff.

thus becomes the medium and guarantee of the eschatological anticipation of the differentiated unity of the people of God.

2. A correspondence obtains between the constituting of the catholic personality and the constituting of catholic ecclesiality. Just as the church, by taking up the whole Christ, realizes its own catholic ecclesiastical being, so also does every communicant (who through baptism has been constituted into a catholic person) realize his own life as a catholic person by taking up the *whole* Christ within the framework of the eucharistic gathering.[175] This yields two consequences for the understanding of person.

First, if personhood is eucharistically determined, then personhood, like ecclesial being as well, is an event rather than a condition. In the act of baptismal rebirth, it is not continual life that is given pre-eschatologically to persons; rather, in baptism they become persons in a punctiliar fashion and at the same time are "admitted" to the eucharistically transpiring, actualistic experience of personhood. Even though no "ontological *permanence*" attaches to this actualistic baptismal and synaxistic process of becoming a person, a certain "eschatological *finality*" does indeed attach to it.[176] What happens between the eucharistic gatherings on this side of the reign of God, however, can only be the struggle of the *individual* against the devil of individualism, notwithstanding Zizioulas's own implied eschatological ontology according to which a human being *is* that which she will be.[177] Second, although the emergence of the person and that of the church are conceived analogously, the being of the church precedes that of the person. Although only someone who has been constituted into a person in baptism can participate in the eucharistic celebration, she receives herself as a person in baptism and in the Eucharist only within the community, since only there can she accept the whole Christ. A person becomes a person only through and in the eucharistic gathering.

It is of significance here that Zizioulas is not able to conceive the reception of Christ in the Eucharist as a conscious act of the person. As we have already seen,[178] the insertion of cognitive activity into the relation of human beings to one another and to God involves their inadmissible individualization, that is, a negation of their personhood. The process of becoming a person must thus always occur in a noncognitive fashion. This also underscores the fact that person and community are not equiprimal in the eucharistic gathering; a con-

---

175. See Zizioulas, *Communion*, 60f.

176. So Zizioulas in reference to ordination (Zizioulas, "L'ordination," 46; Zizioulas's emphasis), which he understands relationally in correspondence to the process of becoming a person (see 4.2.1 below). Cf. the corresponding statements concerning personhood in Zizioulas, *Communion*, 58, note 52.

177. See note 164 above.

178. See 2.3.1 above.

dition of asymmetry obtains in the relation between person and community. Although the community consists of these persons who live in the community, are a part of the community, and are themselves communal (catholic) persons, the community is not constituted through these persons; rather, the latter are first constituted into persons only through the community.[179]

Hence at the lowest ecclesiological level, that of the local church, we actually find a *reversal of the trinitarian relationships.* At the trinitarian level, the one person constitutes the communion; at the ecclesiological level, persons are constituted by the communion. When Zizioulas writes that "communion which does not come from a 'hypostasis,' that is, a concrete and free person . . . is not an 'image' of the being of God,"[180] this cannot refer either anthropologically or ecclesiologically to every person living in the communion, but rather *only to the one* through whom the many are constituted as an ecclesial communion and thus also as persons. As we will see, this is the function of the bishop "representing" the one Christ. The community constituted through this one takes precedence over the individual persons. The only place in Zizioulas's thinking where the relationships between the one and the many run almost symmetrically is the relationships between local churches.

3. Because Zizioulas understands catholicity as the local presence of the whole Christ who incorporates into himself all human beings (or only all Christians?), catholicity always implies universality (without, however, being identical with it[181]). No local church is permitted to live in an isolated, self-enclosed fashion, but rather must live in communion with all other churches.[182] On the other hand, however, the unity of all churches is not to be conceived by way of universality, but rather by way of concrete catholicity. One cannot say that it is first only at the universal level that the church is actually the one church, and yet always exists concretely in the form of many churches (as, e.g., Ratzinger would maintain[183]). The one church does not merely exist in the multiplicity of churches; it *is* this multiplicity, the entire multiplicity and each individual element of this multiplicity. "The one Christ event takes the forms of *events* (plural), which *are as primary ontologically* as the one Christ event itself. The local churches are as primary in ecclesiology as the universal church."[184]

According to Zizioulas, the *one* (numerically identical, so to speak) Eucharist is celebrated in all churches. Accordingly, the universal church is not a "unity in collectivity," but rather a "unity in identity":

---

179. Admittedly, there can be no community without persons.
180. Zizioulas, *Communion,* 18.
181. See ibid., 257.
182. See Zizioulas, Ἡ ἑνότης, 199; *Communion,* 133.
183. See II.2.3 above.
184. Zizioulas, *Communion,* 132f.

Schematically speaking, in the first case the various local churches form *parts* which are added to one another in order to make up a whole, whereas in the latter, the local churches are *full circles* which cannot be added to one another but *coincide* with one another and finally with the body of Christ and the original apostolic church.[185]

Thus are local churches each the one whole church, though with variously differing loci of historical concretization.

In contradistinction to the person, who always receives himself or herself from the community, according to Zizioulas the local church does *not* receive itself from the entire community of churches through some sort of supralocal communal event. The local church *is* the whole church through an emphatically *local* occurrence, namely, that of the Eucharist. It does not become a church through the communion of churches, but rather *shows* merely its catholic ecclesiality (and accordingly also ecclesiality as such) by standing in the universal community. Accordingly, relationships between local churches are fundamentally symmetrical, with no superiority or subordination; every local church is "capable of passing final judgment on everything."[186]

Such an understanding of unity and ecclesiality seems to tend toward a confederation of local churches, even if the communities existing outside this "confederation" would not be considered churches. Zizioulas, however, offsets this tendency through the "one-many" dialectic between the local churches and their bishops, and does so not only at the level of the patriarchate, but also (cautiously) at that of the universal church.[187] This dialectic takes its orientation from trinitarian hierarchical relationships and corresponds to the dialectic between the one (bishop) and the many (priests, laity) within the local church. In the following examination of the structure of the communion, I will question how consistently he carries forward this ecclesiological premise.

4. The Structure of the Communion

From the eschatological catholicity of the eucharistic communities, there emerges not only the communal character of their relationships, but also a certain *structure* of these communities, involving both their internal structure and the structure of their universal unity. Before examining the character of the ecclesial structures at the local and universal levels, I will briefly address the relation between the ecclesial event and the ecclesial institution.

185. Ibid., 158, note 66; cf. Ἡ ἑνότης, 140ff.
186. Zizioulas, "Episkope," 33.
187. See Zizioulas, "Conférences," 505.

4.1. Institution and Event

According to Zizioulas, the need to fulfill certain functions does not suffice to ground the fundamental structures of the church. These structures derive not from the tasks of the church, however articulated, but rather from its eschatological, communal *being*. Because this is realized concretely in the Eucharist, ecclesiastical office acquires "its form, its existence and its theological specification from the typology of the Eucharist."[188] The Eucharist, however, is nothing other than the historical celebration of the eschatological reign of God at a specific place. Hence, ecclesial structures are ultimately grounded in the nature of the reign of God and must correspond to its structure.[189]

Yet how are the structures of the church to be understood if the church is an eschatological *event*, an anticipatory παρουσία ("coming")?[190] According to Zizioulas, the reign is present in history *in and through ecclesial structures*. The structures of the church, however, do not derive from history, but rather are grounded in the eschatological reign itself. First, and still in a rather abstract fashion, the existence of an eschatological community already implies a certain structure, since one must first of all be able to differentiate it from other communities. Second, the eschatological reign is the reign of Christ, who is surrounded by his apostles (as manifest, according to Zizioulas, in the Apocalypse of John). From this follow specific relationships within the reign of God and accordingly also within the church.[191] The *historic* structures in which the reign of God becomes an eschatological event in the Eucharist synaxis are accordingly *eschatologically* determined.

Since the eucharistic celebration and the (eschatological) heavenly liturgy represent an identical reality, the structure of the heavenly congregation as described in the Apocalypse — the throne of God and of the Lamb, surrounded by the elders with "seven spirits" and, before the throne, the "sea of glass" (Rev. 4:2-6) — serves as the model for the structure of the local church. "The 'place (or throne) of God' in the eucharistic synaxis is occupied in reality by the bishop ... who is surrounded by the thrones of the 'presbyters' and assisted by deacons, with the people facing him."[192] The Spirit constitutes the church through the bishop, the presbyters and deacons, and the people in their structured relationships.[193] The undifferentiated being of the church does not precede this differentiation within the church into certain ministries; rather, the church *comes*

---

188. Zizioulas, "Bishop," 26.
189. See Zizioulas, "Mystère," 334; "Episkope," 33; *Communion*, 138.
190. See 3.1.3 above.
191. See Zizioulas, *Communion*, 205f.; "Déplacement," 99.
192. Zizioulas, "L'eucharistie," 40.
193. See Zizioulas, *Communion*, 207.

about through such differentiation: ". . . the particular charismata *do not flow* from the existence of the body of Christ, but rather *form an integral part* of it."[194]

The most decisive elements of the eschatological ecclesial structure are the *bishop* as the head of the eucharistic congregation and the entire Christian *people* from a certain geographic locality assembled around him. The indispensability of the bishop and of the people for the inner structuring of the local church is grounded christologically in the reality of Christ as the one who at the same time unites the many within himself. By contrast, although the presbyters and deacons are indeed important — and Zizioulas takes pains to emphasize especially the significance of the deacons, who tend to be neglected — ecclesiologically they are nonetheless not indispensable; they become "essential elements [of the local church], depending on the 'typology' of the eschatological community one regards as fundamental to one's theology."[195] In what follows, I will restrict myself to an examination of Zizioulas's understanding of the bishop and laity and of the relationship between the two.

4.2. Bishop

1. In order to understand what it means to be a bishop, one must take note of ordination as the procedure through which one becomes a bishop. Zizioulas understands this process to be commensurate with that through which one becomes a person; as we will see, the processes of ordination and of becoming a person partially overlap and are in a certain sense identical.[196] In any case, Zizioulas applies the fundamental distinction between person and individual to ordination as well. Hence it is only logical that he criticizes both the understanding of ordination as a transferal of sacramental grace from one human being to another (the alleged Catholic misunderstanding) and the delegating of someone for the administration of certain functions by the congregation (the alleged Protestant misunderstanding). For both the traditional ontological and the functionalistic understanding of ordination view the ordained human being as an individual; either as a human being graced by God or as commissioned by human beings, he is something in himself quite independent of his living relationship to the congregation.

By contrast, Zizioulas conceives ordination from the perspective of the community. "Ordination *connects* the ordained minister to the community *so*

---

194. Zizioulas, "L'ordination," 44.

195. See Zizioulas, *Communion*, 256, though Zizioulas admittedly takes a different view in "Grundlage," 72: "Without these [the *four* offices] there is no church."

196. See 4.3.1 below.

profoundly and so essentially that in his new status after ordination one cannot conceive him alone; he has become a *relational entity*."[197] At ordination, a person does not merely acquire a function without himself being determined in his own being by the community. Neither does the ordained human being come into the possession of something as an individual over against the community (Zizioulas mentions in this context *character indelebilis*), but rather *becomes* something within the community. Ordination overcomes the self-enclosure of the ordained person and makes him into an ecstatic entity. What he is, he is through the relations in which he stands; "community forms part of the ontology of episcopacy."[198] What it means to be a bishop is fundamentally determined by the congregation; the seal of the Spirit bestowed in ordination cannot exist outside this relationship.[199] This is why at ordination, not only should the congregation be present in order to accompany the ordination with the acclamation ἄξιος ("worthy") and the song Κύριε ἐλέησον ("Lord, have mercy"), but the episcopal κατάστασις ("enthronement") must also be performed by the congregation itself as an essential part of ordination.[200]

According to Zizioulas, episcopal being is determined not simply by the place occupied by the bishop within the general structure of congregations, but rather by his relation to a *specific* congregation; the name of the place at which the diocese of the future bishop is found is mentioned explicitly in the ordination prayer.[201] If a concrete congregation attaches thus to episcopal ontology, then it seems unavoidable that after changing congregations, a bishop must be ordained anew. Within the framework of Zizioulas's ecclesiology, however, this conclusion does not necessarily follow, since every local congregation is a *catholic* congregation and as such is identical with the one church of God. The catholicity of every particular congregation makes it possible for Zizioulas, despite his insistence on the one-time, nonrepeatable nature of ordination, to avoid the distinction between *potestas iurisdictionis* and *potestas ordinis,* a distinction at odds with his ontology of person. The constituting of a person into a bishop, proceeding as it does by way of a specific local church, makes a bishop into a bishop in the one church of God, and for that reason also (potentially) into a bishop in every local church.

2. Since the eucharistic gathering is the εἰχών ("image") of Christ, so also

197. Zizioulas, "Ordination," 9.

198. Zizioulas, *Communion,* 137.

199. See Zizioulas, *Communion,* 165. The institution of titulary bishops is not only "scandalously uncanonical" (Zizioulas, *Communion,* 251, note 6), but also wholly impossible within Zizioulas's ontology of person: a bishop without a congregation is no bishop at all. The necessary ascription of a fictitious congregation to the titulary bishop merely underscores the validity of this assertion.

200. See Zizioulas, *Communion,* 218; "Bishop," 31f.

201. Zizioulas, *Communion,* 166, note 90.

is the bishop, as its head, the εἰκών of Christ. The identification of the church with Christ is the basis for Zizioulas's understanding of the episcopal office. At the eucharistic celebration,

> The presiding head of the community is to be viewed as the image of Christ by virtue of the fact that he does visibly what the Head, Christ himself, does invisibly . . . This presiding head thus himself acquires the prerogatives belonging to Christ.

Zizioulas can even say, "In the eyes of his people, the bishop *is* Christ."[202] He immediately relativizes this identification, since the bishop remains a weak and sinful being. *In the eucharistic synaxis,* however, he *is* Christ, since Christ himself is acting in and through him. In this sense, the bishop's liturgical acts do not take place parallel with Christ's own salvific acts, but rather are *identical* with those acts.[203] A problem arises here which Zizioulas does not address. If every eucharistic gathering is identical with the *whole* church, how in *every* gathering can there then be one bishop whose actions are identical with Christ's own salvific acts? The actions of the different bishops must be a single action, just as the Eucharist is a single Eucharist. Here the particularity of every bishop seems to vanish.

Just as Christ is not an individual, but rather a person incorporating the many into himself, so also is the bishop, acting as an "*alter* Christ," not an individual. Because through ordination he has become a person, in his task as head of the eucharistic gathering he acts as a corporate personality. Only thus can there come about that identity between Christ and the church through which the church is constituted as church. In the bishop as a catholic person *par excellence,* the christological mystery of the one who is simultaneously the many becomes historically concrete; "the One Christ becomes 'Many' — a community — and the many became 'One.'"[204] The bishop mediates between Christ and human beings, but not in such a way that he provides a bridge between Christ and human beings as separate realities. Rather, because he, as a relational entity, *is* both Christ and human being, he functions as an *alter* Christ who unites the many within himself. In this way, the bishop brings "the presence of the eschatological Christ into history in the form in which this presence will be realised in the last days, namely as a communion."[205] This clarifies why the church necessarily possesses an episcopal structure, indeed why without a bishop, "no spiritual experience that is, properly speaking, Christian," is conceivable.[206]

202. Zizioulas, "Mystère," 329 (my emphasis).
203. See Zizioulas, *Communion*, 163.
204. Zizioulas, "Bishop," 30.
205. Ibid., 29.
206. Zizioulas, "Community," 34.

It seems at first that the congregation has priority over the bishop; the status of bishop is determined by the congregation, and the church itself — internally differentiated from the very outset — takes precedence as an eschatological community over the bishop as *alter* Christ. Now, however, the task of the bishop in realizing the christological mystery in an ecclesial fashion and thereby in constituting the church makes it clear that the *bishop has priority over the congregation.* Although the bishop is indeed conditioned by the church, since without it he cannot be bishop (just as Christ is conditioned the church, since without it he cannot be Christ), it is nonetheless the bishop himself who constitutes the church into the church, and only through the bishop does the church live as the church, since the bishop is "the one through whose hands the whole community would have to pass in being offered up to God in Christ."[207] In strict correspondence with Christ — indeed, in identity with him — the bishop stands "*above* his community" precisely by being connected to his community,[208] since "the including one" (Christ or the bishop) obviously has priority over "the included" (the people).[209] Although reciprocity does obtain between bishop and congregation, it is asymmetrical.

Accordingly, one encounters in the relation between bishop and congregation the same asymmetrical structure of communality that according to Zizioulas also attaches to innertrinitarian relationships and to the relationship between Christ and the church; the one (God the Father, Christ, bishop) constitutes the many, but the many are conditioned by the one. It is thus doubtful whether Zizioulas's understanding of the relation between the one and the many genuinely has excluded "all pyramidal notions" from ecclesiology, as he asserts.[210] The "order of precedence" is actually grounded by this very understanding of relation, as Zizioulas himself says.[211] His assertion that this order of precedence "emerges freely from the communion of love" may well be persuasive with regard to the Trinity (presupposing his problematic understanding of trinitarian relationships), since God *is* love. With regard to the relation between bishop and congregation, however, it remains an empty demand in danger of degenerating into ideology.

3. The higher ranking of the episcopal One (Zizioulas speaks of a "decisive preeminence of the bishop"[212]) over the many is additionally underscored by

207. Zizioulas, *Communion,* 153.

208. See Zizioulas, "Bishop," 30 (my emphasis). The other passages where Zizioulas disavows that the bishop stands above the congregation (see Zizioulas, *Communion,* 164) are not meant to deny the higher status of the bishop over the congregation but to underscore that the bishop is part and parcel of the (hierarchically structured) community.

209. Zizioulas, *Communion,* 183.

210. Ibid., 139.

211. See Zizioulas, "Grundlage," 77; cf. "Die pneumatologische Dimension," 141.

212. Zizioulas, "Groupes," 257.

the exclusive right of the bishop to perform ordination. Since the Spirit is given only through the resurrected Christ whose εἰκών ("image") the bishop is, only the bishop can transmit the Spirit (in a noncausal sense).[213] Here it becomes clear that the bishop not only incorporates the many into Christ and thus unites them, but also simultaneously differentiates those thus united "by distributing the ministries and orders of the Church."[214] As the mediator between God and human beings, the bishop structures relationships within the local church so that the latter can live as a catholic unity. All charismatic manifestations must go through the bishop to insure that they become manifestations of the communion rather than degenerate into self-assertions of individuals to the detriment of the communion.[215]

Yet another characteristic of Zizioulas's understanding of communality becomes clear in the exclusive episcopal right to perform ordination. The community can exist only if there is the one who actually constitutes the various "many" into that community. The church can be catholic, and thus transcend all separation and divisions, only through the bishop. To have a collegial head of the local church is impossible, since in that case the unified catholicity of the local church would be lost. "The oneness of the bishop in each local church is a *sine qua non* condition for the catholicity of this church."[216] According to Zizioulas, the ecclesial unity and thus also ecclesiality itself are inconceivable without the singularity of the bishop. The church is "episcopocentric"[217] because the presence of Christ in the church and the catholicity of the church are mediated through the bishop.

4.3. Laity

The laity, however, exists not only *in* the bishop as a catholic person, but also *juxtaposed with him*. Within the eschatologically shaped structure of the eucharistic communion, laypersons occupy an indispensable position. Thus it is necessary to examine the relation between bishop and congregation from the perspective of the laity as well.

1. Zizioulas emphasizes the significance of the laity within the eucharistic communion by viewing them, too, as *ordained*, ordained specifically in the strict sense of χειροτονία ("election, ordination"), and not merely in the sense of the simple χειροθεσία ("laying on of hands"). Since baptism is inseparable from

213. Zizioulas, "Bishop," 29.
214. Ibid., 30.
215. See Zizioulas, "Die pneumatologische Dimension," 140.
216. Zizioulas, "Bishop," 30f.
217. Ibid., 23.

confirmation and always occurs in the context of the Eucharist, the person baptized is not only made into a Christian through baptism, but in the same act is also ordained; under invocation of the Holy Spirit, hands are laid upon her, and she is assigned to a specific *ordo* within the eucharistic gathering. This is why there are no nonordained Christians.[218] Christians are not distinguished one from the other insofar as some are ordained while others are not, but rather insofar as each has a specific task. Even though only those who have been baptized can be ordained to special ecclesiastical offices, those who are ordained do not through this ordination to a specific office (e.g., that of the bishop) receive something that is somehow added to what they received in baptism. Indeed, at ordination they do not receive anything that can be objectified. Rather, ordained persons are assigned *a different place* within the structure of the eucharistic gathering, that is, a structure now determining what they are. Here Zizioulas once more emphasizes the reciprocity within the church.

This reciprocity, however, proves to be asymmetrical as soon as one considers the specific commission of the indispensable *ordo* of the laity in the eucharistic gathering. The laity's task, indeed, its exclusive prerogative, as Zizioulas maintains,[219] is to say the "amen" as a response to the grace they have received. This "amen" is the liturgical expression of the fact that they, as the new people of God, "like the people of Israel, must *follow* Moses and give to him their *approbation through their responses*."[220] If the bishop really is the *alter* Christ, then something other than this "amen" would be inappropriate. This devaluation of the laity, judged from my perspective, corresponds to the soteriological and ecclesiological enhancement of the bishop; whoever assumes "the place of God"[221] must simply be followed. Admittedly, the laity is not to follow the bishop as an individual who simply stands opposite them, but rather as someone who represents them in a very real fashion. This is also why their reception of episcopal guidance is not to be understood as obedience to an order, but rather as the charismatic acknowledgment of a relation expressing their own personal identity.[222]

Given the specific position of the bishop and laity in the congregation, it is understandable why Zizioulas must define relationships within the church as *hierarchical* (even if he denies any differences in value between the laity and clerics by virtue of having derived that concept of hierarchy from his trinitarian theology). His attempt at deriving this hierarchy from the specificity of tasks themselves, however, does not seem cogent,[223] since such specificity of tasks is

218. Zizioulas, *Communion,* 215f.
219. Zizioulas, "Presuppositions," 343.
220. Zizioulas, "L'eucharistie," 41 (my emphasis).
221. Zizioulas, "Grundlage," 70; cf. "Community," 32.
222. See Zizioulas, *Communion,* 241f.
223. See Zizioulas, "Groupes," 260; "Ordination," 11.

clearly compatible with egalitarian relationships. Hierarchical relationships do not arise because each person has specific tasks, but rather because the specific tasks are defined as being in a certain order of precedence. Zizioulas conceives human persons in strict correspondence to the trinitarian persons, and this leads him astray. Because the trinitarian persons can be distinguished only through their mutual relations, the distinction between these persons — in the *immanent* trinity, they are identical with the "specific tasks" of persons — is bound to the preeminence of the Father, who constitutes the Son and Spirit.[224] This is different in the church, since persons are not identical with their tasks but rather persons who are already distinct are assigned to different tasks. This is why one does not need the one who constitutes these persons as different persons.

2. That all members of the body of Christ are ordained implies that they are all charismatic. Now, charismata derive from the eschatological Spirit of the community, from which Zizioulas concludes that the members cannot be understood in and for themselves, as individuals, but rather only in their relations with the other members of the body.[225] Nor can this be otherwise within the framework of his thinking, since reception of a charisma is identical with the personalization taking place in baptism; "being a 'charismatic' means in the final analysis being a member of the church."[226] Charismata are the "particular forms of relationships between people within the congregation."[227]

In this bestowal of charismata, however, persons are said to be constituted not only in their relationality, but also in their *particularity.* "Despite the fact that each person exists existentially in relation to others, he remains absolutely *unique* and there can never be another exactly the same."[228] One might accordingly expect that a specific charisma is bestowed on each individual person, but this is not the case. Although ordination does indeed differentiate and specify the members of the body of Christ, this differentiation is *not person-specific.* It leads the individual into a certain *ordo* in which he or she has a certain function; laypersons, for example, are to say the liturgical "amen." This bestowal of charismata creates a certain structure in the church. If this is so, then it is not clear how a bestowal of charisma can make *each* person unique. Since the bestowal of charisma assigns to a person a certain position in the network of relationships insofar as that person now belongs to a certain *ordo,* this bestowal can only ground the distinction between various

224. See 1.2.2 above.
225. Zizioulas, "L'eucharistie," 46.
226. Zizioulas, "Presuppositions," 343.
227. Zizioulas, "Grundlage," 76.
228. Zizioulas, "Ordination," 11.

types of persons, and not the uniqueness of every person within a certain type. Here again, we encounter the difficulty Zizioulas has in conceiving the particularity of persons.[229]

Zizioulas's understanding of the laity as an *ordo* amplifies the asymmetry between bishop and people.[230] The bishop occupies a position even more superior to that of the individual layperson than to that of the entire *ordo* of the laity; while the *ordo* of the laity is ecclesiologically indispensable, the individual person by contrast seems almost insignificant. Although Zizioulas writes that "the Eucharist requires the gathering of *all* the members of a local community,"[231] this is an excessively harsh, because unfulfillable, condition to impose on the Eucharist. Neither is it required within the framework of Zizioulas's thought. The presence of the *ordo* of the laity suffices.[232] Indeed, Zizioulas's ecclesiology can get along quite well without the presence of the *majority* of those who belong to a given local church.

The task of the *ordo* of the laity in saying the liturgical "amen," and the corresponding task of the *ordo* of bishops to act *in persona Christi,* make the eucharistic gathering into a strictly *bipolar event.* Neither do the various tasks of the presbyters and deacons interrupt this bipolarity. The presbyters and deacons surround the bishop and stand opposite the people; together with the bishop, they constitute the one pole, while the laity represents the other pole. This bipolarity allegedly corresponds to the Pauline church order, according to which the people are to speak the "amen" in the charismatic worship services (1 Cor. 14:16).[233]

---

229. See 2.1.2 above. Neither is it clear how the personalization occurring in the relation of Christ to the Father — this personalization must always occur as the constituting of particular persons — is related to the personalization occurring through the Spirit in the bestowal of charismata. It seems as if Zizioulas is allowing the two to coincide, whereby the second process is to be understood as a historical concretization of the first (see Zizioulas, "Ordination," 10). If this is indeed the case, then it is unclear how on the basis of this *one* relation of Christ that personalizes human beings the differentiation of those human beings into various orders is to occur.

230. Although Baillargeon praises this reciprocity between bishop and people explicated by Zizioulas, he does not draw attention to the asymmetrical character of this reciprocity (see Baillargeon, *Communion,* 83, 89, 115ff.).

231. Zizioulas, "Presuppositions," 348 (my emphasis).

232. McPartlan finds that the idea of corporate personality implies the necessity for all members of a local church to be present at the celebration of the Eucharist. "Corporate personality requires *actual personal presence*" (McPartlan, *Eucharist,* 177; cf. p. 210). Although this may be true, it would lead to the absurd notion that all those who constitute the corporate personality of Christ must *continuously* celebrate the Eucharist.

233. See Zizioulas, "L'eucharistie," 43; "Community," 30. In this regard, see VI.1.2 below.

4.4. Apostolicity and Conciliarity

Since a certain form of relationships with other eucharistic congregations plays a role in the ontology of every eucharistic congregation, translocal as well as local structures are essential to its being as a church. These structures are of an episcopal nature, since in Zizioulas's view only the bishop as the head of the congregation can represent them concretely. The bishop, as a catholic person rather than as an individual, is the real bond between the local church and all other local churches, within both time (apostolicity) and space (conciliarity).

1. The decisive element in Zizioulas's understanding of ecclesiality is the eschatological "continuity" of the church with Christ, something that becomes an event again and again in the eucharistic gatherings. Viewed from this perspective, the bishop is the *alter Christus* who through the Spirit mediates proleptically the eschatological catholicity of the local church. According to Zizioulas, however, the eschatological continuity of the church is inconceivable without its historical continuity. Viewed from this perspective, the bishop is the *alter apostolus* preserving the catholicity of the church within time. He is "responsible for the relation of his church with the first apostolic community, the historical college of the Twelve. Thus through the bishop each local church is united with all the local churches of the past."[234] This is why a person can only be ordained as a bishop by the bishops themselves, who received their own ordination from the apostles in unbroken historical continuity.

Zizioulas does not, however, examine more closely just why the continuity of every local church with the church of the apostles is to be guaranteed precisely and only through ordination in the apostolic succession; given his theological premise, however, this emphasis on apostolic succession does seem consistent. If, that is, pneumatically eschatological communion with the life of the triune God is mediated not cognitively, but rather in the communal eucharistic event, then the continuity of the church with the church of the apostles can hardly be mediated by way of the continuity of doctrine comprehended and transmitted cognitively. The continuity of the church must then also be mediated in an event, more precisely, in a eucharistically situated event of χειροτονία ("ordination").

Not only is ordination to the office of bishop to be performed by someone who has already himself been ordained bishop, but two or three bishops, preferably from neighboring dioceses, should also be present. This expresses the connection of every bishop with all other bishops, a connection constituting the bishop as bishop and the church as church. The bishop

---

234. Zizioulas, "Bishop," 31.

is the instrument of the catholicity of the church not only in terms of escha-tology (*alter Christus*) and of history (*alter apostolus*), but also in terms of catholicity in space; for each local church in order to be catholic must be in communion with all the other local churches in the world.[235]

The catholicity of the church in space, or the unity of churches, is expressed concretely and maintained by the institution of the regional or universal synod. The synod is of an episcopal nature because the local church itself is essentially of an episcopal nature.

Zizioulas's conception of synodal life is guided by two basic convictions. First, all bishops are basically of equal status, and each one represents the highest authority in the church; no bishop is permitted to intervene in the affairs of the diocese of another bishop, nor may decisions within the structures of the regional (and universal) community be made without consulting the individual bishop.[236] The equality and sovereignty of bishops follow clearly from Ziziou-las's understanding of ecclesial unity at the universal level as "unity in identity" rather than as "unity in collectivity."[237] From this it follows that the only exception to the prohibition against other bishops or the synod interfering in the life of a local church involves those cases in which the ecclesial identity of the local church in question is at stake (e.g., in questions of doctrine) or when the internal affairs of the local church directly and substantively affect the life of other churches (e.g., in questions of excommunication).[238]

The second basic conviction regarding the institution of the synod that seems to relativize the equality of bishops is a certain understanding of the relation between the one — the first (πρῶτος) — and the many. Following the thirty-fourth Apostolic Canon, Zizioulas defines the relation between the one and the many as follows: "No bishop should do anything without the consent of the πρῶτος while the πρῶτος will do nothing without the consent of the others."[239] Here again, the bipolar nature of the reciprocity between the one and the many becomes evident, though the status of the one within the synod is to be distinguished from the status of the one within the eucharistic synaxis. This is why Zizioulas insists that among bishops there is "at most an order of precedence of honors,"[240] though recently he seems to have expressly turned away from this view. The first, he now emphasizes, "gives . . to the synod an ontological status, and not simply an honor."[241] Is this an indication that he is

---

235. Ibid., 33.
236. Ibid.
237. See 3.2.3 above.
238. See Zizioulas, "Conférences," 502; "Entwicklung," 55ff.
239. Zizioulas, "Bishop," 33; see *Communion*, 135f.
240. Zizioulas, "Grundlage," 73.
241. Zizioulas, "Conférences," 504.

beginning to conceive the unity of the universal church in strict correspondence to the unity of the local church?[242]

2. In order to answer this question, but also in order to understand correctly the relation between the one and the many in the church, we must examine the status or being of the bishop. What actually constitutes the status or being of the bishop? Obviously, first of all the Holy Spirit, since according to Zizioulas ordination is a work of God and is therefore performed concretely within the context of epiclesis by a bishop standing in the *successio apostolica* and in the presence of other bishops. What, however, guarantees and attests here that at this ordination God himself is acting through the bishops? It is only logical that Zizioulas does not simply refer to the universal church (as does Ratzinger), but rather to the *concrete eucharistic community,* a community identical with the larger church, in which this ordination is performed. If, that is, ordination is a charismatic event, then it must occur within the eschatological context. According to Zizioulas's ecclesiology, this eschatological context can only be the concrete eucharistic gathering with its specific structure. "The Spirit is exclusively possessed by the church."[243] The bishops are not present "as individual originators of ministry," nor as mediators of something that comes by way of the universal church to the congregation and to those to be ordained, but rather "as a presiding college" in a concrete congregation.[244] Thus can Zizioulas assert that "the organic link of ordination with this community is . . . a key for all theology of the ministry: *it* points to divine action."[245] This mediation of the Spirit through the congregation is commensurate with Zizioulas's conviction that the charisma given in ordination lives not so much from the relation of the bishop in question to other bishops as from his relation to the concrete congregation itself, and that outside this relation such charisma will of necessity be extinguished.[246]

Here it becomes clear that the status of bishop, strictly speaking, is not constituted by the Holy Spirit through the relationships with other bishops, and *a fortiori* not through the relation to the first, but rather only *necessarily expresses and attests itself in these relationships* (just as the ecclesiality of the eucharistic gathering derives not from the universal church, but rather necessarily expresses and attests itself in its connection with all churches[247]). If this were not so, the

242. So McPartlan, *Eucharist,* 203-11.
243. Zizioulas, *Communion,* 165.
244. Ibid., 192f.
245. Ibid., 219 (my emphasis).
246. See ibid., 165.
247. The unity of the eucharistic community with other communities is constituted by the power of the presence of Christ in each of them, and not "by virtue of *an external superimposed structure*" (Zizioulas, *Communion,* 157). As we have already seen, the local

priority of the universal church would have to be the point of departure. Zizioulas, however, understands the universal church as the communion of the local churches that are identical with the universal church. In a manner different from the way in which one becomes a Christian, which happens within the eucharistic gathering and thus by way of the bishop, the episcopal being of the bishop in question is not constituted by way of the first in the synod (notwithstanding the participation of the first in the choice of bishops).

At the trinitarian, christological, and local ecclesiological level of Zizioulas's reflections, we encountered the same understanding of the relation between the one and the many in which the one constitutes the many and the many are conditioned by the one; at the level of the relations between the churches and bishops, this relational determination *can be found only in a loose, analogous fashion*.[248] The relationship "individual bishop — the first" does not exactly correspond to the relationship "individual Christian — bishop." The reason for this is that, in contrast to the the case of the individual Christian, every eucharistic gathering is the concrete realization of the eschatological reign in which Christ (the one) is surrounded by the apostles (the many). Moreover, the eucharistic gathering is *the only* realization of the eschatological reign; outside it, no other entity on earth can be called the "body of Christ" or, strictly speaking, "church." This is why the sojourning universal church can indeed have the same structure as the local churches, though the structure itself can be nothing more than a *reflection* of the christological and ecclesiological *reality* found only in the local church.[249] To assert more than this, Zizioulas would have to abandon his original point of departure, the specific shape of his eucharistic ecclesiology, for the sake of a universalistic ecclesiology.[250] The understanding of the relation

churches are churches in the full sense of the word; for this reason, they cannot be added, but rather coincide with one another, being in this way the one body of Christ. "It is for this reason," Zizioulas writes, "that any 'structure of the unity of the church in the churches' . . . renders itself extremely difficult, once it is a *structure*. (It is not an accident that the ancient church never realized such a *structure* in her life in spite of her conciliar activity.)" (Zizioulas, *Communion,* 158, note 66).

248. This is true even though Zizioulas does try to take his orientation for the relations between churches from trinitarian relationships (see Zizioulas, *Communion,* 134f.).

249. This, I think, is how one should understand Zizioulas's assertion that "a ministry of primacy [is] inherent in all forms of conciliarity" and his statement: "The 'many' always need the 'one' in order to express themselves. This mystery of the 'one' and the 'many' is deeply rooted in the theology of the church, in its christological (the 'one' aspect) and pneumatological (the aspect of the 'many') nature" (Zizioulas, "Nature," 344). Here, "deeply rooted in the theology of the church" means nothing more than "corresponds to the model of the eucharistic gathering."

250. Paul McPartlan believes that Zizioulas's most recent publications allow one to conceive the sojourning universal church as a corporate personality with this "one-many" structure (McPartlan, *Eucharist,* 203-11). (Or is this McPartlan's own suggestion?) The rela-

"first — many" at the synodal level is sustained more by the simple conviction that there can be no differentiated unity without the one than by the trinitarian determination of the structure of communality according to which the one constitutes the many in their being while the many are conditioned by the one.[251] Zizioulas's assertion that "the *first* gives . . . ontological status to the synod"[252] thus says merely that the first is constitutive for the "para-ecclesial reality"[253] of the synod and cannot be construed so that the first occupies ecclesiologically the same position with regard to the bishops as does each bishop with regard to individual Christians; the episcopal being of the individual bishop is not constituted through his relation with the first.

3. Because in the local church the many are the condition of the being of the one, their presence is indispensable at episcopal ordination. Without their acclamation (ἄξιος), representing a form of the liturgical "amen," no ordination can take place. Although at first it seems that for this reason the local church should also participate in the choice of bishop, this is not the case. If such congregational participation in the choice of bishop were indeed a presupposition of ordination, then according to Zizioulas the bestowal of charisma would be dependent on the decision of the people made *outside* the eucharistic gathering. God's charismatic activity, however, cannot be bound to any worldly, that is, noneschatological, causal nexus. The charismatic character of the office can be secured only by the immediacy of God's actions within the eucharistic gathering as a pneumatic eschatological event.[254] Zizioulas does anticipate, however, that the choice of bishop by the synod takes place under the chairmanship of the first.[255] A synod, however, is not a eucharistic event. To remain

---

tion "individual Christian — bishop" would have to correspond strictly to the relation "individual bishop — Pope." Then one could conclude "both that jurisdiction is part of the episcopal ordination which the Pope receives like the other bishops, and also that they receive their jurisdiction *from him*" (McPartlan, *Eucharist*, 209). This does not follow for the simple reason that the sojourning universal church is not a eucharistic community and hence does not, strictly speaking, represent a christological-ecclesiological reality.

251. These two understandings of the relation between the one and the many are clearly distinguishable. When one speaks about the one who constitutes the many and about the many who simultaneously condition the one, then both the one and the many are conditioned ontologically by their mutual relation. By contrast, one can very well speak about the one who is necessary for the differentiated unity of the many without having to address that which constitutes the one and the many ontologically.

252. Zizioulas, "Conférences," 504.

253. I have coined the expression "para-ecclesial reality" in analogy to Zizioulas's own expression "para-eucharistic services," which refers to all services not grounded "in the eschatological essence of the eucharist," such as patriarch, metropolitan, lector, and so on (see Zizioulas, "Grundlage," 70ff.).

254. See Zizioulas, *Communion*, 218f.

255. See Zizioulas, "Conférences," 504.

consistent, Zizioulas would have to argue against election by the synod as a condition for ordination. In any case, his ecclesiological assumptions do not explain why the extraeucharistic decision of the bishops should be acceptable while that of the entire congregation is not.

The significance of the congregation evident in Zizioulas's understanding of ordination is underscored yet once more. Although the apostolicity and conciliarity of the church are concentrated and come to expression in the bishop, the bishop as the bearer of apostolicity and catholicity is a catholic person who includes within himself the entire congregation, not an individual separate from that congregation. The fact that the bishop is conditioned in his being by the congregation corresponds first to the fact that apostolic succession is a succession of *local churches*: "[Apostolic succession] should be viewed neither as a chain of individual acts of ordination nor as a transmission of truths but as a sign and an expression of the *continuity of the Church's historical life in its entirety*, as it was realized in each community."[256] The entire congregation embodies in its own specific structure this apostolic continuity. Only thus can the apostolicity of the church be the means of its all-decisive eschatological continuity, a continuity with the reign of God structured in a certain way. Since every church is completely apostolic through the *successio apostolica*, every bishop is the successor of all apostles and sits on the *cathedra Petri*. Only under this condition is episcopal collegiality not merely a collective unity, but rather a unity in identity allowing every local church to be completely the church of Christ and not merely a part of that church.[257]

The understanding of the bishop as a corporate personality also corresponds to the understanding of synods or councils as assemblies not of bishops, but rather of *local churches through their bishops*.[258] This is already expressed in the canonical rule according to which only diocesan bishops may participate in synods or councils (at least when ultimate decisions are at stake).[259] Because it is the churches themselves that participate in synods through their bishops, the structure of the unity of churches is not independent of individual local churches, but rather is identical with relations between these churches. From this it follows that the councils can be fully valid only if received by the local churches. "It is for this reason that a true council becomes such only a *posteriori*; it is not an institution but an *event* in which the entire community participates and which shows whether or not its bishop has acted according to his *charisma veritatis*."[260] The "amen" of the local church as an act of charismatic acknowl-

256. Zizioulas, *Communion*, 168.
257. See ibid., 197, 168.
258. Zizioulas, "Conférences," 501.
259. Zizioulas, *Communion*, 241; "Conférences," 500f.
260. Zizioulas, *Communion*, 242.

edgment is indispensable for all of ecclesial life.[261] Although the reception of the local churches is indeed integrated into a larger context of the one-many relationship at the synodal and universal level, the local church still maintains its priority; at least it must maintain this priority if Zizioulas is to remain true to his original ecclesiological vision.

According to that original vision, the local church stands at the center of ecclesiology. It is identical with the church, indeed, *is* the *whole* church, because it is identical with the Eucharist, at which the whole Christ is present. In the local church, which alone deserves to be called church in the original sense, human beings move from being individuals to being persons through participation in the personhood of Christ, and are thereby integrated into the trinitarian life. This is why their own relationships must correspond to those of the trinitarian persons. Just as in the Trinity the one (the Father) constitutes the many (the Son and the Spirit) and at the same time is conditioned by them, so also does the one (Christ and bishop as *alter Christus*) constitute the many (the church) and at the same time is conditioned by them.

As we saw in chapter I, Ratzinger by contrast associates eucharistic ecclesiology with a different understanding of the Trinity and arrives at a rather different understanding of ecclesial relationships. Just as the divine persons are wholly identical with pure relations of being-from-the-other and being-toward-the-other, so also, ideally, should human persons be wholly identical with such relations; they should be nothing in and for themselves, and should be completely from and for others. But just as the one substance of God has priority over the three persons, so also is the universal church given precedence over the local church, since the local church is a local realization of that universal church. From this it then follows that the Pope has precedence over the bishops, and the bishops over congregations. Whereas in Zizioulas we encounter a mutual (albeit asymmetrical) relation between the one and the many, in Ratzinger we encounter an (almost completely) one-sided relation of the whole and the one to its concrete realizations.

Are Ratzinger's and Zizioulas's understanding of the Trinity, of human persons, and of the church and its structures persuasive? In the following chapters, I will turn my attention to this question. In the process, I will not only critically examine the thinking of both Ratzinger and Zizioulas but in dialogue with them will also sketch out an alternative understanding of the relation between Trinity and church, of human personhood, and of the church and its structures.

261. See Zizioulas, "Reception," 6.

PART II

Chapter III

The Ecclesiality of the Church

Exploring the question of ecclesiality means exploring what makes the church the church. On the one hand, this represents a restricted point of inquiry, since it overlooks much of the rich life and multifaceted mission of the church; our interest is directed not toward how the church *ought* to live in the world according to God's will nor how it *can* live successfully in the power of the Spirit, but rather toward the *sine qua non* of what it means for the church to call itself a church in the first place. Ecclesiality involves that which is indispensable. On the other hand, we simultaneously find that the question of ecclesiality directs our interest toward that which is decisive in the strict sense, toward that which supports and shapes the entire life and mission of the church. The preeminent ecclesiological significance of this question comes fully into view when one considers that its answer must in its own turn involve a consideration of the most important soteriological, anthropological, and trinitarian issues.

Since it is impossible to say everything at once, in this chapter I will examine ecclesiality as such, and only in the following three chapters examine its soteriological and trinitarian presuppositions and its consequences for theological understanding of office and for ecclesiastical law. The final chapter, on the catholicity of the church, will then provide a bridge between the indispensable ecclesial minimum and the comprehensive horizon of the life and mission of the church. The entire second part represents an attempt to get closer, from various angles, to some understanding of *a whole*. Each of its individual chapters can thus be understood correctly only if read in connection with all the others.

1. Identity and Identification of the Church

The all-embracing framework for an appropriate understanding of the church is God's eschatological new creation. According to the message of Jesus, the gathering of the people of God is grounded in the coming of the Kingdom of God in his person.[1] Commensurately, New Testament authors portray the church, which emerged after Christ's resurrection and the sending of the Spirit, as the anticipation of the eschatological gathering of the entire people of God. Paul, for instance, understands the church as "the anticipation of the coming new, obedient world intended by God's δικαιοσύνη (righteousness)."[2] The eschatological character of the church demands that systematic ecclesiological reflection begin not immediately with the church itself, but rather with God's new creation in its relation to God's people.[3]

1.1. What Is the Church?

1. The future of the church in God's new creation is the mutual personal indwelling of the triune God and of his glorified people, as becomes clear from the description of the new Jerusalem in the Apocalypse of John (Rev. 21:1–22:5).[4] On the one hand, the entire city, which in the Apocalypse refers to the people rather than to the place in which the people live, is portrayed as the supradimensional holy of holies (see 1 Kgs. 6:20) filled with the splendor of the presence of God and the Lamb. On the other hand, however, God and the Lamb are portrayed as the temple in which the holy of holies, the people, are found (see Rev. 21:22). "The saints will dwell in God and the Lamb just as God and the Lamb will dwell in them."[5] In a canonical reading of the New Testament, one can understand this reciprocal personal indwelling of God, the Lamb, and the glorified people as the eschatological fulfillment of Jesus' high-priestly prayer, which portrays the unity of believers as communion within the communion of the triune God: "I ask . . . that they may all be one. As you, Father, are in me and I am in you, may they also be in us" (John 17:21).

---

1. See Lohfink, "Jesus" (even though I cannot subscribe to some of the conclusions he draws from the correct assertion that the assembly of the eschatological Israel is a correlate of Jesus' own proclamation of the Kingdom — as, e.g., regarding the allegedly untenable nature of "*all* congregationalist understandings of the church" [p. 93, my emphasis]).

2. Stuhlmacher, *Gerechtigkeit*, 214.

3. I share this eschatological perspective on ecclesiology with Jürgen Moltmann (see *Church in the Power of the Spirit*) and Wolfhart Pannenberg (see "Reich Gottes"). See also Kraus, *Reich Gottes*, 369f.

4. See in this regard Gundry, "New Jerusalem."

5. Ibid., 262.

Such participation in the communion of the triune God, however, is not only an object of hope for the church, but also its present experience. "We declare to you what we have seen and heard so that you also may have fellowship with us; and truly our fellowship *is* with the Father and with his Son Jesus Christ" (1 John 1:3). Faith in this proclaimed "life," life that was with the Father and appeared in this world in an audible and tangible fashion (see 1 John 1:1-4), establishes communion between believers and the triune God and thus also among believers themselves. Present participation in the trinitarian *communio* through faith in Jesus Christ anticipates in history the eschatological communion of the church with the triune God.[6]

Since Ignatius of Antioch, the question regarding ecclesiality has justifiably been answered through reference to the presence of Christ (ὅπου ἂν ᾖ Ἰησοῦς Χριστός, ἐκεῖ ἡ καθολικὴ ἐκκλησία, "Wherever Jesus Christ is, there is the universal church"[7]) or of the Spirit (*ubi Spiritus Dei, illic Ecclesia, et omnis gratia,* "Wherever the Spirit of God is, there is the church, and all grace"[8]). This reference to the presence of Christ or of the Spirit — most precisely, of the Spirit of Christ — is admittedly not sufficient to ground ecclesiality, since the presence of Christ and of his Spirit cannot be restricted to the church alone (see Eph. 1:22-23; Col. 1:12-20). Hence one must distinguish between the general and the particular presence of the Spirit. Wherever the Spirit of Christ, which as the eschatological gift anticipates God's new creation in history (see Rom. 8:23; 2 Cor. 1:22; Eph. 1:14), is present in its *ecclesially constitutive* activity, there is the church. The Spirit unites the gathered congregation with the triune God and integrates it into a history extending from Christ, indeed, from the Old Testament saints, to the eschatological new creation. This Spirit-mediated relationship with the triune God and with the entire history of God's people — a history whose center resides in Jesus' own proclamation of the reign of God, in his death and in his resurrection — constitutes an assembly into a church.

2. As is well known, the presence of the Spirit of Christ cannot be directly ascertained, which is why this particular notion of the identity of the church cannot yet function as an answer to the question of its *identification*. If one is to speak meaningfully about ecclesiality, one must know not only what the church is, but also how a concrete church can be identified externally as a church; one must also be able to say *where* a church is. If the external identifying features of the church are to fulfill this function, they cannot be *purely* external, however; if they do not visibly disclose something essential about the church,

---

6. Concerning the spirituality corresponding to the anticipatory fellowship of the people of God with the triune God in the new creation, see Land, *Spirituality.*

7. Ignatius, *Smyrn.* 8:2.

8. Irenaeus, *Haer.* 3.24.1.

we will be unable to identify the church unequivocally (unless these features happen to represent a specifically ecclesial curiosity having nothing to do with ecclesiality as such, even though they always accompany the phenomenon "church"). Hence all Christian churches have understood the signs of ecclesiality to be externally perceivable and simultaneously necessary *conditions or consequences* of the ecclesially constitutive presence of the Spirit of Christ. These have been either the persons or actions through which the presence of the Spirit is mediated in a congregation (office and sacraments), the effects of this presence itself (*imitatio Christi,* commitment), or both.

Questions about the identity and identification of the church are inseparable. That by which one can identify the church as church is part of its identity; decisions involving the identification of the church *are* decisions involving its identity. Since ecumenical consensus holds that the presence of the Spirit of Christ makes a church a church, it is precisely questions concerning the external conditions of this presence that become ecumenically significant for the identity of the church. By the same token, it is in these very conditions that the *character* of the presence of the Spirit of Christ in the church comes to expression. These two factors — the character of the presence of the Spirit and its external conditions — give to an ecclesiology its specific configuration; it is they that determine the constellation of relationships between individual persons and the local church, and between local churches as such. Hence in what follows I will concentrate on the problem of the identification of the church in its relation to the character of the presence of the Spirit.

1.2. Where is the Church?

1. As I have already explicated in detail, Catholic ecclesiology[9] understands the church as constituted in the Spirit through the sacraments, above all through baptism and the Eucharist, and through the word. However, the *office of bishop* represents the indispensable condition of the sacraments and of the word, since the bishop, standing in the apostolic succession and in communion with all other bishops, is the sign and guarantor of the universal character and thus also of the divine origin of the sacraments and the word.[10] Only those local fellowships of believers that are "united to their pastors" are churches in the full sense

9. Although by "Catholic ecclesiology" I mean "Ratzinger's ecclesiology," this does not mean that I identify Ratzinger's ecclesiology straightaway with Catholic ecclesiology. I am well aware that no ecclesiology is *the* definitive Catholic ecclesiology and that Ratzinger's is not the only possible Catholic version (see chapter I above). The same applies to Zizioulas's version of Orthodox ecclesiology.

10. See I.4 above.

of the word.[11] This is why all other Christian fellowships except the Orthodox Church, an exception which according to Ratzinger's ecclesiological presuppositions seems to be an anomaly,[12] exhibit merely more or less significant *ecclesial elements* but do not qualify as churches.[13]

According to Orthodox ecclesiology, which understands itself as being wholly eucharistic, the church is "episcopocentric."[14] On the one hand, the bishop as *alter Christus* mediates the presence of Christ and secures the catholicity of the local church. On the other hand, as *alter apostolus* he connects all the various local churches in time (apostolicity) and space (conciliarity). In these two functions, the bishop is indispensable for the event of the eucharistic gathering and thus also for the ecclesiality of the local church.[15] From this it follows that no local church standing outside the Orthodox communion of churches can be designated as a church, not even a local church genuinely standing in the apostolic succession, because it lacks synchronic communion with all other churches.

A second condition of ecclesiality both in the Catholic and in the Orthodox traditions is the *people*. According the Ratzinger, laypersons are not the passive objects of the priests' liturgical activity. The priest is the subject only insofar as he embodies the liturgy as an ecclesial event. The real human subject of the liturgy is the "entire *ecclesia sancta*,"[16] and the individual priest is such only insofar as he embodies the larger church. This is why the congregation may not itself "perform liturgical acts," but rather must receive the liturgy from the universal church.[17] According to Orthodox tradition, there can be no eucharistic gathering without the presence of both the bishop and the people: the relation "bishop — laity" at the level of the local church corresponds to the relation "Christ — church" at the level of the universal church. Because the laity alone can say the liturgically necessary "amen," the laity possesses an indispensable status in the eucharistic gathering, albeit, at least from the Free Church perspective, a not particularly dignified status.[18]

2. In addition to the word, the sacraments, and the presence of the people, the early Free Church tradition emphasized two other conditions regarding the constitutive presence of the Spirit of Christ in a church. The first was obedience to Christ's commandments. The members of a true church, writes John Smyth, "are men separated from all known syn, practicing the whol will of God knowne

11. *Lumen gentium* 26; *Unitatis redintegratio* 3.
12. See I.2.2 and I.4.5 above.
13. *Lumen gentium* 26; *Unitatis redintegratio* 3.
14. Zizioulas, "Die pneumatologische Dimension," 140.
15. See II.4.2.2 and II.4.4.1 above.
16. Ratzinger, *Volk*, 149, note 55.
17. See I.5.3 above.
18. See II.4.3.1 above.

vnto them."[19] According to the familiar Puritan *syllogismus practicus,* true faith can reside in a person's heart only if that faith manifests itself in good works, and without true faith there is no indwelling of Christ through the Spirit within human beings. Similarly also with the church: by tolerating impenitent sinners in its midst, it shows that Christ is not present in it and that it is not a true church.

The second condition of Christ's constitutive presence was the "biblical organization of the church." Differently than for the Reformers, the English Separatists did not consider questions of church organization to be part of the ecclesiological *adiaphora.* According to Smyth, "Gods word doth absolutely describe vnto vs the only true shape of a true visible church."[20] Although Smyth richly supports his explications with biblical references, he is by no means arguing from a purely biblicistic perspective. His entire ecclesiology is based on the fundamental *theological* conviction that *Christ's dominion is realized through the entire congregation.* "We say the Church or two or three faithful people Separated from the world & joyned together in a true covenant, have both Christ, the covenant, & promises, & the ministerial powre of Christ given to them."[21] Such a "true visib[l]e church is Christs kingdome."[22] The members of the church are "the children of the kingdom" and govern as such in the church.[23] If for the sake of order they are to subordinate themselves, then they should do so only to the "government of the Church" as a whole, for only in this case can they stand "vnder the government of Christ."[24] Accordingly, Christ can be present only in a congregation in which his dominion is not impeded by the establishment of the rule of certain human beings, namely, bishops.[25] It is for

19. Smyth, *Works,* 253, though this is not to be understood as an attempt to exclude sinners from the church. The English Separatists did not subscribe to a church of the perfect. According to their own confessional definition, the church expressly consists not merely of the perfect; it "consists of *penitent* persons only, and of such as beleeuing in Christ, bring forth fruites worthie amendment of lyfe" (Smyth, *Works,* 744, my emphasis; cf. also "The Orthodox Creed" [1679], xxx, in *Baptist Confessions,* 319; "The Second London Confession" [1677], xxvi.3, in *Baptist Confessions,* 285). To be sure, the English Separatists, together with the Anabaptists, did understand the church as a milieu "in which imperfect, but only sincere, submissive and obedient Christians, spiritually grow and find help to restrain their sinful tendencies" (Davis, "No Discipline," 144).

20. Smyth, *Works,* 252. Cf. John Smyth's rhetorical question: "Is not the visible Church of the New Testament with all the ordinances thereof, the chief and principal part of the Gospel?" (cited in White, *Separatist Tradition,* 116).

21. Smyth, *Works,* 403; cf. 315. See in this regard Shantz, "Resurrected Christ."

22. Smyth, *Works,* 267. See in this regard Shantz, "Resurrected Christ."

23. Smyth, *Works,* 274.

24. Ibid.

25. This Free Church argumentation corresponds almost exactly to the Old Testament polemic against the ideology of kingship in the nations of the ancient Near East. According

this reason that a church organization in which "power" is held by the entire congregation represents an indispensable condition of ecclesiality.[26]

3. As far as the conditions of ecclesiality are concerned, the episcopal and early Free Church traditions differ especially in three respects.[27] The first concerns the bishop standing in the apostolic succession and communion with other bishops. According to the episcopal tradition, the local church *must* have such a bishop, since he alone can ensure the presence of Christ and thus also the church's ecclesiality; according to the Free Church tradition, such a bishop *is not permitted*, since through his very presence the congregation loses the presence of Christ and thus also its ecclesiality. These two positions are mutually exclusive.

Today, such exclusivity is no longer credible. I am thinking less of the sociological fact that exclusive positions in modern societies are unpersuasive than of the observation that the dynamic life and the orthodox faith of the many, quickly proliferating Free Churches make it difficult to deny them full ecclesiality. Let me illustrate this difficulty by referring to a situation that, although doubtless atypical, must nonetheless be the touchstone of any ecclesiology precisely because it is a borderline case. Should, for example, a Catholic

---

to the presentations of Jan Assmann, these ideologies understand the king "in a double relation of representation: he represents God's dominion over human beings and human fellowship with the gods" (Assmann, *Politische Theologie,* 75). By contrast, in Israel the position which in Egypt the pharaoh occupied is "redefined in a twofold manner. First, the pharaoh as suzerain and commander is replaced by Yahweh. . . . Second — and this step is essentially more revolutionary and more consequential — the position of the king — in the other direction of this representation — is replaced by the 'people,' which is 'chosen' just as the Egyptian imperial god chooses the king; the people act before God, receive his guidance, keep his commandments, and function as a subject of history just as did the pharaoh in Egypt" (pp. 75f.).

26. In his study *The Communion of the Saints,* Stephen Brachlow draws attention to the close connection between ecclesiology and soteriology among the radical Puritans and Separatists (pp. 21-76). Here he seems to be thinking especially of that particular obedience — obedience proving faith to be genuine — to the commandments of the Decalogue and of the biblical doctrine concerning church organization. In this way, human beings can attain certainty of salvation through obedience to both moral and "ecclesiological" commandments (see p. 54). This does not yet, however, reveal the *inner connection* betweeen ecclesiology and soteriology. It seems to me that at least John Smyth's congregationalist ecclesiology emerged not only from an emphasis on obedience to the biblical commandments, but also from the *theological conviction* that only an ecclesiology of this sort takes seriously Christ's dominion and thus also his presence in the congregation.

27. I am using the term "episcopal tradition" to refer to that ecclesial tradition according to which the episcopal office possesses theological-dogmatic, and not merely ecclesiastical-practical significance. In the present text, it functions as an abbreviation for "*Catholic and Orthodox* episcopal tradition."

or Orthodox diocese whose members are inclined more to superstition than to faith and who identify with the church more for nationalistic reasons — should such a diocese be viewed as a church, while a Baptist congregation that has preserved its faith through the crucible of persecution *not* be considered such? Would not an understanding of ecclesiality that leads to such a conclusion take us to the brink of absurdity? Equally untenable is the early, though still widespread Free Church position that denies ecclesiality to the episcopal churches. Smyth's conviction that during his age there was no true church is doubtless an expression of sectarian narrow-mindedness and arrogance.[28] And the assertion that bishops represent Christ sacramentally to the church in no way means that they replace Christ.

Second, both models are based systematically on opposing understandings of how Christ's presence comes to the church. According to the episcopal model, Christ's presence is mediated sacramentally and depends on the concrete relation of any given local church to all other churches. By contrast, the traditional Free Church model speaks of Christ's unmediated, direct presence in the entire local church as well as in every believer. The first model is holistic, the second individualistic. Both models underestimate the enormous ecclesiological significance of concrete relations with other Christians, relations through which every Christian becomes a Christian and in which that person lives as a Christian. According to both models, these relations have a great deal to do with spirituality and yet nothing to do with ecclesiality. But is ecclesiology not building its edifice on a fiction here (even if this fiction does find a certain degree of support in ecclesial reality), namely, that the church is constituted through the office of bishop or that the soul can by itself come to terms with its God? Should not ecclesiology take its orientation from ecclesial practice and from the New Testament witness concerning the church?

The third difference between the episcopal and the early Free Church models concerns the subjective dimension of the conditions of ecclesiality. According to the episcopal tradition, the church is constituted through the performance of objective activities, which concern not only the actions of the bishops themselves in administering the sacraments and engaging in proclamation, but also the participation of the laity in liturgical life. Christ's constitutive presence is not bound to the subjective disposition, however articulated, of human beings, except in the minimal sense of the deliberate intention of the person administering the sacraments "to do what the church does,"[29] and in the sense of the absence of any hindrance (*obex*) for the efficacy of the sacrament on the part of the recipient in the Catholic tradition, or of the presence of the

28. See Smyth, *Works,* 757.
29. ". . . *in ministris, dum sacramenta conficiunt et conferunt, non requiri intentionem, saltem faciendi quod facit Ecclesia*" (Denzinger/Schönmetzer, 854).

ordo of the laity speaking the "amen" in the Orthodox tradition. By contrast, in addition to the objective conditions of ecclesiality (word, sacraments, biblical church organization), the Free Church tradition also recognizes subjective conditions, namely, genuine faith and obedience to God's commandments.

A one-sided emphasis on the objective conditions of ecclesiality risks creating a cleft between the "pure bride" and the "sinful whore," and accordingly also between the church that administers the word and the sacraments (the hierarchy), and the church that receives the word and sacraments (the laity). In the extreme case, the church can then "happen" even without its "sons and daughters," at least without its significant majority; and the latter can "somehow" belong to the church even though they may want nothing to do with it. By contrast, a one-sided emphasis on the subjective conditions of ecclesiality risks grounding the church on the faith, holiness, and communal will of its members. In this case, God's church is reduced to a private club of people who think and behave alike and who are often kept together only through subtle and not-so-subtle forms of manipulation.

I intend in what follows to suggest an ecclesial model that does not subscribe to the exclusivity of the episcopal and early Free Church models, and according to which the church is constituted through a consistently communal occurrence in which the objective and subjective conditions of ecclesiality appear as two dimensions of a single process.

2. We Are the Church!

In "Principles and Inferences Concerning the Visible Church," one of his most important works, John Smyth defined the church as follows:

> A visible communion of Saincts is two, three, or moe Saincts joyned together by covenant with God & themselves, freely to vse al the holy things of God, according to the word, for their mutual edification, & Gods glory . . . This visible communion of Saincts is a visible Church.[30]

This definition of the church, based on Matt. 18:20 (". . . for where two or three are gathered in my name, I am there among them"), shaped the entire Free Church tradition.[31] Yet although it was the Free Church theologians who first accorded Matt. 18:20 a key systematic role in ecclesiology, this particular passage actually acquired preeminent importance quite early in church history.[32] Thus

---

30. Smyth, *Works,* 252; see also pp. 386f., 403, 529, 548.
31. See, e.g., Jenkins, *Congregationalism,* 44.
32. Rudolph Sohm correctly writes that "this passage [Matt. 18:20] traverses the entirety of church history" (Sohm, *Wesen,* 49). Concerning the ecclesiological significance of

Ignatius obviously bases his own ecclesiological principle (ὅπου ἂν ᾖ Ἰησοῦς Χριστός, ἐκεῖ ἡ καθολικὴ ἐκκλησία, "Wherever Jesus Christ is, there is the universal church"[33]) on Matt. 18:20. Tertullian explicitly specifies two or three who are gathered together in Christ's name: The Ignatian *ubi Christus, ibi ecclesia* ("Where Christ is, there is the church") finds its correspondence in Tertullian's *ubi tres, ecclesia est* ("Where three are, the church is").[34]

Even Cyprian, who in *De unitate* insists so forcefully on "the unity, undividedness, and indivisibility of the church's salvific authority,"[35] does not in his polemic against the separatistic groups of his age argue against the rectitude of their ecclesiological appeal to Matt. 18:20. Instead he accuses these groups of having "cut up the sense of a single passage" as they have "cut themselves off from the church." They misconstrue the passage in a twofold fashion. First, the text speaks of unity (v. 19: "if two of you *agree* on earth about anything you ask"), whereas these groups set up "conventicles in opposition," thus "creating new sects and schisms," and do not wish to be "in agreement with the body of the church itself and with the brethren as a whole." Second, the text requires that people assemble in the name of Christ. The separatist groups, however, have "cut themselves off from Christ and his gospel" by "cutting themselves off" from the one church "as the source and origin of truth."[36] Despite these weighty qualifications, Cyprian, too, seems to presuppose that Matt. 18:20 is of significance for ecclesiology rather than only for spirituality.

I will join this long tradition by taking Matt. 18:20 as the foundation not only for determining what the church is, but also for how it manifests itself externally as a church. *Where two or three are gathered in Christ's name, not only is Christ present among them, but a Christian church is there as well,* perhaps a bad church, a church that may well transgress against love and truth, but a church nonetheless. I intend to explicate this as yet incompletely formulated

---

Matt. 18:20 in the thought of John Huss, see Huss, *The Church* 2: "From this [Matt. 18:20] it follows that two righteous persons congregated together in Christ's name constitute, with Christ as the head, a particular holy church"; regarding the earlier Reformed tradition, see Marayama, *Ecclesiology,* 26; regarding the more recent Protestant tradition, see Brunner, *Gebot,* 514f.; Barth, *Church Dogmatics,* IV/2.698ff.; Barth, *Priester,* 245; regarding the Evangelical tradition, see "Evangelical," 306; regarding contemporary Catholic theology, see Schillebeeckx, *Menschen,* 269. Pope Paul VI referred to Matt. 18:20 in a speech before the Delegation of Ecumenical Patriarchs (1972), speaking of the *ecclesia* as a "gathering in which we are joined with you . . . gathered together in the name of Christ, and as a result of having him, Christ, our Lord himself, in our midst" (*Towards,* 241).

33. Ignatius, *Smyrn.* 8:2.
34. Tertullian, *De exhort. castit.* 7; see also *De baptismo* 6; *De pudicitia* 21.
35. Adam, "Cyprians Kommentar," 84.
36. Cyprian, *De unitate* 12.

thesis through theological (and not just purely exegetical[37]) reflections on Matt. 18:20. In discussing the internal and external conditions that any group of persons must fulfill if they justifiably are to call themselves a "church," I am also addressing indirectly Cyprian's two fundamental objections to separatist groups, objections containing the crux of the criticism that episcopal churches direct against Free Churches.

2.1. The Church as Assembly

1. The church is first of all an *assembly*: "where two or three are *gathered* in my name, I am there among them." In his book *Versammelte Gemeinde*, Otto Weber correctly designates the church a "visible assembly of visible persons at a specific place for specific action."[38] Doubtless, however, the life of the church is not exhausted in the act of assembly. Even if a church is not assembled, it does live on as a church in the mutual service its members render to one another and in its common mission to the world. The church is not simply an act of assembling; rather, it assembles at a specific place (see 1 Cor. 14:23). It is the *people* who in a specific way assemble at a specific place. In its most concentrated form, however, the church does manifest itself concretely in the act of assembling for worship, and this is constitutive for its ecclesiality.[39]

The New Testament use, and especially the Pauline use, of ἐκκλησία ("church") confirms this understanding of church as an assembled community. Commensurate with secular Greek usage, according to which ἐκκλησία refers to the assembly of the free citizens of a city, ἐκκλησία in the New Testament refers almost exclusively to the concrete assembly of Christians at a specific place.[40]

---

37. Matt. 18:17 ("if he refuses to listen to them [i.e., to two or three witnesses — v. 16], tell it to the church [ἐκκλησία]") seems to suggest that the two or three assembled in Christ's name (v. 20) are not themselves the church, but rather stand next to the church, though the latter is indeed conceived as the assembled local congregation (see Gundry, *Matthew*, 370). On the other hand, it is also certainly possible that the "two or three" in v. 20 refer to the same people to whom v. 18 ascribes the power of the keys. In that case, however, they would be identical with the congregation (ἐκκλησία) (so Luz, "Einheit," 147f.). Here I follow the early church in construing Matt. 18:20 *theologically* as a statement not only about spirituality, but also about the church itself. Whether this possesses ecclesiological cogency depends less on the exegetical determination of the identity of the "two or three" than on the persuasive power of my overall reading of the New Testament and of my ecclesiological-systematic outline.

38. Weber, *Gemeinde*, 32.

39. See in this regard Roloff, "ἐκκλησία," 1003f.

40. Contra Rudolph Sohm, who believes that ἐκκλησία refers not to "a specific empirical entity, nor to any social concept (not even the concept of a local congregation), but rather expresses exclusively a dogmatic value judgment" (Sohm, *Kirchenrecht*, I.19).

Although the church is indeed always and emphatically "the church of *God*" (1 Cor. 1:2), it is such only as the church of *those people* at a specific place, for example, the church of the Thessalonians or of the Laodiceans (see 1 Thess. 1:1; 2 Thess. 1:1). A church is a concrete assembly of those who at a specific place "call on the name of our Lord Jesus Christ" (1 Cor. 1:2). The place need not be a city, since a single city can have several churches that do not stand over against the overall local church as partial churches, but rather each of which is itself a whole church (see Col. 4:15-16).[41] That the New Testament understands the church as a concrete assembly is also indirectly confirmed by the rare use of the designation ἐκκλησία as a reference to several local churches (see Acts 9:31; 20:28).[42] In reference to a particular province, Paul does not as a rule speak about the church in the singular, but rather about *churches* in the plural (1 Cor. 16:1, 19; 2 Cor. 8:1; Gal. 1:2, 22).

The church nowhere exists "*above* the locally assembled congregation, but rather 'in, with, and beneath' it."[43] A congregation *is* the body of Christ in the particular locale in which it gathers together (see Rom. 12:5; 1 Cor. 12:12-13). Despite the fundamental differences between the Orthodox and Free Church ecclesiologies, they do agree on this important point, namely, that the church in the real sense of the word is exclusively the concrete assembly.[44] A particular denomination, the local churches in a cultural or political region, or the totality of local churches can be called "church" only in a secondary rather than a strictly theological sense.

For both exegetical and theological reasons, however, one cannot identify ἐκκλησία simply with a concrete local church.[45] Because the term *qᵉhal 'ēl*, deriving from apocalyptic Judaism, corresponded to the early church's eschatological self-understanding, the early church adopted this term as its own self-

---

41. With Marlis Gielen I believe that house churches are not to be viewed as one form of assembly (a partial church) among others (the whole or overall church) (Gielen, "ἡ κατ' οἶκον ἐκκλησία," 112-17). A house church is a whole church that assembles in one person's house. In contrast to Gielen, however, it does seem to me possible, given Col. 4:15 and Rom. 16:5, 14, 16 (though also given the size of houses in antiquity), that there could have been several such churches in a single city (see Stuhlmacher, *Philemon*, 71f.). Concerning the notion that Rome, too, possibly had several churches that did not assemble at one place, see Cranfield, *Romans*, 22.

42. Paul's statements concerning his own persecution of the "church" (Gal. 1:13; Phil. 3:6; 1 Cor. 15:9) do not constitute proof to the contrary, since he is speaking there not of the overall church, but rather of the congregation in Jerusalem (see Banks, *Community*, 36; Roloff, "ἐκκλησία," 1002).

43. Weber, *Gemeinde*, 33.

44. Concerning the position of the local church in Orthodox ecclesiology, see II.3.2.1 above.

45. For an earlier Free Church polemic concerning this topic, see Dagg, *Manual*, 100-121; Dargan, *Ecclesiology*, 31-34.

designation. That is, it understood itself "as the company elected by God and determined by him to be the center and crystallization-point of the eschatological Israel now being called into existence by him."[46] When Paul later uses the term ἐκκλησία τοῦ θεοῦ ("church of God"; the simple term ἐκκλησία is probably to be understood as an abbreviation of the original expression ἐκκλησία τοῦ θεοῦ) as a designation for the church of Jewish and Gentile Christians, he is preserving this eschatological horizon. As the ἐκκλησία τοῦ θεοῦ, Christians are the eschatological people of God assembling themselves from all the nations at particular places.[47] Thus it should come as no surprise that the Deutero-Pauline letters to the Ephesians and Colossians in particular use the term ἐκκλησία as a designation not only for a local church, but also for the universal church (Eph. 1:22; 2:22; 3:10; 5:22-33; Col. 1:18). It is important to note, however, that ἐκκλησία in this second sense refers not to the Christians *dispersed throughout the world* or to the totality of local churches but primarily to the universal church as a *heavenly and simultaneously eschatological* entity. As the universal church, the ἐκκλησία is the "heavenly" church gathered around the resurrected Christ in anticipation of its eschatological consummation.[48]

2. What, however, is the relation between the local churches and the totality of the eschatological people of God? What is the theologically primary sense of ἐκκλησία?[49] The answer contains important implications regarding the way one conceives the unity of the church. If one starts with the *priority of the local church,* as seems to be required by the Free Church point of departure,[50] then the universal church in the sense of the entire *communio sanctorum* emerges through the addition of the many local churches; the whole eschatological people of God is a sum of all local churches in which individual Christians have gathered together. But how then can every individual local congregation already be the prolepsis of the eschatological people of God, which as a universal reality comes about only through their addition? If the local church has priority, then even its orientation toward the eschatological unity of the entire people of God is secondary and for that reason also incidental.

Zizioulas takes the *identity of every local church with the universal church*

46. Roloff, "ἐκκλησία," 412.

47. See ibid., 1001-1003.

48. See in this regard Banks, *Community,* 43-47; O'Brien, "Church," 93-97; Turner, "The Ecclesiologies," 4. Andrew Lincoln emphasizes the proleptic character of heaven (see Lincoln, *Paradise*). For a similar interpretation of the "heavenly" church in Revelation, see Hofius, "Gemeinschaft," 193.

49. Posing this question by no means implies "that the whole matter is viewed as an organizational problem" (so Nygren, *Christ,* 98), though important "organizational" consequences do emerge from the answer to this question.

50. As a matter of fact, however, many Free Church theologians begin with the priority of the (invisible) universal church (so, e.g., Strong, *Theology,* 887ff.).

as his point of departure. The whole Christ is present in every eucharistic gathering. Because as a corporate personality Christ incorporates all Christians into himself, the entire church is present with him in every eucharistic communion. Thus the local churches are always the one *whole* church existing concretely at various places. As I have shown,[51] Zizioulas's theory of the identity of the local church and the universal church is an example of "overrealized eschatology"; the local church can be identical with the universal church only if it is inextricably connected with Christ, indeed, only if it is identical with him as a corporate personality; if the local church is identical with Christ, then the eschaton itself must become fully realized in the eucharistic gathering.[52] To preserve the eschatological character of every assembly while simultaneously distinguishing between the church and Christ or between the church and the reign of God, the point of departure must be the priority of the entire eschatological people of God over the local church.

Ratzinger emphasizes the *priority of the universal church.* For the local church, the connection with the church at all places and all times is essential, and this relation to the universal church is concretely lived out through the relation with the historically existing larger church. Following the lead of Vatican II, he defines this relation as the realization of the universal church within the local church; the one, holy, catholic and apostolic church is active and present in every local church.[53] The local church participates in the reality of the larger church; the larger church is actualized in the local church.[54] This notion, however, does not seem to take into account adequately the essentially *eschatological* character of the universal church. The heavenly church assembled around the resurrected Christ is not only open to its future in completion, it *is* that which it will be; and it will be that which it is only as the entire eschatological people of God. This is why the local church is to be defined not from the perspective of its relation to the existing *communio sanctorum,* but from the perspective of its relation to the perfected church in the new creation of God.

The category of *anticipation* expresses this situation. The local church is not a concrete realization of the existing universal church, but rather the real anticipation or proleptic realization of the eschatological gathering of the entire people of God. The local church and the already existing universal church (which includes all Christians who have lived and are living) do overlap insofar as the universal church includes all local churches, and every local church is a part of the universal church understood in this way; yet whatever this relation

51. See II.3.1.3 above.
52. See II.3.1 above.
53. *Christus Dominus* 11; *Lumen gentium* 26.
54. See I.2.3 above.

between universal church and local churches may mean for the concrete relationship between every local church and all other churches in time and space, the local church is not what it is simply insofar as the universal church is actualized within it and acts within it. Just as little is the universal church what it is simply insofar as the various local churches and individual Christians form themselves into a whole within it. *It is precisely as partially overlapping entities that both the local church and the universal church are constituted into the church through their common relation to the Spirit of Christ, who makes them both into the anticipation of the eschatological gathering of the entire people of God.* This is why every local church can also be *completely* the church even though it encompasses only a part of the universal church.[55] This is supported by the following analysis of the church as subject and of the "body of Christ."

3. The alleged relation of actualization between universal church and local church as well as the notion of the identity of the two is grounded theologically in a certain understanding of the relation between Christ and church. Both Ratzinger and Zizioulas, each in his own way, have appropriated the Augustinian notion that Christ and the church constitute a single person, the whole Christ. Within this unity, not only is Christ the subject of the church — of the universal church — but the *church itself becomes a subject,* that is, the subjectivity of Christ is transferred to the church. Just as Christ is present in every local church, and acts within it, so also the universal church, which together with Christ is a mystical person, is present in every local church, acting within or identical with it. The presence of the universal church in the local church follows from the notion of "total identification of Christ with the church" (Zizioulas) and from the idea that the church is a "single subject with Christ" (Ratzinger).[56]

I will return later to the weighty soteriological and anthropological consequences of the idea of the "whole Christ."[57] Here I am interested only in its ecclesiological dimension, which at first glance seems to be exegetically well grounded. In 1 Cor. 12:12 Paul seems to identify the local church with Christ.

---

55. If one views only the local church and universal church without seeing both within the larger context of the entire eschatological people of God, one encounters the following difficulty. A church can then be "church" only if it is *the* church (so, correctly, Evans, *Church*, 21); but if *one* church is *the* church, how in the strict sense then can it still be *a* church? Within the framework of the categorical pair "local church — universal church," it is difficult to conceive consistently the *local church* — the Pauline "*you* are the body of Christ" (1 Cor. 12:27); a church is either identical with the church (Zizioulas) and is for that reason strictly speaking not a *local* church at all, but rather the universal church in its manifestation at a specific locale, or a church is part of the church (so the earlier Catholic ecclesiology), or is a realization of the church with which it is not identical (Ratzinger), and for that reason strictly speaking not a church at all.

56. Zizioulas, "Mystère," 328; Ratzinger, "Theologie," 519.

57. See IV.1.1.2 below.

"For just as the body is one and has many members," Paul writes, "so it is with Christ" (see also 1 Cor. 1:13; 6:15). It is doubtful, however, that one may conclude from this that Paul approximates "an equivalency between the congregation and the Christ who lives on."[58] If one interprets the σῶμα Χριστοῦ ("body of Christ") from the perspective that man and woman become one body in marriage, since the woman derives from the body of the man (see 1 Cor. 6:12-20; Eph. 5:22-33; cf. Gen. 2:21-24), as Heon-Wook Park has recently suggested,[59] then one will have to conceive the σῶμα Χριστοῦ not organically as the body of the one person, but rather communally as the *body*, a totality conceived in whatever fashion, *of several persons*.

One might object that the idea of an organism is already contained in the idea of the body of Christ. But the organic character of the unity of the body is *bound to its physicality;* if the physical nature of the body is eliminated, then the idea of the body no longer contains its organic character. As Robert Gundry has persuasively argued, the body of Christ must be understood in a nonphysical manner; the Christian is "one *spirit* with" the Lord (1 Cor. 6:17), and precisely as such is a part of his "body."[60] Because of its nonphysicality, the body of Christ must be viewed as a *metaphor.*[61] Admittedly, this metaphor is not describing and inculcating merely a certain quality of the *moral* relations between Christians,[62] despite the fact that Paul develops the notion "body of Christ" largely in parenetic passages. Rather, it is expressing certain *soteriological* and strictly *ecclesiological* relations that shape the very being of Christians; it stands for an inward and personal communion in the Holy Spirit between Christ and Christians (see 1 Cor. 6:17) or between Christ and the church (see Eph. 5:22-33), and thereby also between Christians themselves (see Rom. 12:4-8; 1 Cor. 12:14-26). Precisely this metaphorical usage makes it possible for every local church to be called the "body of Christ" in an original sense.[63]

58. Schweizer, "σῶμα," 777.

59. See Park, *Leib Christi* (although I cannot subscribe to all of Park's views). Similarly also Ratzinger, *Das neue Volk,* 81f.

60. See in this regard the polemic of Robert Gundry (*Soma,* 223-44) against John A. T. Robinson (*Body,* 49-83).

61. *Every* interpretation according to which the church is not strictly *identical* with the *earthly* body of Christ is construing the body of Christ as a metaphor, including the interpretation according to which the church as the body of Christ is identical with the resurrected body of Christ (see Robinson, *Body,* 49ff.), since a body consisting of a multiplicity of human, corporeal persons can be called a "body" only in a *figurative* sense. The question whether or not Paul is using the body of Christ metaphorically is falsely put; the only correct query concerns the referent for that metaphor in Paul's usage.

62. See Stuhlmacher, "Volkskirche," 160.

63. Ulrich Luz believes that the designation of the local church as the body of Christ is secondary, since it originally "referred to the entire church" ("Einheit," 73). Here he must

Two important ecclesiological consequences emerge from this nonorganic understanding of the body of Christ, an understanding taking its orientation from Gen. 2:21-24. First, Christ cannot be identical with the church. An element of juxtaposition obtains between Christ and the church that precisely as such is constitutive for their unity. Only as the bride can the church be the body of Christ, and not vice versa.[64] To be sure, one should not understand the genitive Χριστοῦ ("of Christ") exclusively in the possessive sense ("the body that belongs to Christ"), but rather must also interpret it in an explicative sense ("the body that *is* Christ").[65] Otherwise the church and Christ would merely be juxtaposed and their specific oneness suppressed (see 1 Cor. 6:15; 12:1-13.). The identification of Christ and the church, however — "your bodies [are] members of Christ" — derives from the union between Christ and Christians, a union that cannot be conceived in physical categories, however articulated, but rather in personal categories, and a union for which the enduring distinction between the two is of decisive importance. Thus the identification of Christ and church stands for *the particular kind of personal communion* between Christ and Christians, a communion perhaps best described as "personal interiority"; Christ dwells in every Christian and is internal to that person as a person.[66] Rather than being thereby suspended, the specifically Christian juxtaposition of Christ and Christians is actually first constituted through the Holy Spirit. If this is correct, then Paul's statement that "all of you are *one* in Christ Jesus" (Gal. 3:28)

---

presuppose that the designation of the church as the body of Christ is actually "a pre-Pauline ecclesiological notion," though he is unable to adduce any information regarding its origin. Moreover, he is unable to explain why Paul uses this appropriated notion with reference to the individual local churches with only one exception (1 Cor. 10:16; Yorke, *Church,* 122, adduces additionally Rom. 12:5 and 1 Cor. 12:12, though this is doubtful; Gal. 3:28 and 1 Cor. 1:12, which Lutz himself adduces [p. 100], do not constitute exceptions). We should probably view the ecclesiological use of "body of Christ" as a Pauline neologism (so, e.g., Schweizer, "σῶμα," 776). Luz is, however, correct in one point, namely, that if one conceives the "body of Christ" organically (as does Luz himself: "All local churches are cells in which the whole lives" [p. 101]), then the expression *must originally* have referred to the overall church; the local churches can then be called the "body of Christ" only insofar as they are manifestations of the universal church. That Paul uses the expression emphatically in reference to the local church, however — "now *you* are the body of Christ" (1 Cor. 12:27) — is for that reason an additional argument *against* interpreting the "body of Christ" on analogy with the organism of a single person.

64. It is perhaps not inconsequential with regard to the relation between Christ and the church that Paul refers to the church as the *bride* rather than as the "wife" of Christ. The term *bride* "resonates with the idea that this association does not yet constitute fulfillment . . . it still implies an element of eschatological reservation" (Wolff, *2 Korinther,* 211; see also Furnish, *2 Corinthians,* 499).

65. So, correctly, Gundry, *Soma,* 231.

66. See IV.3.2.1 below.

does not mean that this "one" is "Christ himself";[67] they are "one" insofar as they are "in Christ" or insofar as "Christ" dwells "within" them.[68]

But is this "one" who is distinguishable from Christ a subject? It should be noted first that social systems can indeed possess characteristics similar to those of a subject (a group can, for example, organize common experience through certain schemata[69]) and yet represent systems quite distinct from conscious systems.[70] This purely socio-philosophical observation alone should prompt caution in claiming that the church is a subject. Because the church is not simply one social system among others, only theological arguments are decisive. If one interprets σῶμα Χριστοῦ ("body of Christ") from the perspective of Gen. 2:21-24, then one can no longer assert that the church is a subject. Just as the man is not the subject of the woman (even if from the biblical patriarchal perspective he may be her master),[71] so also can Christ *a fortiori* not be the subject of the church, which does after all consist of several persons. But if Christ is not the subject of the church, then neither is the church a subject, since it cannot be a subject of its own over against Christ.[72] One can no more infer that the church is a subject from reference to the church as a bride *alone*

67. Schlier, *Galater*, 175.

68. So Bruce, *Galatians*, 190. In order to understand Christ as the one who includes the many within himself, both Ratzinger and Zizioulas refer to the notion of corporate personality. Whether this idea can be found in the Old Testament is exegetically disputed (for criticism, see Rogerson, "Hebrew"; Moule, *Origin*, 52; Porter, "Two Myths"). But of what significance would it be even if it could be found there? For H. Wheeler Robinson, the corporate personality has two meanings. In the weaker sense, it refers to corporate responsibility, and in the stronger sense to "psychical unity between members of the same social group" (Robinson, "Hebrew," 5). Yet even the stronger sense of the corporate personality is too weak to ground the notion of *Christus totus*. Robinson's formulations — "the group to which he belongs, and into which his own personality, so to speak, extends" (Robinson, *Christian*, 8), or "a new kind of individual . . . who, like the true Israelite of old, could never be divorced from his social relationships" (Robinson, *Corporate*, 58) — do not quite assert that Christ in actuality includes all Christians within his own person, and with those Christians constitutes the whole Christ. Although the idea of the corporate personality can indeed serve to make the notion of *Christus totus* plausible, its contents must derive from elsewhere (see Moule, *Origin*, 52). Its source is a particular understanding of the Pauline notion of the "body of Christ" and of being ἐν Χριστῷ ("in Christ"). If I understand it correctly, however, this construal is neither exegetically nor theologically plausible.

69. See Goleman, *Lies*, 159ff.

70. See Luhmann, "Autopoiesis," 426. Cf. also idem, "Individuum," 162f.

71. This applies even if one conceives the New Testament understanding of the man-woman relationship in a strictly subordinationist fashion. For a non-subordinationist reading of the New Testament texts, see, e.g., Fee, *1 Corinthians*, 491ff., 699ff.

72. Both Ratzinger and Zizioulas presuppose that the subjectivity of the church can only be the subjectivity of Christ (see I.1.1.1 and II.2.1.2 above). In his extensive ecclesio-

(see 2 Cor. 11:2-3; Eph. 5:22-33) than one can infer lifelessness from reference to the church as a temple.

The church, both the universal *communio sanctorum* and the local church, is not a collective subject, but rather a communion of persons, though the latter are indeed not self-contained subjects, but rather are interdependent in a twofold fashion. First, they live only insofar as Christ lives in them through the Spirit (see Gal. 2:20; 1 Cor. 6:19). Second, the Christ lives in them through the multiple relations they have with one another (see 1 Cor. 12:12-13). Yet even though Christians are bound into this complex network of relationships, they still remain subjects; indeed, their being subjects is inconceivable without these relationships (see Gal. 2:20).[73] This is why one must also conceive the "one" who Christians are in Christ (Gal. 3:28; see Eph. 2:14-16) not as a "unified person" who "has transcended all differentiation,"[74] but rather precisely as a differentiated unity, as a communion, of those who live in Christ.

Accordingly, the universal church is not a subject that is actualized and acts within the local church, nor indeed is it identical with the local church. Christ, however, who is present in the local church through his Spirit and in this way makes it into the church in a proleptic experience of the eschatological gathering of the entire people of God, connects every local church with all other churches of God, indeed with the entire communion of those who through the same Spirit are "in Christ." But how is this connection to be expressed concretely? And how is the presence of Christ manifested externally, a presence which is, after all, not directly accessible? I will address the second question first.

2.2. The Church and the Confession of Faith

A church is an assembly, but an assembly is not yet a church. An indispensable condition of ecclesiality is that the people assemble *in the name of Christ.* Gathering in the name of Christ is the precondition for the presence of Christ in the Holy Spirit, which is itself constitutive for the church: ". . . where two or three are gathered *in my name,* I am there among them" (Matt. 18:20).

1. The "name of Jesus Christ" unequivocally identifies the person around whom those in the church are gathering. Here we are dealing with the name of

---

logical study (*Una mystica*), Heribert Mühlen has tried to ground the personality of the church in the specific character of the Spirit as a person who is present within the church (see IV.3.2.2 below).

73. See IV.3.2.1 below.
74. Mussner, *Galaterbrief,* 265.

Immanuel, God with us (see Matt. 1:23).[75] According to Matthew's intention, the name Immanuel expresses the unity of the earthly proclaimer Jesus with the resurrected and proclaimed Christ; he who at birth received the name "God with us" will as the resurrected one remain with his disciples until the end of the world (Matt. 28:20).[76] The church manifests itself as church insofar as it understands itself as defined by the entire history of Jesus Christ, by his past, present, and future. Expressed in Pauline terminology, the church is the church *of Jesus Christ* (Rom. 16:16; cf. Gal. 1:22; 1 Thess. 2:14), or it is not a church at all.

This necessary recourse to the entire history of Jesus Christ makes ecclesiality dependent on certain doctrinal specifications. Although these may well vary (just as confessions of faith vary within the New Testament) and even be quite brief (as, e.g., "Jesus is Lord"), the church cannot exist without them. As the emphatic οὕτως in 1 Cor. 15:11 shows paradigmatically — "*so* we proclaim and *so* you have come to believe" — one can relate to Jesus Christ only by believing *something* about him. The content of faith is necessary in order to distinguish Jesus Christ from "another Jesus" and to distinguish his Spirit from "another Spirit" (see 2 Cor. 11:4). The church is the church only if it is built on the Jesus Christ attested by the apostolic writings, which is why Luke reports that the Jerusalem church "held fast to the apostles' teaching" (Acts 2:42). To be sure, doctrine is not an end in itself, but rather merely a means of preserving and fostering the relation between the assembled congregation and Jesus Christ. It serves to identify unequivocally the person in whose name the congregation gathers. In this limited sense, however, it is true that "there is no church without correct doctrine."

2. The purpose of the cognitive identification of Jesus Christ (correct doctrine) is personal identification with him. In order to be a church, the people must assemble *in the name* of Christ. In so doing, they attest that he is the "determining ground" of their lives;[77] in him they have found freedom, orientation, and power. They come together first of all to call upon him as *Savior* and to bear witness to him before each other and before the entire world. They hear the proclamation "in this name" (Acts 5:28), call upon his name in faith (see Rom. 10:13), are baptized in his name (see Acts 2:38), and in this way are "washed," "sanctified," and "justified" through this name (1 Cor. 6:11). He is the source of their lives.[78] Second, people gather together in Christ's name in

75. See Gundry, *Matthew*, 370.
76. Concerning the *inclusio* Matthew makes in 28:20, see Luz, *Mattäus*, 105.
77. Hartman, "ὄνομα," 519-21. The expression "in the name" "introduces a fundamental reference, reason, purpose or capacity of something or of an action" (Hartman, "Baptism," 26).
78. See Bietenhard, "ὄνομα," 273.

146

order to profess faith in him as their *Lord* and as the Lord of the entire cosmos. He determines the fundamental conditions of their individual and communal lives (see 1 Cor. 1:10; 5:4); they gather together "under his authority and with the intention of acting in obedience to him."[79] It is he who gives their lives binding direction. Third, by assembling in Christ's name, Christians acknowledge him as the power in which they live. The "power" and the "name" are intimately connected.[80] Jesus Christ is Immanuel, the God who is *with* them, and in the power of his Spirit they are able to do those works that are commensurate with the new creation and that allow the new creation to shine in the midst of the old (see Luke 10:17; Acts 4:7).

Two conditions of ecclesiality emerge from the church's status as a congregation assembled in the *name* of Christ. The first is the *faith* of those who are thus assembled. The church is essentially *communio fidelium*, whatever else it may be beyond this. Without faith in Christ as Savior, there is no church.[81] Certainly, the church does not stand or fall with the faith of every individual member. "It existed before the individual came to faith, and it will remain even if certain individuals fall away from faith."[82] This is so, however, not because the church would somehow also exist above the *communio fidelium*, but because the individual standing in faith does not constitute the entire church. The church exists even if I do not believe; yet without at least someone believing, there can be no church, and in this sense the existence of the church is bound to the faith of its members in Christ as their Savior and Lord. (This does not turn the church into a human accomplishment, since faith itself is not a human accomplishment.[83])

The second condition of ecclesiality associated with assembling in the *name* of Christ is the *commitment* of those assembled to allow their own lives to be determined by Jesus Christ. Radicalizing the Calvinist tradition, the Free Churches originally took as their point of departure the assertion that faith without fruit is dead; where there is no fruit, there is no true faith, and where there is no true faith, neither is there a church. This ecclesiological use of the *syllogismus practicus* is correct insofar as no common ground exists between God and mammon (Matt. 6:24), between justice and injustice, between love and hate, and for that reason also between the church of God and the assembly of Satan. Yet, the self-appointed church of the saints inevitably degenerates into

---

79. Barrett, *1 Corinthians*, 124.

80. See Hurtado, *One God*, 110.

81. In Lutheran ecclesiology, Paul Althaus (*Die christliche Wahrheit*, 500ff.) emphasized this dimension of the church, though without defining the church simply as *communio fidelium*.

82. Schlink, *Dogmatik*, 588.

83. See IV.1.1.1 below.

a self-righteous church of hypocrites. If the connection between faith and the fruit of the Spirit (Gal. 5:22-23) is to be preserved while simultaneously avoiding hypocrisy, it is better to speak about the necessary *commitment* of believers to take the path of *imitatio*.[84] Without an *acknowledgment* of Christ as Lord, there is no church.

Although the *sancta ecclesia* ought to live "without spot or wrinkle" (Eph. 5:27), its ecclesiality does not depend on the holiness its members can exhibit, but rather exclusively on the presence of Christ sanctifying them, that is, the presence of the Christ who promised to be there wherever people gather together in his name, believe in him as Savior, and acknowledge him as Lord in order to live in the power of the Spirit. Although an absence of the fruit of the Spirit *can* be a sign of Christ's own absence from a congregation (just as the absence of the fruit of the Spirit can be a sign of the absence of true faith), Christ is not absent because a congregation does not bear the fruit of the Spirit; rather, both Christ and the fruit of the Spirit are absent because those assembled call upon Christ as Savior and Lord with their lips rather than with their hearts (see Isa. 29:13; Matt. 15:8), often in order to conceal religiously their own unrighteousness (see Isa. 1:11-17; 58:6-7). The church is not a club of the perfect, but rather a communion of human beings who confess themselves as sinners and pray: *debita dimitte*.[85]

3. Without personal identification with Jesus Christ, cognitive specification of who he is remains empty; without cognitive specification of who Jesus Christ is, however, personal identification with him is blind. In the act of *confessing faith*, this cognitive specification and personal identification coincide.[86] First of all, the confession with which a person professes faith in Jesus Christ (e.g., "Jesus is the Messiah") says *something* about the work of Jesus Christ

---

84. Although one might object that such talk about obligation is too vague, it is questionable whether greater specificity is really desirable. The boundary between those who belong to the church and those who do not should not be drawn too sharply. According to missiologist Paul Hiebert, an analysis of the category "Christian" can benefit from the mathematic distinction between "bounded sets," "fuzzy sets," and "centered sets." "Bounded sets" function according to the principle "either/or": an apple is either an apple or it is not; it cannot be part apple and part pear. By contrast, "fuzzy sets" have no sharp boundaries; things are fluid, without any definite point of reference, and exhibit varying degrees of identity — such as a mountain that turns into a plateau. "Centered sets" are defined by a center, by the distance of individual things from that center, and by movement toward or away from that center. Hiebert correctly believes that the category "Christian" should be understand as analogous to "centered sets." Although a line of demarcation does indeed exist, the issue is to confirm the center rather than to preserve the boundaries (Hiebert, "The Category," 421ff.).

85. Luther, *Werke*, 34/I.276.8-13.

86. This is not the place for a thorough theological analysis of confession; see in this regard Weber, *Gemeinde*, 61ff.; Arens, *Bezeugen*, 169-404.

and about his person.[87] This declarative function of confession is an expression of the cognitive dimension essential for faith itself. Without a statement concerning who this Jesus Christ is in whom one professes (or does not profess) faith, confession to him would be impossible.

Confession of faith itself, however, consists less in verbalizing a particular theological content than in acknowledging him whom the content of the confession is identifying.[88] This is the *preformative* dimension of confession, the dimension that actually makes confession into confession in the first place. Thus, for example, the believer, by professing "Jesus is Lord," acknowledges the crucified Christ "as the Lord whom God raised from the dead and elevated to κύριος πάντων [Lord of all]," subordinates himself or herself to his rule, and "presents to him praise and homage in calling upon his name."[89] As a speech act, confession is essentially *commissive*; I commit myself to something by making this confession. This is why a person can also profess faith in Christ by performing acts of righteousness, that is, one can acknowledge that the claims of the gospel of Christ are obligating for oneself (see 2 Cor. 9:13[90]). The commissive dimension of confession also manifests itself in the meaning of "denying" (ἀρνέομαι), which functions as a fixed antonym to "confessing." Thus it is possible to deny Jesus Christ not only through "false doctrine," but also through a "false life" (see Titus 1:16).

Confession is, moreover, not an individual and private affair. It always takes place "before others" (Matt. 10:32-33) and possesses an essential *social and public* dimension. Although one does indeed believe with one's heart, one confesses with one's lips (Rom. 10:9-10). In a confession of faith, I affirm my own relation to Jesus Christ, a relation that makes me into a Christian, and yet in the same act I acknowledge this relation before others. The confession of faith is essentially communication, and takes place *between* persons. As an interpersonal occurrence, too, the confession of faith preserves the declarative and preformative dimensions; by professing faith in Jesus Christ before others, I am both communicating something to them and simultaneously inviting them to something, actually, to someone. Because Jesus Christ, in whom I profess faith, is the Savior of all human beings and the Lord of the entire cosmos, such confession of faith is always "intended to achieve consent."[91] The universality of salvific grace is reflected in the social and public nature of the confession of faith.

---

87. According to Hans von Campenhausen, the earliest Christian confessions focused especially on Christ's work — "the salvific fulfillment and salvific promise which Jesus is and brings" — whereas later ones (e.g., in 1 John) focused more "on the reality and essence of his person" ("Bekenntnis," 239).

88. See von Campenhausen, "Bekenntnis," 225.

89. Hofius, "Wort Gottes," 156.

90. See in this regard Hofius, "ὁμολογέω," 1257.

91. Jüngel, "Bekennen," 105.

Because of its essential social nature, consisting not only in confessing faith before someone else, but also in confessing *with* someone else, the act of confessing faith seeks expression in preformulated, common confessions. The confession of faith cannot, however, be reduced to the appropriation and public utterance of confessions; it merely acquires its most pregnant expression in such confessions. Every genuinely Christian speech act is, at least formally and implicitly, an act of confession.[92] Thus, for example, a preacher can proclaim Christ as Lord only if the activity of proclamation is accompanied at least formally by the activity of confessing faith in him. Without this confession accompanying and supporting the proclamation, there is no proclamation.[93] By confessing faith in Christ through celebration of the sacraments, sermons, prayer, hymns, witnessing, and daily life, those gathered in the name of Christ speak the word of God both to each other and to the world. This public confession of faith in Christ through the pluriform speaking of the word is *the central constitutive mark of the church*.[94] It is through this that the church lives as church and manifests itself externally as church. Although such confession is admittedly always a result or effect of the "word," just as faith, too, is a result or effect of the "word" (see Rom. 10:8-10),[95] the "word" is proclaimed in no other way than in this pluriform confessing. The confession of faith of one person leads to that of others, thereby constituting the church.

The reverse side of the *objective* performance of this not merely verbal ecclesial utterance is the *subjective* faith of every individual member of the church. The basic condition of ecclesiality accordingly coincides with the basic condition of salvific grace, which consists in the faith of the heart and the confession of the

92. This is only seemingly contradicted by the fact that *promissio dei* precedes confession, since *promissio dei* contains inalienably within itself the implicit act of confessing. The act of proclamation is necessarily structured linguistically so that the proclaimer implicitly must confess that which is proclaimed. "Your sins are forgiven" cannot be uttered in the liturgical context unless the person proclaiming the forgiveness of sins affirms implicitly the reality of forgiveness of sins. The indispensability of confession is confirmed by the results of Mary-John Mananzan's linguistic analysis, according to which "the credal statements appear to be the main spring from which all the other religious uses of language flow" (Mananzan, The "Language Game," 110).

93. It can happen that the proclaimer does not inwardly affirm that which she implicitly confesses in a sermon. This does not contradict my understanding of ecclesiality, since the being of the church is not constituted through the *proclaimer* confessing Christ both inwardly and outwardly, but rather by the assembled people confessing Christ. Those who confess Christ *are* the church, and those who merely "act as if" are precisely not the church. Concerning the boundary between the church and the world, see note 97 below.

94. See Luther, *Werke*, 50.629.28-30: "Wherever you hear such words and see *preaching, believing, confessing, and commensurate behavior,* you can be sure that a proper *ecclesia sancta catholica* must be there" (my emphasis).

95. See Hofius, "ὁμολογέω," 1261.

mouth (Rom. 10:10). It is merely that the temporal and ontological sequence of the subjective and objective sides of the basic condition of ecclesiality and of being a Christian is reversed; that is, the church is constituted first through confessional speech and only then through faith, while the Christian is constituted first through faith and only then through confessional speech.[96] In the pluriform confessing of a Christian assembly, the objective and subjective conditions of ecclesiality, as the two dimensions of the same personal and ecclesial process, coincide; as an intersubjective occurrence, that in which subjective faith expresses and manifests itself simultaneously constitutes and manifests the church. The precedence of the objective processes involved in constituting the church is preserved, however, despite the fact that these objective processes (confession of faith) express subjective faith, or at least must present themselves as processes attesting faith.[97] If the church is constituted through the pluriform, objective-subjective process of communal confessions of faith, then the cleft between persons and processes through which the church is constituted on the one hand, and those people of whom it actually consists on the other, cannot arise. That which the church *is*, namely, believing and confessing human beings, is precisely that which (as a rule) also *constitutes* it. It is not that each person constitutes himself or herself into a member of the church; rather, through their common pluriform confessing all the mem-

---

96. According to this definition, the church can be found only where people confess Christ *consciously*, and not among the poor and oppressed simply as such (a different view is taken, e.g., by Steinacker, *Die Kennzeichen*, 19). This takes seriously not only the intimate connection between faith, baptism, and church membership in the New Testament, but also the self-understanding of the non-Christian poor and of those who perform acts of righteousness and compassion among them; they do not necessarily want to be "anonymous Christians" or belong to a "latent church." At the same time, the presence of Christ is not restricted to the church; that is, Christ is not just active in a manner directly constitutive for the church (see III.1.1.1 above). This is why one can deny that the poor are a church without at the same time denying the presence of Christ among the poor — the fact that he commits himself to them as his "brothers and sisters" (see Matt. 25:40) — or the activity of the Spirit in those who are engaged on their behalf (see Moltmann, "Christsein," 631). As Jürgen Moltmann correctly writes, the least among us do not tell us what or who the church is, but rather "*where* the church *belongs*" (Moltmann, *Kirche*, 149, my emphasis).

97. External confession does not necessarily attest inner faith, even if it is true that confession without faith is not religiously meaningful. This is also why recourse to confession — or to any other understanding of the objective conditions of ecclesiality — cannot, strictly speaking, show *who* the true church is, but rather only *where* the true church is concealed (see Küng, *Kirche*, 318; Althaus, *Die christliche Wahrheit*, 521). Although this may appear to be a defect (of all ecclesiologies), this concern is assuaged — I hope — by considering that the establishment of clear boundaries is usually an act of violence. The advantage of my own understanding of the objective (intraecclesial) conditions of ecclesiality over against the Catholic-Orthodox or traditionally Protestant understanding is that it is more intimately connected with the faith of those involved, and for that reason is also more likely to show who the true church is.

bers together are constituted into the church by the Holy Spirit, even if the various members, commensurate with their individual charismata, participate in this process in different ways.[98]

4. If one takes the communal confession of faith as the basis of ecclesiality, what, then, is the significance of office and of the sacraments for the being of the church? Since the only necessary intraecclesial condition of the constitutive presence of Christ for the church consists in people gathering in the name of Christ to profess faith in Christ before one another and before the world, the presence of Christ does not enter the church through the "narrow portals" of *ordained office,* but rather *through the dynamic life of the entire church.* The presence of Christ is not attested merely by the institution of office, but rather through the multidimensional confession of the entire assembly. In whatever way "office" may indeed be desirable for church life, either in apostolic succession or not,[99] it is *not necessary for ecclesiality.* Ordained office belongs not to the *esse,* but rather to the *bene esse* of the church. This claim does not constitute any devaluation of the particular service of proclaiming God's word, but rather suggests that proclamation should be understood as a dimension of pluriform, communal confession of faith.[100] The human medium through which the church is constituted is *all* those who assemble in the name of Christ in order to profess faith in Jesus Christ as Savior and Lord. Expressed sociologically, the church is thus constituted by the Spirit of Christ *from below* rather than from above.[101] This is why one cannot secure the principle ὅπου ἂν ᾖ Ἰησοῦς Χριστός, ἐκεῖ ἡ καθολικὴ ἐκκλησία ("wherever Jesus Christ is, there is the universal church")[102] by the principle χωρὶς τούτων [διάκονοι, πρεσβύτεροι, ἐπίσκοποι — M.V.] ἐκκλησία οὐ καλεῖται ("without these [deacons, presbyters, bishops] no [group] can be called a church").[103]

By contrast, the *sacraments* — baptism and Lord's Supper — belong to the *esse* of the church. From the very outset, Christian congregations performed baptisms and celebrated Holy Communion; there does not seem to have been any initial period in church history without baptism or the Lord's Supper.[104] Being a Christian means being baptized and participating in the celebration of the Lord's Supper. Through baptism, a person becomes a Christian, and through the Lord's

98. See VI.1.1.2 below.

99. Concerning the status of (ordained) office in the church, see VI.3.1 below.

100. Concerning the integration of the sermon into the overall events of worship and church life, see Althaus, *Die christliche Wahrheit,* 528-30.

101. The position occupied in episcopal ecclesiology by the bishop is occupied here not by Christ or by the Holy Spirit (as Free Church theologians often assert), but rather by *all the members* of the church. At issue here is an alternative manner of human *mediation* of the presence of Christ in the church.

102. Ignatius, *Smyrn.* 8:2.

103. Ignatius, *Trall.* 3:1.

104. So Dinkler, "Taufe," 629.

Supper a person lives as a Christian; through these two sacraments, a person gains access to the salvific grace grounded in Christ's death and resurrection, salvific grace anticipating the eschatological new creation.[105] Insofar as baptism and the Lord's Supper mediate salvific grace, they are constitutive for the church, and are such not only from the perspective of the stronger Lutheran understanding of this "mediation,"[106] but also from that of the weaker Calvinist understanding.[107] Without baptism and the Lord's Supper, there is no church.[108]

To be sure, the sacraments can be an indispensable condition of ecclesiality only if they are a form of the confession of faith and an expression of faith. This is indeed the case. First, they are a public representation of such confession; in baptism, the person baptized professes publicly faith in him in whose name baptism occurs (see Heb. 10:23), and the ecclesial praise of God and of God's salvific activity is constitutive for the Lord's Supper (ἀνάμνησις ["remembrance"] and καταγγέλλειν ["proclamation"] in 1 Cor. 11:25-26).[109] Second, the mediation of salvific grace through the sacraments is bound to the faith of those receiving them. Here, too, Luther's principle applies, namely, "if you believe, you have it; if you do not believe, you do not have it."[110] Thus does faith precede baptism (Gal. 3:26-27; cf. Mark 16:16; Acts 2:38; 16:31-33);[111] and the Lord's Supper is inconceivable without faith, indeed, without those partic-

---

105. On baptism, see Wilckens, *Römer*, 7-33; on the Lord's Supper, see Hofius, "Herrenmahl," 224-26, 237f.

106. See Luther, *Kleiner Kathechismus* in *Bekenntnisschriften der evangelisch-lutherischen Kirche* 515.38–516.2.

107. Calvin, *Institutes*, IV.14.1-26.

108. Contra Volf, "Kirche," 66; Brunner, *Gebot*, 514; Jenkins, *Congregationalism*, 73f. The significance the sacraments possessed for the Free Churches from the very outset is attested not only by their willingness to die for (what they believed was) the correct baptismal practice, but also by John Smyth's unfortunate decision to baptize himself. Although he was aware that one must receive baptism, he nonetheless found himself forced to baptize himself because he knew of no "true church" from which he could receive what he considered to be the requisite baptism (see Smyth, *Works*, 757).

109. See Hofius, "Herrenmahl," 230ff.

110. See Luther, *Werke*, 7.24.13.

111. Concerning the relation between faith and baptism, see Jüngel, "Taufe," 308; idem, "Thesen," 293. In his polemic against the Baptist understanding of baptism, Ulrich Wilckens calls into question the understanding of faith underlying this view of baptism: Faith is allegedly "not constituted through the decision of the believer, through the experiential power and subjective veracity of his conversions . . . but rather through the divine action in Christ which the believer accepts" (Wilckens, *Römer*, 31). However, even with the understanding of faith Wilckens wishes to see among the Baptists, the Baptist understanding of baptism does indeed work, namely, faith as medium of the *reception* of the divine salvific activity in Christ *on the part of the believer*; it also works when faith as the medium of such reception is "understood in strict exclusivity as *creatura verbi*" (Hofius, "Wort Gottes," 157).

ular practices commensurate with the Lord's Supper (1 Cor. 11:20).[112] Although celebration of the sacraments are certainly not a product of faith, they can be what they are *for the persons who receive them,* namely, instruments of God's activity, and to that extent also constitutive for the church, only if they are indeed received in faith. There is no church without sacraments; but there are no sacraments without the confession of faith and without faith itself. The church is wherever those who are assembled, and be they only two or three, within the framework of their pluriform confession of faith profess faith in Christ as their Savior and Lord through baptism and the Lord's Supper.

3. Church and Churches

The pluriform, intersubjective profession of faith in Jesus Christ is the condition of ecclesiality internal to a local church; it is an intraecclesial event even when a congregation professes faith in Christ before the world. The confession of faith, however, cannot be an idiosyncratic act of a local church. If this confession is constitutive for the church, then *every* church must be constituted by the *same* confession. Confession of faith not only distinguishes the church from the nonchurch, it simultaneously connects every church with all other churches. This raises the question of the sense in which the relations to other churches enter into the conditions of ecclesiality of a church. Does the same confession of faith suffice, as often seems to be the view in the Free Church tradition? Or is a fellowship already separated from Christ and thus also from its own ecclesiality insofar as it lives separate from the larger church, as Cyprian and, following him, both the Orthodox and the Catholic traditions believe?[113]

1. In every congregation assembling in Christ's name to profess faith in him, the *one and the whole* Christ is present through his Spirit. For this reason, the congregation is not a part of the church, but rather is the *whole* church. Along with many other Puritans and Congregationalists of his age,[114] John Smyth correctly concluded from this that "every true visible Church is of equal power with all other visible Churches."[115] Since the church exists historically only in locally assembled congregations, it also follows that an alliance of different churches (a denomination or regional church), indeed, even a council of all existing churches, is not only not a church, but also can have no "power" over local churches. To be a church, a local church need not be subordinate to anyone (though subordination as such does not, of course, invalidate its ecclesiality). In this sense, every local church is

---

112. See Hofius, "Herrenmahl," 206.
113. See Cyprian, *De unitate* xii.
114. See in this regard Brachlow, *Communion,* 203-29.
115. Smyth, *Works,* 267.

154

indeed independent or "self-complete."[116] It stands on its own spiritual feet because the whole Christ is present in it through the Spirit.[117]

The differences from the Catholic tradition at this point are considerable. Although according to Ratzinger a local church is indeed church in the full sense, since it has the whole Christ, it always receives Christ and thus also itself from the larger church. This is why the Pope, as shepherd of the larger church, and the council of *all* bishops "can act with legal force, that is, as plenipotentiary for the universal Church,"[118] and as such can also intervene in the affairs of the local church; the latter is subordinated to the larger church. By contrast, Zizioulas emphasizes the identity between the larger church and the local church, and accordingly rejects any hierarchical subordination between local churches. Each local church is "capable of passing *final* judgment on everything."[119] Despite the considerable differences, we encounter a surprising convergence between the Congregationalist and Orthodox traditions with regard to one of the pivotal ecclesiological questions; because the local church alone is church in the strictly theological sense, it cannot be subordinated to any other ecclesial authority.

The "independence" of the local church, however, does not yet mean that other churches are *in every instance* denied the right to intervene in the life of a local church. (Just what concrete form such intervention is to take is a different question altogether, one to be treated independently of the question concerning the right of intervention as such.) Other churches, however, can intervene in the affairs of a local church only *if the ecclesiality of this church is threatened.* This is the case when the integral confession of faith is distorted in a church through the loss of the substance of faith[120] or through permanent resistance in practice to Christ's rule (*status confessionis*).

2. The same presence of Christ through the Spirit that makes each local church "independent" of the other churches simultaneously connects them with one another. There is a broad consensus in the various churches "that the unity [of churches] is given in Jesus Christ. It does not need to be created first."[121] What remains disputed, however, is how this unity should be manifested concretely and how the various means of expressing this unity are related to the constitutive presence of Christ in a church.

116. See Dexter, *Congregationalism,* 523.
117. See Jenkins, *Catholicity,* 104f.; Dexter, *Congregationalism,* 294.
118. Ratzinger, *Church,* 51.
119. Zizioulas, "Episkope," 33 (my emphasis).
120. The view that the Pope — or a synod — can intervene in the life of a local church even in cases when the issue is not the preservation of the substance of faith, but rather the "*situationally appropriate clarification* of the substance of faith" (Fries/Rahner, *Einigung,* 105, my emphasis) seems problematic to me, even if it is true that the line between "preservation" and "situationally appropriate clarification" cannot always be drawn clearly.
121. Vischer, "Schwierigkeiten," 34.

In the Catholic and the Orthodox traditions, this constitutive presence of Christ is given only with the presence of the bishop standing in *communio* with all bishops in time and space. Only in this way can the derivation of the local church from the larger church (Ratzinger) or the identity of the local church with the larger church (Zizioulas) be expressed, and only in this way can the presence of the "whole Christ," head and members, in the local church be ensured, a presence that as such makes a local church into a church. Yet if one conceives the local church apart from the relation to the universal church conceived as subject, but rather by way of the Spirit-mediated relation to the eschatological gathering of the people of God in the new creation,[122] then the constitutive presence of Christ in a church need not be mediated through the concrete sacramental relation to all other churches. A church is a network of relations, and the constitutive presence of Christ is mediated through these relations, that is, through the communal confession of faith. This is why the sacramentally mediated (through ordination) status of being "with-the-larger church" or "from-the-larger church" is not an indispensable condition of ecclesiality.

Neither can the Free Church thesis concerning a *direct* presence of Christ in the church apply here, since it either misunderstands the character of the mediation of faith, or mistakenly presupposes that the constitutive presence of Christ is something other than the presence of Christ in the hearts of believers manifesting itself externally.[123] "Two or three faithful men" as a matter of fact do not "have Christ given vnto them *immediatelie* from heaven," as Smyth asserted,[124] but rather through their relationships to one another and to the other human beings through whom they have become Christians by having believed and having been baptized by them.

If the actual sacramental relations between churches are an excessively strong condition of the ecclesiality of every individual church, can there then be any *inter*ecclesial conditions of ecclesiality beyond the *intra*ecclesial ones? I suggest taking the *openness* of every church toward all other churches as an indispensable condition of ecclesiality.[125] Since the eschatological gathering of

122. See 2.2.3 above.
123. See IV.2.1.2 below.
124. Smyth, *Works,* 548 (my emphasis). The intention behind his assertion, however, is indeed correct; Christ comes to a congregation not "by meanes of any State, Prince, Priest, Prelate whatsoever." Smyth later arrived at a more differentiated position: "I hold as I did hold then, succession being broken and interrupted, it may by two or three gathered together in the name of Christ, be renewed and *assumed againe*" (p. 756, my emphasis). Even though he rejected any succession except that in truth, he asserted that "it is not lawful for every one that seeth the truth to baptize, for then ther might be as manie churches as couples in the world and non have anie thinge to doe with other" (758).
125. I am not so sure that there is a clear tendency among congregations to "turn inward and close themselves off from the overall church" (Lehmann, "Gemeinde," 44).

the people of God, whose foretaste is the local church, is not identical with all churches of the past and present, the ecclesiality of a local church need not depend on the sacramental relation to them. Yet since the eschatological gathering of the people of God will include all these churches as its own anticipations, a local church cannot alone, in isolation from all other churches, claim to be a church. It must acknowledge all others churches, in time and space, as churches, and must at least be open to diachronic and synchronic communication with them.

The requirement of openness also emerges from the character of the confession of faith that makes a church into a church. Such confession is an event in which a congregation appropriates the confession of all churches of God[126] (just as an individual appropriates the confession of the congregation [Heb. 3:1; 4:14; 10:23][127]). This is why a congregation can indeed profess faith in Christ without positive connections with other congregations, but not in express isolation from them. By isolating itself from other churches, a church attests either that it is professing faith in "a different Christ" than do the latter, or is denying in practice the *common* Jesus Christ to whom it professes faith, the Christ who is, after all, the Savior and Lord of *all* churches, indeed, of all the world.

This openness to all other churches is the *interecclesial minimum* of the concrete ecclesial proleptic experience of the eschatological gathering of the whole people of God. Through this openness, however, a church necessarily sets out on the *path* to its future, a path on which it is to express and deepen its communion, that is, its differentiated unity, with all other churches through the common confession of faith and appropriate structures of communion (see Eph. 4:2, 13-16).[128] By refusing to set out on this path within the framework of its perhaps modest possibilities, it shows that it is a private religious club rather than a church of God. This is why even the Congregationalists quite justifiably have insisted not only on the "self-completeness, under Christ, of the local church," but also that these local churches "necessarily owe to each other sisterly affection and activity."[129]

The understanding just presented of ecclesiality and of its interecclesial condition exposes itself to the charge that it allows us to speak only of a plurality of churches rather than of the *one* church. And this is indeed the case. On this

126. In taking recourse to a confession of faith in his argumentation in 1 Cor. 15:1-2, Paul is referring to the faith common to the various churches transmitted from the original apostles and received by the Corinthians (see Luz, "Einheit," 67).

127. See Hofius, "ὁμολογέω," 1261. The relation "church–churches," although analogous to the relation "individual–church," is not identical with it (see VII.4.2 below).

128. Concerning the various forms of communication between congregations in the New Testament period, see Luz, "Einheit," 102ff.

129. Dexter, *Congregationalism*, 523.

side of the eschatological gathering of the whole people of God, there can be no church in the singular. Whether this is to be viewed as an *objection* or as a theologically accurate description of ecclesial reality obviously depends on the notion of unity with which one is operating. As Lukas Vischer has rightly emphasized, the term *communio* better expresses the New Testament understanding of the "unity of the church" than the term "unity" itself, "burdened as it is by a lengthy philosophical tradition."[130] Within history, the one church exists only as the *communion* of churches. Although this communion is not itself a church, it does anticipate under the conditions of history the unity of the whole eschatological people of God.

3. In conclusion, I would like to point out briefly one additional condition of ecclesiality affecting the relation of church and world. Just as professing faith in the one Jesus Christ implies an openness on the part of a church to other churches, so also does professing faith in him as universal Savior and Lord imply an openness on the part of the church to all human beings.[131] No one who professes faith in Christ should be denied entrance into the church and full participation in it. Just as Peter did not merely behave badly by refusing fellowship to Gentile Christians, but rather betrayed the truth of the Gospel itself (Gal. 2:11-14), so also is a discriminatory church not merely a bad church, but no church at all; it is unable to do justice to the catholicity of the eschatological people of God. Even if such a church were to assemble in the name of Christ and profess faith in him with its lips, it could expect only rejection from its alleged Lord: "I never knew you" (Matt. 7:21-23).

In summary, the ecclesiality of the church can be defined as follows. *Every congregation that assembles around the one Jesus Christ as Savior and Lord in order to profess faith in him publicly in pluriform fashion, including through baptism and the Lord's Supper, and which is open to all churches of God and to all human beings, is a church in the full sense of the word, since Christ promised to be present in it through his Spirit as the first fruits of the gathering of the whole people of God in the eschatological reign of God.* Such a congregation is a holy, catholic, and apostolic church. One may rightly expect such a congregation to grow in unity, sanctity, catholicity, and apostolicity, but one may not deny to it these characterizing features of the church, since it possesses these on the basis of the constitutive presence of Christ.

130. Vischer, "Schwierigkeiten," 25f. See V.4.3 below.
131. See VII.3.2.2 below.

Chapter IV

Faith, Person, and Church

As is well known, Friedrich Schleiermacher distinguished between two opposing forms of Christian communion. Protestantism, he maintained, "makes the individual's relation to the Church dependent on his relation to Christ," while Catholicism "makes the individual's relation to Christ dependent on his relation to the Church."[1] Similar to the social models customarily called "individualism" and "holism" (or "collectivism"),[2] these two basic ecclesial models seem to be incompatible. One comes either by way of Christ to the church, or by way of the church to Christ. Yet appearances are misleading here. Only a simplistic theory contains the alternative "person-Christ-church" or "person-church-Christ." In the complex ecclesial reality of *all* churches, the relation of individuals to the church depends on their relation to Christ, just as their relation to Christ depends on their relation to the church; the two relations are mutually determinative.[3] Different confessions and churches differ in this regard only in the *way* they understand these mutually determinative relations and in the *status* they ascribe to one or the other relation. *This* particular issue, however, admittedly involves the central and as yet insufficiently addressed question in

1. Schleiermacher, *Christian Faith*, §24. In his famous work, *Die Einheit in der Kirche* (1825), Johann Adam Möhler felt Schleiermacher's distinction between Protestantism and Catholicism was accurate ("very good") (Möhler, *Einheit*, 405).

2. See in this regard Dumont, *L'individualisme*, 35, 69, 197.

3. Schleiermacher seems to have been aware of this; otherwise, he would not have hoped for the elimination of this opposition between Protestantism and Catholicism without the victory of the one over the other (see *Christian Faith*, §23). Concerning the contradictory elements in Schleiermacher's understanding of the essence of the church, see Bonhoeffer, *Communio*, 101ff., note 18.

contemporary ecumenical encounters, especially within Protestant-Roman Catholic dialogue.[4]

Free Churches seem to represent an extreme case of Schleiermacher's basic Protestant model of Christian fellowship. If every church, viewed from a purely sociological perspective, is constituted "from below" through the interaction of its members, does not everything then become "uncertain and fluid," as Schleiermacher formulated Catholic criticism of Protestantism, and does not ultimately "each individual stand by himself"?[5] The charge of naked ecclesial individualism looms before us. But does it necessarily apply? Or is the relation of human beings to Christ, according to what seems to be an extremely individualistic Protestant ecclesiology, also mediated through their relations with one another, and does it not become real first only within these relations?

In this chapter, I will attempt to answer these questions, in dialogue with Ratzinger and Zizioulas, by examining the understanding of the mediation of faith and of the structure of salvation implied by the basic ecclesiological conviction "We are the church."[6] The chapter will conclude with a brief analysis of the anthropological presuppositions of the soteriological views presented within the chapter.

1. Faith and the Church

Because human beings appropriate salvific grace in faith, the understanding of salvation (and thus also of the church) is shaped in an essential fashion by the way the faith is mediated. Hence an individualistic understanding of the mediation of faith is at once also an individualistic view of salvation, and a communal understanding of the mediation of faith is also a communal view of salvation. I will first examine the role of the church in the process of the mediation of faith, and then address the basic question raised by Zizioulas regarding whether the view that faith is the medium of participation in salvific grace — quite apart from the *way* such faith is mediated — is itself already individualistic.

1.1. Ecclesial Mediation of Faith

1. As the human medium of participation in salvation, faith consists not in pure passivity, but rather in receptive *activity*; regardless of how one may

---

4. See Kasper, "Grundkonsens," 187f. Cf. also Birmelé, *Salut*, 203ff.

5. Schleiermacher, *Christian Faith*, §24.

6. See chapter III above.

understand theologically the activity of faith, it is obviously *human beings* who are believing.[7] Nonetheless, faith is not grounded in the activity of believing human beings. No one can give oneself faith; one must receive it from God precisely as one's own receptive activity. Faith is a work of God's Spirit and God's word, something about which widespread ecumenical consensus does obtain even if it remains a matter of dispute both between the various churches and within these churches themselves whether one may understand faith as a gift of God that can be rejected,[8] or whether one must understand it "in strict exclusivity as *creatura verbi.*"[9] I need not address this question here. Presupposing the necessity of faith for the mediation of salvation,[10] a different question becomes decisive for the problem of soteriological and ecclesiological individualism, namely, *how* faith as a gift of God is mediated concretely to human beings, and especially how the church participates in this mediation of faith. Hence in what follows, I will concentrate on the problem of the instrumentality of the church.[11]

John Smyth advocated the notion of God's *direct* influence on human souls. Although he emphasized that those who have not yet come to faith need means of grace "to stir them vpp the better to performe the condicion of repentance to the remission of sinnes,"[12] he still insisted that "god the father, in our regeneration, *neither needeth nor vseth the helpe of any creature,* but that the father, the word and the holy ghost, *immediately* worketh that worke in the soule."[13] When, however, a person has been born again, that person should no longer need means of grace, since he has "three witnesses in himselfe, the father, the word, and the holie ghost, which are better then all scriptures, or creatures

---

7. See 1.2.2 below. Eberhard Jüngel justifiably qualifies his own formulation that faith is "pure passivity, pure inactivity" with the assertion that one can *let* the love of God happen to one and presumably — if one wishes to participate in "the *experience* of being loved" — must indeed do so (*Gott,* 466, my emphasis).

8. So, e.g., Friedrich, "Glaube," 112.

9. Hofius, "Wort Gottes," 157.

10. See 1.2 below.

11. The questions concerning the participation of individual persons and of the church in the initiation process are two obviously related and yet distinct questions. If one views faith as a condition of salvation to be fulfilled (at least in part) by human beings themselves, then one will also be more inclined to claim that the church acts as a subject in the mediation of salvation, and vice versa. The individual and communal human activities in the mediation of faith correspond to one another. Of course, it is logically possible to allow individual faith as a condition of salvation, and at the same time to reject the participation of the church in salvific activity. And vice versa, it is possible to start with pure passivity on the part of individual human beings and at the same time to affirm the necessity of church cooperation with God's salvific activity.

12. Smyth, *Works,* 743.

13. Ibid. (my emphasis).

whatsoever."[14] In fact, however, Christians cannot do without such means of grace, because of the "weakness of the flesh." Although they stand "aboue the law and scriptures," they are to make use of such means "for the gaininge and supporting of others."[15] Yet, according to Smyth, salvation still takes place, at least ideally, between individual souls and God. Accordingly, the church emerges through the addition of those who, as isolated individuals, have become Christians and now live as Christians.

Against such an individualistic understanding of the mediation of salvation, an understanding still advocated in some Free Church circles (and within Protestantism in general),[16] Ratzinger has emphasized that one receives faith precisely as a gift of God *from* the church. For that reason, a person always believes *with* the church; indeed, the actual believing subject or "I" is the collective "I" of the church. Here the church appears as a mother giving birth to sons and daughters who live with her and through her.[17] Because the church has an essential role in the mediation and discharging of faith, salvation itself possesses an indispensable social dimension. But is this understanding of the church as mother theologically persuasive?

2. My own understanding of ecclesiality is guided by Matt. 18:20, where Christ says, "For where two or three are gathered in my name, I am there among them."[18] According to this text, Christ's presence is promised not to the believing individual directly, but rather to the entire congregation, and only through the latter to the individual.[19] This is why no one can come to faith alone and no one can live in faith alone. Otto Weber has quite correctly emphasized that we cannot have Christ "at all outside the congregation."[20] The church is not only the *filia* of faith, first of all of the Spirit and word of God, then also of faith, but also the *mater* of faith.[21] Appropriately understood, the motherhood of the

14. Smyth, *Works,* 744.

15. Ibid.

16. See, e.g., the criticism of Farley, *Ecclesial Man,* 182f.

17. See I.1.1.2 above.

18. See III.2 above.

19. Origen interpreted Matt. 18:18-20 in this way: "συνάγει ἡ συμφωνία, καὶ χωρεῖ τὸν ἐν μέσῳ τῶν συμφωνούντων γινόμενον Ὑιὸν τοῦ Θεοῦ" (*Comm. in Matth.,* ad loc.).

20. Weber, *Gemeinde,* 36. Cf. also Bonhoeffer, *Communio,* 101. It is certainly correct that it is "only in the body itself" that one receives the very Spirit who "*is active* so that one can enter into the body" (Congar, *Der Heilige Geist,* 168). As we are about to see, however, in the dialogue between the Roman Catholic and Protestant traditions, it remains disputed whether this body is to be conceived as a "subject," and whether it acts as a subject together with Christ in the mediation of salvation. The answer to this question will determine whether the statement that one receives the Spirit in the body of the church is theologically acceptable.

21. See in this regard Calvin, *Institutes,* IV.1.4; Luther, *Werke,* 30/I.188.24f.; 40/I.664.18ff.; 47.20.20f. Concerning Luther's understanding of the church as mother, see Jüngel, "Kirche," 329f.

church is a statement that the transmission of faith occurs through interpersonal ecclesial interaction. God's salvific activity always takes place through the multidimensional confession of faith of the *communio fidelium*.[22] The sacraments, which no person can self-administer and yet which each person must receive personally, symbolize most clearly the essentially communal character of the mediation of faith.

The communal character of the mediation of faith implies that, in a limited but significant sense, every Christian does indeed receive faith from the church; for that which a person believes is precisely that which the previously existing communion of believers has believed. By believing, a person appropriates the Spirit-inspired confession of faith of all churches in time and space. There is no other way to believe, unless one were to create one's own religion. The faith with which I believe is shaped by the ecclesially mediated forms in which it is expressed; there is no pure, ecclesially unmediated faith consisting of pure feeling.[23] Hence, even my most personal faith can only be that which is ecclesially mediated.[24] Moreover, it is only through life in the congregation in whose confession I participate that I discover the meaning of the confession of faith. Although ecclesial socialization does indeed take place through learning the language of faith — this is the most important content and instrument of ecclesial socialization[25] — learning the language of faith nevertheless also presupposes ecclesial socialization. What George Lindbeck says of proclamation is true of every form of the confession of faith: "[it] gains power and meaning insofar as it is embodied in the total gestalt of community life and action."[26]

It is from the church that one receives the content of faith, and it is in the church that one learns how faith is to be understood and lived. This ecclesial activity of mediation is meaningful, however, only if it leads one to entrust one's life to God in faith. The goal of ecclesial mediation must be a person's own *fiducia*.[27] Yet it is precisely this all-decisive faith, understood as trust, that the church in fact cannot give to a person. *Fiducia* is exclusively a gift of the Spirit of God. If the church were to give to a person faith in this sense — insofar as, as Ratzinger explains, the acceptance of persons on the part of the church is an essential constituent part of faith[28] — then it would not only attest salvation with its own words and deeds, but would itself participate actively in God's

22. By "confession [of faith]" I am referring here to the implicit or explicit confessional dimension of all religious speech and activity (see III.2.2.3 above).

23. See in this regard Lindbeck, *Doctrine*, 30ff.

24. See Barth, *Church Dogmatics*, IV/1.685ff.

25. See Berger and Luckmann, *Construction*, 133-39, regarding language and socialization in general.

26. Lindbeck, *Doctrine*, 36.

27. See Althaus, *Theologie*, 56ff.

28. See I.1.2 above.

salvific activity. This is indeed implied by the Catholic doctrine of the motherhood of the church. As *Lumen gentium* maintains, the church "brings forth sons, who are conceived of the Holy Spirit and born of God, to a new and immortal life."[29] By contrast, one must insist that the church is not the subject of salvific activity with Christ; rather, Christ is the *only* subject of such salvific activity. This is the soteriological reason why one must reject the notion of *Christus totus, caput et membra; Christus totus* is incompatible with *solus Christus*.[30] Precisely in order to preserve the principle *solus Christus*, "the loneliness of the believing 'yes' to God," a "yes" that must be pronounced by the self and nobody else, is soteriologically indispensable.[31] The exclusivity of divine salvific activity requires direct[32] personal acceptance of saving grace by human beings.[33]

3. The difference between the Free Church (as well as the general Protestant) and Catholic understanding of the church's *function* as mother corresponds to their different understanding of the church's *identity* as mother. According to

29. *Lumen gentium* 64. Similar formulations concerning the church as mother can also be found in the writings of the Reformers. Thus Luther writes in the Larger Cathechism that the church "begets and carries every Christian" (*Werke*, 30/I.188.24f.). Similarly also Calvin: "For there is no other way to enter into life unless this mother [the church] conceive us in her womb, give us birth, nourish us at her breast . . ." (*Institutes*, IV.1.4; cf. also Huss, *The Church*, 13). In contrast to the statements of the Reformers, those of the Dogmatic Constitution *Lumen gentium* do appear within the framework of a theology of the *church as sacrament*. What is problematic with the notion of the sacramentality of the church is not the idea that God encounters us "not in any purely spiritual manner, but rather within worldly structures" (Pesch, "Sakramentsverständnis," 334). What is problematic is the denial (or at least lack of clear affirmation) that Christ is the *only* subject of this salvific activity (see in this regard Jüngel, "Kirche"; Birmelé, *Salut*, 203-53). A significant ecumenical consenssus does exist, however, about the belief that Christ is "the real subject of all salvific activity in the church" (Kasper, "Kirche," 242), so that the mediation of salvation through the church accordingly "possesses epicletic structure" (Kasper, "Grundkonsens," 180; see also Congar, *Der Heilige Geist*, 488-95). The decisive open question within ecumenical dialogue between Catholics and Protestants, a question not yet enjoying any consensus, concerns the character of the instrumentality of the church (see Birmelé, *Salut*; Kasper, "Grundkonsens," 178) — is the church an instrument in God's hands in such a way that Christ remains the *sole* subject of saving grace, or not?

30. For a critique of this notion, see III.2.1.3 above.

31. Pesch, *Rechtfertigung*, 261. Jesus' proclamation of the reign of God confronted every person directly with God (see in this regard Jüngel, *Gott*, 485f.).

32. This is not to deny that every experience of God is mediated. There is no immediate directness; one's own socially mediated self-experience flows into every experience of God (see Mühlen, "L'expérience," 47ff.).

33. According to Luther, the personal nature of faith and the exclusivity of divine salvific activity are inseparable, "for no one can lay his own faith on another, nor give to him that same faith, though he may indeed pray that that person, too, may be clothed with Christ; but each person must believe for himself, and Christ alone must clothe us all with himself" (*Werke*, 10/I.476.12ff.).

Ratzinger, the mother church is the entire *ecclesia sancta* and is so as a *subject* rather than as a diffuse spiritual space. This subject, which the church is together with Christ, acquires the concrete capacity for action in priests, who receive their consecration from God insofar as they receive it from the entire church. Thus does the motherly function of the church become concentrated in its (still male![34]) hierarchy; the latter possesses the divine authority to proclaim faith and to administer the sacraments, authority deriving from its particular sacramental relation to the entire *sancta ecclesia*. It is the mediation of faith by way of sacramental office that alone makes it possible for individual human beings to receive their faith from outside, from God, instead of having to construct it themselves by designing their own Christianity from the Bible (or from the entirety of the Christian tradition) and by living it according to their own direction.[35] The direct nature of the appropriation of faith seems, according to this argumentation, virtually to negate the exclusivity of divine salvific activity.

Yet are those who interpret the Bible and the Christian tradition for themselves necessarily fashioning their own religion? Does being responsibly mature simultaneously mean being arbitrary or high-handed? On the contrary, it is precisely faith that enables human beings to "judge all things freely; this applies both to the political shape of life and to the organizational forms of the church and its doctrinal formulations."[36] That pseudo-Christian forms of religiosity do indeed arise is clear from the history of sects and movements, and certainly not just within Protestantism! But by surrendering to "authoritative" officials the distinction between true faith and self-made superstition, do we not run the risk that these custodians of faith may degenerate into lords of faith by repressing rather than expressing the genuine *sensus fidelium*? Ultimately, the only way to escape this danger is to trust in the Holy Spirit.[37] Why should it then be misguided to entrust from the outset the process of discernment between faith and superstition to the Holy Spirit active within believers as they study the Bible and the Christian tradition?[38] It is *the Spirit*

<hr/>

34. For persuasive argumentation that the Catholic tradition does not contain any strictly dogmatic reasons proscribing the ordination of women, see Legrand, "Traditio."

35. See I.4 above.

36. Pannenberg, "Reich Gottes," 53.

37. See Rahner, "Kommentar," 227f. According to Walter Kasper, the Catholic Church does agree with the Protestant belief that offices are "no guarantee for the actual transmission of the gospel" (Kasper, "Grundkonsens," 176).

38. It is not enough to speak only about the authority of scripture, since scripture is always read within the context of a certain interpretive tradition. The relationship between scripture and tradition is reciprocal. This view does not surrender scripture as a criterion of tradition — its function as judge over against the church — since the reciprocity between scripture and tradition is *asymmetrical*. Scripture is fixed; tradition is moveable. This is why tradition, which is *one* of the contexts from which scripture is read, can also be influenced

who creates the authentic *sensus fidelium,* and *the Spirit* that simultaneously watches over it. People who believe correctly have not "fashioned" their own faith for themselves, but rather have received it from the Spirit of God through the Bible, through Christian tradition, and through the confession of faith of Christian congregations.

Because one does not receive faith (*fiducia*) from the church (the church is not a secondary subject of salvific activity), but rather *through* the church, and because the church is a communion of persons rather than a subject,[39] the character of faith as a gift does not require a priestly office fundamentally different from the general priesthood of believers through which God gives faith to individuals. True, without such a priestly office, there can be no guarantee that when people act in the mediation of faith, it really is God who is acting as well; but whether this is a defect or a necessary expression of God's sovereignty must yet be examined.[40] In any event, the receptive element can be adequately expressed symbolically[41] by the assertion that the word of God that creates faith always comes to individuals through the multidimensional confession of faith of *others.*[42] Understood in this way, the mother church does *not* stand *over against* individual Christians; rather, Christians *are* the mother church";[43] the mother church is the communion of brothers and sisters that has always existed vis-à-vis the individual Christian. The universal priesthood of believers implies the "universal motherhood of believers."

---

by scripture. Concerning the relationship between tradition and interpretation and rationality in general, see MacIntyre, *After Virtue,* 204-25; idem, *Whose Justice?* 1-11, 349-403; on the relationship between scripture, reason, and the church in Lutheran theology, see Bayer, "Schriftautorität."

39. See III.2.1.3 above.

40. See VI.2.2.3 below.

41. That God's word always comes to a person by way of others can, with regard to the character of faith as gift, have only *symbolic* significance, namely, God's word is spoken to me by others, and this symbolizes the fact that it comes from God. If there were any actual connection between human and divine giving, then the word of God that creates faith would come not only from God *through* human beings, but also from God *and* human beings, in which case those other human beings — the church — would together with God constitute the subjects of salvific activity. That God's word always comes through *certain* other human beings can function as a guarantee for the divine origin of the word, even if no actual connection exists between the respective activities of human and divine giving. When these particular human beings act in a certain way, then God is also always acting; and God acts in a salvifically creative way only if these particular human beings act in a certain way. If the notion of the sacramentality of the church meant *only* this — and not also that these particular human beings are acting *with* Christ — this would constitute ecumenically important progress toward clarifying the question of the church's instrumentality.

42. See III.2.2.3 above.

43. Jüngel, "Kirche," 329f. See also Baur, "Amt," 112; Ratschow, "Amt," 612.17.

Paul's use of the metaphor of conception and birth confirms this understanding of the motherhood of the church. Paul understands himself as father (1 Cor. 4:14-15; 2 Cor. 6:13; 2 Thess. 2:11; Phlm. 10) and as mother (Gal. 4:19; cf. 1 Thess. 2:7) of his congregations and of their members, since as a missionary he was the first to preach the gospel to them, and because their own spiritual birth, their new creation by the Spirit, occurred through him.[44] There is no talk about the church as a subject acting with Christ. The apostle as *proclaimer* and as *individual* apostle is their father and mother; he did not baptize the Corinthians (1 Cor. 1:14-17), and his congregations emphatically have οὐ πολλοὺς πατέρας ("not many fathers," 1 Cor. 4:15), but rather only one. This is also why his fatherhood can only be ἐν Χριστῷ Ἰησοῦ ("in Christ Jesus") and διὰ τοῦ εὐαγγελίου ("through the gospel," 1 Cor. 4:15). C. K. Barrett correctly remarks in this regard that "Christ is the agent and the Gospel is the means by which men are brought to new life."[45]

This thesis of the universal motherhood of believers also corresponds to the actual practice of Christian churches. The mediation of faith for all practical purposes proceeds less by way of officeholders (in whom allegedly the entire church acts)[46] than by way of the various Christian "significant others" (such as family members or friends).[47] And the mediation of faith is supported by the life of all the members of the church (the "remaining others"), who among other things also create the plausibility structures for the mediation of faith.[48] It is through them *all* that the motherly-fatherly triune God begets children into new life.[49] Of course, these "significant others" cannot bring the process of initiation to its conclusion; a person does not become a Christian until he or she is baptized and partakes of the Eucharist, both of which acts emphatically are to take place within the worship service and accordingly also in the *local church*. Only within the framework of the motherhood of the local church can one speak of the motherhood of individual Christians. The universal mother-

44. See Stuhlmacher, *Philemon*, 38.
45. Barrett, *1 Corinthians*, 115.
46. Lehmann, "Gemeinde," 45, also admits this.
47. So also Kress, *Church*, 182f.
48. The "significant others" function in the life of a Christian as the main players in the performance surrounding the person's Christian identity, while the "rest of the others" function as a kind of chorus (so Berger and Luckmann, *Construction*, 150-51, in describing the construction of identity). See VI.1.1.2 below.
49. The New Testament uses both masculine and feminine metaphors to describe this rebirth. A person is born anew not only "of imperishable seed, through the living and enduring word of God" (1 Pet. 1:23), but also "of the Spirit" (John 3:6). The Johannine text clearly compares the Spirit with a mother, contrasting the origin of a person from her mother with her new origin from the Spirit (John 3:4; see Bultmann, *John*, 137). Concerning the motherly dimension of the Spirit's activity, see Moltmann, *Geist*, 171ff.

hood of believers is bound to *common ecclesial* motherhood.[50] In this sense, one must indeed, along with Ratzinger, distinguish between the participation of private teachers and that of the church in the process of initiation.[51]

1.2. Individualism of Faith?

From Zizioulas's perspective, the entire effort to make the communal character of the mediation of *faith* plausible makes little sense. In his view, the appropriation of salvific grace through faith is in and of itself individualistic, quite apart from how faith itself is mediated. Faith presupposes cognitive content. Yet any relation proceeding by way of cognitive content basically leaves a person alone. Although people can enter into relations to others by way of cognitive acts, their inner "makeup" is not then determined by these others. Thus, despite these relationships, they are self-enclosed entities or individuals. In contrast to the being of an individual, personhood presupposes the primacy of love over knowledge, whereby love is an ontological rather than a moral category. Within the relationship between God and human beings, it refers to the relation which Christ, in his freedom, establishes with human beings and which human beings, through the incarnation and the sacraments, experience at a subcognitive (or supracognitive?) level.[52]

1. On the one hand, the primacy of love over knowledge seems quite cogent. If God is a person, then ultimately the issue is not to know something (and certainly not "everything") about God, but rather to encounter God as a person and to stand in personal communion with God. The same applies to one's fellow human beings. Moreover, to focus on a person from an *exclusively* cognitive perspective means to miss precisely that person's being as a person. To know a person in an exhaustive manner would mean to destroy him or her as a person.[53] A person is essentially a mystery.

Problems arise, however, when one construes the primacy of love over knowledge in such a way that love may not be mediated through knowledge. This is unpersuasive even with regard to the relationship between divine love and

50. From this perspective one can also correctly evaluate the work of the para-ecclesial evangelistic and missionary organizations that have become so important today, especially in English-speaking Protestant churches. Without inclusive ties to local churches, their activity in proclamation will remain inadequate.

51. See I.1.2 above.

52. See II.2.3.1 and II.2.3.3 above.

53. So, correctly, Zizioulas, "Person," 46, who denies that one can ascribe to the person "positive qualitative content." By contrast, Ratzinger does ascribe positive content to the person; a person is *pure* relationality. Here he *over*determines the person conceptually and for that reason also reduces it to relations (see I.6.1 above and 3.2.1 below).

divine knowledge. Although God did create the world through the power of his love and knows it only as the created world, yet if God is not to be identified with the world through the assumption of an essential self-alienation on God's part, then God, too, *must first will the world as something to be created and for that reason must also know the world as something to be created.*[54] Divine love is inconceivable without volition and cognition, which under the priority of cognition mutually determine one another.[55] This is even more the case with regard to human loving, for in contrast to God, human beings encounter the world, other human beings, and God not as the results of their own creative activity, but rather as already existing reality. In order to love them — at least in order to love them in a personal way as opposed to remaining in an apersonal relation with them, however articulated — they must know them. They cannot love existing reality without coming to identify that reality as something distinct from themselves, and every identification, indeed, even mere observation itself, must be conceived as an "*operation of designating or describing something on the basis of some distinction.*"[56] Among adult individuals at least, such identification of the person to be loved necessarily always includes some process involving knowledge and recognition, which is why such knowing, in this minimal sense of identifying the element of otherness, must continually accompany love. There can be no communion without knowing, though the reverse is also true, that is, there can be no knowing without communion, since knowing presupposes some relation to what is recognized, however rudimentary that relation may be.[57]

If love and knowing mutually determine one another, then love should be understood not only as an ontological category, that is, as a relation determining the inner constitution of those involved in the relation, but also as an expression of their *will.* In order to conceive love as a *personal* relation, I must first conceive it as a relation that has received voluntary inner affirmation. Such affirmation, however, presupposes not only knowledge, but along with it also that element of free, affirming will which chooses between various (previously recognized) possibilities. Admittedly, this choice must be understood in a weaker sense; the possibilities need not be subjectively perceivable, but merely concretely at hand. I can be free to "decorate" my neighbor's house with graffiti even if this act does not in fact occur to me; but I am not free to do this if in actuality this is not a possibility in the first place (e.g., because his house is guarded by four bloodthirsty Dobermans). Love is inconceivable without knowing and willing. Hence it comes as no

---

54. Jürgen Moltmann quite justifiably states that "from eternity God has *desired* not only himself but the world too" (Moltmann, *Trinity,* 108, my emphasis). This creative will of God presupposes the act of knowing.

55. So Oeing-Hanhoff, "Die Krise," 299.

56. Luhmann, "Autopoiesis," 407.

57. So Moltmann, "Entdeckung," 400.

surprise that both knowledge and will are from the outset part of the structure of the faith that creates communion with God and human beings.

2. *Knowledge* is an essential dimension of faith; this is already the case insofar as faith always arises from ἀκοή ("hearing"), that is, is always *fides ex auditu*,[58] though it certainly cannot be reduced to consent to the cognitive content of the language mediating it. Here certainly the dictum applies that one can know more than one can actually articulate.[59] Accordingly, faith is mediated not only by way of the spoken word, and especially not only by way of the written word.[60] In the case of the missionary work of Paul, who can be considered a theologian of the word, one could not only hear something, but also see something with one's eyes (Gal. 3:1) and experience it on one's body (1 Cor. 2:4; 4:20; Rom. 15:19; 1 Thess. 1:5). Accordingly, faith is also begotten through nonverbal forms of communication.[61] This, however, changes nothing in the fact that faith necessarily has a verbally specifiable cognitive content and that this must be appropriated intellectually. Faith is

> the reception and adoption of the εὐαγγέλλιον τοῦ Χριστοῦ (gospel of Christ) heard in the proclamation, and the recognition and acknowledgment of its content posited by God himself. . . . Faith views as true what the proclamation witnesses and proclaims as the ἀλήθεια τοῦ εὐαγγελίου (truth of the gospel).[62]

Faith includes "in a very elementary fashion a process of viewing as true" certain "*assertorial* sentences and statements."[63] It is never simply *fiducia*, but rather always both *fiducia and assensus*. Therefore, the nonverbal presentation of the gospel must always be accompanied by the verbal proclamation of it.

If consent to certain cognitive content is part of the structure of faith, then the *will* must also constitute an essential dimension of faith. Willing and knowing are mutually inclusive. It is only by way of an act of my own will that I can view some cognitive content as true. "*Natura fidei voluntas*," maintained Martin Luther, whom no one can accuse of turning faith into a human work.[64]

---

58. So Bultmann, *Theology*, §35.

59. See in this regard Polanyi, *The Tacit Dimension*, 3-25. There is a *fides implicita* not only in the genuinely Catholic sense that by professing the basic truths one is implicitly also accepting all Christian truths (see Congar, *Diversités*, 195f.), but also in the sense that one always believes *more* than one is able to articulate through language.

60. Concerning the corporeality of the word according to Luther, see Bayer, "Schrift-autorität," 78.

61. See Kress, *Church*, 162.

62. Hofius, "Wort Gottes," 155.

63. Ibid., 156.

64. Luther, *Werke*, 40/III.50.3ff. Cf. Pesch, *Rechtfertigung*, 199.

The volitional dimension of faith is not to be understood to mean that faith is simply a "free deed of decision,"[65] for faith is a gift of God; yet God does not bypass human will when giving faith to a person. Although it is true that people do not believe "from within themselves," they do believe "as themselves"; they are passive, but their passivity is the *"responsorial* passivity of letting oneself be"[66] (cf. Luke 1:38). This act of "letting oneself be" is inconceivable without the will.

Faith with its cognitive and volitional dimensions is soteriologically indispensable. The frequency with which πίστις ("faith") and πιστεύειν ("to have faith, to believe") occur in the New Testament attests that here, in contrast to Judaism and antiquity at large, faith has become the "prevailing term for man's relation to the divine."[67] The soteriological indispensability of faith and the renunciation of any cognitively and volitionally mediated relation to God, as demanded by Zizioulas, could be compatible if one could understand faith as the *consequence* of a purely sacramentally mediated relation to God, as "sensing the life of God."[68] But this is not the case. For although faith does presuppose the influence of the Spirit (how else could faith be a gift of God?), faith does not, as it were, always lag behind the relation to God that has already been formed. Faith is not a necessary accompanying phenomenon of the fundamental relation to God underlying it, but rather the mode in which this relation itself takes place.

If the relation to God is mediated both cognitively and volitionally, then in an important sense human beings, precisely as believers, do stand over against God. Ludwig Feuerbach saw this correctly, maintaining that to give up faith with its cognitive and volitional dimensions would mean suspending God's autonomy; to affirm faith means to affirm God's autonomy.[69] Accordingly, this juxtaposition with God in faith presupposes anthropologically a certain independence on the part of every human being that is also preserved in the experience of salvation. Does this independence, however, amount to anthropological and soteriological individualism, as Zizioulas believes, or is it a presupposition precisely of the specifically human communal identity? I will return to this question after examining the ecclesial character of salvation.[70]

65. Bultmann, *Theology,* §35.
66. Joest, *Ontologie,* 313 (my emphasis).
67. Bultmann, *Theology,* §9; see Friedrich, "Glaube," 91.
68. Zizioulas, "Die pneumatologische Dimension," 143.
69. See in this regard Jüngel, *Gott,* 458.
70. See 3.1 below.

2. The Ecclesial Character of Salvation

The ecclesial mediation of faith serves to bring human beings into a direct (though not unmediated) relation to God; *they* must in faith accept salvation from *God*. These individual human beings, however, do not remain alone with their God. By entering into this relation to God, supported by the communion of believers, they are simultaneously constituted into the communion of believers. Here I will examine which soteriological status the *communio fidelium* possesses and how inclusion into a concrete church takes place.

2.1. The Ecclesiality of Salvation

1. If salvation takes place between the lonely soul and its God, as John Smyth maintains, then it is individualistic. Nothing changes in this regard if we identify the church with the spiritual army of Christ and assert that "they that are not members of the visible church are no subjects of Christs kingdome."[71] For in this case, membership in a church cannot be an expression of what Christians *are*, but rather only the appropriate consequence of what they are *to do*; "every man is *bound in conscience* to be a member of some visible church established into this true order."[72] If church membership is not to be understood merely as an act of obedience, then according to Smyth's proposal its only purpose can be to support human weakness. The church is necessary — as John Calvin, in whose tradition Smyth stands, asserted — because Christians "have not yet attained angelic rank," but rather behave either as "infants and children," or as rebellious subjects.[73] Thus according to Smyth, the visible church is not grounded in the positive experience of salvation, but rather in a *soteriological deficit*. The church is an "external aid" for a fuller experience of salvation; salvation itself is asocial.

By contrast, the Catholic and Orthodox traditions insist on the essential sociality of salvation. Salvation *is* communion with God and human beings. The self-enclosed individual is caught in the opposite of salvation; this is the fundamental idea underlying the entire ecclesiology of both Ratzinger and Zizioulas. Even if their understanding of the church as communion is unpersuasive,[74] this fundamental idea, grounded as it is in the very character of faith, should be affirmed.

2. The faith human beings receive from God places them into a relation

---

71. Smyth, *Works*, 267f. See in this regard Brachlow, *Communion*, 58.
72. Smyth, *Works*, 256 (my emphasis).
73. Calvin, *Institutes*, IV.1.1.
74. See Chapter III above.

with God. To believe means to enjoy communion with God. Faith is not, however, merely the "flight of the lonely to the lonely" (Plotinus). Because the Christian God is not a lonely God, but rather a communion of the three persons, faith leads human beings into the divine *communio*. One cannot, however, have a self-enclosed communion with the triune God — a "foursome," as it were — for the Christian God is not a private deity. Communion with this God is at once also communion with those others who have entrusted themselves in faith to the same God. Hence one and the same act of faith places a person into a new relationship both with God and with all others who stand in communion with God. These others "are discovered *equiprimally* with the new communion with God as one's neighbors, as those who belong to the same communion."[75] Inclusion into the ecclesial communion is accordingly already given with the reception of salvific grace.

Now, this two-dimensional *communio* should not be domesticated in a pseudo-Protestant fashion as inclusion into the *ecclesia invisibilis*. Although one must indeed distinguish theologically between the *ecclesia visibilis* and the *ecclesia invisibilis*, one may not separate them from one another; doing so runs the risk of misusing alleged communion in the invisible church to justify separation from visible churches. The invisible church — *communio sanctorum* — exists concretely only in the plurality of visible churches,[76] which is why membership in the invisible church is bound to membership in a visible church. A person cannot be fully initiated into the Christian faith without being socialized into a Christian church.[77]

Since church membership depends on communion with God, it is a consequence of communion with God. Communion between a Christian and other Christians, however, is not an addendum to that person's communion with God; although it is indeed secondary, it is so in an ontological rather than a temporal sense. The concrete ecclesial community is the *form* — albeit not the only form — in which this communion with God is lived concretely,[78] just as love is the form in which faith is lived.[79] This is why life in the congregation is not something added to faith and its confession, faith that always occurs with and in the church. Life in the congregation is the *execution* of this confession of faith. Just as faith is confessed through speaking, so also is it confessed through life *in* the fellowship of believers. In this sense, faith

75. Jüngel, *Gott*, 485; my emphasis.

76. Similarly Brunner, *Kirche*, 11f.

77. See 1.1.2 and 1.1.3 above.

78. Concerning the Pauline understanding of the relationship between faith and the church, see Dobbler, *Glaube*, 61, 69ff., 239f.

79. This corresponds to the idea of faith "made effective through love" (Gal. 5:6), but not to the idea of faith shaped through love (see Calvin, *Institutes*, III.11.20).

means entering into *communio, communio* with the triune God and with other Christians.[80]

3. It is soteriologically and ecclesiologically inappropriate to understand the church as an external aid to salvation. The church is not a mere training subject or training ground for the edification of pious individuals. As Emil Brunner correctly emphasized, the church is "not some *externum subsidium fidei,* but rather is the thing itself. . . . Being allied with one another is just as much an end in itself as alliance with Christ."[81] Salvation and the church cannot be separated. The old formula was *extra ecclesiam nulla salus.* Freed from its element of exclusivity, which rightly tarnished its reputation, the formula does accurately express the essentially communal character of salvation. Correctly understood — and as Dietrich Bonhoeffer formulated it, having picked up on it during the struggle between church and state during the period of National Socialism — the formula states that "salvation is inconceivable without the church, and the church is inconceivable without salvation."[82] To experience faith means to become an ecclesial being. Nor can it be otherwise if the church is to be the proleptic experience within history of the eschatological integration of the entire people of God into the communion of the triune God.[83]

The church is not a means, but an end in itself;[84] it is a necessary mode of the life of faith. At the same time, however, the church is also a means of grace, since the processes of ecclesial life — confession of faith by the pluriform, mutual speaking of God's word and through the life of communion — both mediate and support faith. In this way, the encounter with grace and the means of grace overlap. Although they can indeed be distinguished insofar as the means

80. In a study of Luther's writings, Jürgen Lutz has tried to show not only that according to Luther the *communio sanctorum* supports and fosters the justifying *fides,* but also that "each person's justification" takes place as "the *repraesentatio Christi* for others" in the *communio sanctorum* (*Unio,* 76). From this he concludes that the *communio sanctorum* is "an integral aspect of the event of justification" (p. 264). This is theologically persuasive, though it is unclear to me why this notion must be dependent on a *processive* understanding of justification; "only when he [a Christian]," Lutz writes, "*moves forward* in sanctification can he be called a priest" (p. 184, my emphasis). My premise is that every Christian can already be a priest for others through her — ideally not merely external — confession of faith.

81. Brunner, *Kirche,* 12, 15. I do not, to be sure, share Brunner's hostility toward institutions (see VI.2 below).

82. Bonhoeffer, "Kirchengemeinschaft," 231. The formula is false, however, if understood as "a theoretical truth about those who are saved and those who are lost" (ibid.).

83. See III.1.1.1 above.

84. See in this regard Bonhoeffer, *Communio.* My assertion here that the church is an end in itself does not mean that it should isolate itself from the world in some self-satisfying fashion, but rather that it is not a mere means of salvation, but rather is itself a dimension of the salvific experience. Concerning the task of the church in the world, see chapter VII below, and Volf, "The Church."

of grace can also function as means without the underlying experience of grace, yet the means of grace must always, so to speak, bow before the experience of grace. Only the experience of grace that is at least implicitly affirmed can serve as a means of grace.[85] The overlapping of the experience and the means of grace occurs because Christ's constitutive presence for the church is nothing other than Christ's presence within the hearts of believers that has turned toward the outside in the fruit and gifts of the Spirit. Christ's presence through the Spirit makes a person into a Christian and simultaneously leads that person into ecclesial communion, constituting the church thus in a twofold fashion: first, by adding a person to the church and, second, by mediating faith to others through that person. Here again we see that the church as mother and the church as sibling fellowship are identical.

2.2. The Genesis of a Concrete Church

1. According to the Free Church tradition, faith is a necessary but by no means sufficient condition for the emergence of a church. As in most English Separatists, so also in Smyth's ecclesiology the idea of *covenant* plays a preeminent role. For him, the church is "a visible communion of Saincts . . . two, three, or moe Saincts joyned together by covenant with God & themselves, freely to vse the holy things of God, according to the word, and for their mutual edification, & God's glory."[86] Two elements of this definition of the church are of significance here: "joining together" and "covenant." A church comes about only if people voluntarily unite, and it grows insofar as people voluntarily join it. A Christian congregation, however, also includes a covenant — "vowe, promise, oath"[87] — without which it has neither continuity nor stability. According to Smyth, the covenant between believers is merely the external side of the love uniting them (just as the human side of the covenant between God and believers is merely the external side of the faith connecting them with Christ). This covenant consists of "all the duties of love whatsoever."[88]

The decisive element of these two ideas — "joining together" and "covenant" — is that they describe *human activities.* Human activity was so predominant in Smyth's thinking that he was able to coin the most unfortunate expressions, such as "a man Churching himself."[89] Together with other English

85. See III.2.2.3, note 90, above.
86. Smyth, *Works*, 252.
87. Ibid., 254.
88. Ibid.
89. Ibid., 660. This use of language set a precedent. Hence the Baptist theologian Augustus Hopkins Strong wrote that "any number of believers, therefore, may *constitute*

Separatists, he also advocated a mutualistic understanding of covenant. The covenant between God and believers remains valid only if believers fulfill the conditions of the covenant, if they live according to God's commandments, including the implementation of the biblical understanding of church organization.[90] It is not surprising, then, that Free Church ecclesiology has been accused of understanding the church as emerging simply from the act of its members assembling together. Since in this case the church would actually be a free association of independent individuals, it could not be a work of God, but rather would of necessity be a product of believers themselves.[91]

Although this polemic against Free Church ecclesiology is indeed correct, it is not differentiated enough, proceeding as it does from a false alternative, namely, juxtaposing the Free Church notion of "from below" with the Catholic (or Orthodox and allegedly genuinely Protestant) notion of "from above." This position not only erroneously presupposes that Free Church ecclesiology negates the "from above," but also forgets that *no* church can arise and live without *also* being constituted "from below." The Spirit of God, acting through the word of God and the sacraments ("from above"), is the real subject of the genesis of the church. It is *the Spirit* who constitutes the church. *People*, however, must accept the gifts of God in faith (even if this faith is itself a gift of God); *they* must come together, and *they* must remain together. It is understandable that in the static societies of earlier centuries this horizontal dimension of the constituting of the church was passed over. In modern, mobile, post-Christian societies, in which a person does not necessarily already belong to a certain local church simply by virtue of having been born and baptized in a certain locale, this dimension must be considered ecclesiologically as well.

Holding fast to the notion of "from below," however, is not primarily an accommodation to social circumstances, but rather a matter of the *theological* identity of the church. Historically there seems to be little doubt that the churches of the first Christians, viewed sociologically, were "voluntary associations,"[92] a fact reflecting a fundamental theological insight, namely, that in *every* ecclesiology in which the church is a *communio fidelium*, regardless of

---

themselves into a Christian Church, by adopting for their rule of faith and practice Christ's law laid down in the New Testament, and associating themselves together, in accordance with it, for his worship and service" (Strong, *Theology*, 902, my emphasis). See by contrast Walton, *Community*, 117, 164.

90. See in this regard Brachlow, *Communion*, 21ff.

91. See I.2.2 above. Similar criticisms of Free Church ecclesiology can be found in the Orthodox (see Limouris, "Church," 140), Lutheran (see Elert, "Katholizität," 249; Aulen, *Faith*, 312ff.), and Anglican traditions (see Abbott et al., eds., *Catholicity*, 11-12).

92. Scroggs, "Communities," 20; see also Dobbler, *Glaube*, 166ff.

whatever else it may be beyond this, the human will to come together and to abide together as a concrete church must be viewed as a constitutive element of the being of the church.[93] That is, if one defines the church *only* from the perspective of the objective activities (and thus "from above"), the church hovers over the people of God and cannot be identical with that people. If one understands the church as *communio fidelium* and yet eliminates ecclesiologically the element of human will, the church itself is reduced to an amorphous mass of individuals who, driven by the Spirit, come together quite spontaneously; an actual, concrete church exists then only in the act of such fortuitous assembling, and lacks historical continuity. If one wants to preserve the historical continuity of the church, and at the same time to understand it as *the whole people* of God, *including officeholders and laity,* then the question is not whether the church is constituted "from below," but rather *how* one is to reflect theologically on this element of "from below" so that the church is not simply reduced to the result of these believing individuals' need for association. Oddly enough, neither Free Church theologians nor their critics have expended much effort in reflecting in a positive theological fashion on the ecclesiologically indispensable element of the human will in belonging to a concrete church.

2. My own tentative response to the unexplored question posed above picks up on reflections concerning the character and function of faith. If inclusion in the church is already given with the reception of salvific grace through faith, then the human will, which necessarily belongs to life in ecclesial communion, must be conceived in a theologically similar fashion as that will to live in communion with God which is a necessary aspect of faith. When I join a church, I am not making myself into an ecclesial being ("to church oneself"), nor am I thereby making the church into a church; rather, in this, *my own act, the Lord* "adds" me to the church (Acts 2:41, 47). And when I "hold fast to the fellowship" (Acts 2:42), or join a different Christian congregation, this, too, can be the human execution of this divine act of "being added."[94] In this sense, every local church is God's work (see Ps. 100:3).[95] This is clearly expressed by the initiatory sacrament of baptism. Through baptism, whose necessary presupposition is faith and accordingly also the will,[96] one is initiated into a twofold communion — communion with God and a concrete communion with Christians. By wanting to be baptized, I also want to become part of a church.

Already implicit within faith, this will to communion with other Christians

---

93. See Bonhoeffer, *Communio,* 178, 186.
94. See Bonhoeffer, *Communio,* 190.
95. See in this regard Flew and Davis, eds., *Catholicity of Protestantism,* 103.
96. See III.2.2.4 and IV.1.2.2 above.

is also, like faith itself, *mediated ecclesially*.[97] This already follows from the purely sociological observation that, as Niklas Luhmann formulated it, one does not simply decide "to let oneself be socialized."[98] The explicit will to be socialized already presupposes an initial, still rudimentary socialization. A person "cannot be socialized if he or she is not already socialized."[99] The Free Church tradition was not sufficiently mindful of this.[100] It committed the same mistake ecclesiologically that the liberal tradition committed socio-philosophically. According to Jeremy Bentham's excellent formulation, John Locke forgot in his associative understanding of society that an individual does not come to the world having already come of age.[101] Just as a person cannot arise, develop, and live apart from her relationships with others, neither can a Christian exist as a Christian before entering into relation with other Christians; she is first constituted as a Christian *through* these relations. Ecclesial membership is not merely the result of associative will added externally to one's being as a Christian. The church mediated to this person the content of faith, led her to faith, and the faith given her by God placed her into communion with other Christians. Hence she does not merely join a concrete church; she *is* an ecclesially determined being, one destined to live in the church (see 2 Tim. 1:5).[102] She must, to be sure, realize her ecclesial being volitionally by joining and remaining in a church. A reciprocal relationship obtains here between ecclesial being and the volitional ecclesial status of standing-

---

97. Dietrich Bonhoeffer advocated the stronger thesis that the "individual will" to belong to the church can "at most . . . be an . . expression of membership in the church" (*Communio*, 102). This subvolitional (or supravolitional) membership in the church would have to correspond to a subvolitional (or supravolitional) fellowship with Christ. Fellowship with Christ, however, is mediated through faith, for which the cognitive and voluntative dimension is essential (see 1.2.2 above). Just as faith is not an expression of fellowship with Christ, but rather the medium in which this fellowship is realized, so also is the will to belong to a church not an expression of church membership, but rather the medium in which this membership is lived.

98. Luhmann, "Autopoiesis," 427.

99. Ibid. There is no need to examine here how *initial* ecclesial socialization comes about. With regard to the processes of socialization in general, Niklas Luhmann has recourse to the element of chance: "Any element of chance that makes it possible for a person to understand himself as related to social demands may also render such entry possible" (p. 427).

100. See in this regard Walton, *Community*, 156.

101. See Dumont, *L'individualisme*, 82. George Herbert Mead (*Mind, Self and Society*, 233) argues similarly: "The contract theory of society assumes that the individuals are first all there as intelligent individuals, as selves, and that these individuals get together and form society."

102. Edward Farley speaks of a "depth dimension of . . . commitment, rarely formulated or even made the object of reflection" (*Ecclesial Man*, 97). Similarly also John Dewey with regard to social relationships in general (see *Individualism*, 82).

178

in-relation. Ecclesial being is expressed in the will to engage in these relationships, and the will to engage in these relationships shapes ecclesial being.[103] The one cannot be reduced to the other. Both will and being, however, are fruits of the Spirit of communion active in and through the church.[104]

3. The understanding of the ecclesial mediation of faith and of the ecclesial character of salvation just presented presupposes a particular social form of the church. Following Ferdinand Tönnies and his models of "community" and "society," one can distinguish between ideal types of organic and associative social structures.[105] A person is born into an organic social structure, or grows into it; by contrast, a person freely joins an associative social structure. The former is a "living organism" whose parts depend on the whole organism and are determined by it; the latter is "a mechanical aggregate and artifact" composed of individual parts. The former is thus enduring, the latter transient.[106] In short, organic social structures are communities of being, while associative social structures are alliances for a specific purpose.

The church, however, cannot be classified according to this simple two-part schema, and not just because the schema is dealing with ideal types. That the church is neither a social organism nor an association seems plausible once one

103. The mutual relationship of being and will presupposes that one can theoretically distinguish between "the *empirical* subject of word, thought, and will" and "*moral* being, which is independent, autonomous, and thus (essentially) asocial" (Dumont, *L'individualisme*, 69). My premise is that human beings as subjects of thinking and willing are socially conditioned and for that reason precisely *not* essentially asocial beings.

104. One might object to this reconstruction of Christian initiation that there are conversions in which the church participates considerably less than is presupposed here. Such conversions, however, are indisputably exceptions that, it seems to me, confirm rather than disprove the rule. Yet even in the case of a conversion such as that of Saul (Acts 9:1-22), which seems to take place with no ecclesial mediation whatever — the resurrected Jesus reveals himself *directly* to Saul in a vision — the church plays a considerably more important role than is apparent at first glance, since without the intellectual and emotional confrontation with the church he was persecuting, Saul's conversion would have been inconceivable. The heavenly voice alludes to this: "Saul, Saul, why do you persecute me? . . . I am Jesus, whom you are persecuting" (Acts 9:4-5). The resurrected Jesus does not simply reveal himself to Saul, but rather in his self-revelation addresses Saul with regard to the latter's *already existing relation to the church* and thus also to himself. As paradoxical as it may sound, Saul's persecution of the church was the beginning of his ecclesially mediated process of initiation. The positive relation to Christ and to the church that he acquired after conversion (the apostolate) does not simply negate the negative relation he had before conversion (persecution), but rather simultaneously builds on it.

105. Unlike Ferdinand Tönnies's distinction between community and society (see Tönnies, *Gemeinschaft*), my own distinction between organic and associative social structures is intended in a purely descriptive manner and contains no value judgments. For theological criticism of Tönnies, see Moltmann, *Man*, 61ff.

106. Tönnies, *Gemeinschaft*, 5.

considers that membership in the church is based on spiritual *rebirth.* The church cannot be an association, because a person does not simply freely join a church, but rather is re*born* into it. God begets and maintains this new life in the Spirit through the community of discourse and practice called the church. Hence the church is not an aggregate of independent individuals, but rather a communion of ecclesially determined persons. On the other hand, the church cannot simply be a social organism, since a person is not simply born into it, but rather is *reborn.* Christian rebirth presupposes personal faith with its cognitive and volitional dimensions,[107] which is why associative elements are essential for the social structure "church." Hence as I understand it, the church is a mixture of the social type that Max Weber called "church," into which a person is born, and the social type he called "sect," which a person freely joins.[108]

The church does indeed seem to have a "social form *sui generis,*" as Dietrich Bonhoeffer suggested at the end of his study *Sanctorum communio.*[109] Our reflections on the church, however, of necessity make use of metaphors drawn from the social world. "Mother" was the dominant metaphor for the organic understanding of the church. According to Cyprian, the church is a "fixed, unified body" precisely because it is mother: "we are born from her womb, nourished with her milk, and inspired by her spirit."[110] The designation "club" can apply to the associative understanding of the church; like a club, the church appears here as a functional social unit whose members mutually support one another in order to pursue their own or common goals.

If one is to combine these organic and associative elements, as my own analysis requires, it is best to use the two complementary metaphors "siblings"[111] and "friends"[112] — "sibling friends." The metaphor "siblings" derives from the organic social type and expresses the communion of being between the members of the church; the metaphor "friends" derives from the associative social type and expresses the volitional dimension of church membership. The New Testament confirms these two metaphors insofar as the terms "brothers/sisters" and "friends" together constitute the dominant self-designations of the first Christians (although "brother/sister" occurs far more frequently[113]) and insofar as their mean-

---

107. Infant baptism is one of the most important pillars of the organic understanding of the church (see Bonhoeffer, *Communio,* 177, 286 n. 378; Huber, "Kirche," 264f.).

108. M. Weber, "Die protestantischen Sekten," 207-36; E. Troeltsch, *Die Soziallehren,* 967ff.

109. Bonhoeffer, *Communio,* 185.

110. Cyprian, *De unitate* 23.

111. See in this regard Schäfer, *Gemeinde.*

112. Concerning the understanding of the church as a fellowship of friends, see Moltmann, *Church,* 119ff.; 314-17; Klauck, "Freundesgemeinschaft."

113. For the reasons why Paul avoids the terminology of friendship, see Marshall, *Enmity,* 134.

ings converge.[114] The church is the fellowship of siblings who are friends, and the fellowship of friends who are siblings. Of course, these two metaphors describe the relationships within the interior ecclesial sphere and suggest that the church is an intimate group. Other metaphors must complement these to make it clear that the church is an "open" fellowship of friends and siblings who are called to summon enemies and strangers to become friends and children of God and to accept them as friends and siblings. Only such open fellowship is commensurate with the ultimate vision of the church as the eschatological gathering of the entire people of God from all tribes and nations.[115] Yet the mixed metaphor "sibling friends" is confirmed precisely by the description of the eschatological people of God in the Apocalypse of John, which uses two complementary metaphors, one of them alluding to the associative, and the other to the organic social type. "The holy city," as the people, not as the place for the people,[116] is at the same time "the bride, the wife of the Lamb" (Rev. 21:2, 9).

3. Personhood in the Ecclesial Community

The interdependence of ecclesial being and the will to ecclesial life, expressed in the complementary ecclesial metaphors "siblings" and "friends" (or "city" and "bride"), presupposes an anthropology according to which sociality and personhood are two mutually determinative and essential dimensions of human existence. In this section, I will examine the relationship between sociality and personhood in critical dialogue with the tendency to lose "person" within the "whole Christ," a tendency evident in the soteriology and ecclesiology of both Ratzinger and Zizioulas.

3.1. Personhood and Christian Existence

1. Zizioulas's premise is that human beings are constituted as persons through the same trinitarian relation between the Father and the Son. They become persons through baptism precisely because baptism is "the application to humanity of the very filial relationship that exists between the Father and the Son."[117] As I have tried to show, this view surrenders the particularity of each person. The personhood of *different* persons cannot be grounded in one and the same relationship of Christ to the Father; one ends up with human clones

114. See in this regard Klauck, "Freundesgemeinschaft."
115. See Moltmann, *Church,* 119ff.; Klauck, "Freundesgemeinschaft," 6f., 9f.
116. See III.1.1.1 above.
117. Zizioulas, "Human Capacity," 438.

corresponding to Christ.[118] Zizioulas holds fast to his christological grounding of personhood, because otherwise he would have to assert that each human being enters into relation with Christ (through faith) as a person who has already been constituted as such. In his view, however, this would amount to a regression into individualistic anthropology, soteriology, Christology, and ecclesiology all at the same time. Surrendering the particularity of persons in order to preserve their communal aspect, however, is a poor exchange, for surrendering the particularity of a person also means surrendering personhood itself. Spiritual cloning does not produce persons. Can we find a different, anthropologically traversable path to escape individualism?

It seems advisable to take our cue from trinitarian reflection. At the trinitarian level, it is not the same relationship of the Father to the Son and to the Spirit that constitutes the latter two in their particularity, but rather a respectively different relationship, *generatio* and *spiratio* (even if, at least according to the Eastern doctrine of the Trinity, one cannot specify how the two differ). Translated anthropologically, this means that each human being *is constituted into a person by what in each case is a different relation of God to that human being.*[119] A human being becomes a person and enters thus into existence as a human being because he "is addressed by God equiprimally with regard to both God and to himself, and is called to communion with God."[120] On the one hand, God's call is general and is the same for everyone. This grounds common humanity and the equal dignity of every human being. At the same time, however, that call must be specific to each individual; otherwise, abstract personhood, or universal human nature, would be created through the call, but not each particular person distinct from all others, that is, the concrete human being. Unless God's relation to every person is specific in every case, and unless God calls every human being by name (see Gen. 3:9[121]), no human being can declare, "I believe that God created *me.*"[122] It is precisely the uniqueness of God's relation to me that makes me into a unique person.

Yet in God's relation to me, a relation creating me as an individual human being, I do not stand as an individual isolated from other human beings and from my environment. An isolated individual of this sort does not exist.[123] Human beings are in actuality imbedded in a network of multiple and diverse

118. See II.2.1.2 above.

119. Concerning the constituting of personhood through God, see Volf, *Arbeit,* 120ff. (and the bibliography supplied there).

120. Dalferth and Jüngel, "Person," 70.

121. Claus Westermann emphasizes the personal character of God's question to Adam, "Where are you?" (see Westermann, *Schöpfung,* 136ff.).

122. Luther, *Werke,* 30/I.363.2.

123. For a criticism of abstractly uniformizing individualism, see Welker, *Gottes Geist,* 230f.

social and natural relationships; this applies not only to newborn infants, who have not yet become subjects, but even to solitary ascetics, who do, after all, live an imaginary (or, perhaps better, spiritually real) communion and must draw their sustenance from nature. Every human self is conditioned in an essential fashion not only by his or her own corporeal constitution, but also and especially by relationships with other human beings, and by societal structures and institutions. This is why God's own relationship with human beings, a relationship that first constitutes a human being into a person, always realizes itself *through* the differentiated existence of every person in these multiple relations. Hence even though every human being is constituted in his or her personhood exclusively by God, that person's inner "makeup" is still that of a social and natural being. Without other human beings, even God cannot create a human being! Even if God were to create an isolated being, that being would not be a human being. This may be the anthropological significance of the peculiar transition in Gen. 1:27 from singular to plural: "So God created humankind in his image, in the image of God he created *him*; male and female he created *them.*"

God's relationship with human beings keeps the human being as person either from dissolving in the stream of its multiple relationships, or from disintegrating into "a transtemporal society" of "moments of selfhood."[124] In this way, the emergence of a person's continuing character as a subject becomes possible. "Because as a creature addressed by God he is a person and thus a

---

124. Following the process philosophy of Alfred North Whitehead, Catherine Keller (*Broken Web*, 194f.) maintains that the identity of the person through time, which makes it possible to say "I am now the same person as I was a moment ago," is "a (doubtless useful) generalization." This generalization, however, "should not be mistaken for the real actuality in its immediacy" (p. 197). If this identity were real, self-reflection might result, which in its own turn would result in the individualistic "separative self" (pp. 9ff.). Over against the "separative self," Keller advocates the "fluid self" consisting of events (though a self that does not, like the traditional feminine "soluble self," dissolve in this fluidity). Although I share her concerns, it seems that rather than bringing the self into fluidity, she breaks it up into multiple selves, into a "series of self-moments accumulating as my very soul" (p. 212), though my own judgment does reveal that I do not subscribe to process thinking. Let us assume for a moment, however, that Keller's understanding of the person is plausible. The process-philosophical proposal of bringing-the-self-into-fluidity is unable to suspend or sublate the psychological inclination to self-reflection, which is imbedded too deep in our experience of self to be overcome with counterintuitive metaphysical theory. Even if it is true that the "I" cannot *simultaneously* be its own subject and object (see Luhmann, "Autopoiesis," 408), nonetheless our own strong intuition does resist the notion that "the object of its knowing can only be . . . an *earlier* self" (Keller, *Broken Web*, 187, my emphasis). In my opinion, Keller rejects all too quickly H. Richard Niebuhr's grounding of the unity of the socially determined self in "the presence only of One action [the action of God] in all actions upon it" (Niebuhr, *Self*, 126; see Keller, *Broken Web*, 175f.).

human being, a human being's basic feature is this accessibility to communication on the basis of having already been thus addressed, and this feature makes it possible to become a subject in communion with other human beings in the world."[125] It is a human being's personhood as constituted by God that results in a person's not just being determined by the surroundings, but also being able to *encounter* both society and nature *in freedom* precisely as a socially and naturally determined entity.[126] This is why one may not define personhood along with Alistair I. McFadyen as "a structure of response sedimented from a significant history of communication."[127] The person is neither a "pattern of communication" nor the "organizer of communication," nor the two together.[128] Personhood, which differs both from "I" and from self, grounds the two. Personhood marks, as Ingolf U. Dalferth and Eberhard Jüngel write, "the mystery . . . of a human being's origin in God and his destiny to enter into communion with God."[129] On the basis of personhood as grounded in God's creative relationship with human beings, human beings are in a position not simply of having to submit passively to their social and natural relations, but of being able to integrate them creatively into their own personality structure. Without this interactive-integrative activity of being a subject, human beings would exist merely as the reflection of their relationships. Although their personhood would not thereby be lost, they could not live as persons in a manner worthy of a human being.

2. As subjects, human beings stand over against both their own environment and God. Though they live from God's creative relationship with them, they do so in such a way that, as Søren Kierkegaard remarked concerning creation at large, God "by creating gives them independence over against Himself."[130] It is precisely as such persons that human beings experience salvation, namely, as persons who are independent even though they are

125. Dalferth and Jüngel, "Person," 94.

126. Similarly also the conclusion of Wolfhart Pannenberg: "Because selfhood is ultimately grounded in the relation to God, the person can encounter his social situation in freedom" (*Anthropologie*, 234).

127. McFadyen, *The Call*, 114. In his view, the person is "*primarily* a public structure, and only *secondarily* appropriated by individuals" (p. 90, my emphasis). Even apart from confusing personhood with subjecthood, it is still not clear how the "public structure" can turn into the subject ("organizer") that appropriates this structure. To be able to react to social impulses, the "I" may not first be derived only from these impulses — from social interaction taking place outside the "I." George Herbert Mead saw this correctly, though in his thinking one encounters the problem of the unity between "I" and "self" (see Pannenberg, *Anthropologie*, 183).

128. McFadyen, *The Call*, 78.

129. Dalferth and Jüngel, "Person," 94.

130. Kierkegaard, *Concluding Unscientific Postscript*, 232 (II/2, appendix A [" . . . in Danish Literature"]).

indeed conditioned by their environment and stand in relation to God. This has two important consequences. First, human beings are not simply isolated individuals before they experience salvation, as Zizioulas maintains.[131] They are persons constituted by God in the medium of their social and natural relationships, yet persons whose lives are not commensurate with their calling to live in communion with God in faith and in communion with their fellow human beings and fellow creatures in love. Second, the experience of salvation must come about by way of human subjecthood in its cognitive and volitional dimensions; otherwise human beings are bypassed precisely as human beings in the experience of salvation. Zizioulas accordingly has committed two mutually determinative anthropological mistakes in his understanding of Christian initiation. By understanding human beings who live without Christ as isolated individuals, and by negating the cognitive and volitional mediation of salvation,[132] he negates both the essential sociality and the subjecthood of human beings.

The way one becomes a person (anthropology) and the way one becomes a Christian (soteriology) both differ and correspond to one another. The difference emerges from the fact that one is already a subject when one becomes a Christian, which is why a person is as a rule initiated into the Christian faith *as* a subject. This cannot be the case with regard to becoming a person, since personhood is what grounds being a subject in the first place, and thus being a subject is not a precondition, but rather a consequence of becoming a person. Becoming a person and becoming a Christian, however, simultaneously correspond to one another. Just as a human being is constituted into a person by God by way of social (and natural) relationships, so also one is constituted into a Christian by God by way of ecclesial relationships, relationships that are not just social, since the initiatory process comes to its conclusion only through baptism and the Eucharist. Hence as a person and as a Christian, one is indeed an independent, and yet simultaneously a socially conditioned entity.

3.2. Person in the Communion of the Spirit

1. According to Ratzinger, the believing person is socialized not only into a concrete Christian church, but in an even more fundamental fashion into an overall ecclesiastical subject, namely, *Christus totus, caput et membra.* (In his own way, Zizioulas advocates the same idea.[133]) One's understanding of person

131. See Farley, *Ecclesial Man,* 157f.
132. See II.1.1.2 and II.2.3 above.
133. See II.2.1.2 above.

must be accommodated to this soteriological-ecclesiological situation, since human beings must be able to be persons within a comprehensive collective subject. To this end, Ratzinger offers the understanding of person as "total relationality," in correspondence to the Augustinian trinitarian concept of person. The person consists completely and totally of its relations, and possesses nothing of its own. Ratzinger is forced to maintain this because the element of "having something of one's own," applied to every individual person, would all too easily become a disruptive factor in the single collective *subject.*

I have already pointed out that, with regard to personhood, Ratzinger does not distinguish sufficiently between the anthropological and soteriological levels. At the anthropological level, he must tacitly accept a kind of personhood not consisting in pure relationality, for which then pure relationality (occurring only in God) "provides the direction."[134] Yet if the person is in fact also something other than its relations, then it can be integrated into the collective subject only through its elimination as a person having something of its own. Although Ratzinger does insist that personhood, rather than being extinguished in the ecclesial subject surrounding it, is actually first established in that subject, nonetheless this "being established" will be more than an empty cipher only if there is a self distinct from these relations that can then be established *in* its ecclesial relations.[135]

My premise is that the person is constituted by God through its multiple relationships to its human and natural surroundings, and that God gives to the person in this act of constitution the capacity for freedom with regard both to God and to its environment. This freedom presupposes that the person constituted and determined by these relations is in fact not identical with those relations, but rather is able to stand over against and relate to its social and natural environment, and that it is able to make something both of its relationships and of itself as a being that stands in such relationships. If this basic anthropological conviction is not to be obviated soteriologically — the equivalent of its soteriological negation — then salvation cannot be conceived as insertion into the collective ecclesial subject, since this presupposes an understanding of person as pure relationality incommensurate with personhood. Instead, if we assume that God's relation to human beings makes possible their capacity to engage in face-to-face encounter with God and with their surroundings, then salvation must consist in human beings living in such a way that this encounter is not one of opposition to God, their fellow human beings, and the rest of creation, but rather one of standing in an affirming communion with them.

The fact that human beings must be liberated from opposition toward God does not negate their character as subjects given with personhood. Just as the

134. Ratzinger, *Dogma,* 213.
135. See I.6 above.

creator God has given them freedom as persons, so also does the savior God redeem them from misusing that freedom without robbing them of it. They do not become pure relations that have divested themselves of their selves (or who were divested of such). That neither the selfhood of human beings nor their juxtaposition to God is negated in the experience of salvation comes clearly into view in one of the New Testament's basic soteriological texts: "Now it is no longer I who live, but it is Christ who lives in me. And the life I now live in the flesh I live by faith in the Son of God" (Gal. 2:20). As this seemingly paradoxical formulation attests, personhood is not reduced to pure relation in the experience of salvation; although it is indeed no longer I who live, Christ does nonetheless live in *me*, and *I* live in faith.[136] The anthropological thesis that the free person is constituted through God's relation to that person finds its soteriological correspondence in paradoxical formulations such as Gal. 2:20. This correspondence is grounded in the fact that the self retains its creaturely continuity in the experience of grace ("Christ lives in me") despite radical discontinuity ("I do not live").[137] That *the same* self must be meant in both statements becomes immediately apparent when one considers that otherwise no human being could experience salvation; that is, ever new, saved human beings would have to be created *ex nihilo*. The death of the sinner and the resurrection of the human being reconciled with God are the death and resurrection of *the same* human being; at issue are the death of the sinner and "*his [or her]* resurrection," as Otfried Hofius correctly formulates.[138]

Ratzinger's notion of pure relationality eliminates the soteriological dialectic between "I" and "not-I"; the "I" dissolves in its relations and becomes the "not-I." Yet it is of decisive anthropological, soteriological, and ecclesiological significance that this dialectic be maintained. To express this dialectic, I would propose the category of *personal interiority*. As we shall see, this category is originally at home in the doctrine of the Trinity, where it describes the mutual indwelling of the divine persons. The one person is internal to the other persons without the persons suspending their personhood.[139] In soteriology, the cate-

---

136. See also Wilckens, *Römer*, II.131f., on Rom. 8:9. The same applies when the Johannine Christ says "my teaching is not mine" (John 7:16). Commensurate with his own doctrine of the Trinity (see I.6.1 above), Ratzinger interprets this statement as follows: "Christ's doctrine is he himself, and he himself is not his own because his own ego exists *completely* from the perspective of the Thou" (*Dogma*, 214; my emphasis). Jesus' statement, however, lives precisely from the fact that the speaking subject or ego is not reduced to pure relationality.

137. Concerning the problem of continuity and discontinuity, see Dabney, *Kenosis*.

138. Hofius, "Sühne," 46 (my emphasis). This continuity must also be implied in Eberhard Jüngel's penetrating analysis of the "dialectic of being and nonbeing," which belongs to the essence of love (*Gott*, 445), if love is to be described as "the ever greater selflessness *in ever so great self-centeredness*" (p. 509, note 11; see also p. 408).

139. See V.3.2.1 below.

gory of personal interiority serves to express a similar situation, namely, that through the Holy Spirit, Christ is internal to Christians as persons without suspending their status as selves. To this one may object that the idea of personal interiority is vague. And indeed, it can be conceptually specified as little as can the idea of person itself,[140] though it can be rendered plausible on the basis of such phenomena as prophecy. The Spirit and the prophet are not simply juxtaposed to one another. When the prophet speaks, *he* is speaking *in the Spirit* (1 Cor. 14:2), or the *Spirit* is speaking *in him* (1 Cor. 12:4-11). Yet even in the act of prophetic proclamation, the Spirit and the prophet do not simply coincide. The one prophet, says Paul, should let the Spirit wait until the other prophet has spoken (1 Cor. 14:26-33).[141] Here we are standing before the unfathomable phenomenon of personal interpenetration.

2. To conceive the sociality of salvation with the aid of the notion of the *whole Christ* as a collective subject is to make an anthropological and soteriological mistake. According to Paul, the resurrected Christ lives in Christians through the Spirit (see Rom. 8:10-11),[142] just as Christians live in Christ and in communion with one another through the Spirit (see 1 Cor. 12:12-13). Neither can it be otherwise, since it is precisely the Spirit who is the first fruits of the eschatological communion between human beings and God and of communion with one another in God's new world (see Rom. 8:23; 2 Cor. 1:22). This is why one must conceive the sociality of the present experience of salvation *pneumatologically.*

Heribert Mühlen has tried to make ecclesiological use of the notion of the Holy Spirit as "one person in many persons."[143] Even though this formula does not adequately describe the personal trinitarian uniqueness of the Spirit,[144] it does nonetheless accurately describe the soteriological-ecclesiological work of the Spirit. Mühlen, unfortunately, wants to ground the personhood of the church with this formula. If one discards this ecclesiologically mistaken (and, within the framework of his trinitarian theology, insupportable[145]) attempt,

---

140. See 1.2.1 above.

141. Similarly also with glossolalia. "*I* will pray with the *spirit,*" Paul writes (1 Cor. 14:15). See in this regard Fee, "Pauline Literature," 666f.; idem, *1 Corinthians,* 670, 696.

142. See Bruce, *Galatians,* 144; Fee, "Pauline Literature," 669.

143. Mühlen, *Una mystica.*

144. Jürgen Moltmann has critically remarked that according to Mühlen, "a binity" actually exists within God, one which "merely appears outwardly as a unity, thus representing a trinity" (Moltmann, *Spirit,* 14).

145. Mühlen argues that if the Father is the divine "I" and the Son the divine "Thou," then the Holy Spirit as the bond of love between the two is the divine "We" in person; the Spirit is "one person in two persons" (*Una mystica,* 197), in such a way that the Spirit is simultaneously in the Father and in the Son "on the basis of its [the Spirit's] *constitution as person*" (Mühlen, *Geist,* 164). In Mühlen's trinitarian model, it is clear how the Spirit as one

then the formula "one person in many persons" does accurately express the two unique dimensions of the Spirit's activity. The Spirit is both the *presence* and the *counterpart*.[146] Because the Spirit is a *person*, the Spirit is a counterpart; because the Spirit is *in* many persons, the Spirit is the presence.

The relation of person and communion in the church derives from the Spirit's status as personal counterpart and personal presence. The Spirit present in Christians is a person different from them, just as they are persons different from the Spirit. This is why the Spirit present in many persons does not make these persons into a collective person, but rather creates a differentiated communion both with and among them. These persons are neither constituted into an undifferentiated multiplicity through the christological event (Zizioulas), nor dissolved into pure relationality (Ratzinger); rather, they exist with one another in the Spirit, and they do so in such a way that they simultaneously stand as counterparts to the Spirit and to one another (even though they are determined both by the Spirit and by one another). They do not, however, within this juxtaposition dissociate into a multiplicity of individuals standing in isolation from one another, since the same Spirit is present *in every* person, and the same Spirit connects them all with one another. In this way, one can derive the unity of the church already from the plurality of its members instead of grounding it in the claim that the church is a single subject, a unity which does not respect the independence of communally determined persons.

The Spirit present in all Christians "opens" each of them to all others. It starts them on the way to creative mutual giving and receiving, in which each grows in his or her own unique way and all have joy in one another.[147] This path issues in common eschatological communion with the triune God. One can enjoy communion with the triune God at the end of this path, however, only because the triune God already stood at its beginning. The Spirit dwelling through faith in the hearts of human beings "himself issues from his fellowship with the Father and the Son, and the fellowship into which he enters with believers corresponds to his fellowship with the Father and the Son and is therefore a *trinitarian fellowship*."[148]

---

person can be in many persons (in Christ and in Christians) and can unite them with one another; it is not clear, however, how the Spirit can constitute several persons in the church into a "greater 'I.' " Within the Trinity, the Spirit does not constitute the Father and the Son as *one* person or as *one* subject, but rather (according to Mühlen) emerges from the Father and the Son and in this way is itself constituted as a person different from the Father and the Son.

146. Jürgen Moltmann has analyzed the unique, externally active personality of the Spirit as "presence and counterpart" (see *Spirit*, 289).

147. See VII.4.2 below.

148. Moltmann, *Spirit*, 218.

Chapter V

Trinity and Church

Today, the thesis that ecclesial communion should correspond to trinitarian communion enjoys the status of an almost self-evident proposition. Yet it is surprising that no one has carefully examined just where such correspondences are to be found, nor expended much effort determining where ecclesial communion reaches the limits of its capacity for such analogy. The result is that reconstructions of these correspondences often say nothing more than the platitude that unity cannot exist without multiplicity nor multiplicity without unity,[1] or they demand of human beings in the church the (allegedly) completely selfless love of God.[2] The former is so vague that no one cares to dispute it, and the latter so divine that no one can live it. We have as yet no detailed examination of the correspondence between Trinity and church, nor can such be presented within the framework of the present chapter. My goal here is only to sketch out the trinitarian foundation of a nonindividualistic Protestant ecclesiology within the framework of a critical discussion with Ratzinger and Zizioulas. The first step must be to reflect on the possibilities and limits of correspondence between the church and the Trinity.

1. Correspondences and Their Limits

"The mystery of the triunity can be found only in the deity itself, not in the creature," says Erik Peterson at the conclusion to his influential essay, "Mono-

---

1. So, e.g., Forte, *Trinität als Geschichte*, 200f.
2. So, e.g., Ratzinger, *Einführung*, 142ff.

theismus als politisches Problem."3 This *theological principle* not only "breaks in a fundamental fashion with every sort of 'political theology,' "4 but also condemns to failure from the outset every attempt at conceiving the church in correspondence to the Trinity. The unity of the creatures can never correspond to the mysterious unity of the triune Creator.5 According to Peterson, however, faith in the Trinity not only fulfills politically the negative function of depriving the worldly monarch of any theological legitimation by denying the existence of a heavenly monarch, it also emphasizes positively that Christians should pursue political engagement "under the presupposition of faith in the triune God." Yet any serious implementation of this *socioethical principle* relativizes precisely the above-mentioned theological principle; that is, although the triune God cannot bestow legitimacy on political power, there must in created reality still be broken creaturely correspondences to this mystery of triunity. Otherwise, the political engagement of Christians under the presupposition of trinitarian faith is reduced to *pure*, sterile criticism.7

Peterson's ambivalence with regard to the relation between the Trinity and created reality is grounded in the character of this relation itself. On the one hand, God's triune nature remains a mystery that human beings can only worship but not imitate. On the other hand, both the entire history of God with the world and the worship of God constituting the answer to this history aim precisely at the indwelling of the triune God in the world. Any reflection on the relation between Trinity and church must take into account both God's uniqueness and the world's purpose in becoming the dwelling of the triune God, which corresponds to this triune God himself.

1.1. Correspondences

1. The trinitarian conception of God as the highest reality has important consequences for the fundamental question of the relation *between the one and the many,* a question that since Parmenides has accompanied philosophical discussion in the West (and for which significant parallels can be found in various cultures and world religions).8 According to the schematic presen-

3. Peterson, "Monotheismus," 105.

4. Ibid.

5. So Peterson, "Monotheismus," 104, following Gregory of Nazianzus.

6. Peterson, "Monotheismus," 47 (prefatory remark).

7. Trinitarian faith does not for this reason mean the end of every political theology (as Peterson seems to be asserting), but rather only of political theology that justifies the dominance of the one over the many (as Peterson, "Monotheismus" [prefatory remark] suggests). See Assmann, *Politische Theologie,* 23ff.; Meier, "Politische Theologie," 15ff.

8. See Copleston, *Religion;* Habermas, *Einheit,* 11-35.

tation by Odo Marquard, two traditions stand opposed in this discussion. The tradition of universalizing philosophies brings to bear "the precedence of the one before the many. . . . Wherever multiplicity rules, we have an unfortunate situation that must be remedied; it must be universalized, totalized, globalized, egalicized, emancipated, revolutionized." By contrast, the tradition of pluralizing philosophies brings to bear "the precedence of the many before the one." The rule of unity — of the one science as well as of the one party — is "an unfortunate situation that must be remedied; it must be detotalized, decentralized, differentiated, pluralized, traditionalized, regionalized, individualized."[9]

To think consistently in trinitarian terms means to escape this dichotomy between universalization and pluralization. If the triune God is *unum multiplex in se ipso* (John Scotus Erigena), if unity and multiplicity are equiprimal in him, then God is the ground of both unity and multiplicity. Only "unity in multiplicity" can claim to correspond to God.[10] Since God is the one God, reality does not, as Aristotle's metaphor suggests, degenerate into individual scenes like a bad play;[11] yet since the one God is a communion of the divine persons, the world drama does not degenerate into a boring monologue. Trinitarian thinking suggests that in a successful world drama, unity and multiplicity must enjoy a complementary relationship.

Even these brief and abstract considerations concerning the one and the many indicate that the way one thinks about God will decisively shape not only ecclesiology, but the entirety of Christian thought.[12] Of course, quite varied accents are still possible within the respective trinitarian positions arguing against the preeminence of either the one or the many. This is why both those more inclined toward pluralization (political theologians,[13] liberation theologians,[14]

---

9. Marquard, "Einheit," 2.

10. See Kern, "Einheit," 207.

11. See Aristotle, *Metaphysics*, 1076a. According to Aristotle, the universe, like any well-organized community, must have only the one ἀρχή, since multiple rule is anarchy: "The rule of many is not good; let one be the ruler"; in this context, Aristotle cites the *Iliad* in agreement (*Metaphysics*, 1076a). See in this regard Schegler, *Metaphysik*, 2.295f. Thomas Hobbes grounded his preference for the monarchical form through reference to the one God who rules the cosmos, in accord with his own modalistic doctrine of the Trinity (see Hobbes, *Leviathan*, 522; cf. in this regard Palaver, *Politik*, 242-73).

12. Jürgen Moltmann, (*Trinity; Schöpfung; Weg; Geist*) and Wolfhart Pannenberg, (*Theology*), each in his own way, have understood all of theology as an explication of the doctrine of the Trinity. See also Ratzinger, *Einführung*, 147; Kasper, *Gott*, 378ff.; Lossky, *Theology*, 65f.

13. See, e.g., Moltmann, *Trinity*.

14. As a liberation theologian, Leonardo Boff (*Gott*) has picked up on Moltmann's trinitarian writings. Concerning the relation between the trinitarian theology of Moltmann and Boff, see O'Donnel, "Trinity," 15ff.

feminist theologians,[15] and theologians of religion[16]) and those more inclined toward universalization (traditional Orthodox and Catholic theologians) can consider themselves bound to *trinitarian* thinking. In the theological discussion itself, however, it is not so much the preeminent significance of the doctrine of the Trinity, with its denial of the dominance of the one or the many, that constitutes the bone of contention for theological and especially ecclesiological thinking, as it is the concrete manifestation of the trinitarian doctrine and the ecclesiological and social consequences that can and should be drawn from it.

One should not, however, *overestimate* the influence of trinitarian thinking on political and ecclesial reality. Thus, for example, the bishops of the fifth century apparently sensed no contradiction between an affirmation of trinitarian faith and the sacralization of the emperor.[17] By contrast, John Smyth, who apparently advocated modalism, cannot be accused of clericalism.[18] This is why one should not expect too much of any reconceptualization of the doctrine of the Trinity, however necessary it may be. It does not seem that the conceptualization process proceeds simply in a straight line from above (Trinity) to below (church and society) and that social reality is shaped in this way.[19] Ecclesial and social reality on the one hand, and trinitarian models on the other are mutually determinative, just as ecclesial and social models and trinitarian models are mutually determinative. Conceiving the church in correspondence to the Trinity does not mean much more than thinking with theological consistency, all the while hoping that reality will not prove to be too recalcitrant. Of course, thinking about the Trinity and about social relations in light of the Trinity must be shaped primarily by the scriptural narrative of the triune God.

2. The correspondence between trinitarian and ecclesial communion derives not just from the formal demand to conceive the relation of the one

15. Thus does Mary Grey view "the intrinsic link between a mutual, relational understanding of personhood and a relational concept of God" ("Core," 369; see also Keller, *Broken Web,* 136). In her own provocative contribution to the doctrine of God, Sallie McFague takes a different position regarding the significance of the Trinity. In her view, the Trinity is "not necessary"; "settling for three" is "a kind of pragmatism" (*Models,* 184). Father, Son, and Spirit (or the feminist designations "Mother," "Lover," and "Friend," which McFague puts in their place) are merely the various *names* of the one God, who does, however, have *many* names; "God has many names" (182). Yet as the title of her book — *Models of God* — already indicates, she ends up in modalism and hence also — against her own intentions — in a relationally impoverished monism.

16. See Pannikar, *Trinity;* Williams, "Trinity"; D'Costa, "Christ"; Schwöbel, "Particularity."

17. See Grillmeier, "Auriga mundi," 402ff.

18. See Smyth, *Works,* 733. See also Yves Congar's remarks concerning the ecclesiological significance of the *filioque* (*Esprit,* 271ff.).

19. According to Zizioulas, ecclesial experience decisively shaped the development of the patristic doctrine of the Trinity (see Zizioulas, *Communion,* 16f.).

and the many analogously on different levels. In substance, the correspondence is grounded in Christian baptism. Through baptism "in the name of the Father, of the Son, and of the Holy Spirit," the Spirit of God leads believers simultaneously into both trinitarian and ecclesial communion. Churches thus do not emerge from baptism simply as images of the triune God fashioned by human beings, but rather as concrete, anticipatory experiences, rendered possible by the Spirit, of the one communion of the triune God and God's glorified people (see 1 John 1:3-4; Rev. 21-22). From this perspective, it is understandable why insight into the trinitarian character of the church was gradually acquired parallel with the growing consciousness of God's triune nature (see 1 Cor. 12:4-6; 2 Cor. 13:13; Eph. 4:4-6), a consciousness grounded in the activity of the Father, the Son, and the Holy Spirit in salvation history and evidenced in New Testament triadic formulae.[20] If Christian initiation is a trinitarian event, then the church must speak of the Trinity as its determining reality.

Because churches, in the power of the Holy Spirit, already form a communion with the triune God, ecclesial correspondence to the Trinity can become an object of hope and thus also a task for human beings. The correspondence between the trinitarian and ecclesial relationships is not simply formal. Rather, it is "ontological" because it is soteriologically grounded.[21] Jesus' high-priestly prayer, that his disciples might become one "as you, Father, are in me and I am in you, may they also be in us" (John 17:21), presupposes communion with the triune God, mediated through faith and baptism, and aims at its eschatological consummation.[22] The already obtaining communion of the church with the triune God, directed at this consummation, implies that the correspondence between Trinity and church is not purely formal and that it involves more than a certain relationship between the one and the many. The relations between the many in the church must reflect the mutual *love* of the divine persons.

The New Testament witness concerning the relation between the Trinity and the church has shaped the ecclesiological traditions of both the East and the West. Thus, for example, the most important teacher in the early Greek church, Origen, writes that the church is full of the holy Trinity.[23] Similarly,

20. Arthur W. Wainwright concludes his examination of the New Testament witness concerning the Trinity with the suggestion that the problem of the Trinity arose "because of the development of Christian experience, worship, and thought . . . . The whole matter was based on the life and resurrection of Jesus himself, who received the Spirit during his earthly life and imparted the Spirit to others after his resurrection" (*Trinity*, 266f.).

21. Alistair MacFadyen has recently come to a similar conclusion; in his view, the Trinity is not merely a social model, but rather "a consequence of God's redemptive and creative relationship with us" ("The Trinity," 14).

22. See Käsemann, *Wille*, 125ff.

23. ". . . ὁ δὲ ἐν τῇ Ἐκκλησίᾳ τυγχάνων τῇ πεπληρωμένῃ τῆς ἁγίας Τριάδος" (Origen, *Selecta in Psalmos, Patrologia graece* 12.1265в). The Orthodox theologian Boris

Cyprian, who decisively influenced the ecclesiology of the West, views the church as *de unitate Patris, et Filii, et Spiritus Sancti, plebs adunata*.[24] The notion of *imago Dei* influenced both ecclesiological traditions, and both of them developed differently commensurate with their different understandings of the Trinity.[25] Still, it seems that only in our own century has a more sustained, conscious reflection on the trinitarian dimension of the church been undertaken. The topic was treated first in the theology of the Eastern church,[26] especially with regard to the ecclesiological consequences of the *filioque*,[27] but was quickly picked up in other Christian traditions as well,[28] and made its way into various ecclesiastical and ecumenical documents.[29]

3. The idea of a correspondence between church and Trinity has remained largely alien to the Free Church tradition.[30] This is to be expected. If one understands the church as a covenant arising insofar as human beings make themselves into a church, as John Smyth suggests, then one cannot understand the church in analogy to the Trinity.[31] Were the divine persons to unite, as do converted Christians, into a fellowship — as the common Free Church ecclesial model has it — one would have not a Trinity, but rather tritheism. For Smyth, the theological grounding of the church is not trinitarian, but rather *christological*. The church is "the kingdom of Christ"; "the regenerate sitt together with Christ Jesus in heauenly places." In communion with Christ, every Christian is a king, just as every Christian is also a priest and a prophet.[32] If personal faith plays a decisive role in the salvific experience, then this exclusive soteriological-

---

Bobrinskoy bases his own studies of the liturgical life of the church on the theological-ecclesiological principle "the church is full of the Trinity" (*Trinité*, 147-97).

24. Cyprian, *Liber de Oratione Dominica*, 23 (*Patrologia latina* 4.553).

25. See Biedermann, "Gotteslehre," 135, 139.

26. See Larentzakis, "Kirchenverständnis," 73.

27. See Congar, *Esprit*, 271ff.

28. For the Catholic tradition, see Mühlen, *Una mystica*; for the Protestant tradition, see Moltmann, *Trinity*, 200-202; Plantinga, "Images," 59ff.

29. For example, in the documents of the Second Vatican Council (*Lumen gentium* 2–4; *Unitatis redintegratio* 2; see in this regard Kasper, "Communio," 65ff.), in the documents of the official dialogue between Catholic and Orthodox churches ("Mysterium"), or in the "Common Declaration of the Study Group of Protestant and Catholic Theologians" ("Erklärung," 120).

30. Though cf. the most recent document (1989) of the Catholic-Pentecostal dialogue "Koinonia," 29.

31. It is probably no accident that Augustus Hopkins Strong does not mention the church in his analysis of the implications of the doctrine of the Trinity, even though he views the Trinity as the model of interpersonal love — "fatherly giving and filial receiving" (*Theology*, 351). In his view, the church arises through human beings constituting themselves into a church (see *Theology*, 902).

32. Smyth, *Works*, 274f., 740.

ecclesiological concentration on Christ can, strictly speaking, ground only the salvation of the individual, but not the ecclesial salvific community itself. Each person stands directly under the dominion of Christ; what *all together* are to be remains unarticulated, emerging rather simply from that which each is to be in and for himself or herself.

My intention here is to make a contribution to the trinitarian reshaping of Free Church ecclesiology. In chapter IV, I presented an understanding of faith as a simultaneous incorporation into both trinitarian and ecclesial communion.[33] This was the initial cornerstone of a trinitarian understanding of the church, since only by already understanding the initiation process itself in a trinitarian fashion, and only by understanding the church as more than just a fellowship based on will can one arrive at the notion that the fellowship of Christians should reflect the trinitarian unity of God. Here I will try to show how those assembled in the name of Christ, even if they number only three, can be an εἰκών ("image") of the Trinity.[34] Although this thesis may seem radical, it is not new. Tertullian, albeit in his Montanist period, already brought into correspondence the ecclesial and trinitarian "three":

> For the Church is itself, properly and principally, the Spirit Himself, in whom there is a Trinity of one divinity, Father, Son and Holy Spirit. He unites in one congregation that Church which the Lord said consists of three persons. And so, from that time on, any number of persons at all, joined in this faith, has been recognized as the Church by Him who founded and consecrated it.[35]

Tertullian's allusion to Matt. 18:20 is unmistakable. It is precisely as the congregation assembling in the name of Christ that the church is an image of the Trinity.[36] I will develop Tertullian's idea here in dialogue with the Catholic and Orthodox traditions. To this end, I will relate John 17:21 ("as you, Father, are in me and I am in you, may they also be in us") to the following ideas: (a) the ecclesiality of the church, building on Matt. 18:20 ("where two or three are gathered in my name, I am there among them"; chapter III above); (b) the mediation of faith, building on Gal. 2:20 ("I live, but it is no longer I who live, but it is Christ who lives in me"; chapter IV above); and (c) the structure of the church, building on 1 Cor. 14:26 ("when you come together, each one has a hymn, a lesson, a revelation . . . "; chapter VI below). I will let the issues coming to expression in each passage mutually inform and interpret the others.

---

33. See IV.2.1.2 and IV.2.2 above.
34. Concerning ecclesiality, see III.2 above.
35. Tertullian, *De pudicitia* 21.
36. See Ratzinger, *Volk*, 75.

Although any consideration of the relationship between the Trinity and the church presupposes a complete doctrine of the Trinity, a comprehensive trinitarian reflection of this sort is not possible within the framework of this chapter. Instead, I will adopt the general features of the social model of trinitarian relations as proposed especially by Jürgen Moltmann[37] (though also by Wolfhart Pannenberg[38]), developing only certain aspects of this model, especially where required by consideration of the correspondence between the Trinity and the church. Before I can examine these correspondences, however, several preliminary methodological remarks are in order concerning the mediations necessary for understanding the church in correspondence to the Trinity. Here I will briefly clarify the limits of the church's ability to image the Trinity, and I will then try to concretize those insights at various points in the analysis of the actual correspondences between the Trinity and the church.

1.2. The Limits of Analogy

1. Although trinitarian ideas can undeniably be converted into ecclesiological ideas, and indeed are so converted, it is equally undeniable that this process of conversion must have its limits, unless one reduces theology to anthropology or, in a reverse fashion, elevates anthropology to theology. The reasons for this are obvious. Our notions of the triune God are not the triune God, even if God is accessible to us only in these notions. A certain doctrine of the Trinity is a model acquired from salvation history and formulated in analogy to our experience,[39] a model with which we seek to approach the mystery of the triune God, not in order to comprehend God completely, but rather in order to worship God as the unfathomable and to imitate God in our own, creaturely way. Trinitarian models bring God to expression in the same way all language about God does, namely, as a God who is revealed anthropomorphically, but who always remains hidden "*in the light of his own being*"[40] because God dwells "in unapproachable light" (1 Tim. 6:16). As Erik Peterson has emphasized, the *mystery* of triunity is indeed found only in the deity itself.

It does not follow from this, however, that "absolutely *nothing can be acquired for practical life* from the doctrine of the Trinity," as Kant believed.[41]

---

37. See esp. his explications in *Trinität*, 145-94; "Einheit"; *Geist*, 303-24.

38. See Pannenberg, *Theology*, 1.259-336; 422-32, and the earlier essays, "Person," "Die Subjektivität," and "Der Gott."

39. Concerning the doctrine of the Trinity as a model, see LaCugna and McDonnell, "Far Country," 202-5.

40. Jüngel, "Geheimnis," 500.

41. Kant, "Streit," 50.

Strictly speaking, we do not have a "concept" of "a God in several persons,"[42] yet the models (*doctrine* of the Trinity) with which we try to circumscribe the triune God can be translated "into practical life," because they describe God through the categories of our own reality, be those categories psychological or social. Through the idea of innerworldly relationships, we bring to expression the relationships between the divine persons. That we genuinely are bringing to expression God rather than merely the world itself derives from the fact that God's self-revelation comes in a this-worldly fashion; for what else could reference to *revelation* mean if not this? The *this-worldly character* of God's self-revelation makes it possible to convert trinitarian ideas into ecclesiological ideas.

The trinitarian models, however, are not simply projections of ideal social models. Insofar as trinitarian models do in fact speak about the triune God who is to be distinguished from human beings, models of the triune God and of the church must also be distinguished. "Person" and "communion" in ecclesiology cannot be identical with "person" and "communion" in the doctrine of the Trinity;[43] they can only be understood as *analogous* to them. If the *doctrine* of the Trinity represents an initial mediation between the self-revelatory triune God and the church, then we also need a second mediation between any given doctrine of the Trinity and ecclesiology. Because God is accessible to *us* only in our own thoughts about God, the absence of this second mediation risks deifying the church or stripping God of the divine nature.

2. The necessity of these two mediations is grounded in the creaturely nature of human beings. Human beings are creations of the triune God and can correspond to God only in a *creaturely* fashion. A third mediation, however, must also be added, one grounded in the difference between the historical and the eschatological being of Christians. The correspondence of ecclesial to trinitarian communion is always lived on the path between baptism, which places human beings into communion with the triune God, and the eschatological new creation in which this communion is completed. Here the correspondence acquires an inner dynamic, moving between the historical minimum and the eschatological maximum. For a *sojourning* church, only a dynamic understanding of its correspondence to the Trinity is meaningful. If the church remains at a statically understood minimum of correspondence to the Trinity, it misses possibilities God has given it along with its being; if by contrast it reaches for a statically understood maximum, it risks missing its historical reality, and

---

42. Ibid.

43. Studer, "Person-Begriff," 177, is even more radical with regard to the concept of person as it was developed dogmatically in the fourth century and then generally adopted: "If one is trying to compare the personal fellowship and personal development of human beings in some fashion with the divine life of the Father, Son, and Spirit, one is best advised not to introduce this concept of person into the equation."

certainly if it claims to realize this maximum, its self-understanding turns into ideology. In none of these three cases would the correspondence of the church to the Trinity do justice to the character of the church as a sojourning people of God. The ecclesiologically relevant question is how the church is to correspond to the Trinity *within history.*

Accordingly, the methodological decision to understand the correspondence of the church to the Trinity not merely "from above" acquires a substantive grounding in addition to the formal one already mentioned. Although the life and structure of the church should correspond to the divine communion, a communion through which the church is constituted and from and toward which it lives, the conditions under which it lives on this side of God's new creation must be considered in order to know *how* the church is to correspond concretely to the divine communion during its actual sojourn toward eschatological consummation. If to these historical limits one also adds the creaturely restrictions of such correspondence between the Trinity and human communities, it follows that the correspondences between church and Trinity can be demonstrated only *after* the development of anthropology, soteriology, and ecclesiology (even though both anthropology and ecclesiology must be developed in the light of trinitarian doctrine).

2. Trinity, Universal Church, and Local Church

According to the familiar schema, the trinitarian theologies of the Christian West and East differ insofar as for the West, the unity of the divine essence is primary, whereas in the East it is the triplicity of the divine persons.[44] This distinction explains the preference of the West for psychological analogies, and of the East for social analogies for the Trinity. Although both Ratzinger and Zizioulas have reflected in an independent fashion on the Trinity, their respective trinitarian theologies nonetheless still fit this schema quite well. In this section, I will take as my point of departure Ratzinger's and Zizioulas's particular understanding of the Western and Eastern trinitarian traditions in order to analyze the ecclesiological correspondences to the relation of the divine persons to the divine essence[45] and then to draw attention to the communion of the divine persons as that aspect of God which lends itself to the construction of analogies.[46] The correspondence between the church and the communion of the divine persons will then be developed in the next two sections.

44. See in this regard Wendebourg, "Person," 503ff.
45. Regarding this aspect of correspondence between Trinity and church, see Biedermann, "Gotteslehre."
46. Moltmann, "Einführung," 17.

1. Although Ratzinger considers the one substance of God and the three divine persons equiprimal, he takes the dominance of unity as his point of departure. Because he locates this unity at the level of substance, the one substance of God must take precedence over the nonaccidentally conceived persons.[47] The relationship between the universal and local church is then determined in analogy to the relationship between substance and person in God, just as the relationship between local churches is also determined in analogy to the relations between the divine persons.[48] The one universal church (the whole) takes precedence over the many local churches. Although all these local churches are churches in the full sense of the word rather than merely incomplete *parts* of the one church, they are such only insofar as they exist from and toward the whole.[49] Within the framework of Ratzinger's thinking, this means that the local church is to be completely transparent for the whole. What Hermenegild Biedermann says about the relationship between trinitarian doctrine and ecclesiology in the Catholic tradition in general, applies to Ratzinger as well: "Just as the unity of the one divine nature and essence as it were 'sustains' the triplicity of persons, so also does a *universal church* as the common foundation 'sustain' the multiplicity of local churches."[50] Local churches are churches precisely in their relation to the whole.

According to Zizioulas, the unity of God is grounded not in the one divine substance, but rather in the person of the Father, which is why the one substance of God does not enjoy ontological priority over the persons. Quite the reverse is actually the case, that is, God's personal mode of existence (the person of the Father) constitutes the divine substance. In this sense, God's being coincides with his personhood, which is always realized in communion; the substance exists *only as persons.*[51] This yields a completely different analogy between the one divine substance and the church than was the case with Ratzinger. Just as in God's own being there is no substance behind the persons, so also in ecclesial being there is no universal church behind the local churches. Every local church *is,* according to Zizioulas, the universal church at a particular place of its concretization. In order to be identical with the universal church, however (and that means in order to be that which it *is* as church), every local church must stand in communion with other local churches. The one universal church enjoys no precedence before the many local churches, but rather exists precisely *as* these churches, and does so as the one and whole

47. See I.6.2 above.
48. See also 3.1.3 below.
49. See I.2 above.
50. Biedermann, "Gotteslehre," 138.
51. See II.1.1 above.

church in each local church that itself stands in communion with other local churches.[52]

2. Understanding the unity of God by way of the one substance of God seems unavoidably to establish the precedence of the one God before the three persons, and thus also to threaten the triunity of God. By contrast, one must insist with Jürgen Moltmann that "the persons themselves constitute both their differences and their unity."[53] This presupposes that the divinity of the one God does not precede the divine persons, but rather exists concretely as three persons.[54] If this is the case, then God's being coincides with the communion of the three divine persons, something Zizioulas has rightly emphasized, even though the ecclesiological conclusions he draws from this are not fully persuasive.

Although at first glance Zizioulas seems to be correct in maintaining that the coincidence of person and substance in God corresponds to the simultaneity of universal and local church, this raises considerable ecclesiological and trinitarian concerns. One important ecclesiological argument militates against the simultaneity of the universal and local church, namely, that these local churches are not the variously concrete modes of existence of the universal church, but rather are *historical* anticipations of the eschatological gathering of the entire people of God.[55] They are not identical with the universal church in the sense of the church of all ages; rather, these local churches are superordinate to the *existing* "universal church." The universal church arises *by way of* the local churches, just as the local churches themselves arise through the pneumatic anticipatory connection to the yet outstanding gathering of the whole eschatological people of God, that is, to the *eschatological* universal church, if one will. By contrast, the common divine nature arises not by way of the "collection" of the divine persons, but rather is identical with the latter, which is why the relation "divine nature — divine persons" cannot correspond to the relation "universal church — local church." What is capable of such correspondence, however, are the relationships between the divine persons and those between local churches.

The correspondences "divine nature — universal church" and "divine persons — local churches" are similarly to be rejected for trinitarian reasons. If the universal church is to correspond to the divine nature, and if at the same time every local church is to be identical with the one universal church, the three

52. See II.3.2.3 above. Cf. Biedermann, "Gotteslehre," 134 (regarding the general Orthodox understanding of the correspondence of Trinity and church): "just as in the triunity the one divine essence does not signify a 'more' over against the persons," so also is "the universal church to be understood less as the 'comprehensive one' . . . than as the 'multiple-unity.'"

53. Moltmann, *Trinity*, 175.

54. So Staniloae, *Dogmatik*, 1.267.

55. See III.2.2 above.

divine persons must possess the one, numerically identical divine nature, something both the Eastern and the Western traditions do as a rule maintain.[56] In that case, however, one must either assume that the one divine nature exists in addition to the divine persons and is concretized differently in each person, or one is forced into the awkward position of deciding how to distinguish between the persons, each of which is allegedly identical with the one numerically identical divine nature. For this reason, it is advisable to dispense entirely with the one numerically identical divine nature and instead to conceive the unity of God *perichoretically*.[57] That is, each divine persons stands in relation not only to the other persons, but is also as a personal center of action internal to the other persons.[58] In order to speak at the supralocal level of a correspondence between Trinity and church, one must for trinitarian reasons take as point of departure not the relationship "divine nature — divine persons," but rather the relations between the divine persons as such. Just *how* relations between the local churches are to be conceived in analogy to trinitarian relations will be examined more closely later.[59]

3. The distinction between universal and local church involves only the church that finds itself on the way to its eschatological future. When in the eschaton the whole people of God is assembled in the unity of the triune God, this distinction will be eliminated, and human beings will live in perfect communion with the triune God and will reflect the communion of the triune God in their own mutual relationships. Because every local church is a concrete anticipation of this eschatological community, it is decisive that one understand and live the *relationships within* a given local church in correspondence to the Trinity. Whereas these relationships are eschatologically abiding, those between local churches as local churches are merely historically determined and accordingly transient. The Trinity indwells in the local churches in no other way than through its presence within the persons constituting those churches, since the church *is* those who gather in the name of Christ.[60] This is why although *inter*ecclesial correspondence to the Trinity is important, it can nonetheless be conceived only in analogy to the pivotal *intra*ecclesial correspondence to the Trinity.

Can the relationship "divine nature — divine persons" have significance for relations within a local church? If one presupposes the one, numerically identical divine nature (which, as we have already seen, is to be rejected), then

---

56. This does not, however, seem to have been the Nicene doctrine (see Kelly, *Doctrines*, 234ff.).

57. So, e.g., Moltmann, *Trinity*, 174ff.; idem, "Einheit," 124ff.; Siebel, *Geist*, 25ff., 87ff.

58. See 3.2 below.

59. See 3.1.3 and 3.2.4 below.

60. See III.2.1.1 above and 3.2.4 below.

the relations within the church can no more be understood in correspondence to the relationship "divine nature — divine persons" than relations between churches can. For within interpersonal relations there is nothing that might correspond to the numerically identical divine nature, unless one were to conceive the unity of humankind anthropologically as the unity of the one human nature and to assert (as does Ratzinger) that all human beings constitute "one single human being" destined to become one single human being in Christ.[61] Although this particular notion has enjoyed a venerable history,[62] it is both anthropologically and ecclesiologically unacceptable.[63] For both trinitarian and ecclesiological reasons, the one numerically identical divine nature can play no role in the analogy between the Trinity and the church. As with relations between local churches, one must also understand those within any given local church in correspondence to the *communion of the divine persons.*

3. Trinitarian Persons and the Church

Although one cannot separate the trinitarian persons and relations, one must distinguish between them. Hence I will examine first the correspondences between the character of the trinitarian persons — their relationality and their mutual interpenetration — on the one hand, and that of ecclesial persons and local churches on the other. In the following section, I will then inquire what significance the processions and structure of the divine relations possess for structuring ecclesial relations.

3.1. Relational Personhood

1. Ratzinger defines trinitarian personhood as *pure* relationality; *persona est relatio.* This understanding of the trinitarian persons has two important consequences. First, the persons become so transparent that it is difficult to distinguish them from the one, sustaining divine substance.[64] The consequence is not only that the one substance gains the upper hand over the three persons, but also that the three persons actually become redundant. If behind the actions of the divine persons there is no "I" of these persons, then the three persons

---

61. Ratzinger, "Wurzel," 223.

62. See, e.g., Gregory of Nyssa, *Quod non sint tres dii* (*Patrologia graeca* 45.117ff.).

63. See III.2.1.3 and IV.3 above.

64. See I.6 above. Similarly also Gunton, *Promise,* 42, in his analysis of Augustine's doctrine of the Trinity.

65. LaCugna, *God,* 99.

are superfluous in the economy of salvation, and "the Triune God's relationship to us is . . . unitary," as Catherine LaCugna correctly maintains with regard to Augustine's doctrine of the Trinity.[65] Second, the persons seem to dissolve into relations; the Father becomes fatherhood; the Son, sonship; and the Spirit, procession. Understood in this way, these persons are not only superfluous but also incapable of action. Pure relations — the "act of begetting," the activity of being begotten, and that of procession — can no more act in salvation history than they can be petitioned in prayer or praised in worship.[66]

To do justice to the salvation history from which knowledge of the Trinity is actually acquired, one must conceive the trinitarian persons *as subjects*. God's external works are not to be attributed to the one undifferentiated divine essence, but rather proceed from the divine persons. Accordingly, personhood cannot be conceived as pure relation, any more than relation can be conceived merely as a manifestation of personhood. Rather, person and relation emerge simultaneously and mutually presuppose one another. This is one of the basic insights in Jürgen Moltmann's doctrine of the Trinity: "Here there are no persons without relations; but there are no relations without persons either. Person and relation are complementary."[67] The divine persons are constituted through *generatio* and *spiratio* as subjects who, though different, are mutually related from the outset and are inconceivable without these relations; furthermore, they manifest their own personhood and affirm that of other persons through their mutual relations of giving and receiving.[68]

2. In strict correspondence to the trinitarian persons, Ratzinger tries to conceive human persons as pure relations as well. Although this understanding of personhood is ultimately unpersuasive with regard to the divine persons, it can still exhibit a certain degree of plausibility if one understands divine being

66. So Moltmann, "Einheit," 123f. Walter Kasper, *Gott*, 351, shares this opinion. From the fact that one "cannot petition, worship, and glorify" (p. 351) the relations or the distinct modes of subsistence, however, he concludes only that one should maintain the concept of persons, but not that one cannot really understand personhood as pure relation in the first place. This, however, merely conceals linguistically rather than eliminates the theological difficulties with persons as "pure relations." When one worships, one only acts "as if" the Father, Son, and Spirit are persons — at least this is what those do who understand what they are doing in worshiping God. Following Ratzinger's dialogical understanding of the Trinity, Kasper defines the three divine persons as "pure self-articulation," "pure hearing," and "pure reception" (p. 353; see also pp. 375f.), albeit without, like Ratzinger (see *Einführung*, 144), expressly denying that the Father is "the one speaking," the Son "the one corresponding in obedience," and the Holy Spirit "the one purely receiving" (p. 353). Kasper does not, however, explain how "the *pure* self-articulation" can simultaneously be "the one speaking." Ratzinger is more consistent in this regard.

67. Moltmann, *Trinity*, 172 [final sentence not included in English translation — translator's note].

68. See 4.2 below.

as pure actuality.[69] With regard to human persons, however, it is wholly inappropriate. It is true that for Ratzinger the notion of "pure relation" is the soteriological-eschatological goal of the human person rather than its anthropological definition. In reality, the human person is not simply identical with its relations; rather, these are "something extra added to the person."[70] Yet precisely this is what the experience of salvation is to overcome. With regard to Christ, a believer is "pure relation," just as with regard to the Father, Christ is "pure relation." Although the "most absolute [sic] unity" results from this,[71] for just that reason the human persons together with the divine persons dissolve into the one undifferentiated substance of God. Although this is admittedly not Ratzinger's intention, it is the consequence of his concept of person.

If one understands trinitarian persons and relations as complementary, it is possible to conceive ecclesial personhood in correspondence to trinitarian personhood. Here I will address only the relationality of the divine and ecclesial persons, and will discuss their subjectivity in the context of a consideration of the structure of trinitarian and ecclesial relations.[72] Like the divine persons, so also ecclesial persons cannot live in isolation from one another; Christians are constituted as independently believing persons through their relations to other Christians, and they manifest and affirm their own ecclesial personhood in mutual giving and receiving (see Phil. 4:15). Within the context of the complementary nature of person and relation, the structure of personal life can indeed be described accurately with Ratzinger's notion of "being from and toward," though this "being" is now no longer "pure, [and] unreserved."[73] A Christian lives from and toward others.

Although the relations of the ecclesial and trinitarian persons correspond, a distinction does remain between the two. I am not referring to the fact that human beings remain persons even if they live isolated from one another, whereas the trinitarian persons are inconceivable without the most intimate of communion. Human beings can live *as human beings* in isolation from or even in hatred toward one another (even though in reality they always become human beings through others and remain related to others even in hatred, indeed, even in indifference). This derives from their being constituted as human beings through *God's relation* to them by way of their relations to their environment, rather than through *their* relation either to God or to their environment. [74] *As Christians*, however, human beings cannot live apart from

---

69. So Siebel, *Geist*, 14.
70. Ratzinger, *Introduction*, 131; cf. Ratzinger, "Personenverständnis," 213.
71. Ratzinger, *Introduction*, 135.
72. See section 4 below.
73. Ratzinger, *Introduction*, 134.
74. See in this regard Pannenberg, *Theology*, 1.431.

fellowship with other Christians. Salvation has an indispensable ecclesial structure,[75] and in this sense relations between trinitarian and ecclesial persons do correspond.

Yet the difference between the two remains. It consists, first, in the fact that human beings, though determined by one another, *are* not simply communion, as is the Trinity, but rather must always be held together by an implicit or explicit covenant. Because of the creaturely nature of human beings, ecclesial communion is always a communion of the will (even if their ecclesial being and their ecclesial will are mutually determinative).[76] This applies in an important sense to the eschatological people of God as well. To be sure, the communion of this people is final; its past being would, as Karl Marx said of communism, contradict the pretension of its essence;[77] and the possible end of this communion will not even appear on the horizon of the consciousness of those who are redeemed in this ultimate fashion. Yet the finality of this communion is *bestowed,* and for that reason it presupposes the possibility of its nonbeing, nonbeing which in reality will never occur.

Second, ecclesial communion on this side of God's new creation can correspond to the perfect mutual love of the trinitarian persons only in a broken fashion. The church's fellowship is always in transit between the historical minimum and the eschatological maximum of the correspondence to the love in which the trinitarian persons live. The minimum consists in "being from others" and "being together with others," for only a *communion* of persons can correspond to the Trinity. The maximum consists in perfect "being toward others," in the love in which they give of themselves to one another and thereby affirm one another and themselves.

3. Ratzinger defines relations between (local) churches in analogy to the pure relationality of the Trinity. Only when churches have given up all "holding onto one's own" can the "coalescence into unity" come about.[78] This corresponds exactly to the analogy "universal church — divine substance" and "local church — divine person."[79] Such a union, emerging from *pure* relationality, results, however, in a dissolution of the respective individual identities of the various local churches. If one starts with the complementary nature of person and relation, then not only do ecclesial persons, but also ecclesial communities appear as independent and yet mutually related entities affirming one another in mutual giving and receiving (see Rom. 15:26f.; 2 Cor. 8:14).

---

75. See IV.2 above.
76. See IV.2.2.2 above.
77. See *Marx Engels Werke Ergänzungsband*, 1.536.
78. Ratzinger, *Introduction*, 135.
79. See 2.1 above.

But are local churches necessarily characterized by being "from" and "toward" as required by correspondence to the Trinity? I think not. Nor is Ratzinger able to apply this structure of communality consistently to the relations of local churches. Although an alliance in love is indeed desirable between local churches, it is *not an absolute condition* of ecclesiality, unless one were to understand love objectively, as Ratzinger does, following Augustine, as "standing in" the eucharistic communion; this results, however, in an elimination of the aspect of love involving "being toward others." Ratzinger himself uses the word *love* equivocally. In a trinitarian and maximal-ecclesiological sense, it refers to the "from/toward" structure; in a minimal-ecclesiological sense, however, it refers to the "from/with" structure. This reflects the position of Catholic tradition, which asserts that only "being from others" and "being together with others, " but not "being toward others," is indispensable for ecclesiality. The sojourning church corresponds only partially to the Trinity.

The question arises, however, whether actual "being with others" is indispensable for the *minimum* of correspondence between Trinity and church. It is true that a local church, even as a fellowship of mutual giving and receiving, could not correspond to the Trinity if it intentionally separated itself from other churches and did not seek communion with those churches; for the Trinity is precisely an open and inviting communion. If a church is open to other churches, however, it already corresponds partially to the triune God, just as by seeking communion with other churches it corresponds to the eschatological gathering of the entire people of God in communion with the triune God, and in so doing is actually a church in the first place.[80] Hence the minimum of interecclesial correspondence to the Trinity seems to consist not in actual "being with all others," but rather in "being from others" and "*seeking* to be toward all others."[81]

3.2. Perichoretic Personhood

1. In their mutual giving and receiving, the trinitarian persons are not only interdependent, but also *mutually internal,* something to which the Johannine Jesus repeatedly refers: "so that you may know and understand that the Father is in me and I am in the Father" (John 10:38; cf. 14:10-11; 17:21). This mutually internal abiding and interpenetration of the trinitarian persons, which since Pseudo-Cyril has been called περιχώρησις,[82] determines the character both of the divine persons and of their unity.

80. See III.3.2 above and VII.2 below.
81. Concerning the relations between churches, see III.3.2 above and 3.2.4 below.
82. See Prestige, *God,* 296.

Perichoresis refers to the reciprocal *interiority* of the trinitarian persons.[83] In every divine person as a subject, the other persons also indwell; all mutually permeate one another, though in so doing they do not cease to be distinct persons. In fact, the distinctions between them are precisely the presupposition of that interiority, since persons who have dissolved into one another cannot exist in one another. Perichoresis is "co-inherence in one another without any coalescence or commixture."[84] This is why both statements can be made: "Father and Son are in one another," and "Christians are in *them*" ("in *us*" — plural!; John 17:21). Being in one another does not abolish trinitarian plurality; yet despite the abiding distinction between the persons, their subjectivities do overlap. Each divine person acts as subject, and at the same time the other persons act as subjects in it, which is why the Johannine Jesus can formulate paradoxically: ἡ ἐμὴ διδαχὴ οὐκ ἔστιν ἐμὴ ("My teaching is not mine," John 7:16). This statement acquires its full theological weight only if one does not resolve the tension between "mine" and "not mine" on one side or the other, but rather emphasizes both equally. Within personal interiority, "mine" is simultaneously "not mine" without ceasing to be "mine," just as "not mine" is simultaneously "mine" without ceasing to be "not mine."

From the interiority of the divine persons, there emerges what I would like to call their *catholicity*. "The Father is in me and I am in him" (John 10:38) implies that "whoever has seen me has seen the Father" (John 14:9-10). The one divine person is not only itself, but rather carries within itself also the other divine persons,[85] and only in this indwelling of the other persons within it is it the person it really is. The Son is Son only insofar as the Father and the Spirit indwell him; without this interiority of the Father and the Spirit, there would be no Son. The same applies to the Father and to the Spirit. In a certain sense, each divine person *is* the other persons, though is such in its own way, which is why rather than ceasing to be a unique person, in its very uniqueness it is a

83. So Staniloae, "Relations," 38.

84. Prestige, *God*, 298. The objection immediately seems to arise that the notion of "co-inherence without coalescence" is just as difficult to conceive as is the idea criticized above regarding personhood as pure relationality. It is important to note, however, that the respective points of departure are different. Perichoresis starts with persons who are then to be conceived as distinct persons in their mutual interiority; the understanding of person as pure relationality starts with relations which must then "harden" into persons. The idea of perichoresis starts with the story of revelation (Father, Son, and Spirit as acting and speaking persons), and then admittedly leads into what comes close to being a conceptual labyrinth; the idea of pure relationality, by contrast, must proceed first through the conceptual labyrinth in order to arrive at the story of revelation in the first place. As already seen above (see IV.3.2.1), the idea of perichoresis also acquires a certain degree of plausibility if one considers such religious phenomena as prophetic speech from a strictly phenomenological standpoint. The prophet and the Spirit are *both* — each in a different way — subjects of the prophetic message (though prophecy admittedly involves a one-sided rather than a mutual personal interiority).

85. Similarly Staniloae, *Dogmatik*, 1.275.

completely *catholic* divine person. Of course, the catholicity of the divine persons is also open for creation and its history, and consists not only in this mutual interiority, but also in all creation "being in God." Only thus can God — and each of the three divine persons — "be all in all" (1 Cor. 15:28).

This reciprocal interiority of the divine persons determines the character of their unity. The notion of perichoresis offers the possibility of overcoming the alternatives *unio personae — unitas substantiae*.[86] The unity of the triune God is grounded neither in the numerically identical substance nor in the accidental intentions of the persons, but rather in their *mutually interior being*.[87] "By the power of their eternal love, the divine persons exist so intimately with, for, and in one another that they themselves constitute themselves in their unique, incomparable and complete union."[88] The unity of the divine essence is the obverse of the interiority and catholicity of the divine persons.

2. In a strict sense, there can be no correspondence to the interiority of the divine persons at the human level.[89] Another human self cannot be internal

86. See Hilary of Poitiers, *De trinitate* 4.42: "*Unum sunt, non unione personae sed substantiae unitate*" (*Patrologia latina* 10.128).

87. It is often assumed that perichoresis and the oneness of the divine substance are two complementary ways of conceiving the unity of God. Perichoresis is "the exact reverse of the identity of ousia," writes G. L. Prestige (*God,* 298). No less a thinker than John of Damascus juxtaposes the two ideas, asserting that God is one (among other things) διὰ δὲ τοῦ ὁμοουσίου, καὶ τοῦ ἐν ἀλλήλαις εἶναι τὰς ὑποστάσεις (*De fide,* I, VIII, *Patrologia graeca* 825f.). It is questionable, however, whether the two ideas are compatible. If one presupposes the one numerically identical substance of God, then the only content of the divine persons consists in their relations of origin. The Father, for example, has everything in common with the Son except being begotten. The persons are nothing more than the ἀγεννησία, γέννησις, and ἐκπόρευσις, and are such as "ways in which the one indivisible divine substance distributes and presents Itself" (Kelly, *Doctrines,* 266). If under the presupposition of the unity of the divine substance one wishes to speak of the coinherence of persons, then one must assert that the ἀγεννησία is in γέννησις, which is obviously nonsense. Although the Father can be in the Son (see note 84 above) — at least according to the Johannine Jesus — Fatherhood cannot be in Sonship. The coinherence of persons can come about only if the persons, while essentially standing in relations, nevertheless are not identical with those relations. This, however, presupposes that one abandons the numerical identity of the divine substance.

88. Moltmann, "Einheit," 124. See idem, *Trinity,* 174f. When O'Donnell writes that the "union which Moltmann describes is only a moral union" ("Trinity," 21), he overlooks precisely the decisive point, namely, that the divine persons *are* in one another. While this being in one another does presuppose the constitution of the persons (see Wendebourge, "Person," 508, note 35), the persons are constituted as being mutually internal to one another; they do not only later become mutually internal to one another.

89. Contra Harrison, "Perichoresis," 65. Siebel speaks "of two persons in the third person." Yet because this third person can be only a "moral" rather than a "natural" person, he must seek refuge in a "quasi-person" (*Geist,* 48f.), thereby underscoring for all practical purposes the impossibility of personal interiority at the human level.

to my own self as subject of action. Human persons are always external to one another *as subjects.* One might at most adduce the experience of mutual love as proof to the contrary; yet despite all the selflessness of love, it is not the beloved Thou who is the subject of love within the loving self, but rather the loving self itself, even if the love of the self is kindled only on the beloved Thou in the first place.[90] A self in this sense, one that through love has become self-less, is indeed a self that can embrace or "enter empathetically" into the other, but it is not a self that can indwell as a self that other.[91] The indwelling of other persons is an exclusive prerogative of God.

But even the divine persons indwell human beings in a qualitatively different way than they do one another. This is evident already from the fact that the interiority of the divine persons is strictly reciprocal, which is not the case in the relation between God and human beings. To be sure, it is not only the Spirit, and together with the Spirit also the Son and the Father, that is in human beings; human beings are also in the Spirit (see Rom. 8:9).[92] They are not, however, internal to the Spirit as subject; otherwise, they would also be the subjects of the Spirit's actions just as the Spirit is the subject of theirs; the Spirit does, after all, "blow where it chooses." If human beings were *personally* interior to the Spirit in the same way the Spirit is personally interior to human beings, the conclusion "the wind blows where it chooses . . . *so* it is with everyone who is born of the Spirit" (John 3:8) would be reversible. But it is not. This personal interiority is one-sided. The Spirit indwells human persons, whereas human beings by contrast indwell *the life-giving ambience of the Spirit,* not the person of the Spirit.

At the ecclesial level (and at the creaturely level in the broader sense), only the *interiority of personal characteristics* can correspond to the interiority of the divine persons. In personal encounters, that which the other person is flows consciously or unconsciously into that which I am. The reverse is also true. In this mutual giving and receiving, we give to others not only something, but also a piece of ourselves, something of that which we have made of ourselves in communion with others; and from others we take not only something, but also a piece of them. Each person gives of himself of herself to others, and each person in a unique way takes up others into himself or herself. This is the process of the mutual internalization of personal characteristics occurring in the church

90. Eberhard Jüngel, *Gott,* 430ff., has persuasively demonstrated that love is not *pure* selflessness.

91. Even a relation as close as that of pregnancy does not involve the phenomenon of personal interiority. Although the child is a person (in the theological sense), it has as yet no subjectivity, and exists not in the self of the mother, but rather in her body (which she admittedly not only possesses, but rather *is* as well).

92. Concerning the presence of the Son in human beings and of human beings in the Son, see John 6:56; 14:20.

through the Holy Spirit indwelling Christians. The Spirit opens them to one another and allows them to become *catholic persons* in their uniqueness. It is here that they, in a creaturely way, correspond to the catholicity of the divine persons. This catholicity of Christians, however, cannot be limited ecclesially. That is, a catholic person involves the internalization not only of that person's Christian siblings and friends, but also of the person's *entire* "environment" — of the Creator as well as of every creature. Every person is a catholic person insofar as that person reflects in himself or herself in a unique way the entire, complex reality in which the person lives.[93]

3. The mutual giving and receiving presupposes an already existing connection of some sort, however rudimentary. If I am utterly isolated from others, I can neither give nor receive anything from them. This is why the communion of persons precedes their catholicity (just as the interiority of persons precedes their full unity). Because human persons cannot be internal to one another as subjects, their unity cannot be conceived in a strictly perichoretic fashion, as is often suggested.[94] Does this not make the (local) church, quite differently than the Trinity, into a subsequent union of Christians? Does not precisely the correspondence between the unity of the church and the unity of the triune God require the mutual interiority of human persons, and does not the New Testament also conceive unity by way of the mutual interiority of persons? Thus does Jesus in John 17:21 request "that they may all be one, *as* you, Father, are in me and I am in you." Yet already for *theological* reasons, this "as" (καθώς) may not be interpreted in the sense of identity, but rather must be interpreted in the sense of similarity.[95] In that case, however, human perichoretic unity does not necessarily follow from divine perichoretic unity; one must ask rather in what the comparison between divine and human unity consists. This theological consideration is confirmed exegetically insofar as the statement "as you, Father, are in me and I am in you" is continued not by "may they also be *in one another,*" but rather by "may they also be *in us.*" Human beings can be in

93. According to the anthropology of Catherine Keller, "*everything* in some way is *really* part of me" (*Broken Web,* 184, first emphasis mine). Differently than my own explications, however, her feminist theological anthropology stands in the tradition of the process philosophy of Alfred North Whitehead, who within the framework of his own metaphysics tried to show that "every actual entity" is in "every other actual entity" (*Process,* 92f.; see in this regard, Welker, *Universalität,* 80ff.).

94. So, e.g., Kasper, *Gott,* 346; Plantinga, "Images," 62f. As the parallel in 1 Chron. 12:39 suggests, the proverbial expression "one heart and soul" (Acts 4:32) is not to be interpreted in the sense of an interiority of persons, even though "heart" does refer to the personal center of a human being. See also Aristotle, *Ethics* 1168b, where μία ψυχή ("one soul") appears in the context of the ethics of friendship.

95. Bultmann, *John,* 513. So also Lightfoot, *John,* 299, who renders καθώς as "resemble."

the triune God only insofar as the Son is in them (John 17:23; 14:20); and if the Son is in them, then so also is the love with which the Father loves the Son (John 17:26). Because the Son indwells human beings through the Spirit, however, *the unity of the church is grounded in the interiority of the Spirit* — and with the Spirit also in the interiority of the other divine persons — *in Christians.* The Holy Spirit is the "one person *in* many persons."[96] It is not the mutual perichoresis of human beings, but rather the indwelling of the Spirit common to everyone that makes the church into a communion corresponding to the Trinity, a communion in which personhood and sociality are equiprimal. Just as God constitutes human beings through their social and natural relations as independent persons, so also does the Holy Spirit indwelling them constitute them through ecclesial relations as an intimate communion of independent persons.[97] As such, they correspond to the unity of the triune God, and as such they are instantiations of *the one* church.

4. If human persons cannot be internal to one another, then churches as fellowships of persons can be such even less. Accordingly, the divine perichoresis cannot serve as a model of *inter*ecclesial unity. Nor are churches subjects that the Holy Spirit might indwell apart from the Spirit's indwelling the hearts of those of whom the church consists.[98] Hence in the Holy Spirit the churches are related to one another not so much insofar as those churches are collective subjects, but rather insofar as the *people* of whom they consist stand in some relation, be they laity or officeholders. In modern societies, this takes place not only directly, in personal encounter, but also through mediating institutions and mechanisms of interaction.

Nevertheless, the perichoresis of the divine persons also possesses interecclesial relevance. Here, the correspondence between Trinity and church builds on the *catholicity* of the divine persons. Like individual persons, so also do entire communities have their specific identifying characteristics, acquired either by way of the cultural context in which they abide or through exceptional personalities active among them; they now transmit these characteristics to other churches. By opening up to one another both diachronically and synchronically, local churches should enrich one another, thereby increasingly becoming catholic churches. In this way, they will also increasingly correspond to the catholicity of the triune God, who has already constituted them as catholic churches, because they *are* anticipations of the eschatological gathering of the entire people of God.[99]

96. Mühlen, *Una mystica.* See IV.3.2.2 above.
97. See IV.3.2 above.
98. See IV.2.1.3 above.
99. See VII below.

4. The Structure of Trinitarian and Ecclesial Relations

The relations between the persons and their personal interiority logically presuppose the "generation" of the Son and the "procession" of the Spirit, since only persons who are already constituted can relate to one another and exist in one another. In discussion of the Trinity, the structure of trinitarian relations has been consistently determined by the notions of generation and procession. Here I will examine in what sense generation and procession structure trinitarian relations, and I will inquire concerning which particular aspect of the Trinity ought to be reflected in ecclesial structures.

1. As I have tried to show, although Ratzinger conceives relations within the church in a trinitarian fashion, he conceives the structure of the church monistically. The paradox is only apparent. Because the persons are "pure relations," God can act externally only as the one undifferentiated divine being, that is, as *one* "person."[100] This one divine nature acting externally corresponds to the one church that together with Christ constitutes one subject and thus itself becomes capable of action. Hence for both the Trinity and for the church, the "one" is structurally decisive: the one divine Nature, the one Christ, the one Pope, and the one bishop. This in its own turn corresponds to the filioquistic linear doctrine of the Trinity; the Spirit is the third who proceeds from the Son and who accordingly within the economy of salvation cannot determine the Son. This is why although the Spirit can indeed vivify the structures of the church, the Spirit can hardly determine their form.

The strictly hierarchical structure of the church derives from the systemic dominance of the one and from the precedence of the whole. Because only the one can ensure the unity of the totality, the Pope must rank above the bishop, just as the bishop must rank above the congregation. Although their power, in analogy to the divine "pure relationality," is theoretically always purely "vicarial power" (it is Christ who acts through them), concretely it is always realized as personal power, at least on this side of God's new creation. If one conceives the relations of ecclesial persons in analogy to the pure trinitarian relations, the many of necessity remain defenselessly subject to this personal power of the one. Personal rights cannot be derived from this understanding of persons as "pure relation." This concept of person erroneously presupposes realized eschatology and is unable to do justice structurally to the abuse of power. Because persons understood in this way are also embedded in a monistic hierarchical structure of relations, the understanding of person as pure relation can easily degenerate into repressive ideology.[101]

---

100. This is the implication of Augustine's doctrine of the Trinity (see Hill, *God*, 61; cf. Studer, "Person-Begriff," 174).

101. See I.6.2 above.

Zizioulas conceives the structure of ecclesial relations in a consistently trinitarian fashion. He does so on the basis of a nonfilioquistic trinitarian theology that accords primacy to the person of the Father. The relations between the one and the many are reciprocal. Just as the Father constitutes the Son and the Spirit and is simultaneously conditioned by them, so does Christ constitute the church and is simultaneously conditioned by it in the Spirit, and so also does the bishop as the image of Christ constitute the ecclesial community and is conditioned by that community as a pneumatic entity.

For Zizioulas, however, this reciprocal relation between the one and the many is asymmetrical. The Father constitutes the Son and the Spirit, while the Son and the Spirit only *condition* the Father; Christ constitutes the church, while the church only *conditions* Christ. Accordingly, the bishop constitutes the church, but is only *conditioned* by the church. The monarchy of the Father and the subordination of the Son and the Spirit ("a kind of subordination," Zizioulas writes[102]) are reflected not only in the dominion of Christ over the church, but also in the hierarchical relations within the church itself. Like the trinitarian person, so also is the ecclesial person inconceivable without hierarchy.[103] The function of the *ordo* of laypersons is exclusively responsorial; they follow the bishop acting *in persona Christi* and speak the liturgical Amen. Moreover, Zizioulas understands the *ordo* of laypersons as an undifferentiated unity; all have the same liturgical function. Laypersons are thus placed into a hierarchically structured bipolarity of the one and the many in which they not only remain subordinated as a whole, but are also virtually insignificant as individuals.[104]

2. I have argued that we should conceive the trinitarian persons and relations as complementary, and I have defined the trinitarian persons as perichoretic subjects. Father, Son, and Spirit are, as Wolfhart Pannenberg formulates it, not "different modes of being of the one divine subject," but rather "living realizations of separate centers of action."[105] Accordingly, God also cannot act externally as the one tripersonal divine self, but rather only as a communion of the different persons existing within one another. But how are the relations of the divine persons as subjects structured?

Trinitarian theology usually identifies the processions with relations,

102. Zizioulas, *Communion*, 89.

103. See Zizioulas, "Die pneumatologische Dimension," 141. At least to me as an outsider, Zizioulas's unrestricted affirmation of hierarchy seems to correspond more to Orthodox ecclesial reality than does the polemic against subordination in the church (directed esp. against Catholic ecclesiology) to which some Orthodox theologians are inclined (see Harkianakis, "Petrusdienst," 285).

104. See II above.

105. Pannenberg, *Theology*, 1.319. A different view is taken by Heribert Mühlen, who assumes only "a single personal center of action in the deity" (*Geist*, 166).

something that can occur in a twofold fashion. Either the relations dissolve into processions, or the processions are understood as mutual relations. In the first case, the result is unilinear hierarchical relations between the divine persons; the Father begets the Son and spirates (together with the Son?) the Spirit, and sends the Son and (with him?) the Spirit. The Father alone is engaged in giving, and any retroactivity of the Son and Spirit on the Father appears as an anomaly. In the second case, the divine persons dissolve into a common divine nature; all the persons mutually constitute and are conditioned by one another, and for that reason none can be distinguished from the others,[106] unless following Hegel one completely equates the immanent and economic Trinity and from the outset understands the Son as the incarnate divine person and the Spirit as the person who brings the world to God.[107]

The one constituting and the one constituted, however, are to be distinguished both conceptually and substantively from the constitutive process itself.[108] This is why one must distinguish between the constitution of the persons and their relations. The Son and the Spirit are constituted by the Father. The Father is the source from which the Son and the Spirit receive their divinity; he constitutes the "hypostatic divinity" of the Son and Spirit. Just *how* all three divine persons exist as God, however, or their "innertrinitarian form," is determined by their mutual relations.[109] The constitution of the persons and their

106. See Zizioulas, *Communion*, 45, note 40. Wolfhart Pannenberg, who disputes the distinction between the level of constitution and that of relation, understands the constituting of the persons as strictly reciprocal. This leads him to insist on the *future* monarchy of the Father, for otherwise one could not distinguish between the persons. The monarchy of the Father is thus less a requirement of the unity of the divine persons — the *divine* unity, which is the "result" of the perfect and loving "common operation of the three persons" (*Theology*, 1.325), does not need the monarchy of the Father as its "seal" — than the presupposition of their distinctions. If the future monarchy of the Father really were necessary for the unity of the triune God, then Pannenberg would be unable, as Ingolf Dalferth has critically remarked, "to present a trinitarian-theological solution to the problem of the unity of God that was more than an eschatological consolation in a future 'later'" (Dalferth, *Der auferweckte*, 194). For a critique of Pannenberg's understanding of the strict reciprocity of innertrinitarian relations, cf. Jansen, *Relationality*, 178; O'Donnell, "Pannenberg's Doctrine of God," 96.

107. So Schoonenberg, "Trinität," 116: "The immanent Trinity is a Trinity of persons insofar as it is the economic Trinity." Yves Congar has rightly objected that the statement "the economic Trinity is the immanent Trinity" is correct only if it is irreversible (*Geist*, 333ff.). "The immanent Trinity reveals itself in the economic Trinity. But does it reveal itself completely?" (p. 337). See in this regard Oeing-Hanhoff, "Die Krise," 301f.; Koslowski, "Hegel," 124ff.

108. So Wiegand Siebel, *Geist*, 32ff., who continues Jürgen Moltmann's distinction between the level of constituting and that of relation (see Moltmann, *Trinity*, 165f., 175f.), albeit without referring to Moltmann.

109. Moltmann, *Geist*, 321.

relations are, of course, not to be conceived as two temporally sequential steps, but rather as two dimensions of the eternal life of the triune God.[110] The constitution of persons through generation and procession grounds the distinctions among the persons, who are simultaneously constituted as standing in relations; these distinctions then manifest themselves in the salvation-historical differentiation of the persons.

If this distinction between the "hypostatic divinity" (constitutional level) of the trinitarian persons and their "innertrinitarian form" (relational level) is persuasive, then the unilinear hierarchical relations can disappear from the trinitarian communion, since maintaining that the Father constitutes the Son and Spirit says nothing as yet about *how* the relations between them are structured. In any case, within salvation history they do appear as persons standing in reciprocal relationships to one another.[111] With regard to the immanent Trinity, salvation history thus allows us to infer the fundamental equality of the divine persons in their mutual determination and their mutual interpenetration; even if the Father is the source of the deity and accordingly sends the Son and the Spirit, he also gives everything to the Son and glorifies him, just as the Son also glorifies the Father and gives the reign over to the Father (see Matt. 28:18; John 13:31-32; 16:14; 17:1; 1 Cor. 15:24). Moreover, within a community of perfect love between persons who share all the divine attributes, a notion of hierarchy and subordination is inconceivable. Within *relations* between the divine persons, the Father is for that reason not the one over against the others, nor "the First," but rather the *one among the others*.[112] The structure of trinitarian relations is characterized neither by a pyramidal dominance of the one (so Ratzinger) nor by a hierarchical bipolarity between the one and the many (so Zizioulas), but rather by a polycentric and symmetrical reciprocity of the many.

3. If one starts from the trinitarian model I have suggested, then the structure of ecclesial unity cannot be conceived by way of the one, be it the Pope, the patriarch, or the bishop. Every ecclesial unity held together by a mon-archy, by a "one-[man!]-rule," is monistic and thus also un-trinitarian. Reflecting on the fact that no *one* human being can correspond to the trinitarian relational network, Heribert Mühlen has concluded that ecclesiastical *office* is to be exercised collegially, even the office of the Pope![113] This is a step in the

110. One can maintain that Moltmann's distinction between the level of constituting and that of relation is the equivalent of an affirmation of "ontological monarchism" (so Olson, "Trinity," 226) only if one ascribes ontological status exclusively to the relations of origin, and not to the perichoretic relations.

111. See in this regard Pannenberg, *Theology*, 1.308ff.; idem, "Der Gott," 123ff.

112. So Moltmann, *Geist*, 323.

113. He speaks of the "trinitarianization" of the Pope, adding, however, that this "does not *necessarily* mean that the latter must consist in establishment of a triumvirate" (Mühlen, *Entsakralisierung*, 257, my emphasis).

right direction. Such a "trinitarianization" of office would correspond to the collegial exercise of office in the early church (see Phil. 1:1; 1 Thess. 5:12; Rom. 12:8).[114] Yet this step would not suffice, for the correspondence between the structure of the Trinity and the church would still be conceived ecclesiologically in an overly hierarchical fashion. Although this would break the dominance of the one, the bipolarity between the now "trinitarianized" determinative office and the congregation that says "amen" would remain in effect. This is unavoidable if one distinguishes in principle rather than in function between universal and particular priesthood. The *ordo* of the priests then corresponds to the triune God and acts in God's name over against the congregation.

Conceiving the structure of the church in a consistently trinitarian fashion means conceiving not only the institution of office as such, but also the *entire (local) church* itself in correspondence to the Trinity. The high-priestly prayer of Jesus brings all who believe in him into correspondence with the unity of the triune God (John 17:20; cf. 1 John 1:3). Paul, too, seems to be arguing from a trinitarian perspective[115] when he admonishes the Corinthian congregation to unity (1 Cor. 12:4-6; cf. Eph. 4:3-6).[116] The various gifts, services, and activities that all Christians have correspond to the divine multiplicity. Just as the one deity exists as the Father, Son, and Spirit, so also do these different divine persons distribute different gifts to *all* Christians. That these gifts are distributed

---

114. Concerning the collegial exercise of office in the Pastorals Epistles, see Fee, *Timothy,* 20ff.

115. Although one cannot understand the New Testament triadic formulae as evidence of a fully developed doctrine of the Trinity, one should read them theologically in the light of the trinitarian history of God attested by the New Testament, a history from which the doctrine of the Trinity later arose.

116. Heinrich Schlier finds in the New Testament evidence of a trinitarian grounding of the unity of the church ("Einheit," 162-64), though he seems to view especially the one Father, the one Christ, and the one Spirit — *each in and for itself* — as the ground of this unity rather than the divine persons in their triunity. Hence despite the trinitarian appearance, the unity of the church is still conceived *monistically.* A similar conceptual schema can be found in *Lumen gentium* (2–4); from a theological, christological, and pneumatological perspective respectively, "the whole of the church is examined" (Grillmeier, "Kommentar," 161), but the *structure of ecclesial relations* is not conceived in analogy to the structure of trinitarian relations. Even this limited trinitarian grounding of unity has far-reaching ecclesiological consequences and represents a clear advance over the earlier Christo-monistic understanding of the church (see in this regard Legrand, *Réalisation,* 210ff.; idem, "Entwicklung," 151-67; in Protestant circles, H. Richard Niebuhr especially has criticized the unitarianism of the Father, Son, and Spirit [see "Trinity"]). When *Unitatis redintegratio* 2 goes one step further and conceives the structure of the church in analogy to trinitarian relations, this occurs in connection with explications concerning the *one Christ* with whom the Holy Spirit unites the church, and concerning the *one hierarchy* at whose head the "one" — namely, the successor of Peter — stands.

for the benefit of *all,* however (1 Cor. 12:7), corresponds to the divine unity; *the same* Spirit, *the same* Lord, and *the same* God (the Father) are active in all these different gifts.[117] The symmetrical reciprocity of the relations of the trinitarian persons finds its correspondence in the image of the church in which *all* members serve one another with their specific gifts of the Spirit in imitation of the Lord and through the power of the Father. Like the divine persons, they all stand in a relation of mutual giving and receiving.[118]

At the trinitarian level, unity does not presuppose the unifying one, but rather is constituted through perfect love, which is the very nature of God and through which the divine persons exists in one another. By contrast, ecclesial (as well as every other creaturely) unity is inconceivable without the one, though this one cannot be part of the ecclesial communion itself, since this would contradict the structure of trinitarian relations. It is no accident that the New Testament attests no particular charisma of unity (although, for example, people with episcopal charisma are to expend special effort on behalf of unity on the basis of the specific character of their function[119]). Not until the letters of Ignatius does the preservation of unity become a specific task of the bishop. Here, the συνέδριον τοῦ ἐπισκόπου ("council of the bishop") corresponds to the ἑνότης θεοῦ ("unity of God").[120] The bishop is thereby in a position to preside within the church εἰς τόπον θεοῦ ("in the place of God") and thus to ensure its unity.[121] The New Testament itself does not yet attest this understanding. There, the unity of the church seems especially to come about through the indwelling of the *one* Spirit (and with it of the entire holy triunity) *in every person.*[122] Accordingly, and in analogy to the Trinity, *every* person as a bearer of the Spirit participates in the constitution of unity.[123] This is also commensurate with the New Testament admonitions to foster

117. This theological interpretation of 1 Cor. 12:4-6 is plausible only given two pre-suppositions, namely, (1) that "Spirit," "Lord," and "God" are not simply different names of the one person, but rather references to different persons (see in this regard Wainwright, *Trinity;* Fee, "Pauline Literature," 669f.) and (2) that "gifts of grace," "services," and "activities" describe different dimensions of the same reality — the charismata (see in this regard Fee, *1 Corinthians,* 586).

118. See in this regard, Gelpi, *Pentecostalism,* chapter IV.

119. See Luz, "Einheit," 70, 145ff.

120. Ignatius, *Phld.* 8:1.

121. Ignatius, *Magn.* 6:1.

122. It is perhaps not without significance that both in 1 Cor. 12:4-6 and in Eph. 4:3-6, texts admonishing readers to unity, the sequence in the triadic formulae is not "God (Father) — Lord — Spirit," but rather "Spirit — Lord — God (Father)."

123. Schlier, "Einheit," 166ff., has emphasized that the "bearers of charismata" are "*mediators* [and guards] of the salvific unity of the church." He distinguishes, however, the bearers of such charismata from the bearers of office, who mediate the unity of the church "in a different sense."

unity, which are in fact directed to all the members of the congregation (see 1 Cor. 1:10-17; Eph. 4:3).

4. If the person is not identical with relations, then one can also conceive the *rights* of ecclesial persons in correspondence to the Trinity. It would, of course, be utterly inappropriate to ascribe rights to the divine persons in an effort to ascribe them analogously to ecclesial persons as well. "Rights legitimate the social practice of claiming goods on moral grounds."[124] For the divine persons, however, such "practice of claiming goods" is inconceivable, since they live in perfect love; they are internal to one another as persons and mutually *give everything* to one another. Hence they can have no formal rights that might legitimate this "practice of claiming goods" (and that might be asserted through commensurate sanctions). These rights presuppose the possibility of persons being abused, and they are meaningless without this possibility. With regard to the divine persons, however, this presupposition is counterfactual.

The understanding of the divine persons as (interdependent and mutually internal) autonomous centers of action corresponds to the understanding of ecclesial persons as interdependent and catholic, albeit autonomous subjects. In order to protect the persons from abuse, not only for their own sake (the equivalent of an individualistic understanding of human rights), but also because of their communion with others and with God,[125] one must ascribe inalienable rights to those not (yet) living in perfect love. People in the church *can* have these rights, because they are persons who are to correspond to the relations of the divine persons as centers of action; but they *must* have these rights if they are to live in correspondence to the divine persons, because they are living on this side of God's new creation. The rights of all the members of the church, of officeholders as well as of all other Christians, are grounded in the correspondence of the *sojourning church* to the Trinity.

Personal rights, of course, cannot replace mutual love between persons. Rather, properly understood, rights presuppose such love; they protect against the abuse of persons and are an expression of love on this side of God's new creation. Because they are also grounded in the Trinity, they simultaneously point toward their own suspension in God's new creation, a creation in which human beings in communion with the triune God will reflect perfect divine love.

---

124. Wolterstorff, "Christianity," 212.

125. Paul Ramsey has defined these rights as "whatever it is necessary for me to have in order to be with and for fellow man" (*Ethics,* 37; see also Hauerwas, "Right," 238ff.).

Chapter VI

Structures of the Church

Ecumenical discussion about the church has in recent decades concentrated largely on the problem of ecclesial structures, and primarily on the question of office. It seems apparent enough why this is the case. Ecclesial life in most churches (of the First World?) proceeds by way of priests and pastors and is realized in the proclamation of the Gospel and in the celebration of the sacraments, primarily baptism and the Eucharist, events in which officeholders play key roles. Thus ecumenical dialogue concerning the question of office not only takes place around a well-defined issue, but is also immediately relevant for the life of local churches. At the theological level as well the question of office is fertile ground for ecumenical discussion, since an entire ecclesiology is always reflected in a certain understanding of office, that is, of what officeholders are to do in the church and how they are to become officeholders.

This intimate connection between the nature of the church and that of office not only explains the ecumenical and ecclesiological significance of the question of office, but simultaneously makes clear why concentration on this particular question was bound to run quickly into insuperable difficulties.[1] For behind the question of office there lurks the fundamental problem of one's understanding of the church, a problem that, while approachable by way of the question of office, can by no means be solved through it. The *BEM (Baptism, Eucharist, and Ministry)*

---

1. Hans-Martin Barth, *Priester,* 19ff., criticizes the centrality of the question of office in ecumenical discussion without acknowledging the preeminent ecclesiological significance of this question; the Catholic church, he believes, has "forced" this onto the Protestant church, which "begins with an ecclesiologically different point of departure" (p. 20). However, the *question* of office is also of central significance for an ecclesiology in which office itself occupies a peripheral position.

document and the resultant discussion demonstrated this clearly.[2] Without an ecumenical agreement of what the church is, one can either allow the diverging understandings of office to stand unreconciled next to one another, or one can try to cloak them with merely verbal convergences. Either way, unity is feigned rather than genuinely attained. This is why in recent years the question of the character of the church, especially of the understanding of the church as communion, has moved into the center of ecumenical dialogue.

Reflection on ecclesial structures obviously presupposes reflection on the church. If the structures of the church really are to be the structures *of* the church rather than structures *over* the church, then the church must take precedence over its structures. Accordingly, one must first determine what the church is (chapter III), how salvation is mediated within it (chapter IV), and how it is to correspond to the Trinity as its ground and goal (chapter V). Only after dealing with these fundamental ecclesiological questions can one reflect meaningfully on the structures of the church. In this chapter, I will examine the problem of ecclesial structures by first addressing the problem of participation in church life. I will then discuss ecclesial institutions and the allocation of persons to particular roles. Commensurate with my own primary interest in relations between persons, I will not expressly examine the sacraments here, which together with offices are part of the structures of the church.

Each of the three problems just mentioned — the relationship between universal and particular priesthood, between Spirit and church law, and the understanding of ordination, to use theological instead of sociological terminology — is extremely complex, and the attendant secondary literature dealing with exegesis, church history, systematic theology, and canon law is endless. I cannot address these problems in any detail here. In a study of the church as communion, it should suffice merely to point out which consequences regarding the theology of office and one's understanding of canon law can be drawn from the basic ecclesiological decisions I have presented in the three preceding chapters.

1. Charismata and Participation

The church lives through the participation of its members, that is, the laity and the office holders, and is constituted through them by the Holy Spirit. All

---

2. See M. Thurian, ed., *Churches*. In its own answer to the *BEM* Document, the Russian Orthodox Church rightly emphasized that the question of a recognition of offices is secondary to the recognition of churches: "The fundamental ecclesiological problem of unity lies not in an 'ecumenical' mutual recognition of 'ministry,' but in recognition of the church, in which this ministry is exercised, as a 'true Church' confessing the faith of the apostles" (M. Thurian, ed., *Churches*, I.9; cf. IV.147).

churches agree on this point. What is disputed is *how* this occurs. First, I will advocate a particular Protestant understanding of the constitution and life of the church, and I will contrast this with the Catholic and Orthodox understanding. Then I will explicate this understanding by reflecting on the charismata.

1.1. Bishop or Everyone?

1. Catholic and Orthodox ecclesiologies are emphatically *episcopocentric.* In the ecclesiologies of both Ratzinger and Zizioulas, the bishop plays a respectively different role, but for both of them his preeminent position in the church is decisively associated with the notion of the church as a subject, a notion in its own turn sustained by the idea of the "whole Christ," head and members. The church needs the bishop as the one human subject in order itself to be concretely capable of acting as a subject. The bishop acts *in persona Christi* and simultaneously *in persona ecclesiae.* These two are as intimately connected as are the head and body in the one organism of Christ, which according to both Ratzinger's and Zizioulas's understanding is the church.

For Ratzinger, emphasis on the church as subject means a strong affirmation of the significance of the whole church. If the church is one subject with Christ, then it also acts soteriologically with Christ. This activity of the whole church becomes concrete in the liturgical ministry of the priest; in him, the church realizes its participation in Christ's own mediatorship.[3] I have already pointed out that this understanding ascribes too much soteriological significance to the church.[4] This "too much" with regard to soteriology corresponds simultaneously, however, to "too little" with regard to the laity. Despite the universal priesthood of all who have been baptized,[5] the priest *in principle* cannot be replaced by other believers. Only a priest who has received his authority sacramentally from the whole church can act *in persona Christi* and *in persona ecclesiae.* Although laypersons are indeed also subjects of worship activity insofar as they are part of the *ecclesia catholica* acting with Christ in the priest, they are always acting through the priest. Accordingly, Ratzinger understands the *actuosa participatio* less in the sense of external activity than in the sense of personal participation in worship events.[6] Although on one level the

3. See Ratzinger, *Prinzipienlehre,* 287.

4. See IV.1.1.2 above.

5. See *Lumen gentium* 10.

6. See I.5.1 above. For a richer understanding of the *actuosa participatio* in Catholic ecclesiology, see Legrand, *Réalisation,* 181ff.; Kasper, "Communio," 79ff. Catholic theologians in Latin America have reflected with particular intensity on the role of the laity in the church, and in the process have advocated theses radically different from those of Ratzinger (see Boff, *Die Neuentdeckung;* idem, *Kirche*).

bipolarity between priest and *ecclesia catholica* as well as between priest and concrete congregation is suspended insofar as both participate in liturgical activity, on another level this same bipolarity is still underscored. That is, in the liturgy it is the priest who acts *in persona Christi* and *in persona ecclesiae;* the entire congregation and each individual person internalize this activity receptively, and only in being thus receptive are they authentically active in worship.

According to Zizioulas, the being of officeholders, that is, of bishops, is both christologically and ecclesiologically determined. The bishop represents Christ to the congregation and simultaneously embodies in himself the whole congregation. On the one hand, the bishop does not simply stand opposite the congregation according to this model, since he is not a *persona privata,* but rather a communal entity, a corporate personality. On the other hand, in the liturgy the bishop alone acts *in persona Christi.* The congregation *receives* his activity. It follows the bishop, at least theoretically, in pneumatic willingness and speaks the liturgical "amen." Despite the fact that the bishop is conditioned by the congregation, the situation of bipolarity — more specifically, asymmetrical bipolarity — remains between bishop and congregation for Zizioulas as well; the bishop, who is conditioned by the congregation, acts; and the congregation, which is constituted by the bishop, receives.[7]

2. Over the course of this investigation, I have tried to show (1) that the church is not a single subject, but rather a communion of interdependent subjects, (2) that the mediation of salvation occurs not only through officeholders, but also through all other members of the church, and (3) that the church is constituted by the Holy Spirit not so much by way of the institution of office as through the communal confession in which Christians speak the word of God to one another.[8] From these three basic theological convictions, it follows that the life and structure of the church cannot be episcopocentric. The church is not a monocentric-bipolar community, however articulated, but rather fundamentally a *polycentric community.*[9]

Paul seems to envision such a model of ecclesial life with a polycentric participative structure when he tries to reestablish peace within the enthusiastic and chaotic congregation in Corinth (see 1 Cor. 14:33).[10] As a kind of summary of his own ecclesiologically extremely significant instructions in 1 Corinthians

7. See II.4.3 above.

8. See III.2.1.3, IV.1.1.3, and III.2.2 above.

9. According to Michael Welker, the "simple hierarchical structures . . . still characterizing our churches" should be replaced by "the development of new forms making it possible for the congregation to participate in producing and shaping worship services, including the content of such services" (Welker, *Kirche im Pluralismus,* 125f.). Within the framework of Catholic hierarchical ecclesiology, Avery Dulles has advocated an understanding of the church as a "polycentric community" (Dulles, *Catholicity,* 126).

10. See also 3.1.1 below.

12–14, he writes: "When you come together, *each one* has a hymn, a lesson, a revelation, a tongue, or an interpretation. Let all things be done for building up the congregation" (1 Cor. 14:26; cf. 1 Pet. 2:5-10; 4:10).[11] During the Protestant Reformation, Luther rediscovered the participative model of ecclesial life with his notion of the universal priesthood of believers, a priesthood he never understood merely soteriologically, but rather always ecclesiologically as well.[12] In the German-speaking sphere, it was then especially Philipp Jakob Spener, Nicholas Ludwig Graf von Zinzendorf, and Johann Hinrich Wichern who tried to vivify Luther's ecclesiological insight here, an insight also unable to establish itself within Protestantism.[13] In the English-speaking sphere, it was especially the various Free Church groups who undertook this, such as the Baptists,[14] Congregationalists,[15] Quakers,[16] and Pentecostals.[17]

The polycentric character of the church has a twofold theological grounding, namely, in the Christian call to faith and in the charismata. Christians are called to enter into communion with Jesus Christ (1 Cor. 1:9) and to confess and witness him with words and deeds (1 Pet. 2:9). At their initiation, they receive from God's Spirit the authority and capacity for this ministry. The call to faith and ministry is general, one-time, and permanent, whereas the particular forms of ministry change, just as do both the bearers of ministry and the situations in which they function. For that reason, this calling can ground only a general priesthood that is the same for all members of the church; it cannot

---

11. See in this regard Fee, *1 Corinthians*, 690. In support of his bipolar understanding of church life, Zizioulas adduces the Pauline instructions in 1 Corinthians 12–14, the same text from which I draw my own understanding of the church as a polycentric community. According to Zizioulas, the people were to speak the "amen" in charismatic worship services (1 Cor. 14:16; Zizioulas, "L'eucharistie," 43). One can find a bipolar understanding of the church in 1 Cor. 14:16 only if one interpolates later liturgical structures into the Pauline letters, since for Paul it is not the task of an *ordo* within the church to speak the "amen," but rather the task *of all members without distinction* to give such a response to the liturgical contribution that can come from *every* member (see 1 Cor. 14:26). The polycentrality in church life stands here over against the bipolarity insofar as every person can contribute in the worship service, while simultaneously all are to speak the liturgical "amen."

12. See Althaus, *Theologie*, 254ff.

13. On the notion of universal priesthood in Protestant theology, see Eastwood, *Priesthood*; see also Barth, *Priester*, 29-103, 191-250. The apex in Hans-Martin Barth's explications, which closely resemble my own views (already presented in Volf, "Kirche," 55-60), reads: "The Protestant church is the church of the universal priesthood — or it does not exist" (p. 103).

14. See Walton, *Community*, 102.

15. See Eastwood, *Priesthood*, 164-71.

16. See Gwyn, *Apocalypse*, 166.

17. The most influential earlier Pentecostal lay theologian, Donald Gee, spoke of "open" worship services characterized by "general liberty for all to take part as the Spirit moved upon the members of the congregation" (Gee, *Gifts*, 15). See also Lim, *Spiritual Gifts*, 34ff.

ground the various and changing ministries of each member. The specific way in which each Christian realizes his or her general priesthood must be established through the individual, specific charismata, even if it is true that each Christian already receives a specific charisma (or specific charismata) in the general call as such. For the charismata are empowerments for pluriform service in the church and in the world, empowerments which come from God's grace and which can change and overlap.[18] The relationship between calling and charismata can be defined as follows. The call to new life and to practices commensurate with this life comes to everyone without distinction through the words of the gospel. At the point of its individual appropriation, this general call becomes specific in the gifts given to each person for concrete and changing tasks in church and in world.[19] *That* all Christians have a task in church and world is grounded in Christian calling; *which* concrete ministry (or ministries) they have is determined by the gifts of the Spirit given to them at the moment.

Commensurate with their calling and endowment by God's Spirit, all the members of a church are stewards of God's manifold grace through their deeds and words (see 1 Pet. 4:10-11), and all have something to contribute in worship and in the entire life of the church.[20] The church arises and lives insofar as salvation is mediated through mutual service with the pluriform gifts of the Spirit. It is true, of course, that not everyone participates in the same way and with the same intensity in the mediation of faith. Although one should in particular not underestimate the preeminent significance of officeholders, who have an indispensable role in the church, the whole life of the church is not ordered around them. Different persons can become the soteriologically "significant others" for other persons. Beyond this, all the members of the church create the "plausibility structures" in which the mediation of faith and life in faith become possible in the first place.[21] Thus the Spirit does not constitute

18. Norbert Baumert, "Charisma und Amt," has recently called into question Ernst Käsemann's thesis that Paul uses the term "charisma" as a *terminus technicus* (Käsemann, "Amt," 109). My own argumentation is not dependent on the veracity of Käsemann's thesis. Here I am not strictly following the Pauline use of "charisma," but rather *am construing a theology of charismata.* In the process, I am taking as my guide not only the direct Pauline statements concerning charismata, but also his general explications regarding church services and functions.

19. See Volf, "Arbeit," 419ff. for a brief theological reflection on charismata. For theological-historical studies of the charismata, see Norbert Baumert's articles "Semantik," "Begriffsgeschichte," and "Fremdwort."

20. The following presentation is not to be understood as a continuation of the inappropriate polemic against liturgical worship services traditionally practiced in Free Church circles (see Smyth, *Works,* 270ff.), but rather as an invitation to understand and shape the liturgy in a certain way.

21. See in this regard Berger and Luckmann, *Construction,* 157ff.

the church exclusively through its officeholders, but also through every member serving others with his or her gifts.[22] The point of this polycentric-participative model of church life is not, of course, simply to outdo the Catholic understanding of the church, as it were, in a Free Church fashion, so that the worship service itself becomes a salvific *work* performed by all believers. The acting priest is not simply replaced by the acting congregation; rather, the mediation of the *exclusive* salvific activity of Christ is now enjoined on all believers.[23]

3. In the following section, I will define more closely this polycentric-participative model of church life in a brief reflection on several ecclesiologically relevant features of the charismata. First, however, let me briefly examine the practical consequences of this model.

This model involves first only a *reinterpretation* of what is already actually happening in churches. The model according to which the Spirit constitutes the church through officeholders (ordained in the apostolic succession) obscures the ecclesiologically highly significant fact that in all churches, faith is mediated and kept alive above all by the so-called laity, that is, in families, in one's neighborhood, or in the workplace; without this lay activity of faith mediation, there would be no living church.[24] Ecclesiologically, the model that assigns priority to officeholders also suppresses the contribution of the laity in worship. In all churches, the laity participates in the worship service through singing, praying, the reading of scripture, the confession of faith, or simply through their mere presence. All these activities must be acknowledged ecclesiologically as constitutive for the church, for it is through these activities that people confess Christ before one another as Savior and Lord, and it is in this way that the Spirit of God constitutes them into a church.

Theological reinterpretation of what has always in fact taken place in the church is simultaneously an important presupposition for a new church practice. For the ecclesiological obscuring of the lay role in constituting the church is one of the most important *theological* factors contributing to lay passivity. If laypersons are constituted into a church by taking the sacraments and/or by hearing the proclaimed word, then active participation in the mediation of faith is something external to their ecclesial being; they are church in their passivity, and their activity is something added to their being as church, or perhaps also not added. If by contrast the church is constituted by the confession of all its members, then the mediation of faith is a dimension of their ecclesial being;

22. So also Hans-Martin Barth in his interpretation of Luther (*Priester*, 37).
23. See IV.1.1.2.
24. What the Church of South India remarks in its reponse to the *BEM* Document concerning "rural congregations" applies to *all* churches: "the light of the gospel is kept by ordinary people by their faithful commitment to the gospel" (M. Thurian, ed., *Churches*, II.78).

they are church in their activity of faith mediation (which is, of course, merely the reverse side of their receptive passivity and is first made possible only by that passivity).

The passivity of laypersons admittedly also stems from factors other than merely theological ones. Sociological factors especially play an important role. Following Max Weber and Ernst Troeltsch, Hervé Legrand rightly explains the tendency to disqualify the laity religiously in part

> from the necessary division of labor in every society . . . one can see that the identity of the clergy is dialectically related to the religious dispossession of the laity (the "clerics" inculcate in the "laity" the latter's lack of knowledge and know-how) and to the parallel affirmation by the clergy of its own proper election and of its own proper superiority.[25]

An initial step toward countering this sociological tendency is a theological elevation of the laity into the medium through which the church is constituted by God's Spirit.

1.2. The Charismatic Church

1. Because the church is born through the presence of Christ in the Holy Spirit, the thesis that the church is constituted by way of the entire called and charismatically endowed people of God presupposes that the exalted Christ himself is acting in the gifts of the Spirit. According to the Pauline understanding of the charismata, this is indeed the case, since, as Ernst Käsemann emphasizes, a gift of the Spirit is "the specific portion of the individual in the dominion and glory of Christ."[26] This is why the charismata are not gifts that can be separated from the concrete presence of Christ in human beings and be at the latter's free disposal. Christ himself is "present in his gifts and in the ministries attesting those gifts and made possible by those gifts."[27] Since all Christians, as we will shortly see, have charismata, Christ is also acting through all the members of the church, and not merely through its officeholders.[28]

The connection between the charismata and Christ's constitutive presence in the church by the Spirit also demonstrates clearly the intimate relation

25. Legrand, *Réalisation*, 184.

26. Käsemann, "Amt," 111.

27. Ibid., 118.

28. Many churches have critically made this point in their response to the *BEM* Document over against the text that over-emphasizes official representation of Christ (see *Baptism, Eucharist and Ministry*, 36 [M11]; see M. Thurian, *Churches*, II.78, 207; III.175; IV.36, 181; "Evangelical," 306).

between the charismata and the constitutive activity of confession.[29] Confession of Christ as Savior and Lord is an essential dimension of charismatic activity. Although not the only feature, confession is the indispensable feature distinguishing the charismata from other activities in which people engage in the church and world (see 1 Cor. 12:2-3). This cannot be otherwise. If Christ is to act in the charismata, then he must be implicitly or explicitly confessed by charismatics themselves and through their charismatic activities as the one who he is, namely, Savior and Lord. Just as every charisma is a concrete manifestation of Christ's grace,[30] so also is every charismatic activity a concrete form of confession to him.

Although every charismatic activity is a confession, not every confession is charismatic, since confession occurs through the entire life of Christians, through everything they speak or do. Although all of Christian life is lived in the Spirit, it is not charismatic as a whole.[31] Charisma has a narrower meaning in its reference to a particular capacity given by the Spirit of Christ for a particular ministry in church or world. If this is the case, then the thesis that the church is constituted by the Spirit of God through charismatic activity, although correct, is a simplification, albeit a much more complex simplification than the thesis that the church is constituted with the help of officeholders. For the Spirit of God can also use people to perform certain ministries who have no particular gifts for these ministries, perhaps an ecclesial "manager" in order to strengthen faith, or an academic in order to console. What a person contributes to the life of the church, through secondary ministries or even through the living, spiritual "aura" surrounding a person,[32] goes far beyond the particular charismata given to an individual. It is meaningful, however, to speak about the church being constituted through the charismata insofar as the activity of the Spirit through every member of the church becomes evident in a particularly concentrated fashion in these charismata.

2. The second identifying feature of the charismata is their *universal distribution*. According to the New Testament texts, charismata are not "phenomena limited to a certain circle of persons, but rather are universally present in the church" (see 1 Cor. 12:7; Rom. 12:3; Eph. 4:7; 1 Pet. 4:10).[33] In the

29. See III.2.2.3 above.

30. Käsemann, "Amt," 117.

31. Contra Käsemann, "Amt," 116. Ulrich Brockhaus has persuasively argued against Käsemann's ethical expansion of the charismata (Brockhaus, *Charisma*, 220ff.).

32. Concerning the "aura" as a form of communication separate from language, see Berger and Luckmann, *Construction*, 163.

33. Küng, *Kirche*, 226; see also Boff, *Kirche*, 267ff.; Duffield and Van Cleave, *Foundations*, 329. *Lumen gentium* 12 apparently takes a different view when it maintains that these gifts are distributed "*inter* omnis ordinis fideles" (my emphasis; see in this regard Gerosa, *Charisma*, 69f.). It does not seem evident to me that the universal distribution of charismata

community as the body of Christ, there are no members without charisma. The Spirit poured out upon all flesh (see Acts 2:17-21) also distributes gifts to all flesh; these gifts are "a present dispensed without distinction and without conditions."[34] This is why a division into those who serve in the congregation and those who are served is ecclesiologically unacceptable; every person is to serve with his or her specific gifts, and every person is to be served in his or her specific need. In actuality, however, many members are passive in churches. Hence although not every baptized person can be called a charismatic, the charismata are nonetheless present "in embryonic form" in every person, as Karl Rahner expresses it.[35] Commensurate with the measure to which the charismata are given to a person (see 1 Pet. 4:10)[36] — no one is to be coerced into activity! — these gifts are to be acknowledged, vivified, and employed in service to the church and world.

Universal distribution of the charismata implies *common responsibility* for the life of the church.[37] Such common responsibility is compatible with the particular charismata of leadership ("office").[38] In the context of universal distribution of charismata, however, such leadership acquires a new profile. It cannot be the task of leaders, ordained or not, to do everything in the church themselves. This would lead to hypertrophy of this one member of the body of Christ and to a fateful atrophy of all other members. The task of leaders is first to animate all the members of the church to engage their pluriform charismatic activities, and then to coordinate these activities.[39] Second, leaders are responsible for a mature church that is called to test every manifestation of the Spirit (see 1 Thess. 5:21).[40]

Common responsibility implies *mutual subordination* (see Eph. 5:21).[41]

---

is to be understood to mean that each person has "his own charisma" on the basis of his own uniqueness (so Baumert, "Charisma," 31). Just as it is a useful abstraction (actually, an abstraction first making verbal communication possible to begin with) to speak of "deacons," even though each has a specific task and performs that work in his own way, so also is it meaningful to speak about a charisma of διαϰονία.

34. Brockhaus, *Charisma*, 170.

35. Rahner, "Charisma," 1028.

36. See Wilckens, *Römer*, III.11.

37. See Banks, *Community*, 139; Dunn, "Models," 107.

38. I am here presuppposing the institution of "office" and will ground it later below in the section on "Ordination."

39. So also Barth, *Priester*, 234.

40. One extraordinary feature of Pauline correctives to his congregations is that Paul does not address the leaders in those congregations as authorities whose task is to implement his instructions; this is best understood if one starts with the notion of the common or shared responsibility of all for the life of the church.

41. So also Mühlen, *Entsakralisierung*, 438.

Although Paul demands that his congregations acknowledge certain members · and be subordinate to them (see 1 Thess. 5:12; 1 Cor. 16:15-16), the authority of these members is relativized in several respects and precisely thereby also protected. First, such authority is not absolute, since the members of the church owe unconditional obedience only to their common Lord. Second, it is based less on their formal position than on their active service in the congregation (see 1 Thess. 5:13).[42] Ultimately, obligatory subordination to leaders stands within the framework of the obligatory mutual subordination of all, which is why Christian obedience can only be free "obedience to the respectively different charismata of others."[43]

3. The third characteristic feature of the charismata is their fundamental *interdependence*. All members have charismata, but not every member has all charismata. The fullness of gifts is to be found in the entire (local) church.[44] Paul emphasizes in several passages that, commensurate with their functions, the members of the body of Christ have *"different* gifts" (Rom. 12:6; cf. 1 Cor. 12:7-11). The church is not a club of universally gifted and for that reason self-sufficient charismatics, but rather a community of men and women whom the Spirit of God has endowed in a certain way for service to each other and to the world in anticipation of God's new creation.

Since the members of the church are interdependent, their life must be characterized by mutuality.[45] The church is a community "of [mutual] giving and receiving" (Phil. 4:15). The "charismata of office" must be integrated into this mutuality. Officeholders do not stand opposite the church as those acting exclusively *in persona Christi*. Since the Spirit of Christ acts in them not by the power of their office, but rather in the execution of their ministry,[46] their actions do not differ in principle from those of any other member of the church. Insofar as each person contributes in his or her own specific way to the various aspects of church life, that person is acting as a "representative" of Christ to those affected by that action. This does not eliminate the inevitable polarity between ministry *in persona Christi* and the congregation, but it does decentralize it and in so doing overcome the bipolarity between "officeholders" and "congregation." Spiritual activity and receptivity are no longer assigned to two different groups of persons, but rather represent two basic activities of every person; that is, every person acts *in persona Christi* and every person receives this activity.

4. The *sovereign Spirit of God* allots the charismata "as the Spirit chooses"

42. Cf. Dunn, "Models," 106; Käsemann, "Amt," 120.

43. Küng, *Kirche*, 474.

44. For a similar understanding within the framework of Catholic ecclesiology, see Legrand, "Entwicklung," 151.

45. See in this regard Lohfink, *Gemeinde*, 116-24.

46. See Schweizer, "Konzeptionen," 331.

(1 Cor. 12:11).[47] The Spirit works, first, *as* the Spirit chooses; no church, neither an entire (local) church nor any stratum in the church, can prescribe which gifts the Spirit is to bestow upon which members. Furthermore, the Spirit works *when* the Spirit chooses; the church cannot determine at which time the Spirit is to bestow its gifts. This clearly reveals that the church lives from a dynamic not deriving from itself. The problem of who is to do what in the church is in an important sense not a church matter at all. It is not the church that "organizes" its life, but rather the Holy Spirit. Hence the *pneumatological structure* of the church follows from the sovereignty of the Spirit in the bestowal of charismata.

The church is first of all structured by *apersonal* institutions, those that need not be conceived anew with every changing situation, but rather which are already given. These include different, more or less stable ecclesial ministries (such as that of overseeing or serving).[48] These institutions, however, are inconceivable without personal bearers.[49] The *personal participative structure* of these institutions is determined by the sovereign Spirit, who bestows the charismata when and upon whom the Spirit chooses. In this way, the Spirit opposes "any possible self-isolation of the church in its institutional and traditional habits and allows it to be a permanently 'open system.'"[50]

But how are the charismata bestowed by the sovereign Spirit? They are often described as "surprising" or "punctiliar," so that one can do nothing other than "open oneself to them" (or perhaps also not).[51] This then yields the juxtaposition of charisma and office. Charisma is "immediate" and "not at one's disposal," whereas office can be transmitted sacramentally.[52] But this model of the bestowal of charismata is too simple. Paul demands that one "strive" (ζηλόω) for the charismata and "pursue" (διώκω) them (1 Cor. 12:31; 14:1).[53]

47. See Baumert, "Charisma," 34, 37.

48. Although apersonal institutions include the sacraments, these cannot be examined within the framework of this chapter.

49. The ecclesiological distinction between apersonal institutions and personal participative structure corresponds to the sociological distinction between "key roles" in a social system and to the "allocation of human capacities and human resources among tasks" (Parsons, *Institutions*, 120). A further distinction must be made between the institutions and persons on the one hand, and the service rendered by persons through these institutions on the other. Hence according to the Protestant understanding, proclamation of the word of God is constitutive for ecclesiality, whereas certain institutions through which this service is carried out are not.

50. So M. Kehl in a lecture, after the citation of Baumert, "Charisma," 34, n. 31.

51. So Baumert, "Charisma," 32ff., 45.

52. Concerning the juxtaposition of charisma and office, see Bittlinger, *Im Kraftfeld*, 129.

53. My premise is that the charismata are not necessarily punctiliar events (so also, e.g., Ridderbos, *Paul*, 443ff.). Merely distinguishing between the momentary and the enduring charismata by no means constitutes the first "step toward ascribing special status to

This presupposes recognition of one's own, inborn or learned capabilities as well as of the needs of the church; in order to serve others, one must know both what they need and what one has or does not have to offer oneself. Of course, I cannot simply choose my charisma according to my own evaluation of the situation. Striving for certain charismata makes sense only if I am prepared to have my own evaluation of myself and of others corrected by the evaluation others have of me and of themselves, since those others must want to accept my service. Thus does one arrive at the *interactional model* of the bestowal of charismata.[54] I acquire the charismata from the Spirit of God through interaction with myself, that is, with that which I am by nature and that which I have become in society on the basis of my disposition and abilities, *and* through interaction with the church and world in which I find myself. Although charismata are gifts of the sovereign Spirit of God, they are not found in the isolated individual, but rather in persons in their concrete natural and social state. Precisely as gifts of the sovereign Spirit, the charismata are ecclesial not just in their direction, but *already in their bestowal.*

5. The *synchronic and diachronic plurality* of charismata is also ecclesiologically relevant. According to Paul, a person can have several charismata at the same time. Although he does not mention any universally gifted personalities who might live independently of the community, within the framework of ecclesial interdependence he is concerned precisely that each person have charismata "in abundance" (1 Cor. 14:12).

With regard to the structures of the church, diachronic plurality is even more important than synchronic. In contrast to calling, charismata in the theological sense of a combination of calling and endowment for a specific ministry in church and world are not "irrevocable" (Rom. 11:29). Various charismata can replace one another over time, something implied by the interactional model of their bestowal. Over the history of the congregation and of its individual members, the charismata with which these members serve in the congregation can also change; certain charismata come to the fore at certain times, while others become unimportant (either for the congregation itself or for the bearers of these charismata). This does not mean that the divine calling and endowment for a certain ministry cannot be a lifelong affair; but it is not *necessarily* such. In any case, there is no correlation between the permanence of a particular charisma and its divine origin. The Spirit of God is the Spirit of life, and the Spirit's gifts are accordingly as varied and dynamic as is ecclesial life itself.

---

officeholders and to subordinating the rest of the congregation members to them," as Ulrich Brockhaus believes (*Charisma*, 215). This is the case only if one has already tacitly identified the enduring charismata with office.

54. Similarly also Veenhof, "Charismata," 90f.

2. The Trinity and Ecclesial Institutions

According to a view widespread in Protestant circles, the Spirit of God and church institutions stand in contradiction. "Where the Spirit of the Lord is, there is freedom" (2 Cor. 3:17); by contrast, institutions are perceived as mechanisms of repression. If this view were correct, then resolute "pneumatic anarchy" would be the only appropriate "structure" for a charismatic church.[55] This view, however, is prejudiced, and anyone sharing it fails to recognize both the character of ecclesial institutions and the way the Spirit of God acts.

2.1. The Trinity as Model

1. According to Peter Berger and Thomas Luckmann, "institutionalization occurs whenever there is a reciprocal typification of habitualized actions by types of actors."[56] Institutions are in this view the stable structures of social interaction, and they arise in every social situation that endures beyond its own origin, including when two people do the same thing together repeatedly.[57] The identity of a social unit presupposes institutionality, since identity is inconceivable without the formally or informally fixed regularity and predictability of relations and their implicit or explicit legitimation through explanation and justification.[58] Every social unit, as a group defining itself over against other social units, is already an institution. Concrete sociality and institutionality are inseparable.

The answer to the question whether the *church* is an institution obviously depends on the character of the church. If the church is "a number of parallels that cross only in infinity," as Adolf von Harnack, in a well-known polemic, formulated Rudolph Sohm's understanding,[59] and if it appears only as a punctiliar event, then it cannot be an institution because it is not a social unit. But if the essence of the church is also "that it establishes communities on earth,"[60] then it can exist in no other way than as an institution. As I have tried to show,[61] salvation possesses an essentially social dimension. Accordingly, one can become and live as a Christian only through institutionalized procedures, that is, through confessing Jesus Christ as Savior and Lord, through baptism in the name of the triune God, through the Eucharist, which celebrates communion

---

55. Sohm, *Wesen*, 54; see also Brunner, *Kirche*, 18ff.; Kraus, *Reich Gottes*, 376.

56. Berger and Luckmann, *Construction*, 51. Concerning the problem of institutions, see also Parsons, *Institutions*, 117-252; Neal, "Institution."

57. See Berger and Luckmann, *Construction*, 52ff.

58. See Anderson and Carter, *Behavior*, 119ff.; Neale, "Institution."

59. Harnack, *Kirchenverfassung*, 148f.

60. Ibid., 149.

61. Concerning the sociality of salvation, see V.2.1 above.

with the triune God and with one another.[62] The essential sociality of salvation implies the essential institutionality of the church. The question is not *whether* the church is an institution, but rather *what kind* of institution it is.

2. An appropriate answer to the question of the character of the church as an institution should be given through reference to the doctrine of the Trinity. The church reflects in a broken fashion the eschatological communion of the entire people of God with the triune God in God's new creation.[63] Its institutions should thus correspond to the Trinity as well. That they are able to do this derives from the character of the charismata that structure the church. As I have already shown, relations between charismatics are modeled after trinitarian relations (see 1 Cor. 12:4-6).[64]

The institutionality of the church can be conceived in correspondence to the Trinity only because the Trinity itself is in a certain sense an "institution." This becomes apparent as soon as one understands institutions as stable structures of social interaction. For the Trinity is inconceivable without stable relations between the divine persons; the identity of the divine persons cannot be determined without such stable relations. Of course, the Trinity is an institution only analogously. For example, the divine persons do not exhibit any possibility for a *typology* of agents of the sort required for institutionalization,[65] since *per definitionem* only one divine person is available for any one trinitarian "role"; the "roles" are not interchangeable between the persons, since their respective uniqueness as distinct persons is defined by these "roles."

Of course, the correspondence of ecclesial institutions to the Trinity cannot be determined just "from above," from the Trinity itself. The limits of analogy applicable to the church must also be considered, limits grounded in the church's creaturely and historical nature.[66] Hence a double access to the institutionality of the church is necessary; it must be viewed both as a communion living from its fellowship with the triune God and as a human social phenomenon. An exclusively sociophilosophical grounding of this institutionality would neglect the inner essence of the church as a communion with the triune God;[67] an exclusively trinitarian grounding would, by contrast, fail to do justice to the character of the church as a human community on its way to its goal.

---

62. Since faith has a cognitive dimension (see IV.1.2.2 above) and since the content of faith is therefore the same for everyone, the personal faith of every individual is a "role" and implies the institutionalization of conduct (for a sociological consideration of "roles," see Berger and Luckmann, *Construction*, 72ff.).

63. See III.1.1.1 above.

64. See V.4.3 above.

65. See Berger and Luckmann, *Construction*, 53.

66. See V.1.2 above.

67. For a Catholic polemic against deriving church rights from a sociophilosophical *apriori* — *ubi societas, ibi ius* — see Müller, "Communio," 484.

3. The character of an institution depends primarily on two factors: the pattern of power distribution and the manner of its cohesion. With regard to the distribution of power, one can distinguish between symmetrical-polycentric and asymmetrical-monocentric models; with regard to cohesion, one can distinguish between coerced and freely affirmed integration. The combination of these factors in their concrete implementation yields the multiple forms of institutions with two extreme models (which never occur in reality in their pure forms): institutions with asymmetrical-monocentric distribution of power and (formally or informally) coerced integration, and institutions with symmetrical-decentralized distribution of power and freely affirmed integration.

As I have already shown,[68] Ratzinger and Zizioulas understand the Trinity hierarchically and ground the hierarchical relations within the church in part on this basis. For Ratzinger, relations in the Trinity and in the church are monocentric; since the persons are "pure relations," the Trinity can have but one center. Although Zizioulas abandons monocentricity, he does maintain the hierarchy; the relationship between the one (the Father) and the many (the Son and the Spirit) is asymmetrical in favor of the "one." Both Ratzinger and Zizioulas insist on freely affirmed integration in both the Trinity and the church; yet because on this side of God's new creation freely affirmed integration in the church must remain an unattainable ideal, hierarchical relations within the church grounded in the Trinity must always be lived concretely as partially coerced subordination of the many to the dominant one.

In following Jürgen Moltmann, I by contrast take as my premise the symmetrical relations within the Trinity.[69] This yields the ecclesial principle that the more a church is characterized by symmetrical and decentralized distribution of power and freely affirmed interaction, the more will it correspond to the trinitarian communion. Relations between charismata, modeled after the Trinity, are reciprocal and symmetrical; all members of the church have charismata, and all are to engage their charismata for the good of all others.[70]

4. Polemic against the institutionality of the church is often presented in the name of "completely spontaneous" interaction interpreted as love that corresponds to the Trinity.[71] But can love understood in this way be the only law of a *human* community? According to Talcott Parsons, there are two presuppositions for "the stabilization of a love-dominated community." The first is "some

68. See V.4.1 above.
69. See V.4.2 above. The ecumenical problem with regard to the institutionality of the church resides less in the "*realization* of the communio-principle in the law of the church" (Pirson, "Communio," 45, my emphasis) than already in one's *understanding* of the trinitarian and ecclesial *communio*-principle.
70. See V.4.3 above; Moltmann, *Church*, 305f.
71. Brunner, *Kirche*, 66.

cognitively intelligible definition of what this [i.e., mutual love] entails with respect to their [i.e., the members' of the community] own conduct and their expectations of reciprocal conduct from each other and from others with whom they interact." The second presupposition is "responsiveness to appropriate leadership initiative in defining the obligations, rights, and tasks of . . . [a] collectivity. . . . A viable collective entity . . . must have rules — rules that can be communicated and understood in cognitive terms."[72] Complete spontaneity in the *objective* sense is an impossibility within a community of love, at least within a human community, since in contrast to God, who *is* love, human beings can love one another only if they participate in God's own love. Hence if they are to love one another, they cannot simply behave toward one another however they will. Although the Augustinian principle "love and do what you will" is correct, still in order to love one must at least implicitly acknowledge and follow quite specific rules of interaction.

Behavior in correspondence to such rules of interaction can occur in a subjectively spontaneous manner. In God's new creation, the individual and communal lives of people will coincide in the communion with the triune God, and they will *want* to do what love, which is God, commands. Although the Spirit of the new creation has already poured out God's love into the hearts of Christians (Rom. 5:5), their individual and communal lives do not yet coincide completely.[73] Hence within the church on this side of God's new creation, one will not be able to do without rules of interaction that are at least partially *external* to every member.

The pivotal question is accordingly not whether freely understood love or rules of interaction are to determine the social life of the church, but rather whether the rules of interaction specifying the practice of love are to be formalized, or whether, in anticipation of eschatological *subjective* spontaneity in communal life, they are to determine the life of the church only as internalized rules of habit. That such rules of habit are not formally specified should not lead one to the conclusion that they are not *fixed rules.*[74] Although after successful socialization "a certain mode of conduct does usually develop 'spontaneously,'" it always does so "*along institutionally prescribed lines.*"[75] More-

72. Parsons, "Religion," 319f.
73. This is also to be asserted contra the Marxist understanding of communism, unless one were foolish enough to understand communism as the reign of God (see *Marx Engels Werke, Ergänzungsband,* 1.535, 538f.; *Marx Engels Werke,* 1.370; 2.138. Cf. in this regard Volf, *Arbeit,* 22-24).
74. The development of strong rules of habit can be observed quite well in the "house-church" movement. In these churches, a strongly hierarchical, informal system "of paternal relations" often develops between the congregation and "charismatic delegates from the ascended Christ" (see Walker, *Restoring,* 141, 171).
75. Berger and Luckmann, *Construction,* 60 (my emphasis).

over, although such rules of habit can be more repressive than formalized rules, at the same time they are not strong enough to counter the "law of fish," namely, that the large eat the small. Hence much argues for legal formalization of the rules of interaction. Although legality cannot generate love, it can create space for love by specifying duties and rights.[76] Such legal statutes in the church, however, must be open to change in light of the love displayed in the communion of the triune God. For if these statutes are to be *church* law, this law, too, must correspond to the essence of the church as an image of the triune God.[77]

There is no contradiction between the church of love and the church of law; rather, both together stand in opposition to the church of lawlessness and injustice.[78] An essential distinction, however, does obtain between the church of love and the church of law. The church of law is the *pre-eschatological* form of the eschatological church of love. Although the church is essentially an institution, it is not essentially an institution in which interaction must be specified *externally*. Legal regulation of interaction is the manner in which trinitarian relations within the church are reflected on this side of God's new creation. However such *external specification* of this interaction may be articulated, it is not only an anticipatory sign of the new creation in the church, but also a sign of the *distance* from its eschatological goal.[79] For a law makes sense only if the possibility exists that what it commands might not be followed; it is "meant not for the innocent . . . but for the lawless and disobedient" (1 Tim. 1:9). There follows from this a tendentiously minimalist understanding of church statutes; the less ecclesial life must be legally regulated, and the more the institutions of the church are lived as the fellowship itself of siblings and friends, the more will these institutions correspond to their own future in which they will be identical with the realization of the communion of the church with the triune God.

5. Because the formal rules of interaction are not only an image of the new creation in the church, but also a sign of the church's distance from its goal, they are not only preliminary but also alterable. Like all other social phenomena, churches, too, abide in a permanent state of morphogenesis with regard to their rules of interaction (one that does, however, stand in constant tension with a parallel tendency toward morphostasis). The direction in which

---

76. See in this regard Herms, *Kirche*, 111.

77. The thesis that church law must correspond to the essence of the church enjoys wide acceptance today among theoreticians of church law (see in this regard Heckel, "Begrenzung," 943f.).

78. So Kasper, "Sakrament des Geistes," 38. Concerning the relationship between love and law, cf. the persuasive argumentation of Michael Welker, *Gottes Geist*, 239ff.

79. See Duquoc, *Churches*, 58f.

these formal rules of interaction are to develop is indicated in a binding fashion by the trinitarian communion. As Ernst Wolf has emphasized, the statement *ecclesia reformata semper reformanda est* applies to church law as well.[80]

The concrete forms of reflection of the Trinity in the church are shaped not only by the binding model of the Trinity, but also by the various cultural contexts in which the church finds itself. From the very outset, the social organization of the church was a result of both the negation and adoption of existing forms of socialization. Because the church lives in differing cultural spheres, both diachronic and synchronic pluriformity of church orders is to be expected. Rather than being lamented as a deficit, that is, as a violation of unity, such pluriformity can be understood as the institutional dimension of the necessary process of ecclesial enculturation.

2.2. *Spirit, Institutions, and the Mediation of Salvation*

Trinitarian relations can serve as a model for the institutions of the church because the triune God is present in the church through the Holy Spirit, shaping the church in the image of the Trinity. Through this activity of the Spirit, salvific grace is mediated and the church is constituted. But what is the relation between the ecclesial institutions, shaped according to the trinitarian model, and this constitutive activity of the Spirit? This is the most disputed ecumenical question with regard to the institutionality of the church, one I will address by examining the relationship between the activity of the Spirit and its human bearers.

1. According to Ratzinger, a purely functional understanding of ministry in the church would be incommensurate with the essence of the church. The "pneumatic character of the church" is necessarily expressed "in the pneumatic character of its ministries."[81] Because the actions of the Holy Spirit in the church are conceivable only as the actions of a whole (the *whole* Christ, head and members, acts through the Spirit), the pneumatic character of ministries demands spiritual officeholders representing that whole. Because the Holy Spirit is bound to these officeholders, they are able to function with spiritual authority in the church and to interpret in a binding fashion the word of God.[82] They guarantee that people in the church are dealing with God rather than merely with themselves.

According to Zizioulas, the structures of the church are the structures of the reign of God as realized in every eucharistic gathering. The structure of the

---

80. Wolf, *Rechtsgedanke*, 72.
81. Ratzinger, *Prinzipienlehre*, 276.
82. See I.4.4 and 4.5 above.

church, however, includes not only officeholders, that is, bishops surrounded by presbyters and deacons, but also the laity. The Spirit acts through both, and does so through their (emphatically asymmetrical) mutual relationship; the congregation can do nothing without the bishop, and the bishop nothing without the "amen" of the congregation. Hence the local church as a whole, including its fixed structure, guarantees that God is acting within it; only what the bishop (in communion with other bishops) decides *and* what the local church (in communion with other local churches) receives derives from the spirit of truth. Commensurate with the pattern of trinitarian relations between the one and the many, the *charisma veritatis*, although given to the bishop, is at the same time contingent on the local church.[83]

2. If the church is an anticipation of the eschatological communion of the entire people of God, and if it is constituted as such through the Spirit of Christ,[84] then the ministries in the church must indeed be understood pneumatically; otherwise, they could not contribute to the life of the church *as church*, since they would be external to the church.[85] Rudolph Sohm has seen this quite clearly, and has rightly insisted that only two possibilities exist for carrying out ministries in the church, namely, on the basis either of the spiritual charismata or of holy law.[86] I have already advocated the charismatic character of church ministry. Here I will explore the relationship between charismata, ecclesial institutions, and church law.

If the charismata were purely punctiliar events, they could have little to do with ecclesial institutions. At best, the institutions would resemble a house, to draw on a metaphor of Hans Dombois, into which one would have to move charismatically.[87] The Spirit would then necessarily be external to the institutions themselves. Although the Spirit would indeed be active through the institutions, the latter would not actually be a result of the Spirit's activity, but rather merely a human framework for a divine occurrence. An actualistic understanding of charismata, however, is faulty.[88] Although certainly rendered possible by God, even a charisma as extraordinary as prophecy is according to Paul nonetheless an *enduring* gift. Reference to "prophets" (1 Cor. 12:28) presupposes this. Prophets engage in habitualized activities also acknowledged by the church as activities of a certain type. Prophecy is an institution in the sense defined

83. See II.4.2 and 4.3 above.

84. See III.1.1.1 above.

85. Here I will discuss only the *theologically significant* personal institutions of the church, but not those with a purely bureaucratic character. The latter are theologically significant "only insofar as they are able to make the theological meaning of the primary institutions transparent" (Kehl, "Kirche," 178, note 1).

86. See Sohm, *Wesen*.

87. Dombois, *Recht*, I, 903.

88. See 1.2.4 above.

above.[89] The same applies to all other charismata. They do not stand in opposition to institutions, nor do they merely occur within institutions; charismata *are* (more or less flexible) institutions (which does not mean, of course, that all ecclesial institutions are charismatic).

Considering that no member of the church is without a charisma, this definition of the relationship between charisma and institution has one important consequence: The members of the church do not stand over against the church as an institution; rather, their own actions and relations *are* the institution church. Although the institutional church is not their "product," but rather is a "product" of the Spirit, the church does not stand over against them as a kind of objectified, alien entity, but rather is the manner in which they relate and behave toward one another. These relations between members are, however, not arbitrary, but rather are played out in (more or less flexible) "roles." They do not have to create these roles ever anew, but rather grow into already existing roles (while simultaneously shaping those roles through their own uniqueness). If the actions and relations of persons are ecclesial institutions, it is important to note that these institutions themselves first make possible the specific participation of every member in the life of the church. Without institutions, the church cannot become an "event."[90] This principle is correct, however, only if it is also reversible; unless the church becomes an event, it cannot be the kind of institution it is supposed to be.

3. Protestant circles often perceive the tying of the Spirit to institutions, that is, to the ministers as the bearers of the Spirit, as problematic. But if charisma is enduring rather than punctiliar, then the Spirit is necessarily bound to the charismatics, albeit through a bond realized not by human beings but by the Spirit of God. The crucial question is whether this self-binding of the Spirit to institutions can be *formalized* in the form of church law. The answer must be: No! The reason is not that such law necessarily contradicts the salvific mediating activity of the Spirit of God. For it is indisputable that "the legal system already inheres within the structural elements of the economy of salvation."[91] Still, one cannot derive from this a system of *holy* law, as Libero Gerosa has recently attempted. The crucial question is whether the legal system genuinely contained in the economy of salvation may be formulated and practiced as *spiritually binding* church law. This legal system derives from the activity of the Spirit, which, as Rudolph Sohm has rightly emphasized, cannot

---

89. In his analysis of the relationship between prophecy and institution, Hans Walter Wolff understands prophecy in opposition to religious and political institutions. He does this because he is using a narrower definition of institution than I am. He himself, however, does speak of an "institution of prophecy," albeit one appearing in three types rather than as a unified phenomenon (Wolff, "Prophet," 89).

90. Marsch, *Institution,* 123.

91. Gerosa, *Charisma,* 120.

be formalized.[92] Such formalization would first of all negate the sovereignty of the Spirit, since such law would have to presuppose the Spirit of God "as a calculable element."[93] Second, one could not clearly differentiate between the action of the church and that of Christ; one could easily mistake the Spirit of God for the Spirit of the church.[94] Third, any legal formalization of spiritual activity would result in a false liberation of people; formal certainty that in the actions of others one is actually encountering God would come at the price of one's own freedom of faith, since church law can provide religious certainty only by tethering religious life.[95]

Because one can never know ahead of time how long the Spirit of God will bestow a particular charisma on a person, all charismata (as institutions!) presuppose a perpetual process of spiritual discernment. Every charismatic is acknowledged by the congregation as a charismatic (or perhaps also not so acknowledged), and his or her charisma is received ever anew in the practice of ministry. The ecclesial process of reception has a critical and a receptive dimension: "but test everything; hold fast to what is good" (1 Thess. 5:21; cf. 1 Cor. 14:29; 1 John 4:1). To give primacy to the critical dimension would certainly be inappropriate, for critical testing does not occur for its own sake but aims at proper reception of the Spirit's activity. Still, discernment must accompany every charismatic activity in the congregation, since the charismata always depend on the concrete activity of the Spirit, which cannot simply be presupposed.

The whole process of reception is not something added to the charismata, but rather is an essential part of the charismata themselves. According to the interactional model of the bestowal of charismata, the latter are not given to individuals in an isolated fashion and then exercised in the congregation. They are bestowed precisely as gifts of the Spirit in the mutual interplay between the charismatic individual and the receiving congregation. The charismata are al-

92. Rudolph Sohm's not quite accurate thesis that "church law stands in opposition to the essence of the church" (*Kirchenrecht*, I.1) is based on the correct insight that formal law and the sovereign activity of the Spirit of God stand in opposition. Life with God cannot be legally regulated (see Sohm, *Wesen*, 14), which is why Sohm himself advocates a charismatic form of church organization. My own conception differs from his essentially insofar as I begin with an *ecclesial mediation of the charismata*, mediation always occurring through the concrete local churches. By contrast, he seems to be thinking primarily of the individual charismatics and the individual members of the universal church standing over against them, members who through voluntary obedience subordinate themselves to the activity of the Spirit through these charismatics (see Sohm, *Kirchenrecht*, I, 26ff.; idem, *Wesen*, xxiv).

93. Pirson, "Communio," 41.

94. See Harnack, *Entstehung*, 128.

95. See Sohm, *Wesen*, 22.

ways partly determined by the concrete church.[96] A church can therefore either implicitly or explicitly decide concerning the presence of charismata among its individual members, or at least concerning the presence of the charismata with which ministry can occur in this concrete church.

Exercising charismata is essentially *an open ecclesial process.* It cannot be the purpose of legal regulations to restrict this process, but rather to protect it in its openness. Legal precautionary measures serve to create the space in which the complex mutual interdependence between individual charismatics and the congregation can be realized. Such an understanding of church law comes to expression in a paradigmatic fashion in the Pauline instructions concerning prophecy. "Let two or three prophets speak, and let the others weigh what is said. . . . for God is a God not of disorder but of peace" (1 Cor. 14:29, 33). Church law serves to overcome disorder and to establish peace rather than formal order, which precisely in its formality has a repressive effect.[97] This law is structured in such a way that it protects the open ecclesial interaction in which *all* (πάντες), one by one (καθ' ἕνα), can speak and be heard, and in which *others* (ἄλλοι) can test and thus *all* (πάντες) learn and be encouraged (1 Cor. 14:31). Only church law conceived in this way would do justice to the church itself and be commensurate with the fact that the pluriform ecclesial ministries actually derive from the sovereign Holy Spirit present both in individuals and in the congregation as a whole[98] as the firstfruits of the eschatological reign of peace.

4. If it is true that the charismata are ecclesial institutions through which salvation is mediated, then ecclesial institutions cannot be a purely human product.[99] And yet, although the Holy Spirit generates them, neither are they a purely divine product. Even though the Spirit acts through ecclesial interaction, we cannot specify in advance where and how the Spirit will act. Although one can indeed hear "the sound of it," one cannot know "where it comes from or where it goes" (John 3:8). Identification of a person as a charismatic is not an infallible judgment based on a specifiable rule but a spiritual process played out on the basis of past experience. We can say "this woman is a prophetess" because she has exercised such prophetic activity in the past. Yet as soon as we have identified a person as a charismatic, we are simultaneously anticipating the future. The statement "this man is a deacon" not only expresses the experience of the past, but simultaneously our expectations (our hope!) for the

---

96. The charismata are not given *by* the church — they are gifts of the *Spirit,* not of the church — but rather *through* the church.

97. See in this regard Moltmann, *Church,* 291.

98. Similarly also Pirson, "Communio," 44.

99. So, e.g., Hasenhüttl, "Kirche," 8 (albeit with a significantly narrower understanding of institution).

future. Because the identification of charismatics always comes about through human experience and expectation, ecclesial institutions are not only a divine, but also a human product. Like the church itself, its institutions have both a divine and a human dimension.

The human dimension of ecclesial institutions requires that the assignment of certain individuals to certain roles (charismata) must always be viewed as provisional. This is the case not because such assignment itself is provisional, but rather because our own knowledge of it always remains provisional. Cognitive anticipations of future experience with the sovereign Spirit of God are *per definitionem* provisional; we *do not know* whether a person will have a certain charisma in the future as well. Moreover, our determination on the basis of past experience that a person has a charisma is also provisional; strictly speaking, *we do not know* whether a certain action on the part of an individual really has come about on the basis of the charisma bestowed by the Spirit. We are only able to evaluate provisionally that this is so. Because the activity of the Spirit is unpredictable and because our human knowledge of the activity of the Spirit is limited, any (formal or informal) ecclesial acknowledgment that a certain person has a certain charisma must always remain subject to revision.

5. Just as (from the human perspective) the bestowal of charismata is provisional, so also are the ecclesial activities rendered on the basis of these charismata provisional, activities such as interpretation of the word of God or the power of the keys.[100] Though God's revelation is complete and trustworthy, there is no such thing as an infallible interpretation of this revelation, no ecclesiastical truth of obligatory character for one's conscience,[101] no ecclesiastical truth concerning what one is to believe and to do, and thus no ecclesiastical truth concerning who belongs to the church and who does not. "For we know only in part," and thus it will remain until "the complete comes" (1 Cor. 13:9-10). Every denial of such provisionality and every fascination with *certitudo* betray a dangerous proximity to blind fundamentalism.

Nevertheless, the church cannot avoid specifying the content of faith and (at least implicitly) deciding concerning membership in the church. This derives in part from the fact that both the content of faith and the kind of life commensurate with faith are essentially part of faith itself.[102] Yet here, too,

---

100. Commensurate with my interest in this entire chapter in *personal* ecclesial institutions, I am expressly not considering the sacramental activities accompanying baptism or the Eucharist.

101. Even if one believes that *all* statements of faith, including the statement that "God has revealed himself in Christ," are provisional (see Pannenberg, *Wissenschaftstheorie,* 312ff.; cf. also Clayton, *Explanation,* 136ff.), one must at the same time distinguish between the provisional character of revelation itself and the church's formulations of this revelation.

102. See IV.1.2.2 above.

the church can do nothing but follow after the Spirit of truth, the firstfruits of the new creation, and make its decisions in a provisional fashion in anticipation of later perfection and completion. These decisions, too, are in principle subject to revision. What is not subject to revision is the divine revelation itself (even though this revelation, too, and certainly our own knowledge of it, is open to eschatological completion). Insofar as the church proclaims this revelation in the power of the Spirit, its own proclamation also participates in the truth of the revelation. This is why the church can proclaim not only its opinion on the word of God, but the word of God itself. This is also why it is not built on itself, but rather on Jesus Christ as the Savior and Lord of the entire world.

3. Ordination

In the preceding discussion, I have simply presupposed "office" and "ordination." In so doing, I am following the long Protestant and Free Church tradition which, apart from a few exceptions such as the Society of Friends or the Plymouth Brethren, has not questioned the institution of office as such. John Smyth was in any case by no means hostile to ordained office. He wrote that "members . . . received into communion are of two sorts. 1. prophets 2. private persons."[103] Together with other English Separatists, he felt indebted to the Reformed tradition, which held the institution of office in high esteem, even if he did try to tilt the delicate Puritan balance between the "aristocratic" and "democratic" elements in the relationship between officeholders and the congregation in favor of "democracy."[104]

Smyth's grounding of ordained office was based exclusively on the interpretation of biblical passages. This is unobjectionable as long as one is aware that the New Testament does not contain any unified, theologically reflected view of church organization, but rather only the various witnesses concerning the manner in which the early churches regulated their own lives within various cultural spheres. Hence any biblical grounding must be placed within a theological framework if it is not to degenerate into mere biblicism. In what follows, I will try to ground the institution of office and ordination *theologically* by first discussing the character and necessity of ordained office and of ordination, and then by examining how the election of officeholders should be carried out.

103. Smyth, *Works,* 255.
104. See in this regard Brachlow, *Communion,* 157-202.

3.1. Office and Ordination

1. "Offices" are a particular type of charismata.[105] Like any other ministry in the church, the ministry of (ordained) officeholders is based on the baptism common to all Christians and on the charismata bestowed especially on office-holders.[106] Since *all* Christians are not only baptized but also have the various charismata specific to each of them, there can be no difference in principle between officeholders and other members of the church (though neither can office be understood as "merely a typological diaconal culmination of the universal charisma of the Spirit at the level of those commissioned by the church,"[107] since all Christians have [partially] *different* charismata). The distinction between the general and the particular priesthood does not divide the church into two groups, one of which has merely the general, while the other has also the particular priesthood,[108] but rather refers to *two dimensions in the service of every member of the church*. On the basis of common baptism, all have become priests, and all realize their priesthood in their own way on the basis of their respective charismata. Hence all members of the church, both office-holders and "laypersons," are fundamentally equal.[109]

If one's premise is the equality of all ministries in the church, then the necessity of (ordained) office is not apparent. Since all ministries in the church

105. So also Baumert, "Charisma," 36, note 38.

106. See 1.1.2 above.

107. Schillebeeckx, *Menschen*, 250.

108. The formulation from *Lumen gentium* that is generally (and correctly) perceived in Protestant ecclesiology to be problematic and according to which "the general priesthood of believers" and "the priesthood of service" differ "in nature and not merely in degree" (no. 10) would be *correct* if the two terms were not referring to *two different groups* in the church. What this formulation rejects does indeed need to be rejected, since the thesis of a gradual distinction between general and particular priesthood — one person is *more* of a priest than another — basically reaffirms and underscores hierarchical relations. What the formulation is asserting, namely, that an essential distinction does obtain between general and particular priesthood, is correct insofar as the distinctions between all charismata and ministries are indeed *qualitative* rather than quantitative. Wolfhart Pannenberg takes a similar view, though for him it suffices for the essential distinction asserted by *Lumen gentium* between general and particular priesthood "to remain encompassed by the life context of the community of believers" ("Ökumenisches Amtsverständnis," 272). By contrast, I am concerned with affirming the qualitative differences between the charismata within the framework of a polycentric and egalitarian, i.e., an emphatically nonmonocentric-bipolar understanding of the church.

109. According to Carl Heinz Ratschow, equality in the church undermines "office in its very foundations," since office stands or falls "with the so-called hierarchical *auctoritas*" (Ratschow, "Amt VII," 595, 50ff.). But office can be based on no other *auctoritas* than are all other charismata of all other Christians, namely, the authority of Christ, which is why this *auctoritas*, from the inner-ecclesiastical perspective, emphatically cannot be hierarchical.

are charismatic, office cannot simply be derived by way of charisma; it must be grounded by way of the particular features of those ministries performed by officeholders and of the charismata bestowed upon them for those ministries. The specific element attaching to the charismata of office is their *reference to the entirety of the local church.*[110] As Wolfhart Pannenberg has emphasized following the *Confessio Augustana* XIV, the particular task of officeholders consists in being "publicly responsible for the concerns common to all Christians."[111] This involves not only representing the congregation, but also *serving* the congregation as congregation; it involves not only acting in the name of the congregation before God, individual members of the congregation, or the world, but also acting in the name of Christ before the congregation as a whole.

For both Ratzinger and Zizioulas, the totality of the congregation cannot be conceived without the unity of office; the one must always be a reference to the whole, for only in this way can the unity of the whole be guaranteed and thus the whole exist precisely as a whole. Both Ratzinger and Zizioulas derive their (in part different) understandings of the relationship between the one and the whole from a hierarchical doctrine of the Trinity in which the one is dominant.[112] By contrast, I have advocated a symmetrical understanding of the relations between the trinitarian persons, which yields a basically collegial understanding of ecclesiastical office of the sort actually attested by the New Testament writings (see, e.g., Phil. 1:1; 1 Tim. 3:1–4:8; 5:17; Titus 1:5-7[113]; 1 Pet. 5:1). Each of the various officeholders focuses in a specific way on the whole of the local church, for example, as a preacher or a deacon. In 1 Cor. 14:31, the emphatic threefold πάντες ("all") is made possible by the καθ' ἕνα ("one by one"). Here, too, the "one" stands in correlation to "all." Different than Ratzinger and Zizioulas, Paul places the "one" into a linear series of multiple "ones," a situation corresponding to the polycentric structure of the congregation.

In every officeholder, a certain dimension of the unity of the whole local church comes to expression, and all together are a sign of church unity.[114] Such a conception of office also makes it fairly easy to agree on a threefold (not tri*level*) understanding of office, as proposed by the *BEM* Document,[115] insofar as all important functions involving the local church as a whole can easily be

110. So, e.g., Althaus, *Wahrheit*, 508; Ratschow, "Amt," 614, 617ff.

111. Pannenberg, "Ökumenisches Amtsverständnis," 278.

112. See I.6 and II.1.1 above.

113. For a collegial understanding of office in the Pastoral Epistles, see Fee, *Timothy*, 21ff.

114. A different view is taken by Wolhart Pannenberg, who (commensurate with his doctrine of the Trinity, see V.4.2 above, note 106) wants to place "the symbolic function of the officeholder as a sign of the unity of the church" in the "center of a theology of ecclesiastical office" (Pannenberg, "Reich," 134).

115. See *Baptism*, nn. 22ff.

subsumed under the titles ἐπίσκοποι ("bishops"), πρεσβύτεροι ("presbyters"), and διάκονοι ("deacons").

2. Like all other charismata, so the charismata of office must be recognized by the congregation in order to be constituted as charismata at all and to function as such in a local church. This presupposes that one should conceive "the gifts" and "the power of using gifts," which John Smyth (together with other Separatists) actually strictly distinguished, as aspects of a single reality. According to Smyth, officeholders have received these gifts directly from God; "the power of using those gifts they have from the head Christ by the means of the body."[116] If one operates with an interactional model of charismatic endowment,[117] then both "the gifts" and "the power of using them" are given by God "by the means of the body." Thus recognition on the part of the congregation enters into the ontology of office, to use Zizioulas's terminology. Whether this recognition is explicit or implicit is of secondary significance; what is decisive is *that* it is present. Before examining ordination as the explicit form of the ecclesial recognition of the charismata of office, let me first discuss the consequences of this understanding of office for the relation between office and the ecclesiality of the church.

I have argued that the church is constituted through the multiple mutual public confession of faith in Jesus Christ.[118] In this sense, office really does not belong to the *esse* of the church. Even a congregation that has no official officeholders can be a church in the full sense. But no local church can endure over time and remain true to its own calling without at least implicitly recognized offices, that is, without charismata focused on the entire local church. Ministries performed by officeholders are indispensable for the church. To survive as a church at all, every church must act internally or externally, must secure its own foundations in its confession of faith in Jesus Christ, and celebrate the sacraments. For this, it also needs leaders, teachers, and deacons. Although the bearers of these roles can often change within a church, and must not necessarily be explicitly recognized, they must nonetheless be there. In this limited sense, (ordained and nonordained) offices are a necessary part of ecclesial life.

3. Three important conclusions for a theology of ordination can be drawn from this charismatic understanding of office.[119] First, since the charismata are actually gifts of the Spirit, the charismata of office can be based neither on

116. Smyth, *Works,* 424.
117. See VI.1.2.4 above.
118. See III.2.2.4 above.
119. For the opposing view of the following three aspects of ordination in the Roman Catholic Church, see *Lumen gentium* 21; for similar views recently presented on the Protestant side as well, see Hahn, "Grundfragen," 343f.

delegation on the part of the congregation (as is often asserted in the Free Church tradition[120]) nor on a sacramental act of bishops (as understood in episcopal churches). If the charismata of office were generated through delegation, they would be reduced to a purely human commission and authorization. If, by contrast, they were to result from a sacramental act (either of the universal church or of the local church), the sovereignty of the Spirit would be endangered since one would have to know beforehand when, with regard to whom, and how the Spirit of God will 'act. Instead, ordination is to be understood as *a public reception of a charisma given by God and focused on the local church as a whole.*[121] Only thus can one simultaneously maintain that the Spirit appoints officeholders (1 Cor. 12:28; cf. Acts 20:28) and does so "just as the Spirit chooses" (1 Cor. 12:11). It would, of course, be inadequate to view this reception as something simply external to the charisma of office, a mere acknowledgment of an already existing situation. As already explained, ecclesial reception is an important dimension of the *bestowal* of the charismata; this applies to the charismata of office as well. Ordination is a public and solemn conclusion to a much longer ecclesial process of reception, one that as a whole is part of the constitution of the charisma of office itself. It follows that ordination is essentially a divine-human act.

Because the ministry of officeholders involves the entire local church, the charismata of office require reception by the entire congregation. Thus in the second place, *ordination is an act of the entire local church led by the Spirit of God,* and not simply of one stratum within the church perpetuating itself through the very institution of ordination (see Acts 6:1-6;[122] 13:1-3). This does justice to the concrete ecclesial mediation of the charismata of office. Although the local church can, and in most instances does, perform ordination through its representatives (officeholders acting in its name; see 1 Tim. 4:13-14), the local church itself must always be present at ordination, since precisely *it* is the human subject of ordination. The divine calling and endowment of an officeholder are recognized by the ordaining activity of the entire congregation, so that one can say with John Smyth: "They are sent by God to preach whom the church sendeth."[123]

Apart from the debate concerning the sacramental understanding of ordination, John Smyth's principle is ecumenically unchallenged, the question being

---

120. See, e.g., Flew and Davis, eds., *The Catholicity of Protestantism,* 106. Similarly also Luther (e.g., *Werke* 6.407.34ff.; see in this regard Althaus, *Theologie,* 279ff.).

121. This does not exclude the possibility that a charisma can be given at ordination, as 1 Tim. 4:13-14 (cf. 2 Tim. 1:6-7) seems to attest. It is questionable, however, whether this particular New Testament passage is to be understood as New Testament confirmation of the sacramental understanding of ordination.

122. For the arguments according to which Acts 6:1-6 is presenting the Seven as being "ordained" by the entire congregation, see Dunn, *Jesus,* 181.

123. Smyth, *Works,* 256.

merely what one understands by "church." Ratzinger and Zizioulas understand this to be the entire catholic church, each in his own way commensurate with their respective understandings of catholicity.[124] Thus both insist that ordination always be performed by a bishop standing in diachronic and synchronic communion with all other bishops. Only this ensures that an officeholder is being commissioned by the entire church, which is one subject with Christ, and that he accordingly enjoys divine commission. But is this line of thought persuasive? That at every ordination by the ordaining bishop or Pope it is always the entire church that is acting is a theological postulate that lacks plausibility. Zizioulas tries to concretize this participation of the entire church at ordination by requiring the "amen" of a concrete congregation to validate ordination in addition to the presence of the bishop *in successione apostolica* (and bishops of surrounding dioceses). These conditions for ordination, however, can have only *symbolic* value; they do not constitute a sure sign that at a given ordination the entire church and so also Christ as its head really are acting. Moreover, these conditions are meaningful only if by "church" one understands the entire existing universal church, the *communio sanctorum* (which for Zizioulas is identical with every local church). But this is not the case. As I have already tried to show, the universal church understood in this way is a theological abstraction. On this side of God's new creation, the church exists concretely only in the individual local churches anticipating the eschatological gathering of the whole people of God.[125] Thus, too, only the local churches can be the human subjects of ordination,[126] whereby the diachronic and synchronic communion of the officeholders performing the ordination in the name of the local churches can function as an important *sign* of the unity of local churches.

Third, ordination is not *necessarily* to be understood as appointment to a lifelong task (although it certainly *can* be such and in many cases indeed is). Like every other charisma, the charisma of office is not irrevocable. The Spirit who has freely given the charisma of office can replace it with a different charisma. Were this not so, the sovereignty of the Spirit would again be called into question; one would, as Rudolph Sohm has correctly seen, be exercising spiritual office "on the basis of formal acquisition," and spiritual office would be "an enduring right."[127] Furthermore, the charisma of office, like every other charisma, needs the acknowledgment of the congregation in order to function

---

124. See I.4.5 and II.4.4.1 above.

125. See III.2.1.2 and III.3.1 above.

126. Understanding the entire local church as the human subject of nonsacramentally understood ordination certainly does not risk viewing the church as the "producer" of office (so Ratzinger) any more than does understanding the bishop and in him the universal church as the human subject of sacramentally understood ordination.

127. Sohm, *Wesen*, 65.

as the charisma of office in the first place. Hence although office can indeed be enduring, it cannot be acquired once and for all. Thus the charismata of office in their two crucial dimensions, namely, in divine bestowal and ecclesial reception, are not necessarily lifelong. The New Testament passages involving the laying on of hands and "ordination" (see Acts 6:6; 13:3; 1 Tim. 4:14; 2 Tim. 1:6) confirm this understanding of ordination insofar as in them, ordination always remains bound to a concrete task.[128] This is why ordination, in contrast to baptism, can be repeated, and is not necessarily a one-time event.[129]

Because the act of ordination is the public conclusion to a spiritual and ecclesial process of reception, it always remains bound to a certain local church, something the Free Church tradition correctly saw from the very outset.[130] Certainly a previous ordination in a local church will be of significance for a different local church into which the ordained person is transferred, and it will be the more so the more intimate is the communion between the local churches involved. In other words, the attachment of ordination to a local church does not exclude the possibility that at the (first) ordination a person simultaneously acquires "recognition" within a territorial church, denomination, or even (the yet yearned for) "universal church" quite independent of any possible transferal to a different congregation. Although such recognition, which would derive from spiritual qualities and professional competence, might be one presupposition of ordination, it must be distinguished theologically from "ordained status" as such. Each local church must itself receive the particular charismata involving it as a whole. Through such (always provisional) reception and the resultant ordination, a particular charisma of office becomes a charisma of office *for this particular local church.*

These three features of ordination demonstrate the impossibility of conceiving office as belonging to petrified institutions and the charismata as belonging to the sphere of pure spiritual freedom. Neither are offices institutionalized charismata that must exist for the sake of order in addition to noninstitutionalized charismata. Offices, like all other charismata, are institutions, and they are distinguished from them according to the kind and degree of institutionalization. Whereas ecclesial recognition is an essential dimension of all charismata, because offices are tied to a local church as a whole the ecclesial recognition they involve is as a rule explicit and public. This is why the charismata of office are (potentially) more stable institutions than the other charismata.

128. See in this regard the persuasive contribution of Williams, "Rukopolaganja," 63-67.

129. The fundamental openness for temporally limited exercise of office corresponds to modern, mobile societies characterized by synchronic plurality and diachronic vocational change (see Volf, *Work,* 108f.; idem, "Arbeit," 425ff.).

130. See Brachlow, *Communion,* 162, 170.

3.2. Ordination and Election

Ordination obviously presupposes election; in order to be ordained, the office-holder must first be selected. In what follows, I will try to define more closely the actual mode of such election. This particular problem, however, simultaneously and paradigmatically evokes the general problem of participation in the decision-making within the church.[131]

1. Commensurate with his construal of the relationship between the one and the many, which builds on his particular understanding of the Trinity, Zizioulas believes that the bishop constitutes the church and yet is simultaneously conditioned by the church. Despite this contingent nature of the bishop with regard to the church, expressed at ordination in the liturgical acclamation "ἄξιος" ("worthy"), an election by the people is, according to Zizioulas, not a condition of episcopal consecration. On the contrary, such election would, argues Zizioulas, make the bestowal of the charisma of office dependent on a decision made outside the eschatological context of the Eucharist. What is his alternative? To be consistent, it would seem that he would have to advocate something like the election of bishops through the casting of lots (see Acts 1:26) within a eucharistic gathering. In fact, however, he has *the synod* making this choice through what is manifestly an extra-eucharistic procedure.[132] Although he is doubtless trying here to preserve symbolically the connection or even the identity between the local church and the universal church, does not, contrary to his own intentions, the universal church now gain the upper hand?

By contrast, Ratzinger does not shy away from election within an extra-eucharistic context, since he expressly affirms the priority of the universal church over the local church. On the one hand, the assembled congregation is indeed a church in the full sense, and as such it is the subject of the worship event; this is why it should also participate in the election of its office holders. "Appointment to office is . . . never to come about *only* from above."[133] On the other hand, however, every local church is "church" only if it stands in sacramental communion with the whole Catholic Church, and it is a subject only if encompassed by the larger subject, which is "the whole Christ" — the head and the body. Full authority always comes from the whole. From this it follows that appointment to office is never to come about only from the individual congregation, but rather must "always *also* include the larger church."[134] The schema "never only from above" and "always also from above" seems to point to a

131. See in this regard Volf, "Demokratie."
132. See II.4.4.3 above.
133. Ratzinger, "Demokratisierung," 41.
134. Ibid.

symmetry between the local and universal church. Considering, however, that the local church is a church only insofar as the universal church is realized and acts within it, according to this schema the local church is clearly in danger of sinking into insignificance.

John Smyth's premise was that the true visible church is the Kingdom of Christ. Its members are the children of the Kingdom and rule within the church.[135] With regard to the election of officeholders, the principle then emerged that "election is by most voyces of the members of the Church in ful communion."[136] Precisely because Christ is the sole king, church constitution is, as August Hopkins Strong formulates it, "an absolute democracy," though it is such only "so far as regards the interpretation and execution of his will by the body."[137] The basic principle of church organization is that Christ rules wherever the whole church rules. His polemical point is that Christ cannot rule where a single stratum in the church (the bishops) rules. This basic principle of Free Church organization is a mirror image of the basic principle of episcopal church organization, namely, that Christ rules wherever the bishop rules who stands in communion with all other bishops in time and space. The polemical point of the latter principle is that Christ cannot rule where ultimate authority rests in the hands of an entire local church.

Both models rightly emphasize that it is not human beings who are sovereign in the church, neither bishops nor laity, but rather the triune God. Each model, however, denies that the other model is preserving the sovereignty of God in the church. Thus each is exclusive and each denies the ecclesiality of the other.[138] From the preceding considerations of ecclesiality, it follows that the question of the electoral mode of officeholders involves not the being of the church as church, but rather the correct way to live as church today. I am assuming that Christ can rule in the church both through bishops and through the whole people, which is why I am trying here only to demonstrate the plausibility of the understanding of the electoral mode of officeholders implied in the preceding ecclesiological outlines, and not to prove that this particular understanding is the only permissible one. The thesis that a participative church structure is the only correct one for all times and places is just as false as the thesis that the hierarchical church structure is God's unalterable decree. This applies even if the strictly *theological* arguments with which the hierarchical understanding of church organization is justified are in *every* context false (which, with regard to a participative understanding of church organization, is not the case). Edward Schillebeeckx has correctly pointed out that the only real

---

135. See III.1.2.2 above.
136. John Smyth, *Works*, 256. See in this regard Strong, *Theology*, 920.
137. Strong, *Theology*, 903.
138. See III.1.2.3 above.

argument for the hierarchical form of the church is "in reality a mere reference to twenty centuries of nondemocratic cultures."[139] The only good reasons that can be adduced in support of a hierarchical understanding of church organization are *cultural*. And these reasons should not be taken lightly, since it is only successful enculturation that makes possible the successful mission of the church.[140] At the same time, however, cultural reasons in favor of a certain understanding of church organization are of limited value; since they are culturally specific, they cannot be universalized.

2. I have already taken issue with the primary theological arguments supporting a hierarchical understanding of church organization, arguing that the Trinity is not to be understood hierarchically,[141] and that the church is not a subject such that divine authority must always come by way of the whole (the whole Christ) and accordingly by way of the one.[142] My argumentation for the election of officeholders by the entire church[143] picks up on the previously developed understanding of the charismata. To this one can object with Ratzinger that charisma

> is a pneumatic rather than democratic principle, that is, an expression for authorization from above that is inaccessible to arbitrary control; it is not an expression of authority commonly accessible from below. Hence it is only appropriate that the concept of charisma should disappear from any debate concerning democratization, where it has no place.[144]

Ratzinger's argumentation, however, presupposes either that the charismata are given by God without any human mediation, or that the divine "from

139. Schillebeeckx, *Menschen*, 275.

140. See in this regard Kottje and Risse, *Wahlrecht*, 44.

141. See V.4 above.

142. See III.2.1.3 above.

143. I am consciously avoiding speaking about "democracy" in the church. Political democracy of the sort that has developed with its various institutions (periodic elections, distinction between the state and the pluralistic civil society) in the past centuries in the Western world is merely a culturally determined form of political participation presupposing specific socioeconomic circumstances. Elevating modern democracy to the status of an imperative applicable to all churches means being imprisoned by a specific culture. Moreover, one can object persuasively that the premodern societies were in principle more open to genuine participation in decision making by all members of society than are modern democracies. One must also consider that the church will differ from society if it remains true to its calling, so that one must ask (a) which elements of modern democracies are transferable to the church and (b) at which points churches should affirm and strengthen and at which they are to criticize and alter modern democratic practice (see Welker, *Kirche im Pluralismus*, 11-36; Hauerwas, *Against the Nations*, 122-31).

144. Ratzinger, "Demokratisierung," 26f.

above" necessarily implies the human "from above." But both presuppositions are mistaken. According to the interactional model of the bestowal of charismata,[145] although the latter are indeed given by God, they are always given through a concrete local church; reception of the charismata is an integral part of their constitution. The charismata of office are no exception. Ordination is the (provisional) conclusion to the *explicit and formal* ecclesial reception of the charismata of office whose beginning is represented by the election of officeholders, a reception that is meaningful, however, only as the continuation of the perpetual, ongoing process of *informal* reception. The conscious election of officeholders should be understood as one moment in this complex process of reception. Charismatic grounding of office thus does not contradict participation of the whole congregation in the election of officeholders, nor is it merely neutral with regard to participation,[146] but rather calls for such participation.[147]

That *officeholders* can and should *be elected* is grounded in the character of the charismata of office, that is, in their essential attachment to a concrete local church. That the *members* of a local church can and should *elect* officeholders is grounded in their calling and in their baptism. All those who are baptized share responsibility for the church and thus must be able to participate in church decisions, including the election of officeholders.[148] In this context, however, baptism should not be viewed in an isolated fashion;[149] it is a one-time event and says little about one's willingness at any given time to take the path of discipleship. Similarly, baptism is valid for all churches and says nothing about one's inclusion in a concrete local church. Reception of the charismata, however, presupposes both the capacity for spiritual discernment and participation in the life of the local church in question, including in the Eucharist. Hence baptism gives the right to participate in the election of officeholders only to those who through baptism have in fact been initiated into the Christian faith and incorporated into a concrete church. Baptism bestows the right of election only as that which it is in the full sense, namely, as the portal into the life of a concrete local church.[150] From this perspective it is understandable why

---

145. See 1.2.4 above.

146. So Schillebeeckx, *Menschen*, 262: charismatic grounding of office says "*nothing about how officeholders must be appointed*" (my emphasis).

147. Concerning charismatic grounding of the election of officeholders by the whole congregation in the Roman Catholic tradition, see Mühlen, *Entsakralisierung*, 435f.

148. So also Schillebeeckx, *Menschen*, 264.

149. So also does *Lumen gentium* 14 define church membership not only through baptism, but simultaneously through "possessing the Spirit of Christ," i.e., not in a purely institutional fashion apart "from the inner status of the person affected" (Ratzinger, *Das neue Volk*, 242ff.; see also Müller, "Communio," 496).

150. See IV.2.2.2 above.

Smyth presents the following principle for the election of officeholders: "Election is by most voyces of the members of the Church *in ful communion*."[151]

3. With regard to the electoral process, understanding election as reception means abandoning the schema according to which people choose between various candidates by means of simple acts of the will. This schema is much too simple, neglecting as it does the relation between potential officeholders and congregation obtaining before the election. Election is the beginning of the formal and explicit ecclesial reception of a charisma of office, but it is also the end of the informal and implicit reception. The latter, however, is an essential part of the *bestowal* of the charismata of office. Before an election ever comes about, the persons up for election have been shaped by the congregation choosing them. Yet just as reception has an aftereffect on the persons whose charisma is being received, so also do these persons affect the recipient congregation. They do not simply present themselves to the congregation as an "electoral possibility." In a certain sense they "impose" themselves in response to the call and gifting of God's Spirit upon the congregation through ministry, a ministry whose faithfulness is subject to the community's discernment. This is the power factor in every charismata of office, one that becomes repressive only if that power does not halt before the critical reception on the part of the congregation. The electoral process of officeholders can be described correctly only as this complex interaction of mutual giving and accepting (or also rejecting) between officeholders and the congregation.

Understanding election as reception means starting theologically with the priority of divine action. The sociological process of officeholders imposing themselves upon the congregation, however, is not to be interpreted as a sign of the priority of divine action. No correlation obtains between the two. The Spirit of God acts neither solely through (future) officeholders insofar as they insert themselves into the life of the community, nor solely through the recipient congregation, but rather through *both in their interaction*. Regarding the priority of divine action, it bears emphasizing that this interaction should not be understood primarily as a human event. Through this interactional electoral process, the members of a church single out those whom *God* has already called (see Acts 13:2). Nor can this be otherwise if ordination is not to be reduced to the delegation of power by the congregation. If God does not stand at the beginning of the explicit process of reception, neither can God be found at its end; appointment by God (see Acts 20:28) presupposes calling by God (see Acts 13:2); otherwise, the divine action in this process of appointment becomes merely a subsequent religious confirmation and justification of human electoral action. Thus all traditions have always viewed the election of officeholders "as concurrence in the will of God or as the emanation of the activity of the Holy

---

151. Smyth, *Works*, 256. See also Jenkins, *Congregationalism*, 46.

256

Spirit."[152] Like ordination itself, election is a spiritual event, something of which Smyth was aware; "election," "approbation," and "ordination," he believed, "must be performed *with fasting and prayer*."[153]

4. This makes it clear that the polycentric participative model of the church cannot simply be realized through structural changes. It is not enough simply to establish participative ecclesial institutions. The sociophilosophical debate on democracy has made it increasingly clear that democratic institutions cannot function without corresponding internalized values and practices. This applies to the church as well.

A participative model of the church requires more than just values and practices that correspond to participative institutions. The church is not first of all a realm of moral purposes; it is the anticipation, constituted by the presence of the Spirit of God, of the eschatological gathering of the entire people of God in the communion of the triune God. Hence the church needs the vivifying presence of the Spirit, and without this presence, even a church with a decentralized participative structure and culture will become sterile, and perhaps more sterile even than a hierarchical church.[154] For it will either have to get along without the participation of most of its members, or it will have to operate with more subtle and open forms of coercion. Successful participative church life must be sustained by deep spirituality. Only the person who lives from the Spirit of communion (2 Cor. 13:13) can participate authentically in the life of the ecclesial community.

152. Kottje and Risse, *Wahlrecht*, 14.
153. Smyth, *Works*, 256 (my emphasis).
154. So also Gee, *Gifts*, 15.

Chapter VII

The Catholicity of the Church

All churches want to be catholic, though each in its own way. This is the paradox of catholicity on this side of God's new creation. Though it stands for totality (ὅλος), it is always based on a certain particularity. No church is catholic purely and simply; each is catholic *in a certain way*. Thus also arises the dispute concerning catholicity.

In entering this dispute in the following discussion, I will summarize the preceding explications concerning ecclesiality, the mediation of faith, the relationship between the Trinity and the church, and the structures of the church (chapters III–VI) by inquiring of their implications for the catholicity of the church. In addition, I will direct my attention briefly to the relationship between churches, the multiple cultures in which they live, and the catholicity of their individual members, in whom we will find reflected a *catholic* church that is open to all cultures and all churches.

1. The Question of Catholicity

1. It is in the dispute concerning catholicity that the episcopal churches and Free Churches have stood at opposite extremes. Since their inception, Free Churches have represented for both the Catholic and the Orthodox Church the quintessence of what is uncatholic. Because catholicity qualifies all other essential attributes of the church, all the ecclesiological capital sins of Free Churches can be understood as transgressions against catholicity. The Free Church understanding of unity, of holiness, and of apostolicity is problematic precisely because it is uncatholic. The unity of Free Churches is uncatholic because it lacks the concrete forms of communion with all other churches, that is, with

the whole church. Their holiness is uncatholic because it is exclusive; according to the Free Church idea, all who do not consciously believe and live commensurately are to be excluded from the church. The apostolicity of Free Churches is uncatholic because it lacks the connection to the whole church in its history, which is assured by the *successio apostolica*. Moreover, the specific ecclesiological characteristic of Free Churches resides precisely in their understanding of unity, holiness, and apostolicity. Were they to become catholic, they would, according to the argumentation of the episcopal churches, have to surrender their very identity. A catholic Free Church is a contradiction in terms; it understands itself as free precisely with regard to those relationships that would tie it to the whole and thus make it catholic in the first place.

This picture changes significantly from the Free Church perspective. Together with other churches deriving from the Reformation, Free Churches have from the very outset subscribed to catholicity and have simultaneously denied this attribute to the Catholic Church.[1] The unity of the Catholic Church is uncatholic because the Pope (or bishop), to use Luther's words, "declares that his own court alone is the Christian church."[2] Its holiness is uncatholic because it maintains a distance from its sinful members (*casta meretrix*) and is never willing to pray for the forgiveness of its own sins (*ecclesia sancta et immaculata*).[3] The apostolicity of the Catholic Church is uncatholic because it insists too much on the form of preserving apostolicity (*successio apostolica*), binds church doctrine to certain formulations from the past, and in this way renders them uniform. According to Free Church argumentation, the Catholic (and implicitly also the Orthodox) Church refuses to accept its own particularity, and thus denies (full?) catholicity to other churches.[4] This sort of exclusive claim to

1. For the Lutheran tradition, see Luther, *Werke,* 5.597.28; 8.96.12; 50.625.15; also Elert, "Katholizität," 241; for the Reformed tradition, see Calvin, *Institutes,* IV.1.2; also Berkhof, *Katholizität,* 16ff.; for the Free Church tradition, see Smyth, *Works,* 745 (albeit without this specific term); also Flew and Davis, eds., *The Catholicity of Protestantism.* It seems at first that the well-known congregationalist *Savoy Declaration* (1658) contests the catholicity of the church: "Besides these particular churches, there is not instituted by Christ any Church more extensive or Catholique." It is imperative, however, that one read the continuation: ". . . entrusted with power for the administration of his Ordinances, or the execution of any authority in his name" ("Die Plattform der Savoy-Declaration," VI, in Müller, *Bekenntnisschriften,* 653). Accordingly, the *Savoy Declaration* is not contesting the catholicity of the church, but rather a certain understanding of the catholicity of the church.

2. Luther, *Werke,* 50.283. See the *Confessio helvetica posterior* (1562) XVII (in Müller, *Bekenntnisschriften,* 196, 5f.); *Consensus Bremensis* (1595) I.2 (in ibid., 740, 11ff.).

3. So also *Unitatis redintegratio* 3. A different accent does, however, seem intended in *Lumen gentium* 8.

4. The Second Vatican Council designated all other Christian communities besides the Catholic Church as non-catholic, including the Orthodox and Anglican churches (see *Unitatis redintegratio* 13, 17; Dulles, *Catholicity,* 132).

260

catholicity is from the Free Church perspective narrow, intolerant, and thus profoundly uncatholic. To be catholic, the Catholic and Orthodox Churches would have to understand themselves as churches among other churches. But by doing so would they not surrender their own identities?

Thus congregationalist and episcopal churches seem to have diametrically opposed understandings of catholicity, which are rooted deeply in their respective ecclesial identities.

2. Obviously, one can fill the concept of "catholicity" with radically different content. Yet if both the Catholic Church and the Free Churches call themselves "catholic," and at the same time mutually deny each other that very catholicity, does not catholicity itself become an empty cipher used in an emotional fashion as a concept with a positive theological charge (anchored as it is in old church confessions) for the sake of strengthening one's own ecclesial identity? Is not the entire dispute concerning catholicity then sterile?

To be sure, the content of the concept of catholicity is not entirely arbitrary. Although catholicity is not a universally accessible *nota ecclesiae* about which one can meaningfully argue outside a given understanding of the church, it is a *proprietas* of the church, its essential characteristic, which (together with other essential characteristics) "expresses the essence of the church with which it is identical."[5] According to the well-known dictum of Karl Barth, the church is "catholic, or it is not the church."[6] From this it follows that the content of the concept of catholicity always depends on the respective understanding of the church. The dispute concerning catholicity can thus be fruitful because it is always a struggle to come to a correct understanding of the church.[7] Insofar as a certain understanding of catholicity qualifies all other essential attributes of the church and makes them problematical for one's ecumenical dialogue partner, the question of the catholicity of the church becomes one of the main questions, if not *the* main question, of dialogue between congregationalist and episcopal churches.[8]

3. Regardless of the theological content with which one fills the concept of catholicity, the discussion of catholicity always involves the fundamental question of the relationship between *unity and multiplicity*. This is already apparent from the term "catholic" itself; to be catholic means to be comprehensive and complete. "A whole," Aristotle writes in his *Metaphysics*, "means (1) that from which is absent none of the parts of which it is said to be by

5. Congar, "Wesenseigenschaften," 364.

6. Barth, *Church Dogmatics*, IV/1.702.

7. See Barth, *Church Dogmatics*, IV/1.701ff.; Lochman, "Notae ecclesiae," 33.

8. Nikos A. Nissiotis believes that the problem of catholicity is "the *primary question of ecclesiology*" and "the core of the primary problem in the dialogue between Christians estranged from one another" (Nissiotis, "Katholizität," 259).

nature a whole, (2) that which contains the objects contained in such a way that they are one."[9] Discounting for a moment the notion of a homogeneous totality, which cannot be applied to a social structure such as the church, one can define totality as *differentiated unity*.[10] Accordingly, any church claiming catholicity must include multiplicity in its unity and must be the one church in that multiplicity; the *catholica* is necessarily, as Pacian of Barcelona said with reference to Psalm 44:10, a queen in colorful clothing.[11]

These terminological considerations also explain why ecumenical consensus holds that both unity and multiplicity are constitutive for the catholicity of the church.[12] If one negates multiplicity, catholicity dissolves into a completely uniform and thus false totality; if one surrenders unity, the *catholica* dissolves into unintegrated and thus false particularities. An appropriate understanding of catholicity can dispense with neither unity nor multiplicity. With regard to the problem of unity and multiplicity, the various understandings of catholicity differ in the *degree* of unification and differentiation they either require or permit. The normative determination of this degree depends on the respective basic ecclesiological decision providing the concept of catholicity with its theological content. Thus one can meaningfully criticize particular understandings of catholicity as totalitarian or individualistic only *in a perspectival way*; this criticism should not be understood as an objective description of a given state of affairs from a neutral standpoint, but rather should be formulated consciously from the perspective of a certain understanding of the church.

4. The relationship between unity and multiplicity is first of all an internal problem of every church, even though attitudes toward multiplicity in one's own ranks cannot be separated from attitudes toward others outside those ranks. The external side of the problem of unity and multiplicity is the problem of the relationship between *exclusivity and inclusivity*. Thus the discussion of catholicity involves not only the inner life of the church, but also the existence of churches in the world. In fact, one can even call the question of catholicity *the* primary problem of churches in their external relations.

As is the case with other social structures, for churches, too, it is the inner dynamic of social life itself that repeatedly evokes the problems of unity and multiplicity, of exclusivity and inclusivity. Moreover, the involvement of churches in contemporary social and cultural life increases the urgency of this

9. Aristotle, *Metaphysics*, 1023b.

10. For the distinction between a homogeneous totality consisting (as does a glass of water) of similar parts, and a heterogeneous totality consisting (as does the human body) of dissimilar parts, see Thomas Aquinas, *Summa Theologiae*, I.11.2.2.

11. See in this regard Beinert, *Um das dritte Kirchenattribut*, 53ff.

12. For Orthodox ecclesiology, see Lossky, "Third Mark," 179; for Catholic ecclesiology, see Dulles, *Catholicity*, 31; for Protestant ecclesiology, see Pannenberg, "Apostolizität," 105f.

problem within the sphere of the church. Two mutually determinative developmental tendencies can be observed today. On the one hand, there is increasing universalization and uniformization, accompanied on the other hand by increasing pluralization and differentiation. According to Odo Marquard, the processes of technological uniformization (primarily through the natural sciences and the global economy) are countered by the "traditional, historical, and aesthetic processes of pluralization"; processes of social uniformization (equality of human beings) are countered by "processes of individualistic pluralization fostering a separation of powers."[13] The world itself is becoming increasingly uniform and in the process is revealing itself in all its multiplicity. Churches are faced with the question to what extent they can identify with the emerging unity of the world as well as with the multiplicity becoming evident within it, and to what extent their catholicity can be inclusive or must be exclusive with regard to the existing tendencies of universalization and pluralization. The theology of catholicity is thus faced with the question of whether ecclesiology is to begin in the tradition of universalization with the priority of the one, or in the tradition of pluralization with the priority of the many. Or is it perhaps possible to escape this alternative altogether?[14]

Contemporary Christian discussion concerning the relations between religions also moves within the traditions of universalization and pluralization. Until recently, Christianity has taken as its premise the thesis deriving from the tradition of unity: *extra ecclesiam nulla salus.* The more inclusive thesis *extra Christum nulla salus* (which was the goal the first thesis tried to make concrete) also gives priority to the one over the many. It is only a "pluralistic theology of religions" that first crosses this "theological Rubicon," "moving away from insistence on the superiority or finality of Christ and Christianity toward a recognition of the independent validity of other ways."[15] This raises the question

13. Marquard, "Einheit," 4. I do not intend to enter the discussion concerning whether the relation of compensation and balance between the two tendencies as asserted by Marquard actually obtains.

14. See V.1.1.1 above.

15. Knitter, "Preface"; also Hick, *God.* In his Gifford Lectures 1986-87, Hick thinks this radical premise of pluralistic theology of religion through to its conclusion: "The Real *an sich* . . . cannot be said to be one or many, person or thing, substance or process, good or evil, purposive or non-purposive" (Hick, *Interpretation,* 246). Hick's position, however, is not a stable one, and threatens to tip over either into relativism or into inclusivism or even exclusivism. Epistemologically it must presuppose a universal rationality (see Apczynski, "John Hick's Theocentrism"), a presupposition incommensurate with pluralistic thinking; ethically he begins with the universality of the commandment of love, which he is able to anchor only in "the Real as variously experienced-and-thought by different communities," but not in "the Real *an sich.*" Love can serve as a criterion of religions only because the commandment of love happens to be central to the great religions. Are we thus not setting out down the path toward an exclusivism of the world religions?

whether one should conceive catholicity within the context of a plurality and thus also relativity of salvific experiences in the various religions, or whether properly understood catholicity requires universality and thus also the absoluteness, however articulated, of Christ.

This brief outline of the great sociological, philosophical, and theological questions raised by the discussion of catholicity serves merely to illustrate that catholicity "includes an entire confession of faith within itself," as Alexis Khomiakov, the well-known, nineteenth-century Russian lay theologian maintained at the end of his life with regard to the concept of *sobornost,* a concept closely related to catholicity.[16] In the following attempt to present an alternative understanding of the catholicity of the local church, I cannot address all these questions. I refer to them here merely in order to indicate the comprehensive framework within which any reflections on catholicity must move.

Just as an adequate consideration of the catholicity of the local church is impossible without an examination of this comprehensive framework, so also is it impossible without exploration of each individual component of the picture itself without an analysis of the catholicity of its individual members. Just how one conceives the church as a whole obviously depends on how one conceives its members as "parts," and vice versa. At the end of my discussion of the catholicity of the church, I will therefore examine the relationship between person and community by considering the catholicity of the person and its relation to the catholicity of the church. The local church stands in the middle between its individual members and the comprehensive whole with regard to which it can be called catholic in the first place. Hence one must examine this comprehensive whole in its relationship to the local church before one can speak of the catholicity of the local church. But before I can discuss these interrelated topics, I must address the disputed question whether catholicity represents a quantitative or qualitative entity.

2. Catholicity and New Creation

The theological content with which one fills catholicity obviously depends on the intended referent of the ὅλος ("whole") contained in the term "catholicity." As the referents change, the partially overlapping meanings of catholicity vary, including the geographical (found everywhere), the anthropological (encompassing all human beings), the revelational (containing all salvific truths), creational (healing all creation), soteriological (containing all salvific goods), or christological (bearing the whole Christ). I will not deal specifically with each

16. *L'Église Latine et le Protestantisme au point de vue de l'Église d'Orient,* 399, cited after Plank, *Katholizität,* 72.

of these different meanings. Beginning with the established classification into a quantitative (extensive) and qualitative (intensive) understanding of catholicity, in this section I will first criticize the quantitative understanding and then present a case for a particular qualitative understanding.

1. Whatever may have been the case with the disputed initial ecclesiological use of the adjective καθολικός by Ignatius of Antioch,[17] the term *catholicity* acquired very early a geographic meaning (unity in spatial and cultural universality) which was then quickly associated with the notion of correct faith. The Catholic Church is the true church, and its universal expansion serves as the emblem of its correct faith.[18] Now, universality is obviously of little help if one is dealing with a false church, and the truth of the church cannot be demonstrated through its universal expansion. The catholicity of the church conceived as geographic universality can at most console its members that they "at least share their error with a great many others," as Ratzinger has fittingly formulated the matter.[19] Universal expansion is not an inherent attribute, but rather a task of the church; hence, it cannot be a defining feature of the true church. Catholicity initially had nothing to do with the actual universal expansion of the church. The church was already catholic, as Henri de Lubac correctly noted, "on the morning of Pentecost, when a small room was still big enough for all its members."[20]

According to a historically influential formula of Vincent of Lérins, catholic is *quod ubique, quod semper, quod ab omnibus creditum est* ("what has been believed everywhere, always, by all").[21] Here the "idea of universality . . . is coupled with that of continuity . . . catholicity refers to identity maintained through the ages."[22] Yet the words *ubique, semper,* and *omnes* would have to be conceived with strict universality if they were to specify adequately that which is to be believed. Otherwise the question remains open regarding just who, for example, belongs to "all" and thus also just what the nature of faith is that embodies the identity of the church through the ages. This is why Martin Chemnitz augmented the formula of Vincent of Lérins by adding *ex*

---

17. Ignatius, *Smyrn.* 8:2. The history of how catholicity has been understood is reflected in the history of the interpretations of this first use of the adjective καθολικός by Ignatius. I am inclined to follow André de Halleux, who believes that the expression ἡ καθολικὴ Ἐκκλησία in *Smyrn.* 8:2 serves to designate the church in its totality. The following conclusion can then be drawn for understanding the catholicity of the church: "the first patristic attestation of the expression ἡ καθολικὴ Ἐκκλησία has without a doubt nothing to do with the theology of catholicity" (de Halleux, "L'Église," 24).

18. See Kelly, "Katholisch," 11ff.

19. Ratzinger, *Volk,* 29.

20. De Lubac, *Katholizismus,* 44.

21. Cited after Beinert, *Um das dritte Kirchenattribut,* 64.

22. Steinacker, "Katholizität," 75.

Scriptura: quod semper, quod ubique et ab omnibus fidelibus ex Scriptura constanter receptum fuit ("what has always, everywhere, and by all the faithful been constantly received from Scripture").[23] If this reference to *Scriptura* is taken seriously, however, then the reference to "always, everywhere, and by all" threatens to become superfluous. *Scripture* attests which faith is to be believed always, everywhere, and by all. Catholicity defined with *ubique, semper,* and *omnes* can in this case have merely an (admittedly important) auxiliary hermeneutical function.

The quantitative understanding of catholicity as the universal expansion of the church or as that which is universally believed is not convincing, and hence a *qualitative* understanding has been proposed in which the ὅλος implied in catholicity is seen primarily as *fullness* and only secondarily as universality. There seems to be a widespread ecumenical consensus today that the church is catholic because the *fullness of salvation* is realized within it.[24] What remains disputed is how the presence of this fullness of salvation in churches (or in the church) is to be conceived.

2. This qualitative understanding of catholicity as the fullness of salvation picks up directly on soteriological and ecclesiological statements found in the New Testament. "And he [God] has put all things under his [Christ's] feet and has made him the head over all things for the church, which is his body, the fullness of him who fills all in all" (Eph. 1:22-23). "For in him [Christ] the whole fullness of deity dwells bodily, and you have come to fullness in him, who is the head of every ruler and authority" (Col. 2:9-10; cf. John 1:14-16). My premise is that these and all other fundamental soteriological and ecclesiological statements in the New Testament can be understood properly only within a comprehensive *eschatological framework*. Like the analysis of ecclesiality, so the exploration of catholicity begins with a reflection on the eschatological new creation of God.[25]

As we have already seen, the new creation is the mutual indwelling of the triune God and his glorified people in a new heaven and a new earth (cf. Revelation 21–22). The entire history of human beings and of the world, freed by judgment from negativity, will also be integrated into this comprehensive reality of the new creation. The new creation will thus be a recapitulation of the entirety of creation from the beginning on, a totality in which God, his

23. Cited after Elert, "Katholizität," 252.

24. For Catholic theology, see esp. Beinert, *Um das dritte Kirchenattribut,* and Dulles, *Catholicity;* for Orthodox theology, see Zizioulas, *Communion,* 143ff.; for Protestant theology, see Berkhof, *Katholizität.*

25. See III.1.1.1 above. Similarly also Pannenberg, "Apostolizität," 92ff.; Moltmann, *Church,* 347ff.; Staniloae, *Dogmatik II,* 222; Flew and Davis, eds., *Catholicity of Protestantism,* 23.

entire people, and the entire cosmos will constitute a differentiated unity, a communion, such that the triune God will be "all in all" (see Eph. 1:10; 1 Cor. 15:28).[26] The eschatological catholicity of the people of God can be understood properly only within the framework of this eschatological totality of God's new creation. *The catholicity of the entire people of God is the ecclesial dimension of the eschatological fullness of salvation for the entirety of created reality.*

From the eschatological definition of catholicity it follows that the intensive (qualitative) and extensive (quantitative) understandings of catholicity are inseparable. Precisely in taking as one's starting point the intensive understanding of catholicity, one unavoidably encounters the extensive dimension. For there can be no fullness of salvation for some without the fullness of salvation for all; nor can there be the fullness of salvation for human beings without the fullness of salvation for the entirety of created reality. Because of its own dynamic, intensive catholicity pushes toward extensive catholicity. It would be a mistake, however, to confuse the intensive-extensive eschatological catholicity of the people of God for the totality of the reign of God.[27] According to the Apocalypse, the new Jerusalem, that is, the people of God in whom the triune God indwells, descends from heaven *down to* the new earth, and is not simply identical with glorified reality (see Rev. 21:1-4). Despite their relationship with one another, the glorified children of God and the glorified world of God (see Rom. 8:21) are to be distinguished, which is why the catholicity of the people of God remains not only constitutively related to something greater, namely, to the triune God, but simultaneously integrated *into* something greater, namely, into the new world of God. The eschatological catholicity of the people of God is to be conceived as a *particularity* that has been opened up both to God and to the entirety of creation.

3. If the catholicity of the church is to be defined eschatologically, then the nature of the relationship between the sojourning church and the new creation possesses crucial significance for understanding the historical catholicity of the church. The relationship between the church and the new creation is, if one follows the New Testament witnesses, best understood with the aid of the concept of *anticipation*. As we have already seen, the anticipatory character of the church is grounded in the presence of the Spirit of Christ, which constitutes it into a church;[28] for the Holy Spirit, through whom Christians are baptized into one body of Christ (1 Cor. 12:12), is according to Paul given to them as the firstfruits and first installment of the new creation (see Rom. 8:23;

---

26. See in this regard Moltmann, *Weg,* 284ff.; von Balthasar, "Absolutheit," 132ff. On judgment in relation to history, see Volf, *Work,* 119-21.

27. As Balthasar, "Absolutheit," 135, apparently does.

28. See III.1.1.1 and 2.1.2 above.

2 Cor. 1:22; Eph. 1:14). If the ecclesiality of the church has anticipatory character, then so does its catholicity. The church is catholic because the Spirit of the new creation present within it anticipates in it the eschatological gathering of the whole people of God.

Very early in the history of theology, the miracle at Pentecost (see Acts 2) was rightly understood as a primal catholic event.[29] The Spirit of God comes over the first Christians and allows them to experience salvation concretely by removing the communication breach caused by the language confusion of the Tower of Babel (see Gen. 11:1-9). They speak and are understood, and thus does the ecclesial community emerge from the Babylonian dispersal. It would, however, be reductionist to understand with Avery Dulles the events at Pentecost simply as "Babel in reverse."[30] At Pentecost, the first Christians did not all speak *one* language; such a miracle would represent an ill-fated return to the uniformity of Babel (which can be viewed as a precondition of the megalomaniacal construction of the tower). In the event of Pentecost, communication comes about through the speaking of *different* languages.[31] The eschatological catholicity of the people of God is thereby reflected in a broken fashion in history. It is a catholicity in which the unity of all is coupled with the affirmation of the uniqueness of each person.

4. Just as the anticipatory character of the catholicity of the church grounds the correspondence between eschatological and historical catholicity, so does it simultaneously *relativize* historical catholicity. If the Spirit of God is present in the church only as the firstfruits of the still outstanding new creation, then each church can be only *partially* catholic. Wolfhart Pannenberg has rightly emphasized that "only in the glory of the eschatological consummation . . . will the church of Christ be realized fully and completely as catholic."[32] Within history, each church is catholic insofar as it always reflects its full eschatological catholicity historically only in a broken fashion. This is why no church can claim full catholicity for itself.

The soteriological and ecclesiological *plērōma* ("fullness") statements (Eph. 1:23; Col. 2:10) on which this understanding of catholicity is based seem to contradict the incomplete or broken character of catholicity. They describe the church simply as "the fullness of him who fills all in all." These statements, however, are describing a heavenly, eschatological church,[33] and with regard to

---

29. See in this regard Volf, *Exclusion and Embrace*, 226-31; de Lubac, *Katholizismus*, 50f.

30. Dulles, *Catholicity*, 173.

31. See Welker, *Gottes Geist*, 215ff.; Volf, "Justice," 471ff.; Dempster, "Moral Witness"; Macchia, "Sighs Too Deep for Words."

32. Pannenberg, "Apostolizität," 105.

33. See III.2.1.1 above.

earthly churches they are to be interpreted theologically in an anticipatory sense. This is also suggested by a closer reading of the letters to the Ephesians and Colossians themselves, which seem to distinguish between "fullness" and the "*whole* fullness"; the church is already "the fullness of him who fills all in all" (Eph. 1:23) because it participates in the "whole fullness" that dwells in Christ (Col. 1:19; 2:10). At the same time, however, Christians — who do not represent an entity different from the church, but who rather themselves *are* the church[34] — are to become so "filled" that they attain the "*whole* fullness of God" (Eph. 3:19; see also Eph. 5:18; 4:11-13).[35] That which can still be filled up is obviously not yet completely full. The *plērōma* statements are thus describing an eschatological reality reflected historically in churches by the Spirit, one which precisely thereby sets free within them an inner dynamic pushing toward this very reality. This dynamic itself, however, demonstrates not only that catholicity is present in actuality, but that it is at the same time also partial.

5. This eschatological perspective enables us to make the ecumenically significant distinction between that which one can call the (eschatological) maximum and the (historical) minimum of catholicity. There is a widespread consensus regarding the maximum of catholicity (notwithstanding the differences in understanding the character of catholicity). This is already significant in and of itself, since it attests the presence of agreement concerning the goal toward which churches are to be moving. By contrast, questions concerning the optimal form of historical catholicity and its minimum remain disputed. Thus the problem of the minimum of catholicity is of crucial importance in ecumenical relations. As in the preceding reflections on ecclesiality, so in the following reflections on catholicity I will address primarily the question of which conditions a church must fulfill in order to be called catholic at all.

Before I discuss the problem of the catholicity of local churches, let me point out that, as far as the qualitative definition of catholicity is concerned, the conditions of catholicity largely coincide with those of ecclesiality. If one defines catholicity as the fullness of salvation, then one must with Wolfgang Beinert view catholicity as the "*most pronounced expression of the essence*" of the church.[36] This means that there is no church that is not catholic, and that recognition of the ecclesiality of a community simultaneously implies recognition of its catholicity.

34. See III.2.1.1 above.
35. See in this regard Schnackenburg, *Epheser*, 81.
36. Beinert, *Um das dritte Kirchenattribut*, 530 (emphasis in the original).

3. The Catholicity of the Local Church

The Reformed tradition, from which the Free Churches derive, ascribed catholicity above all to the *ecclesia invisibilis*. According to the *Westminster Confession* (1647), the one catholic church is invisible and consists of all the elected "that have been, are, or shall be gathered into one."[37] The nascent Free Churches exhibit a similar understanding of catholicity. John Smyth writes that "the Catholique church is the company of the elect," and then expressly adds that it is invisible.[38] It is, of course, an ecclesiological platitude to say that the invisible church is catholic, for if *it* were not catholic, how then could the visible church be such? The theologically decisive question involves the catholicity of concrete, visible churches.

Leaving in abeyance the catholicity of the *ecclesia invisibilis*, one can in Free Church ecclesiology speak only about the catholicity of *local churches*. The reason is apparent enough, since in the strictly theological sense this ecclesiology allows for no other church than the local church.[39] On the other hand, precisely this exclusive concentration on the local church seems to leave no room for any theology of catholicity. Since every church is to be autonomous, and every Christian is permitted to seek (and even change!) a church freely, it seems unavoidable that Free Churches fall prey to local particularism and special interests, and for that reason must again and again prove to be uncatholic. This is the Free Church dilemma of catholicity. Although only the local church can be catholic, in fact it is precisely the local church that seems unable to be catholic. Can one escape this dilemma? How are the famous "two or three" providing the orientation for the Free Church definition of the church to be catholic?[40] I will attempt to respond to this question by examining how the catholicity of the local church arises from the "manifold grace of God" (1 Pet. 4:10) and from its encounter with the richness of creation.

3.1. Catholicity and Grace

1. The definition of the church in article 11 of the influential first Baptist confession of faith, *A Declaration of Faith of the English People* (1611), brings clearly to expression the qualitative understanding of catholicity (albeit without using the specialized theological term "catholic" itself):

37. In Müller, *Bekenntnisschriften*, 597; see also Calvin, *Institutes*, IV.1.2. On the catholicity of the invisible church in the Lutheran tradition, see Elert, "Katholizität," 242.
38. Smyth, *Works*, 251. See *Baptist Confessions*, 285, 318.
39. See III.2.1.1 above.
40. See III.1.1.3 above.

[We believe] that though in respect off CHRIST, the Church bee one, Ephes. 4.4. yet it consisteth off divers particuler congregacions, even so manie as there shall bee in the World, every off which congregacion, though they be but two or three, have CHRIST given them, with all the meanes off their salvacion. Mat. 18.20. Roman. 8.32. 1 Corin. 3.22. Are the Bodie off CHRIST. 1. Cor. 12.27. and a whole Church. 1. Cor. 14.23.[41]

Aside from the possible terminological inconsistency (given the original meaning of "particular,"[42] the expression "particular congregation" presupposes an ecclesiology whose premise is the primacy of the universal church and that accordingly has no place in Free Church ecclesiology), this citation attests a specifically Free Church understanding of catholicity. Every church ("congregation") has the whole Christ along with all means of salvation and is for that reason not part of the church, but rather is a *whole* church and is in this sense catholic. Here catholicity means *the wholeness of a congregation or church based on the presence of the whole Christ.* "Every true visible Church," Smyth writes, "hath title to [the] whole Christ and all the holy things of God."[43] Hence it is catholic.

Assuming the qualitative understanding of catholicity, there is no disagreement that the catholicity of the local church is constituted by the presence of Christ through the Spirit. What remains open is which relationship between the local church and the universal church (in the most comprehensive sense of *ecclesia triumphans* and *ecclesia militans*) the catholicity of the local church presupposes. The documents of Vatican II state that in every local church "the one, holy, catholic and apostolic Church of Christ is truly present and active."[44] A local church is catholic because in it the universal church is realized. Ratzinger conceives this realizational relation with the aid of the notion of church as a subject[45]; the one church is one subject with Christ and as such is present in every local church. Thus the local church is constituted into a catholic church only insofar as "it receives its being from a totality, and it gives itself back to this totality in return."[46] In Orthodox ecclesiology, Zizioulas has contested the priority of the universal church over the local church.[47] The whole Christ, who incorporates *all* Christians into himself, is present in every eucharistic communion. From this it then follows that the local church is identical with the universal church; local churches are each the

---

41. In McBeth, *Sourcebook,* 40.

42. "Belonging to, or affecting, a part, not the whole" (*The Oxford English Dictionary* [1989]).

43. Smyth, *Works,* 267.

44. *Christus dominus* 11; see also *Lumen gentium* 26.

45. See in this regard Chapter I above.

46. Ratzinger, *Feast,* 66.

47. See in this regard Chapter II above.

one whole church, though with differing locales of concrete realization. Here catholicity is the identity of the local church with the universal church. Hence according to both traditions, the catholicity of the local church is constituted through the presence of Christ, though by way of its relation to the existing universal church, either by way of the relation of identity between the two or by way of the relation of the presence of the universal church in the local church.

Without a doubt, a local church can be catholic only by way of a connection with an ecclesiological whole transcending it. The question is whether it is accurate to define this whole as the existing (in heaven and on earth) universal church. According to the model I proposed above,[48] this whole is the eschatological indwelling of the triune God in God's whole people. If this is the case, then one cannot conceive the relation of the whole to the local church with the categories "realization" or "concretization," since this whole, the eschatological people of God, with regard to which the church can be called "catholic," does not represent an already existing reality, but rather an object of hope. Thus, too, the catholicity of a local church cannot be the realization or concretization of the already existing universal church, but rather an anticipation of the still outstanding gathering of the whole people of God, albeit an anticipation in which communal eschatological salvation is experienced concretely.[49] The catholicity of the local church is a historical anticipation of the eschatological catholicity of the people of God in the totality of God's new creation.

That the constituting of the catholicity of every local church does not proceed by way of the existing universal church does not, of course, mean that every local church calling itself catholic can live in isolation from other concrete local churches past and present. What I am questioning here is only that the catholicity of the concrete local church is to be conceived as a realization of the existing universal church. This leaves open the question regarding the nature of concrete relations with other local churches in which the catholicity of each local church must manifest itself.[50]

2. If a local church is to have the fullness of salvation in an anticipatory fashion, then it must also contain all the ministries necessary for the mediation of this fullness. The catholicity of the local church thus has not only a soteriological dimension, but also a *ministerial* dimension. The catholicity of salvific grace presupposes the catholicity of charismata. In article 11 of the *Declaration of Faith of the English People* cited earlier, one reads further that

> diverse particuler congregacions . . . have . . . all the meanes off their salvacion . . . [and are] a whole Church. . . . And therefore may, and ought, when they

48. See III.1.1.1 above.
49. See III.2.1.2 above.
50. See 3.1.3 below; see in this regard also III.3 above.

are come together, to Pray, Prophecie, breake bread, and administer in all the holy ordinances, although as yet they have no Officers, or that their Officers should bee in Prison, sick, or by anie other meanes hindered from the Church. 1:Pet.4.10 & 2.5.[51]

All the members of a church have the right to act with regard to spiritual matters in the church or to elect the "officers," for, as John Smyth wrote, "the brethren joyntly have *all* powre both of the Kingdom & priesthood *immediately* from Christ."[52] From the Free Church perspective, the catholicity of charismata thus means that each congregation contains *all* ministries within itself necessary to mediate salvation, and that the totality of its members is the bearer of these ministries. Here catholicity means *the fullness of spiritual gifts allotted to the local church.*

Free Churches share with episcopal churches the conviction that the soteriological dimension of catholicity presupposes the ministerial one. They differ, however, with regard to how the local church's ministerial catholicity is to be conceived. According to the episcopal tradition, the local church has all the ministries necessary for its life, though in the Catholic tradition these ministries come to the local churches essentially *from the outside.* According to Ratzinger, a person is a bishop only insofar as he stands in synchronic and diachronic "communion with other bishops."[53] Ministries in the local church live fundamentally from the whole of the church. A local church is thus also catholic with regard to its offices precisely insofar as it is a *particular church,* that is, insofar as its ministries come from the universal church and live in a fashion directed toward the universal church. It must be so if the church is one subject with Christ and if its authority derives only from the ecclesial whole.[54]

In the Orthodox tradition according to the reconstruction of Zizioulas, the indispensable context of episcopal ordination is the eucharistic gathering, since "the Spirit is exclusively possessed by the Church."[55] In addition, ordination requires the presence and actions of other (neighboring) bishops in the apostolic succession. Both these conditions of episcopal ordination clearly demonstrate that a local church is catholic also with regard to its ministries insofar as it is *identical* with the universal church, that is, insofar as its bishop is constituted by other bishops, representing its necessary bond with all other churches, in the eucharistic gathering, a gathering in which the local church is identical with the eschatological reign of God.[56]

51. In McBeth, *Sourcebook,* 40.
52. Smyth, *Works,* 315 (my emphasis).
53. Ratzinger, *Das neue Volk,* 116.
54. See I.4 above.
55. Zizioulas, *Communion,* 165.
56. See II.4.2 above.

Just as according to the Free Church model the catholicity of salvation, or the presence of the whole Christ in the Spirit, is not constituted through any reference to the existing universal church, so also according to this model the catholicity of ministries does not require connection with the universal church. The Spirit, present in the church as the firstfruits of the new creation and making it thus into a catholic church, bestows upon it in the same act various gifts necessary for its life. The grace of the new creation is "manifold." When people receive grace, they receive not only the gift of salvation, but simultaneously also the various gifts of the Spirit with which they are to serve one another; as recipients of the grace of salvation they simultaneously become its "stewards" (see 1 Pet. 4:10). The local church is catholic in the full sense because its members are able to transmit further, in the power of the Spirit and through mutual service and common action in the world, the entirety of grace they have received.[57] The local church's catholicity of ministry means that it is *in the power of the Spirit and through the totality of its members that the church itself is constituted as a church and is able to live as a church.*

3. Of course, every Christian group can maintain that it is a catholic church. Mere subscription to catholicity, however, does not immediately make it into a catholic church. What are the *external* marks of catholicity? The qualitative understanding of catholicity cannot avoid this question, since it focuses above all on the interior side of the church (on the fullness of salvific grace). The church is, to be sure, as *Lumen gentium* correctly emphasizes, a "complex reality which comes together from a human and divine element."[58] Although one can indeed distinguish the internal from the external side of the church, one cannot separate the two. This makes the search for the external marks of catholicity meaningful; that is, even if the presence of these marks cannot prove catholicity, their absence can falsify or at least damage the credibility of a community's claim to catholicity. Here I will examine only the two identifying marks of catholicity and will later address yet a third mark involving the creational dimension of catholicity.[59]

One mark of the catholicity of the local church involves its *relations to other churches.* Differently than in the Catholic tradition, however, the sacramentally mediated origin "from the universal church" and movement "toward the universal church" (Ratzinger) does not represent a necessary condition of catholicity according to the Free Church model. Nor is communion with other local churches in space and time on the basis of apostolic succession and on the basis of bishops standing in sacramental communion with one another (Zizioulas) an indispensable factor in determining the catholicity of the local

57. See IV.1.1.3 and VI.1 above.
58. *Lumen gentium* 8.
59. See 3.2.2 below.

church. Such relations between churches can certainly be desirable from the Free Church perspective, but they are not a necessary condition of catholicity. The minimal requirement for catholicity with regard to relations between churches is the *openness* of each church to all other churches. A church that closes itself off from other churches of God past or present, or a church that has no desire to turn to these churches in some fashion, is denying its own catholicity. A church cannot reflect the eschatological catholicity of the entire people of God and at the same time isolate itself from other churches. The catholicity of the local church presupposes that the channels for synchronic and diachronic communication between all churches remain open.

Openness to all other churches of God is, however, only the *minimum* for the catholicity of a church. It cannot be absent if one wishes to call a particular church catholic. It would be a mistake, however, to confuse the minimum of catholicity with its optimum. Although a church that were *only* open to all other churches would indeed be a catholic church, it would clearly be a *poor* catholic church. Every catholic church is charged with maintaining and deepening its ties to other churches past and present. The church that refuses to do this would not be a catholic church and thus would be no church at all. Openness to other churches should lead to a free networking with those churches, and as the image of the net also suggests, these mutual relations should be expressed in corresponding ecclesial institutions.[60]

Openness to all other churches is a formal identifying feature of catholicity. As such, this feature itself is still insufficient, since it is unable to identify those Christian groups to whom a church must be open if it is to be catholic. Hence to this feature we must also add *loyalty to the apostolic tradition*. All churches view loyalty to the apostolic tradition as the basic identifying feature of catholicity, even if they interpret this loyalty differently and seek to secure it through different means. For only from the perspective of the apostolic tradition can that which the catholicity of the church is be determined in the first place, just as it is only by way of the church's (explicit or implicit) confession of faith that it can be distinguished from other social units. According to the Free Church model, catholicity is not constituted through recourse to the universal church, but rather directly by way of the presence of the Spirit of the new creation; so also does the connection with the apostolic tradition, a connection demonstrating and guaranteeing catholicity, need no recourse to the existing universal church with the one at its head,[61] but rather comes about through direct access to the historically mediated apostolic scriptures. Even in such dealings with the apostolic scriptures, however, the catholic demand for openness to all churches remains in effect. An adequate interpretation of the apostolic

60. See in this regard III.3. above.
61. See I.3 above.

scriptures, and thus also the identification of the apostolic tradition, can take place only through synchronic and diachronic ecclesial communication.[62]

3.2. Catholicity and Creation

1. Yves Congar has rightly drawn attention to two sources of catholicity for the church.[63] One is God's grace; the triune God transmits to creation the totality of salvation by taking up dwelling in the communion of those who believe in Christ. The other source of catholicity is creation itself. Creation is certainly not a source of catholicity independent of the grace of the triune God. God the Savior comes into creation as a reality that God as Creator has made and in which God as Sustainer is present. Nonetheless, if the distinction between creation and salvation is meaningful, then it is also possible to view creation as a second source of the catholicity of the church.

Yet how can one understand creation as a source of the church's catholicity if one defines catholicity eschatologically, as I have done? Does not this eschatological perspective lead to disdain for the world of the sort that has so often characterized the Free Church attitude toward culture? The answer obviously depends on how one conceives the relationship between creation and new creation (just as this theological decision is often shaped by the social position of church communities). My premise is that God's eschatological action does not stand in opposition to God's protological action. The new creation does not arise only after the destruction of the old creation as a new *creatio ex nihilo*, but rather through the latter's renewal or rebirth.[64] Just as the nations will bring their "glory" and wealth into the new Jerusalem (Rev. 21:24, 26 — the people, not the city!), so also must churches remain open for the entire natural and cultural wealth of human beings. Churches can reflect historically the eschatological catholicity of the people of God only by becoming places where the salvation of concrete human beings is experienced insofar as their natural and cultural uniqueness is accepted, sanctified, and reconciled. This admittedly presupposes the kind of prophetic criticism that first makes it possible to identify within the various cultures that which corresponds to God's eschatological new creation.[65]

2. The Free Church model seems to be in tension with the creational

---

62. In this limited sense, and only in this sense — namely, of a reading of scripture within comprehensive ecclesial communication — one can genuinely also say that the church gives scripture its meaning (so Hauerwas, *Unleashing*, 27).

63. Congar, "Wesenseigenschaften," 487ff.

64. See in this regard Volf, *Work*, 98ff.

65. See in this regard, Volf, "Church."

dimension of catholicity. This tension derives less from the tendency toward dualism already mentioned, dualism not inherent in the model itself, than from the constitutive role this model ascribes ecclesiologically to covenant and to free choice. Each person can freely choose the church to which he or she wishes to belong. Since, as Aristotle already noted, "like tends toward like," the catholicity of Free Churches is genuinely at risk. They can too easily degenerate into religious clubs in which those of the same race, social class, and political views mutually confirm their one-sidedness within a religious framework. "Homogenous units," to use the phrase popularized by the Church Growth movement, cannot be catholic. Arguably, this criticism presupposes too simple an understanding of the will to belong to a church, since it does not take into account the mutual influence between this will and ecclesial being as such;[66] still, although taking this into account does indeed ease the problem, it does not solve it.

To escape this difficulty, Zizioulas insists on the territorial principle according to which only *one* church is permitted in a specific locality (city) to which *all* Christians from the locality must then belong.[67] The church can be catholic in the creational sense only if it embodies "the totality of its milieu."[68] Is this solution persuasive today?[69] It is difficult to imagine how this territorial precondition of catholicity advocated by Zizioulas can be realized in big cities, not to speak of the modern megalopolis. A purely territorial understanding of locality no longer seems meaningful today. For what we have today is both geographic pluralization of the spheres of life (especially the separation of place of residence and place of work) and cultural pluralization within any given sphere of life; people live multilocally, and locales are multicultural. Hence any attempt at securing the ecclesial imaging of the eschatological catholicity of the people of God *territorially* seems off the mark.[70] Is one to forbid a mobile and multicultural population from attending regularly a church outside its residential area? If one wishes to reject this implicit or explicit prohibition but still affirm the principle of territoriality, one will have to define a local church through officeholders and geographic location without recourse to actual church members, unless one eliminates entirely any notion of liturgical and communal life from the definition of the church. The transcending of all boundaries between people, a process deriving from the experience of salvation itself, must today be lived in the freedom of personal decision. It was no different in New Testament times. The fact that Jews and

---

66. See IV.2.2.2 above.

67. See II.3.2.1 above.

68. Zizioulas, "Groupes," 268. Similarly also Ratzinger, *Gemeinschaft*, 73.

69. For Orthodox criticism, see Erickson, "Local Churches," 9ff.

70. The American sociologist Robert Wuthnow writes: "Geographic mobility, urbanization, and occupational specialization have all eroded the relationship between religion and communities of residence" (*Restructuring*, 309).

Greeks, slaves and free, men and women belong together in the Christian church is, in any case, based on their faith and their baptism (see Gal. 3:26-28; 1 Cor. 12:12-13; Col. 3:10-11). So it is not surprising to find several house churches in a single city during New Testament times.[71]

Each of several churches in a given geographic locale can be catholic; the concrete appropriation of the totality of a geographically circumscribed milieu into the church is not a necessary condition of catholicity. Just as the ecclesial dimension of catholicity becomes manifest through the openness of a particular church to all other churches of God, so also is the creational dimension of catholicity made manifest through its *universal openness* for all human beings who confess faith in Christ without distinction. Any church that excludes certain people on the basis of race or social class, or that is willing to tolerate such exclusion with indifference, is denying its own catholicity. There can be no catholicity without a willingness to accept other Christians and other churches precisely in their otherness (see Rom. 14:1–15:13)![72] Being open to all human beings, however, represents only the minimum of catholicity. Beyond this universal openness, churches should strive to reflect historically the eschatological shalom of the whole people of God through positive integration (not assimilation!) of the entire breadth of cultural wealth within God's rich creation.[73]

4. The Catholicity of Person

1. The catholicity of the church is inconceivable without the catholicity of its members, for its members are not the individual pieces of a larger or smaller ecclesial puzzle who must fit into the whole without themselves having to be complete or whole. Because the "parts" of the church's totality are persons and thus subjects of action, churches will be catholic only if each member is catholic as well. All church traditions have thus reflected on the *catholicity of persons,* though the Catholic and Orthodox traditions have done so much more intensively than has the Protestant.[74]

71. See III.2.1.1 above. This suggests that one insists with such vehemence on the principle of territoriality less in order to secure the catholicity of the local church than to maintain the unidimensional structures of authority and subordination that can be consistently implemented only under the assumption of the principle of territoriality (see in this regard Kaufmann, "Organisation" [English edition: *Concilium,* v.91.73]).

72. See Welker, *Kirche ohne Kurs,* 55ff.

73. Concerning the catholicity of the local church, see the fine argumentation of Lesslie Newbigin, "What is," 19ff.

74. For the Catholic tradition, see Congar, "Wesenseigenschaften," 396; for the Orthodox tradition, see Zizioulas, "Human Capacity," 408; Lossky, "Third Mark," 175; for the Free Church tradition, see Flew and Davis, eds., *Catholicity of Protestantism,* 21.

A consensus obtains between these traditions concerning the ultimate grounding of the catholicity of person. Just as every church is a catholic church because the whole Christ is present in it through the Holy Spirit, so also is every believer a catholic person because the whole Christ indwells every one through the Holy Spirit. This understanding of the catholicity of person not only follows from the qualitative understanding of catholicity, but also draws clear support from biblical statements. Through faith and baptism, every Christian participates in the fullness of the deity dwelling in Jesus Christ (Col. 2:9-12; cf. John 1:14-16). The differences between church traditions with regard to the catholicity of person emerge immediately as soon as one inquires of the role the church plays in the constitution of the catholicity of person.

2. The Catholic and Orthodox traditions conceive the catholicity of person in analogy to that of the local church. Just as a local church becomes catholic insofar as the universal church — *ecclesia triumphans* and *ecclesia militans* together — is realized within it, so a person becomes catholic insofar as the universal church is realized in that person. The individual is catholic because the whole is present in that individual. Moreover, the universal church is conceived here as *subject*. Ratzinger and Zizioulas agree that the "I" of the church is that of Christ.[75] The church, together with Christ, constitutes a single mystical person, the "whole Christ." Thus the individual is catholic because Christ together with the whole church is present within him or her. The catholicity of persons is grounded in their incorporation into the collective person "church," whereby the collective person becomes the internal structure of every individual person.

This particular understanding of the catholicity of person takes its orientation from a widely accepted, traditional understanding of the relationship between soul and body. "If the hand could think," writes Hans Urs von Balthasar, "it would understand that it is an organic expression of a totality transcending its members."[76] Now, the members of the church are not thinking organs, but rather interdependent and still autonomous persons. Persons are constituted by God in the medium of their social relationships. Sociality is essential for personhood.[77] The social surroundings through which a person is constituted, however, are not the social totality active in every person, but rather the concrete — fixed and fleeting, deep and superficial — relations in which a person lives. Accordingly, an ecclesial person is not constituted by the Spirit of God through that person's relation to a whole, however articulated, present and active within him or her,[78] but rather through that person's

---

75. For Ratzinger, see I.1.1.1 above; for Zizioulas, see II.3.1.2 above.
76. Von Balthasar, *Katholisch*, 8.
77. See IV.3.1.1 above.
78. So also de Lubac, *Katholizismus*, 293.

multiple relations to other, concrete Christians, especially through the relations to the concrete congregation in which the person has come to faith and been baptized.[79]

But how are we to conceive the catholicity of persons who are constituted into Christians through their concrete relations to other persons? Taking as our premise the eschatological understanding of catholicity, we may conceive the catholicity of ecclesial persons as the anticipation of the eschatological gathering of the whole people of God in the new creation. The Spirit who is the firstfruits of the new creation is given not only to the whole community, but also to every person in that community; the Spirit dwells "in the hearts" of individuals (see 2 Cor. 1:22). This is why Paul can express the anticipation of the new creation in very personal terms: "So if *anyone* is in Christ, there is a new creation" (2 Cor. 5:17). Every person who is in Christ through the Spirit anticipates in a broken fashion the eschatological indwelling of the triune God in God's whole people.

No Christian, however, can be a catholic person alone, separated from other Christians. Because the catholicity of person anticipates the eschatological catholicity of God's people, it cannot come about through a process taking place merely between the Spirit of God and the hearts of individual persons. Communion of the whole people of God can be anticipated only if one lives in such communion. The issue here is not that the individual must be a member of the overall organism so that the latter can express itself in that member, but rather that if a person is to be catholic, her inner constitution must be determined by an ecclesial community. I am a catholic being only if my relations to other Christians, to a congregation, are part of my ecclesial personhood itself; the essential relationality of the person reflects the comprehensive sociality of the people of God in the new creation. Precisely because the catholicity of the individual Christian is unthinkable without this relationality,[80] it presupposes the catholicity of the church.

From this it follows that the relationship "Christian — other Christians" does not correspond to the relationship "church — other churches." A church can reflect in and of itself the eschatological catholicity of the people of God (albeit in a broken fashion) because it is itself a communion. By contrast, a Christian alone would be an isolated individual, unable to reflect the catholicity of the people of God. Accordingly, openness to all other churches can suffice as a condition of catholicity with regard to a church, whereas *standing* in an ecclesial community is an indispensable condition for the catholicity of person. Thus the catholicity of person is the personal side of the essential sociality of salvation.[81]

79. See IV.1.1.3 and VI.1.1.2 above.
80. See V.3.2.2 above.
81. See IV.2.1.2 above.

3. It is not enough, however, to understand the catholicity of the ecclesial person as relationality, since this objective catholicity of person, "being from others," can also be lived individualistically. Ecclesiological individualism — as any other individualism — does not consist so much in the absence of relations that define the being of the person as in the conscious or unconscious denial of being conditioned by these relations and in the refusal both to enrich others and to allow oneself to be enriched by them. In actuality, every human being is shaped by others. The individualist lacks what I call the *subjective* dimension of the catholicity of person, namely, one's self-understanding as a relational being and the conscious attempt to live one's own relationality within a community of mutual giving and receiving.

Ratzinger defines the subjective catholicity of person as its process of becoming *anima ecclesiastica;* the individual Christian should become a microcosmic image of the universal church. Since this can take place only through a process of internalization, the liturgy of the universal church as well as forms of spirituality one receives from the universal church (rather than invents oneself) are of decisive significance for the emergence of the *anima ecclesiastica*.[82] The Orthodox tradition speaks similarly of the "openness" of the individual "to the whole and to being filled by the whole."[83] This understanding of subjective catholicity is accompanied by the notion of an indissoluble relation between Christ and the universal church, the "whole Christ." Becoming a catholic person is identical with deepening one's experience of salvation because it occurs through internalization of the "whole Christ."

According to the eschatological understanding of catholicity, the catholicity of person will come to fulfillment only in the person's comprehensive relations to the whole people of God in which the triune God dwells. From this the following rule emerges: The more comprehensively a Christian's personal makeup is determined by other Christians past and present, the more catholic that person will be. In this sense, every Christian should become an *anima ecclesiastica,* though the catholicity of person involves less that person's relation to a whole that is thought of as a subject than that person's relation to Christ through *relations to concrete Christians.* (These Christians can, however, occupy different positions of importance in the life of a person, as, for example, the apostle Paul, my own mother, Thomas Aquinas, or an elder in my church.) So the subjective catholicity of person cannot consist only in the internalization of what is common to all; it must also consist in the adoption of what is specific to each. According to the New Testament witness, the Spirit of the new creation is not only the Spirit of salvation common to all, but simultaneously the Spirit of gifts unique to each. The same Spirit baptizes all into one body of Christ and

82. See I.5.4 above.
83. Staniloae, *Dogmatik II,* 221; see Lossky, "Third Mark," 186.

simultaneously "allots to each one individually just as the Spirit chooses" (1 Cor. 12:11-13). This twofold activity of the Spirit in unifying and differentiating prevents false catholicity of either church or persons from emerging in which the particular is swallowed up by the universal. The Spirit of communion opens up every person to others, so that every person can reflect something of the eschatological communion of the entire people of God with the triune God in a unique way through the relations in which that person lives.[84]

---

84. See in this regard Volf, *Exclusion and Embrace*, 50ff.

Bibliography

Abbott, E. S. et al., eds. *Catholicity: A Study in the Conflict of Christian Traditions in the West*. London: Dacre, 1952.

Adam, Karl. "Cyprian's Kommentar zu Mt. 16,18 in Dogmengeschichtlicher Beleuchtung." In *Gesammelte Aufsätze zur Dogmengeschichte und Theologie der Gegenwart*, edited by F. Hofmann, 80-122. Augsburg: Haas, 1936.

Ad gentes. In *Das Zweite Vatikanische Konzil: Dokumente und Kommentare. Lexikon für Theologie und Kirche*, 14.22-125. Freiburg: Herder, 1966-68.

Afanassieff, Nicolas. "The Church which Presides in Love." In *The Primacy of Peter*, by J. Meyendorff, et al., 57-110. London: Faith Press, 1963.

————. "Statio orbis." *Irénikon* 35 (1962): 65-75.

Althaus, Paul. *Die christliche Wahrheit: Lehrbuch der Dogmatik*. 7th ed. Gütersloh: Mohn, 1966.

————. *Die Theologie Martin Luthers*. 5th ed. Gütersloh: Mohn, 1980.

Ammerman, Nancy Tatom. *Congregation and Community*. New Brunswick: Rutgers University Press, 1997.

Anderson, R. E., and I. Carter. *Human Behavior in the Social Environment: A Social System Approach*. New York: de Gruyter, 1984.

Apczynski, John V. "John Hick's Theocentrism: Revolutionary or Implicitly Exclusivist." *Modern Theology* 8 (1992): 39-52.

Arens, Edmund. *Bezeugen und Bekennen: Elementare Handlungen des Glaubens. Beiträge zur Theologie und Religionswissenschaft*. Düsseldorf: Patmos, 1989.

Aristotle. *Metaphysics*. Translated with Commentaries and Glossary by Hippocrates G. Apostle. Bloomington: Indiana University Press, 1966.

Aristotle. *Nicomachean Ethics*. Loeb Classical Library. Cambridge: Harvard University Press, 1975.

Assmann, Jan. *Politische Theologie zwischen Ägypten und Israel*. Munich: Carl Friedrich von Siemens Stiftung, 1992.

Auer, Johann. *Gott — Der Eine und Dreieine: Kleine katholische Dogmatik II*. Edited by J. Auer and J. Ratzinger. Regensburg: Pustet, 1978.

Aulén, Gustaf. *The Faith of the Christian Church.* Philadelphia: Fortress, 1972.

Baillargeon, Gaëtan. *Perspectives Orthodoxes sur L'Église Communion: L'œuvre de Jean Zizioulas.* Bréches théologiques 6. Paris: Médiaspaul, 1989.

Balthasar, Hans Urs von. "Die Absolutheit des Christentums und die Katholizität der Kirche." In W. Kasper, *Absolutheit des Christentums,* 131-65. Freiburg: Herder, 1977.

———. *Katholisch: Aspekte des Mysteriums.* Kriterien 36. Einsiedeln: Johannes, 1975.

Banks, Robert. *Paul's Idea of Community: The Early House Churches in Their Historical Setting.* Exeter: Paternoster, 1980.

Baptism, Eucharist and Ministry. St. Louis: Association of Evangelical Lutheran Churches, 1982.

Barna, George. *Marketing the Church.* Colorado Springs: NavPress, 1988.

Barna, George, and William Paul McKay. *Vital Signs: Emerging Social Trends and the Future of American Christianity.* Westchester, N.Y.: Crossway, 1984.

Barrett, C. K. *Commentary on the First Epistle to the Corinthians.* Black's New Testament Commentary. London: Black, 1968.

Barth, Hans-Martin. *Einander Priester sein: Allgemeines Priestertum in ökumenischer Perspektive.* Kirche und Konfession 29. Göttingen: Vandenhoeck & Ruprecht, 1990.

Barth, Karl. *Church Dogmatics.* Volume IV/1. Edinburgh: Clark, 1956.

Bate, H. N., ed. *Faith and Order: Proceedings of the World Conference Lausanne, August 3-21, 1927.* Garden City, N.Y.: Doubleday, 1928.

Baumert, Norbert. " 'Charisma' — Versuch einer Sprachregelung." *Theologie und Philosophie* 66 (1991): 21-48.

———. "Charisma und Amt bei Paulus." In *L'apôtre Paul: Personnalité, style et conception du ministère,* edited by A. Vanhoye. Bibliotheca Ephemeridum theologicarum Lovaniensium 73. Leuven: Leuven University Press, 1986.

———. "Das Fremdwort 'Charisma' in der westlichen Theologie." *Theologie und Philosophie* 65 (1990): 395-415.

———. "Zur Begriffsgeschichte von χάρισμα im griechischen Sprachraum." *Theologie und Philosophie* 65 (1990): 79-100.

———. "Zur Semantik von χάρισμα bei den frühen Vätern." *Theologie und Philosophie* 63 (1988): 60-78.

Baur, Jörg. "Das kirchliche Amt im Protestantismus: Skizzen und Reflexionen." In *Das Amt im ökumenischen Kontext: Eine Studienarbeit des Ökumenischen Ausschusses der Vereinigten Evangelisch-Lutherischen Kirche Deutschlands,* 103-38. Stuttgart: Calwer, 1980.

Bayer, Oswald. "Schriftautorität und Vernunft — ein ekklesiologisches Problem." In *Autorität und Kritik: Zu Hermeneutik und Wissenschaftstheorie,* 39-58. Tübingen: Mohr-Siebeck, 1991.

Beinert, Wolfgang. *Um das dritte Kirchenattribut: Die Katholizität der Kirche im Verständnis der evangelisch-lutherischen und römisch-katholischen Theologie der Gegenwart.* Koinonia 5. Essen: Ludgerus, 1964.

Bilezikian, Gilbert. *Community 101: Reclaiming the Local Church as Community of Oneness.* Grand Rapids: Zondervan, 1997.

Berger, Peter L. *The Heretical Imperative: Contemporary Possibilities of Religious Affirmation.* Garden City, N.Y.: Doubleday, 1979.

————. "Market Model for the Analysis of Ecumenicity." *Social Research* 30 (1963): 77-93.

Berger, Peter, and Thomas Luckmann. *The Social Construction of Reality: A Treatise in the Sociology of Knowledge.* Garden City, N.Y.: Doubleday, 1966.

————. "Secularisation and Pluralism." *Internationales Jahrbuch für Religionssoziologie* 2 (1966).

Berkhof, Hendrik. *Die Katholizität der Kirche.* Zurich: EVZ, 1962.

Biedermann, Hermenegild. "Gotteslehre und Kirchenverständnis: Zugang der orthodoxen und der katholischen Theologie." *Theologisch-praktische Quartalschrift* 129 (1981): 131-42.

Bietenhard, H. "ὄνομα." In *Theological Dictionary of the New Testament.* Vol. 5. Edited by G. Friedrich. Translated and edited by G. W. Bromiley. Grand Rapids: Eerdmans, 1967.

Birmelé, André. *Le Salut en Jésu Christ dans les dialogues œcuméniques.* Cogitatio fidei 141. Paris: Cerf, 1986.

Bittlinger, Arnold. *Im Kraftfeld des Heiligen Geistes.* 4th ed. Marburg: Ökumenischer Verlag, 1971.

Bobrinskoy, Boris. *Le Mystère de la Trinité: Cours de théologie orthodoxe.* Paris: Cerf, 1986.

Boff, Leonardo. *Der dreieinige Gott.* Translated by J. Kuhlmann. Düsseldorf: Patmos, 1987.

————. *Kirche: Charisma und Macht. Studien zu einer streitbaren Ekklesiologie.* Translated by H. Goldstein. 3rd ed. Düsseldorf: Patmos, 1985.

————. *Die Neuentdeckung der Kirche: Basisgemeinde in Lateinamerika.* Translated by H. Goldstein. Mainz: Matthias-Grünewald, 1980.

Bonhoeffer, Dietrich. *Sanctorum Communio: Eine dogmatische Untersuchung zur Soziologie der Kirche* [= *Dietrich Bonhoeffer Werke* 1]. Edited by J. von Soosten. Munich: Kaiser, 1986.

————. "Zur Frage nach der Kirchengemeinschaft." *Evangelische Theologie* 3 (1936): 214-33.

Bori, Pier Cesare. "L'unité de l'Église durant les trois premiers siècles." *Revue d'histoire ecclésiastique* 65 (1970): 56-68.

Brachlow, Stephen. *The Communion of the Saints: Radical Puritan and Separatist Ecclesiology 1570-1625.* Oxford Theological Monographs. Oxford: Oxford University Press, 1988.

Brockhaus, Ulrich. *Charisma und Amt: Die paulinische Charismenlehre auf dem Hintergrund der frühchristlichen Gemeindefunktionen.* Wuppertal: Brockhaus, 1972.

Bruce, F. F. *The Epistle of Paul to the Galatians: A Commentary on the Greek Text.* New International Greek Testament Commentary. Exeter: Paternoster, 1982.

Brunner, Emil. *Das Gebot und Ordnungen: Entwurf einer protestantisch-theologischen Ethik.* Zurich: Zwingli, 1939.

————. *Das Misverständnis der Kirche.* 2d ed. Zurich: Zwingli, 1951.

Bultmann, Rudolf. *The Gospel of John: A Commentary.* Philadelphia: Westminster Press, 1971.

————. *Theology of the New Testament.* 3rd ed. London: SCM, 1959.

Calvin, John. *Unterricht in der christlichen Religion.* Neukirchen: Verlag der Buchhandlung des Erziehungsvereins Neukirchen, 1955. English edition, *Institutes of the*

Christian Religion. 2 vols. Edited by John T. McNeill. Translated by Ford Lewis Battles. Library of Christian Classics 20-21. Philadelphia: Westminster, 1960.

Campenhausen, Hans Freiherr von. "Das Bekenntnis im Urchristentum." *Zeitschrift für die Neutestamentliche Wissenschaft* 63 (1972): 210-53.

Chandler, Russell. *Racing Toward 2001: The Forces Shaping America's Religious Future*. Grand Rapids: Zondervan, 1992.

Christus Dominus. In *Das Zweite Vatikanische Konzil: Dokumente und Kommentare. Lexikon für Theologie und Kirche*, 13.128-247. Freiburg: Herder, 1966-68.

Clayton, Philip. *Explanation from Physics to Theology: An Essay in Rationality and Religion*. New Haven: Yale University Press, 1989.

Collinson, Patrick. "Toward a Broader Understanding of the Early Dissenting Tradition." In *Godly People: Essays on English Protestantism and Puritanism*, 527-62. London: Hambledon, 1983.

Congar, Yves. "Bulletin d'ecclésiologie." *Revue des sciences philosophiques et théologiques* 66 (1982): 87-119.

————. *Diversités et Communion: Dossier historique et conclusion théologique*. Cogitatio fidei 112. Paris: Cerf, 1982.

————. *Je crois en l'Esprit Saint*. 3 vols. Paris: Cerf, 1979-80. English edition, *I Believe in the Holy Spirit*. 3 vols. New York: Seabury, 1983.

————. *Der Heilige Geist*. Translated by A. Berz. Freiburg: Herder, 1982.

————. "Die Wesenseigenschaften der Kirche." In *Mysterium Salutis IV/1: Das Heilsgeschehen in der Gemeinde*, edited by J. Feiner and M. Löhrer, 357-594. Einsiedeln: Benziger, 1972.

Copleston, Frederick. *Religion and the One: Philosophies East and West*. New York: Crossroad, 1982.

Cox, Harvey G. *The Silencing of Leonardo Boff: The Vatican and the Future of World Christianity*. Oak Park: Meyer Stone, 1988.

Cranfield, C. E. B. *A Critical and Exegetical Commentary on the Epistle to the Romans*. 2 vols. International Critical Commentary. Edinburgh: Clark, 1975.

Dabney, D. Lyle. "Die Kenosis des Geistes: Kontinuität zwischen Schöpfung und Erlösung im Werk des Heiligen Geistes." Diss., Tübingen, 1989.

Dagg, J. L. *Manual of Theology*. The Baptist Tradition. New York: Arno, 1980.

Dalferth, Ingolf U. *Der auferweckte Gekreuzigte: Zur Grammatik der Christologie*. Tübingen: Mohr-Siebeck, 1994.

Dalferth, Ingolf U. and Eberhard Jüngel, "Person und Gottebenbildlichkeit." In *Christlicher Glaube in moderner Gesellschaft*, edited by F. Bröckle et al. 30 vols., 24.57-99. Freiburg: Herder, 1981.

Dargan, Edwin C. *Ecclesiology: A Study of the Churches* (Louisville: Dearing, 1897.

Davis, Kenneth R. "No Discipline, No Church: An Anabaptist Contribution to the Reformed Tradition." *Sixteenth Century Journal* 13, no. 4 (1982): 43-58.

D'Costa, Gavin. "Christ, the Trinity and Religious Plurality." In *Christian Uniqueness Reconsidered: The Myth of a Pluralistic Theology of Religions*, 16-29. Faith Meets Faith. Maryknoll: Orbis, 1990.

Dempster, Murray. "The Church's Moral Witness: A Study of Glossolalia in Luke's Theology of Acts." *Paraclete* 23 (1989): 1-7.

Dewey, John. *Individualism Old and New*. New York: Minton, Balch & Co., 1930.

Dexter, Henry Martyn. *The Congregationalism of the Last Three Hundred Years*. London: Hodder & Stoughton, 1880.

Diekamp, Franz. *Katholische Dogmatik nach den Grundsätzen des heiligen Thomas*. 13th ed. 3 vols. Edited by K. Jüssen. Münster: Aschendorffsche Verlagsbuchhandlung, 1957.

Dinkler, Erich, "Taufe II: Im Urchristentum." In *Religion in Geschichte und Gegenwart*, edited by K. Galling, 627-37. 3rd ed. Tübingen: Mohr-Siebeck, 1962.

Dobbler, Axel von. *Glaube als Teilhabe: Historische und semantische Grundlagen der paulinischen Theologie und Ekklesiologie des Glaubens*. Wissenschaftliche Untersuchungen zum Neuen Testament 2.22. Tübingen: Mohr-Siebeck, 1987.

Dombois, Hans. *Das Recht der Gnade: Ökumenisches Kirchenrecht I*. Forschungen und Berichte der Evangelischen Studiengemeinschaft 20. Witten: Luther, 1961.

Dudley, R. L., and C. R. Laurens. "Alienation from Religion in Church Related Adolescents." *Sociological Analysis* 49 (1988): 408-20.

Duffield, Guy P., and Nathaniel M. Van Cleave. *Foundations of Pentecostal Theology*. Los Angeles: L.I.F.E. Bible College, 1983.

Dulles, Avery. *The Catholicity of the Church*. Oxford: Clarendon, 1985.

Dunn, James D. G. *Jesus and the Spirit: A Study of the Religious and Charismatic Experience of Jesus and the First Christians as Reflected in the New Testament*. Grand Rapids: Eerdmans, 1997.

————. "Models of Christian Community in the New Testament." In *The Church Is Charismatic: The World Council of Churches and the Charismatic Renewal*, edited by A. Bittlinger, 99-116. Geneva: World Council of Churches, 1981.

Dumont, Louis. *Essais sur l'individualisme: Une perspective anthropologique sur l'idéologie moderne*. Paris: Seuil, 1983.

Duquoc, Christian. *Provisional Churches: An Essay in Ecumenical Ecclesiology*. Translated by J. Bowden. London: SCM, 1986.

Durkheim, Emile. *The Elementary Forms of the Religious Life*. Translated by J. W. Swain. London: Allen & Unwin, 1915.

Eastwood, Cyril. *The Priesthood of All Believers: An Examination of the Doctrine from the Reformation to the Present Day*. London: Epworth, 1960.

Elert, Werner. "Katholizität." In *Morphologie des Luthertums I: Theologie und Weltanschauung des Luthertums hauptsächlich im 16. und 17. Jahrhundert*, 240-55. Munich: Beck, 1952.

Erickson, John. "The Local Churches and Catholicity: An Orthodox Perspective." *The Jurist* 52 (1992): 490-508.

"An Evangelical Response to *Baptism, Eucharist and Ministry*." *Evangelical Review of Theology* 13 (1989): 291-313.

Evans, Gillian R. *The Church and the Churches: Toward an Ecumenical Ecclesiology*. Cambridge: Cambridge University Press, 1994.

Eyt, Pierre. "Überlegungen von Pierre Eyt." In J. Ratzinger, *Die Krise der Kathechese und ihre Überwindung*, 40-62. Translated by H. Urs von Balthasar. Einsiedeln: Johannes, 1983.

Fahey, Michael. "Joseph Ratzinger als Ekklesiologe und Seelsorger." *Concilium (Einsiedeln)* 17 (1981): 79-85.

Farley, Edward. *Ecclesial Man: A Social Phenomenology of Faith and Reality*. Philadelphia: Fortress, 1975.

Fee, Gordon D. *First and Second Timothy, Titus.* New International Biblical Commentary 13. Peabody, Mass.: Hendrickson, 1988.

———. *The First Epistle to the Corinthians.* New International Commentary on the New Testament. Grand Rapids: Eerdmans, 1987.

———. "Pauline Literature." In *Dictionary of Pentecostal and Charismatic Movements,* edited by S. M. Burgess and G. G. McGee, 665-83. Grand Rapids: Zondervan, 1988.

Finke, Roger, and Rodney Stark. "How the Upstart Sects Won America: 1770-1850." *Journal for the Scientific Study of Religion* 28 (1989): 27-44.

Flannery, Austin P., ed. *Documents of Vatican II.* Grand Rapids: Eerdmans, 1975.

———. *Vatican Council II: More Postconciliar Documents.* Grand Rapids: Eerdmans, 1982.

Flew, R. N. and R. E. Davies, eds. *The Catholicity of Protestantism.* London: Lutterworth, 1950.

Förster, Winfried. *Thomas Hobbes und der Puritanismus: Grundlagen und Grundfragen seiner Staatslehre.* Hamburg: Dunker & Humbolt, 1969.

Forte, Bruno. *Trinität als Geschichte: Der lebendige Gott — Gott der Lebenden.* Grünewalt-Reihe. Translated by J. Richter. Mainz: Grünewald, 1989.

Friedrich, Gerhard. "Glaube und Verkündigung bei Paulus." In *Glaube im Neuen Testament: Festschrift Hermann Binder,* edited by F. Hahn and H. Klein, 93-113. Biblisch-theologische Studien 7. Neukirchen-Vluyn: Neukirchener Verlag, 1982.

Fries, Heinrich, and Karl Rahner. *Einigung der Kirchen — Reale Möglichkeit.* Quaestiones Disputatae 100. Freiburg: Herder, 1983.

Furnish, Victor Paul. *2 Corinthians: Translation with Introduction, Notes and Commentary. Anchor Bible* 32A. Garden City, N.Y.: Doubleday, 1984.

Gallup, George, and Jim Castelli, Jr. *The People's Religion.* New York: Macmillan, 1989.

Gee, Donald. *Concerning Spiritual Gifts.* Springfield, Mo.: Gospel Publishing House, 1972.

Gelpi, Donald L. *Pentecostalism: A Theological Viewpoint.* New York: Paulist, 1971.

"Gemeinsame Erklärung des Arbeitskreises evangelischer und katholischer Theologen." In *Glaubensbekenntnis und Kirchengemeinschaft: Das Modell des Konzils von Konstantinopel (381),* edited by K. Lehmann and W. Pannenberg, 120-25. Dialog der Kirchen 1. Göttingen: Vandenhoeck & Ruprecht, 1982.

Gerosa, Libero. *Charisma und Rechte: Kirchenrechtliche Überlegungen zum 'Urcharisma' der neuen Vereinigungsformen in der Kirche.* Sammlung Horizonte. Neue Folge 27. Einsiedeln: Johannes, 1989.

Gielen, Marlis. "Zur Interpretation der paulinischen Formel ἡ κατ' οἶκον ἐκκλησία." *Zeitschrift für die Neutestamentliche Wissenschaft* 77 (1986): 109-25.

Goleman, Daniel. *Vital Lies — Simple Truth: The Psychology of Self-Deception.* New York: Simon and Schuster, 1985.

Grey, Mary. "The Core of Our Desire: Re-imaging Trinity." *Theology* 93 (1990): 363-73.

Grillmeier, Alois. "Auriga mundi: Zum Reichskirchenbild der Briefe des sog. Codex Encyclicus (458)." In *Mit ihm und in ihm: Christologische Forschungen und Perspektiven,* 386-419. Freiburg: Herder, 1975.

———. "Kommentar zum Ersten Kapitel der Dogmatischen Konstitution über die Kirche (Art. 1-8)." In *Das Zweite Vatikanische Konzil: Dokumente und Kommentare. Lexikon für Theologie und Kirche,* 12.156-76. Freiburg: Herder, 1966-68.

Guardini, Romano. *Vom Sinn der Kirche*. Mainz: Grünewald, 1955.

Guinness, Os. *Dining with the Devil: The Megachurch Movement Flirts with Modernity*. Grand Rapids: Baker Book House, 1993.

Gundry, Robert H. *Matthew: A Commentary on His Literary and Theological Art*. Grand Rapids: Eerdmans, 1982.

—————. "The New Jerusalem: People as Place, not Place for People." *Novum Testamentum* 29 (1987): 254-64.

—————. *Soma in Biblical Theology with Emphasis on Pauline Anthropology*. Society for New Testament Studies Monograph Series 29. Cambridge: Cambridge University Press, 1976.

Gunton, Colin. "The Church on Earth: The Roots of Community." In *On Being the Church: Essays on the Christian Community*, edited by Colin E. Gunton and Daniel W. Hardy, 48-80. Edinburgh: Clark, 1989.

—————. *The Promise of Trinitarian Theology*. Edinburgh: Clark, 1991.

Gwyn, Douglas. *Apocalypse of the Word: The Life and Message of George Fox (1624-1691)*. Richmond: Friends United Press, 1984.

Habermas, Jürgen. "Die Einheit der Vernunft in der Vielheit ihrer Stimmen." In *Einheit und Vielheit. XIV: Deutscher Kongress für Philosophie, Giessen, 21.-26. September 1987*, edited by O. Marquard, 11-35. Hamburg: Meiner, 1990.

Hahn, Ferdinand. "Grundfragen von Charisma und Amt in der gegenwärtigen neutestamentlichen Forschung: Fragestellungen aus evangelischer Sicht." In *Charisma und Institution*, edited by T. Rendtorff, 336-49. Gütersloh: Mohn, 1984.

Halleux, André de. "'L'Église catholique' dans la lettre ignacienne aux Smyrnoites. *Ephemerides theologicae Lovanienses* 58 (1982): 5-24.

—————. "Personalisme ou essentialisme trinitaire chez les Pères cappadociens? Une mauvaise controverse." *Revue théologique de Louvain* 17 (1986): 129-55, 265-92.

Häring, Hermann. "Joseph Ratzinger's Nightmare Theology." In *The Church in Anguish: Has the Vatican Betrayed Vatican II*, edited by H. Küng and L. Swidler, 75-90. San Francisco: Harper & Row, 1987.

Harkianakis, Stylianos. "Kann ein Petrusdienst in der Kirche einen Sinn haben? Griechisch-orthodoxe Antwort." *Concilium* (Einsiedeln) 7 (1971): 284-87.

Harnack, Adolf. *Entstehung und Entwicklung der Kirchenverfassung und des Kirchenrechts in den zwei ersten Jahrhunderten*. Leipzig: Hinrichs, 1910.

Harrison, Verna. "Perichoresis in the Greek Fathers." *St. Vladimir's Theological Quarterly* 35 (1991): 53-65.

Hartman, Lars. "Baptism 'Into the Name of Jesus' and Early Christology: Some Tentative Considerations." *Studia theologica* 28 (1974): 21-48.

—————. "ὄνομα." In *Exegetical Dictionary of the New Testament*. Vol. 2. Grand Rapids: Eerdmans, 1990-93.

Hasenhüttl, Gotthold. "Kirche und Institution." *Concilium* (Einsiedeln) 10 (1974): 7-11.

Hatch, Nathan O. *The Democratization of American Christianity*. New Haven: Yale University Press, 1989.

Hauerwas, Stanley. *Against the Nations: War and Survival in a Liberal Society*. Minneapolis: Winston, 1985.

—————. "On the 'Right' to be Tribal." *Christian Scholar's Review* 16 (1987): 238-41.

—————. *Unleashing the Scripture: Freeing the Bible from Captivity to America*. Nashville: Abingdon, 1993.

BIBLIOGRAPHY

Heckel, Martin. "Zur zeitlichen Begrenzung des Bischofsamtes." In *Gesammelte Schriften: Staat — Kirche — Recht — Geschichte,* edited by K. Schlaich, 2.934-54. Jus ecclesiasticum 38. Tübingen: Mohr-Siebeck, 1989.

Herms, Eilert. *Erfahrbare Kirche: Beiträge zur Ekklesiologie.* Tübingen: Mohr-Siebeck, 1990.

Hick, John. *God Has Many Names.* Philadelphia: Westminster, 1982.

———. *An Interpretation of Religion: Human Responses to the Transcendent.* New Haven: Yale University Press, 1989.

Hiebert, Paul G. "The Category 'Christian' in the Mission Task." *International Review of Missions* 72 (1983): 421-27.

Hill, William J. *The Three-Personed God: The Trinity as a Mystery of Salvation.* Washington: Catholic University of America Press, 1982.

Hobbes, Thomas. *Leviathan.* Edited by C. B. McPherson. Harmondsworth: Penguin, 1968.

Hocken, Peter. "The Challenge of Non-Denominational Charismatic Christianity." In *Experience of the Spirit,* edited by J. A. B. Jongeneel, 221-38. Frankfurt: Lang, 1989.

Hofius, Otfried. "Gemeinschaft mit den Engeln im Gottesdienst der Kirche. Eine traditionsgeschichtliche Skizze." *Zeitschrift für Theologie und Kirche* 89 (1992): 172-96.

———. "Herrenmahl und Herrenmahlparadosis: Erwägungen zu 1 Kor 11,23b-25." In *Paulusstudien,* 203-40. Wissenschaftliche Untersuchungen zum Neuen Testament 51. Tübingen: Mohr-Siebeck, 1989.

———. "ὁμολογέω." In *Exegetical Dictionary of the New Testament.* Vol. 2. Grand Rapids: Eerdmans, 1990-93.

———. "Sühne und Versöhnung: Zum paulinischen Verständnis des Kreuzestodes Jesu." In *Paulusstudien,* 33-49. Wissenschaftliche Untersuchungen zum Neuen Testament 51. Tübingen: Mohr-Siebeck, 1989.

———. "Wort Gottes und Glaube bei Paulus." In *Paulusstudien,* 148-74. Wissenschaftliche Untersuchungen zum Neuen Testament 51. Tübingen: Mohr-Siebeck, 1989.

Huber, Wolfgang. "Die wirkliche Kirche: Das Verhältnis von Botschaft und Ordnung als Grundproblem evangelischen Kirchenverständnisses im Anschluss an die 3. Barmer These." In *Kirche als "Gemeinde von Brüdern" (Barmen III),* edited by A. Burgsmüller, 1.249-77. Gütersloh: Mohn, 1980.

Hurtado, Larry W. *One God, One Lord: Early Christian Devotion and Ancient Jewish Monotheism.* Philadelphia: Fortress, 1988.

Huss, John. *The Church.* Translated by D. S. Schaff. New York: Scribner's Sons, 1915.

Jenkins, Daniel. *Congregationalism: A Restatement.* New York: Harper and Brothers, 1954.

———. *The Nature of Catholicity.* London: Faber and Faber, 1941.

Jansen, Henry. "Relationality and the Concept of God." Diss., Amsterdam, 1995.

Joest, Wilfried. *Ontologie der Person bei Luther.* Göttingen: Vandenhoeck & Ruprecht, 1967.

Jones, Serene. "This God Which Is Not One: Irigaray and Barth on the Divine." In *Transfigurations: Theology and the French Feminists,* edited by C. W. Maggie Kim et al., 109-41. Minneapolis: Fortress, 1993.

Jüngel, Eberhard. "Anthropomorphismus als Grundproblem der neuzeitlichen Hermeneutik." In *Wertlose Wahrheit: Zur Identität und Relevanz des christlichen*

Glaubens. Theologische Erörterungen III, 110-31. Beiträge zur evangelischen Theologie 107. Munich: Kaiser, 1990.

———. "Bekennen und Bekenntnis." In *Theologie in Geschichte und Kunst: Festschrift Walter Elliger*, edited by S. Herrmann and O. Söhngen, 94-105. Witten: Luther, 1968.

———. *Gott als Geheimnis der Welt: Zur Begründung der Theologie des Gekreuzigten im Streit zwischen Theismus und Atheismus*. 3rd ed. Tübingen: Mohr-Siebeck, 1978.

———. "Einheit der Kirchen — konkret." In *Wertlose Wahrheit: Zur Identität und Relevanz des christlichen Glaubens. Theologische Erörterungen III*, 335-45. Beiträge zur evangelischen Theologie 107. Munich: Kaiser, 1990.

———. "Die Kirche als Sakrament?" In *Wertlose Wahrheit: Zur Identität und Relevanz des christlichen Glaubens. Theologische Erörterungen III*, 311-34. Beiträge zur evangelischen Theologie 107. Munich: Kaiser, 1990.

———. "Thesen zu Karl Barths Lehre von der Taufe." In *Barth-Studien*, 291-94. Ökumenische Theologie 9. Zurich: Benziger, 1982.

———. "Verweigertes Geheimnis? Bemerkungen zu einer unevangelischen Sonderlehre." In *Vernunft des Glaubens: Wissenschaftliche Theologie und kirchliche Lehre. Festschrift Wolhart Pannenberg*, edited by J. Rohls and G. Wenz, 488-501. Göttingen: Vandenhoeck & Ruprecht, 1988.

———. "Zur Kritik des Sakramentalen Verständnisses der Taufe." In *Barth-Studien*, 295-314. Ökumenische Theologie 9. Zurich: Benziger, 1982.

Kant, Immanuel. "Der Streit der Fakultäten." In *Werke in sechs Bänden*. Edited by W. Weischedel. Darmstadt: Wissenschaftliche Buchgesellschaft, 1964.

Karl Marx, Friedrich Engels: Werke. Ergänzungsband. Berlin: Dietz, 1967-1968.

Käsemann, Ernst. "Amt und Gemeinde im Neuen Testament." In *Exegetische Versuche und Besinnungen*, 1.109-34. 6th ed. Göttingen: Vandenhoeck & Ruprecht, 1970.

———. *Commentary on Romans*. Translated by Geoffrey W. Bromiley. Grand Rapids: Eerdmans, 1980.

———. *Jesu letzter Wille nach Johannes 17*. Tübingen: Mohr-Siebeck, 1966.

Kasper, Walter. *Der Gott Jesu Christi*. Mainz: Grünewald, 1982.

———. "Grundkonsens und Kirchengemeinschaft: Zum Stand des ökumenischen Gesprächs zwischen katholischer und evangelisch-lutherischer Kirche." *Theologische Quartalschrift* 167 (1987): 161-81.

———. "Kirche als Communio: Überlegungen zur ekklesiologischen Leitidee des Zweiten Vatikanischen Konzils." In *Die bleibende Bedeutung des Zweiten Vatikanischen Konzils*, edited by F. Cardinal König, 62-84. Schriften der Katholischen Akademie in Bayern 123. Düsseldorf: Patmos, 1986.

———. "Kirche als Sakrament des Geistes." In *Kirche — Ort des Geistes*, edited by W. Kasper and G. Sauter, 13-55. Kleine ökumenische Schriften 8. Freiburg: Herder, 1976.

———. "Die Kirche als universales Sakrament des Heils." In *Theologie und Kirche*, 237-54. Mainz: Grünewald, 1987.

———. Review of *Einführung in das Christentum*, by Joseph Ratzinger. *Theologische Revue* 65 (1969): 182-88.

———. "Theorie und Praxis innerhalb einer Theologia Crucis: Antwort auf J. Ratzingers 'Glaube, Geschichte und Philosophie.'" *Hochland* 62 (1970): 152-59.

Kaufmann, Franz-Xaver. "Kirche als religiöse Organisation." *Concilium* (Einsiedeln) 10 (1974): 30-36.

———. "Kirche und Religion in der spätindustriellen (modernen) Gesellschaft." In *Charisma und Institution,* edited by T. Rendtorff, 406-19. Gütersloh: Mohn, 1985.

———. *Religion und Modernität: Sozialwissenschaftliche Perspektiven.* Tübingen: Mohr-Siebeck, 1989.

———. *Zur Zukunft des Christentums: Soziologische Überlegungen.* Veröffentlichungen der Katholischen Akademie Schwerte 8. Schwerte: Katholische Akademie, 1981.

Kehl, Medard. "Kirche als Institution." In *Handbuch der Fundamentaltheologie 3: Traktat Kirche,* edited by W. Kern, H. J. Pottmeyer, and M. Seckler, 176-97. Freiburg: Herder, 1986.

Keller, Catherine. *From a Broken Web: Separatism, Sexism, and Self.* Boston: Beacon, 1986.

Kelly, J. N. D. "Begriffe 'Katholisch' und 'Apostolisch' in den ersten Jahrhunderten." In *Katholizität und Apostolizität,* edited by R. Groscurth, 9-21. Kerygma und Dogma B.2. Göttingen: Vandenhoeck & Ruprecht, 1971.

———. *Early Christian Doctrines.* 5th ed. London: Black, 1971.

Kenneson, Philip D. "Selling [Out] the Church in the Marketplace of Desire." *Modern Theology* 9 (1993): 319-48.

Kern, Walter. "Einheit-in-Mannigfaltigkeit: Fragmentarische Überlegungen zur Metaphysik des Geistes." In *Gott in Welt: Festschrift Karl Rahner,* edited by H. Vorgrimler, 1.207-39. Freiburg: Herder, 1964.

Kierkegaard, Sören. *Concluding Unscientific Postscript.* Translated by Walter Lowrie. Princeton: Princeton University Press, 1944.

"Kirche als Communio: Ein Dokument der Glaubenkongregation." *Herder-Korrespondenz* 46 (1992): 319-23.

Klauck, Hans-Josef. "Kirche als Freundesgemeinschaft? Auf Spurensuche im Neuen Testament." *Münchener Theologische Zeitschrift* 42 (1991): 1-14.

Knitter, Paul F. Preface to *The Myth of Christian Uniqueness: Toward a Pluralist Theology of Religions,* edited by J. Hick and P. F. Knitter. Maryknoll, N.Y.: Orbis Books, 1987.

Koslowski, Peter. "Hegel — 'der Philosoph der Trinität'? Zur Kontroverse um seine Trinitätslehre." *Theologische Quartalschrift* 162 (1982): 105-31.

Kottje, Raymund, and Heinz Theo Risse. *Wahlrecht für das Gottesvolk? Erwägungen zu Bischofs-und Pfarrerwahl. Raymund Kottje antwortet Heinz Theo Risse.* Das theologische Interview 4. Düsseldorf: Patmos, 1969.

Kraus, Hans-Joachim. *Reich Gottes: Reich der Freiheit. Grundriss Systematischer Theologie.* Neukirchen: Neukirchener Verlag, 1975.

Kress, Robert. *The Church: Communion, Sacrament, Communication.* New York: Paulist, 1985.

Krieg, Robert A. "Kardinal Ratzinger, Max Scheler und eine Grundfrage der Christologie." *Theologische Quartalschrift* 160 (1980): 106-22.

Küng, Hans. *Die Kirche.* Munich: Piper, 1977.

LaCugna, Catherine Mowry. *God for Us: The Trinity and the Christian Faith.* San Francisco: Harper & Row, 1991.

LaCugna, Catherine Mowry, and Kilian McDonnell. "Returning from 'The Far Country':

Theses for a Contemporary Trinitarian Theology." *Scottish Journal of Theology* 41 (1988): 191-215.

Lake, Peter. *Moderate Puritans and the Elizabethan Church.* Cambridge: Cambridge University Press, 1982.

Land, Steve. *Pentecostal Spirituality: A Passion for the Kingdom.* Sheffield: Sheffield Academic Press, 1993.

Larentzakis, Grigorios. "Trinitarisches Kirchenverständnis." In *Trinität: Aktuelle Perspektiven der Theologie,* edited by W. Breuning, 73-96. Quaestiones Disputatae 101. Freiburg: Herder, 1984.

Legrand, Hervé-Marie. "Die Entwicklung der Kirchen als verantwortliche Subjekte: Eine Anfrage an das II. Vatikanum. Theologische Grundlagen und Gedanken zu Fragen der Institution." In *Kirche im Wandel: Eine kritische Zwischenbilanz nach dem Zweiten Vatikanum,* edited by G. Alberigo et al., 141-74. Düsseldorf: Patmos, 1982.

—————. "Le métropolite Jean Zizioulas, docteur honoris causa de l'Institut Catholique de Paris." *Service Orthodoxe de Presse* 148 (May 1990): 19-22.

—————. "La Réalisation de L'Eglise en un lieu." In *Initiation à la pratique de la théologie: Dogmatique III,* edited by B. Lauret and F. Refoulé, 143-345. Paris: Cerf, 1983.

—————. "A Response to 'The Church as a Prophetic Sign.'" In *Church, Kingdom, World: The Church as Mystery and Prophetic Sign,* edited by G. Limouris, 145-51. Faith and Order Papers 130. Geneva: World Council of Churches, 1986.

—————. "*Traditio perpetue servate?* The Non-ordination of Women: Tradition or Simply an Historical Fact?" *Worship* 65 (1991): 482-508.

Lehmann, Karl. "Gemeinde." In *Christlicher Glaube in moderner Gesellschaft,* edited by F. Böckle et al., 29.6-65. Freiburg: Herder, 1982.

Lightfoot, R. H. *St. John's Gospel: A Commentary.* Oxford: Clarendon, 1956.

Lim, David. *Spiritual Gifts.* Springfield, Mo.: Gospel Publishing House, 1991.

Limouris, Gennadios. "The Church: A Mystery of Unity in Diversity." *St. Vladimir's Theological Quarterly* 31 (1987): 123-42.

Lincoln, Andrew T. *Paradise Now and Not Yet: Studies in the Role of the Heavenly Dimension in Paul's Thought with Special Reference to His Eschatology.* Society for New Testament Studies Monograph Series 43. Cambridge: Cambridge University Press, 1981.

Lindbeck, George A. "Confession and Community: An Israel-like View of the Church." *Christian Century* 107 (1990): 492-96.

—————. *The Nature of the Doctrine: Religion and Theology in a Postliberal Age.* Philadelphia: Westminster, 1984.

Link, Christian. "Die Bewegung der Einheit: Gemeinschaft der Kirchen in der Ökumene." In *Sie aber hielten Fest an der Gemeinschaft: Einheit der Kirche als Prozess im Neuen Testament und heute,* by Christian Link, Ulrich Luz, and Lukas Vischer, 187-271. Zurich: Benziger, 1988.

Lochman, Jan Milic. "Die 'notae ecclesiae.'" In *Die Kirche und die letzten Dinge,* by F. Buri, J. M. Lochman, and H. Ott, 31-33. Dogmatik im Dialog 1. Gütersloh: Mohn, 1973.

Lohfink, Gerhard. "Jesus und die Kirche." In *Handbuch der Fundamentaltheologie 3: Traktat Kirche,* edited by W. Kern, H. J. Pottmeyer, and M. Seckler, 49-96. Freiburg: Herder, 1986.

—————. *Wie hat Jesus Gemeinde gewollt? Zur gesellschaftlichen Dimension des christlichen Glaubens.* Freiburg: Herder, 1982.

BIBLIOGRAPHY

Lossky, Vladimir. "Concerning the Third Mark of the Church: Catholicity." In *In the Image and Likeness of God,* edited by J. H. Erickson and T. E. Bird, 169-81. Crestwood, N.Y.: St. Vladimir's Seminary Press, 1975.

————. *The Mystical Theology of the Eastern Church.* Crestwood, N.Y.: St. Vladimir's Seminary Press, 1976.

Lubac, Henri de. *Katholizismus als Gemeinschaft.* Translated by H. U. von Balthasar. Einsiedeln: Benziger, 1943.

————. *Zwanzig Jahre danach: Ein Gespräch über Buchstabe und Geist des Zweiten Vatikanischen Konzils.* Translated by W. Bader. Munich: Neue Stadt, 1985.

Luhmann, Niklas. "Die Autopoiesis des Bewusstseins." *Soziale Welt* 36 (1985): 402-46.

————. "Individuum, Individualität, Individualismus." In *Gesellschaftsstruktur und Semantik: Studien zur Wissenssoziologie der modernen Gesellschaft,* 3.149-357. Frankfurt: Suhrkamp, 1989.

————. *Funktion der Religion.* Frankfurt: Suhrkamp, 1977.

————. "Society, Meaning, Religion — Based on Self-Reference." *Sociological Analysis* 46 (1985): 5-20.

Lumpkin, William L., ed. *Baptist Confessions of Faith.* Valley Forge, Pa.: Judson, 1959.

Luther, Martin. *D. Martin Luthers Werke: Kritische Gesamtausgabe.* Weimar: Böhlan, 1883-.

Lumen gentium. In *Das Zweite Vatikanische Konzil: Dokumente und Kommentare. Lexikon für Theologie und Kirche,* 12.139-347. Freiburg: Herder, 1966-68.

Luntley, Michael. *Reason, Truth and Self: The Postmodern Reconditioned.* London: Routledge, 1995.

Lutz, Jürgen. *Unio und Communio: Zum Verhältnis von Rechtfertigungslehre und Kirchenverständnis bei Luther: Eine Untersuchung zu ekklesiologisch relevanten Texten der Jahre 1519-1528.* Konfessionskundliche und kontroverstheologische Studien 55. Paderborn: Bonifatius, 1990.

Luther's Works. 55 vols. Ed. Theodore G. Tappert and Helmut T. Lehmann. Philadelphia: Fortress, 1958-1967.

Luz, Ulrich. "Unterwegs zur Einheit: Gemeinschaft der Kirche im Neuen Testament." In *Sie aber hielten fest an der Gemeinschaft: Einheit der Kirche als Prozess im Neuen Testament und heute,* by Christian Link, Ulrich Luz, and Lukas Vischer, 43-183. Zurich: Benziger, 1988.

————. *Das Evangelium nach Mattäus.* Evangelisch-katholischer Kommentar zum Neuen Testament 1/1. Zurich: Benziger, 1985.

Macchia, Frank D. "Sighs Too Deep for Words: Towards a Theology of Glossolalia." *Journal of Pentecostal Theology* 1 (1992): 47-73.

McBeth, H. Leon. *A Sourcebook for Baptist Heritage.* Nashville: Broadman, 1990.

McFadyen, Alistair I. *The Call to Personhood: A Christian Theory of the Individual in Social Relationships.* Cambridge: Cambridge University Press, 1990.

————. "The Trinity and Human Individuality: The Conditions for Relevance." *Theology* 95 (1992): 10-18.

McFague, Sallie. *Models of God: Theology for an Ecological, Nuclear Age.* Philadelphia: Fortress, 1987.

MacIntyre, Alasdair. *After Virtue: A Study in Moral Theory.* 2d ed. Notre Dame: University of Notre Dame Press, 1984.

————. *Whose Justice? Which Rationality?* Notre Dame: University of Notre Dame Press, 1988.

McPartlan, Paul Gerard. *The Eucharist Makes the Church: Henri de Lubac and John Zizioulas in Dialogue.* Edinburgh: Clark, 1993.

Mananzan, Mary John. *The "Language Game" of Confessing One's Belief: A Wittgensteinian-Austinian Approach to the Linguistic Analysis of Creedal Statements.* Tübingen: Niemeyer, 1974.

Marayama, Tadatka. *The Ecclesiology of Theodore Beza: The Reform of the True Church.* Geneva: Libraire Droz, 1978.

Marquard, Odo. "Einheit und Vielheit: Statt einer Einführung in das Kongressthema." In *Einheit und Vielheit: XIV. Deutscher Kongress für Philosophie, Giessen, 21.-26. September 1987,* edited by O. Marquard, 1-10. Hamburg: Meiner, 1990.

Marsch, Wolf-Dieter. *Institution im Übergang: Evangelische Kirche zwischen Tradition und Reform.* Sammlung Vandenhoeck. Göttingen: Vandenhoeck & Ruprecht, 1970.

Marshall, Peter. *Enmity in Corinth: Social Conventions in Paul's Relations with the Corinthians.* Wissenschaftliche Untersuchungen zum Neuen Testament 2/23. Tübingen: Mohr-Siebeck, 1987.

Martin, David. *Tongues of Fire: The Explosion of Protestantism in Latin America.* Oxford: Blackwell, 1990.

Marty, Martin E. *The Public Church: Mainline-Evangelical-Catholic.* New York: Crossroad, 1981.

McClendon, James W. "The Believers Church in Theological Perspective." Unpublished paper, 1997.

Mead, George Herbert. *Mind, Self and Society from the Standpoint of a Social Behaviorist.* Edited by C. W. Morris. Chicago: University of Chicago Press, 1934.

Mead, Sidney E. *The Lively Experiment: The Shaping of Christianity in America.* New York: Harper & Row, 1963.

Metz, Johann Baptist. "Das Konzil — 'der Anfang eine Anfangs.'" *Orientierung* 54 (1990): 245-50.

Meyendorff, John. Foreword to *Being as Communion: Studies in Personhood and the Church,* by John Zizioulas. Crestwood, N.Y.: St. Vladimir's Seminary Press, 1985.

Meyer, Heinrich. "Was ist Politische Theologie? Einführende Bemerkungen zu einem umstrittenen Begriff." In *Politische Theologie zwischen Ägypten und Israel,* edited by Jan Assmann, 7-19. Munich: Siemens, 1992.

Möhler, Johan Adam. *Die Einheit in der Kirche oder das Prinzip des Katholizismus: Dargestellt im Geiste der Kirchenväter der drei ersten Jahrhunderte.* Edited by J. R. Geiselmann. Darmstadt: Wissenschaftliche Buchgesellschaft, 1957.

Moltmann, Jürgen. "Christsein, Menschsein und das Reich Gottes: Ein Gespräch mit Karl Rahner." *Stimmen der Zeit* 203 (1985): 619-31.

————. *The Church in the Power of the Spirit: A Contribution to Messianic Ecclesiology.* New York: Harper & Row, 1977.

————. "Einführung: Einige Fragen der Trinitätslehre heute." In *In der Geschichte des dreieinigen Gottes: Beiträge zur trinitarischen Theologie,* 11-21. Munich: Kaiser, 1991.

————. "Die einladende Einheit des dreieinigen Gottes." In *In der Geschichte des dreieinigen Gottes: Beiträge zur trinitarischen Theologie,* 117-28. Munich: Kaiser, 1991.

‒‒‒‒‒. "Die Entdeckung der Anderen: Zur Theorie des kommunikativen Erkennens." *Evangelische Theologie* 50 (1990): 400-414.

‒‒‒‒‒. *Geist des Lebens: Ganzheitliche Pneumatologie.* Munich: Kaiser, 1991.

‒‒‒‒‒. "'Die Gemeinschaft des Heiligen Geistes': Trinitarische Pneumatologie." In *In der Geschichte des dreieinigen Gottes: Beiträge zur trinitarischen Theologie, 90-105.* Munich: Kaiser, 1991.

‒‒‒‒‒. *Gott in der Schöpfung: Ökologische Schöpfungslehre.* Munich: Kaiser, 1985.

‒‒‒‒‒. *Kirche in der Kraft des Geistes: Ein Beitrag zum messianischen Ekklesiologie.* Munich: Kaiser, 1975.

‒‒‒‒‒. *Man: Christian Anthropology in the Conflicts of the Present.* Philadelphia: Fortress Press, 1974.

‒‒‒‒‒. *Politische Theologie — Politische Ethik.* Fundamentaltheologische Studien 9. Munich: Kaiser, 1984.

‒‒‒‒‒. *The Spirit of Life: A Universal Affirmation.* Minneapolis: Fortress, 1992.

‒‒‒‒‒. *The Trinity and the Kingdom: The Doctrine of God.* New York: Harper & Row, 1981.

‒‒‒‒‒. *Der Weg Jesu Christi: Christologie in messianischen Dimensionen.* Munich: Kaiser, 1989.

Moule, C. F. D. *The Origin of Christology.* Cambridge: Cambridge University Press, 1977.

Mühlen, Heribert. "L'expérience chrétienne de l'Esprit: Immédiaté et médiations." In *L'expérience de Dieu et le Saint Esprit: Immédiaté et médiations. Actes du colloque,* 47-79. Le Point theologique 44. Paris: Beauchesne, 1985.

‒‒‒‒‒. *Entsakralisierung: Ein epochales Schlagwort in seiner Bedeutung für die Zukunft der christlichen Kirchen.* Paderborn: Schöningh, 1971.

‒‒‒‒‒. *Der Heilige Geist als Person. In der Trinität, bei der Inkarnation und im Gnadenbund: Ich — Du — Wir.* 4th ed. Münsterische Beiträge zur Theologie 26. Münster: Aschendorff, 1980.

‒‒‒‒‒. *Una mystica persona: Die Kirche als das Mysterium der heilsgeschichtlichen Identität des Heiligen Geistes in Christus und den Christen: Eine Person in vielen Personen.* 3rd ed. Munich: Schöningh, 1968.

Müller, Ernst F. Karl. *Die Bekenntnisschriften der Reformierten Kirche.* Leipzig: Deichert, 1903.

Müller, Hubert. "Communio als Kirchenrechtliches Prinzip im Codex Iuris Canonici von 1983?" In *Im Gespräch mit dem dreieinen Gott. Elemente einer trinitarischen Theologie. Festschrift zum 65. Geburtstag von Wilhelm Breuning,* 481-98. Düsseldorf: Patmos, 1985.

Mussner, Franz. *Der Galaterbrief.* Herders theologischer Kommentar zum Neuen Testament 9. Freiburg: Herder, 1974.

"Das Mysterium der Kirche und der Eucharistie im Lichte des Geheimnisses der Heiligen Dreieinigkeit: Erstes approbiertes Dokument der gemischten Kommission für den theologischen Dialog zwischen der römisch-katholischen und der orthodoxen Kirche." *Ökumenisches Forum* 5 (1982): 155-66.

Neale, Walter C. "Institution." *Journal of Economic Issues* 21 (1987): 1177-1206.

Nachtwei, Gerhard. *Dialogische Unsterblichkeit: Eine Untersuchung zu Joseph Ratzingers Eschatologie und Theologie.* Erfurter theologische Studien 54. Leipzig: St. Benno, 1986.

Newbigin, Lesslie. "What Is 'A Local Church Truly United'?" In *In Each Place: Towards a Fellowship of Local Churches Truly United,* 14-29. Geneva: World Council of Churches, 1977.

Nichols, Aidan. *The Theology of Joseph Ratzinger: An Introductory Study.* Edinburgh: Clark, 1988.

Niebuhr, H. Richard. "The Doctrine of the Trinity and the Unity of the Church." *Theology Today* 3 (1946/47): 371-84.

———. *The Responsible Self: An Essay in Christian Moral Philosophy.* New York: Harper & Row, 1963.

Nietzsche, Friedrich. *Zur Genealogie der Moral.* In *Werke: Kritische Gesamtausgabe 14/2.* Edited by G. Colli and M. Montinari. Berlin: de Gruyter, 1968.

Nissiotis, N. A. "Die qualitative Bedeutung der Katholizität." *Theologische Zeitschrift* 17 (1961): 259-80.

Nygren, Anders. *Christ and His Church.* Philadelphia: Westminster, 1956.

O'Brien, P. T. "The Church as a Heavenly and Eschatological Entity." In *The Church in the Bible and the World: An International Study,* edited by D. A. Carson, 88-119. Exeter: Paternoster, 1987.

O'Donnell, John. "Pannenberg's Doctrine of God." *Gregorianum* 72 (1991): 73-97.

———. "The Trinity as Divine Community: A Critical Reflection Upon recent Theological Developments." *Gregorianum* 69 (1988): 5-34.

Oeing-Hanhoff, Ludger. "Die Krise des Gottesbegriffs." *Theologische Quartalschrift* 159 (1979): 285-303.

Olson, Roger. "Trinity and Eschatology: The Historical Being of God in Jürgen Moltmann and Wolfhart Pannenberg." *Scottish Journal of Theology* 36 (1983): 213-27.

Palaver, Wolfgang. *Politik und Religion bei Thomas Hobbes: Eine Kritik aus der Sicht der Theorie René Girards.* Indian Theological Studies 33. Innsbruck: Tyrolia, 1991.

Panikkar, Raimundo. *The Trinity and World Religions: Icon-Person-Mystery.* Inter-Religious Dialogue 4. Madras: Christian Literature Society, 1970.

Pannenberg, Wolfhart. *Anthropologie in theologischer Perspektive.* Göttingen: Vandenhoeck & Ruprecht, 1983.

———. "Die Bedeutung der Eschatologie für das Verständnis der Apostolizität und Katholizität der Kirche." In *Katholizität und Apostolizität,* edited by R. Groscurth, 92-109. Kerygma und Dogma Beiheft 2. Göttingen: Vandenhoeck & Ruprecht, 1971.

———. "Der Gott der Geschichte: Der trinitarische Gott und die Wahrheit der Geschichte." In *Grundfragen Systematischer Theologie: Gesammelte Aufsätze.* Göttingen: Vandenhoeck & Ruprecht, 1980.

———. "Ökumenisches Amtsverständnis." In *Ethik und Ekklesiologie,* 219-40. Göttingen: Vandenhoeck & Ruprecht, 1977.

———. "Person und Subjekt." In *Grundfragen Systematischer Theologie: Gesammelte Aufsätze.* Göttingen: Vandenhoeck & Ruprecht, 1980.

———. "Reich Gottes, Kirche und Gesellschaft in der Sicht der systematischen Theologie." In *Christlicher Glaube in moderner Gesellschaft: Enzyklopädische Bibliothek in 30 Teilbanden,* edited by Franz Böckle et al., 29.119-35. Freiburg: Herder, 1982.

———. "Reich Gottes und Kirche." In *Theologie und Reich Gottes,* 31-61. Gütersloh: Mohn, 1971.

———. "Die Subjektivität Gottes und die Trinitätslehre: Ein Beitrag zur Beziehung zwischen Karl Barth und der Philosophie Hegels." In *Grundfragen Systematischer Theologie: Gesammelte Aufsätze*. Göttingen: Vandenhoeck & Ruprecht, 1980.

———. *Systematic Theology*. 3 vols. Grand Rapids: Eerdmans, 1991-97.

———. *Wissenschaftstheorie und Theologie*. Frankfurt: Suhrkamp, 1977.

Park, Heon-Wook. "Die Vorstellung vom Leib Christi bei Paulus." Diss., Tübingen, 1988.

Parsons, Talcott. *On Institutions and Social Evolution: Selected Writings*. Edited by L. H. Mayhew. Chicago: University of Chicago Press, 1982.

———. "Religion in Postindustrial America: The Problem of Secularization." In *Action Theory and the Human Condition*, 300-322. New York: Free Press, 1978.

———. *The Social System*. Glencoe, Ill.: Free Press, 1951.

Pelchat, Marc. Review of *Le Cardinal Ratzinger et la théologie contemporaine*, by Jacques Rollet. *Laval théologique et philosophique* 45 (1989): 322-24.

"Perspectives on Koinonia: Final Report of the International Roman Catholic/Pentecostal Dialogue (1985-89)." *Pneuma* 12 (1990): 117-42.

Pesch, Otto Hermann. "Das katholische Sakramentsverständnis im Urteil gegenwärtiger evangelischer Theologie." In *Verifikationen: Festschrift G. Ebeling,* edited by E. Jüngel et al., 317-40. Tübingen: Mohr-Siebeck, 1982.

———. *Theologie der Rechtfertigung bei Martin Luther und Thomas von Aquin: Versuch eines systematisch-theologischen Dialogs*. Walberger Studien 4. Mainz: Grünewald, 1967.

Peterson, Erik. "Der Monotheismus als politisches Problem." In *Theologische Traktate*, 45-147. Munich: Kösel, 1951.

Pirson, Dietrich. "Communio als Kirchenrechtliches Leitprinzip." *Zeitschrift für evangelisches Kirchenrecht* 29 (1984): 35-45.

Plank, Bernhard. *Katholizität und Sobornost: Ein Beitrag zum Verständnis der Kirche bei den russischen Theologen in der zweiten Hälfte des 19. Jahrhunderts*. Das östliche Christentum. Neue Folge 14. Würzburg: Augustinus, 1960.

Plantinga, Cornelius, Jr. "Images of God." In *Christian Faith and Practice in the Modern World: Theology from an Evangelical Point of View,* edited by M. A. Noll and D. F. Wells, 51-67. Grand Rapids: Eerdmans, 1988.

Polanyi, Michael. *The Tacit Dimension*. London: Routledge & Kegan Paul, 1966.

Porter, Stanley E. "Two Myths: Corporate Personality and Language/Mentality Determinism." *Scottish Journal of Theology* 43 (1990): 289-307.

Prestige, G. L. *God in Patristic Thought*. London: S.P.C.K., 1956.

Rahner, Karl. "Charisma." *Lexikon für Theologie und Kirche,* 2.1025-30. Freiburg: Herder, 1957-67.

———. "Kommentar zum Dritten Kapitel der Dogmatischen Konstitution über die Kirche (Art. 18-27)." In *Das Zweite Vatikanische Konzil: Dokumente und Kommentare. Lexikon für Theologie und Kirche,* 12.210-47. Freiburg: Herder, 1966-68.

Raiser, Konrad. "Ökumene vor neuen Zielen: Gespräch mit dem Theologen Konrad Raiser." *Evangelische Kommentare* 25 (1992): 412-16.

Ramsey, Paul. *Christian Ethics and the Sit-In*. New York: Abingdon, 1961.

Ratschow, Carl Heinz. "Amt/Ämter/Amtsverständnis VII." In *Theologische Realenzyklopädie*, 2.593-622. Berlin: de Gruyter, 1976-95.

Ratzinger, Joseph Cardinal. *Auf Christus Schauen: Einübung in Glaube, Hoffnung, Liebe*. Freiburg: Herder, 1989.

―――. "Buchstabe und Geist des Zweiten Vatikanums in den Konzilreden von Kardinal Frings." *Internationale Katholische Zeitschrift "Communio"* 16 (1987): 251-65.

―――. *Die christliche Brüderlichkeit.* Munich: Kösel, 1960.

―――. *Church, Ecumenism, and Politics: New Essays in Ecclesiology.* New York: Crossroad, 1988.

―――. "Demokratisierung der Kirche?" In *Demokratie in der Kirche: Möglichkeiten, Grenzen, Gefahren,* edited by J. Ratzinger and Hans Maier, 9-46. Werdende Welt 16. Limburg: Lahn, 1970.

―――. *Dogma and Preaching.* Chicago: Franciscan Herald, 1984.

―――. *Dogma und Verkündigung.* Munich: Wewel, 1973.

―――. "Dogmatische Konstitution über die Göttliche Offenbarung: Kommentar." *Lexikon für Theologie und Kirche,* 13.498-528, 571-81. Freiburg: Herder, 1957-67.

―――. "Ein Versuch zur Frage des Traditionsbegriffs." In *Offenbarung und Überlieferung,* by K. Rahner and J. Ratzinger, 25-69. Quaestiones Disputatae 25. Freiburg: Herder, 1965.

―――. *Introduction to Christianity.* London: Burns & Oates, 1969.

―――. *Eschatology, Death and Eternal Life.* Washington, D.C.: Catholic University of America Press, 1988.

―――. *The Feast of Faith: Approaches to a Theology of the Liturgy.* San Francisco: Ignatius, 1986.

―――. *Die Geschichtstheologie des Heiligen Bonaventura.* Munich: Schnell & Steiner, 1959.

―――. "Glaube, Geschichte und Philosophie: Zum Echo auf 'Einführung in das Christentum.'" *Hochland* 61 (1969): 533-43.

―――. "Glaubensvermittlung und Glaubensquellen." In *Die Krise der Kathechese und ihre Überwindung,* 13-39. Translated by H. Urs von Balthasar. Einsiedeln: Johannes, 1983.

―――. "Identifikation mit der Kirche." In *Mit der Kirche leben,* by J. Ratzinger and K. Lehmann, 13-40. Freiburg: Herder, 1977.

―――. "Kirche II, III." *Lexikon für Theologie und Kirche,* 6.172-83. Freiburg: Herder, 1957-67.

―――. "Leib Christi II. Dogmatisch." *Lexikon für Theologie und Kirche,* 6.910-12. Freiburg: Herder, 1957-67.

―――. "Die letzte Wurzel für den Hass gegen das menschliche Leben liegt im Verlust Gottes: Das Referat von Kardinal Joseph Ratzinger auf der Kardinalsversammlung." *Herder-Korrespondenz* 45 (1991): 223-27.

―――. "Liturgie und Kirchenmusik." *Internationale Katholische Zeitschrift "Communio"* 15 (1986): 242-56.

―――. *Das neue Volk Gottes: Entwürfe zur Ekklesiologie.* Düsseldorf: Patmos, 1969.

―――. "Pastorale Konstitution über die Kirche in der Welt von heute: Kommentar." *Lexikon für Theologie und Kirche,* 14.313-54. Freiburg: Herder, 1957-67.

―――. *Das Problem der Dogmengeschichte in Sicht der katholischen Theologie.* Cologne: Westdeutscher Verlag, 1966.

―――. *The Ratzinger Report: An Exclusive Interview on the State of the Church. Joseph Cardinal Ratzinger with Vittorio Messori.* San Francisco: Ignatius, 1985.

―――. *Die sakramentale Begründung christlicher Existenz.* 4th ed. Freising: Kyrios, 1973.

————. *Schauen auf den Durchbohrten: Versuche zu einer spirituellen Christologie.* Einsiedeln: Johannes, 1984.

————. "Schriftauslegung im Widerstreit: Zur Frage nach Grundlagen und Weg der Exegese heute." In *Schriftauslegung im Widerstreit,* edited by J. Ratzinger, 15-44. Quaestiones Disputatae 117. Freiburg: Herder, 1989.

————. "Theologie und Kirche." *Internationale Katholische Zeitschrift "Communio"* 15 (1986): 515-33.

————. *Theologische Prinzipienlehre: Bausteine zur Fundamentaltheologie.* Munich: Erich Wewel, 1982.

————. *Volk und Haus Gottes in Augustins Lehre von der Kirche.* Münchener theologische Studien 2/7. Munich: Zink, 1954.

————. "Vorwort." In *Schriftauslegung im Widerstreit,* edited by J. Ratzinger, 7-13. Freiburg: Herder, 1989.

————. "Warum ich noch in der Kirche bin." In *Zwei Plädoyers,* by H. Urs von Balthasar and J. Ratzinger, 57-75. Munich: Kösel, 1971.

————. *Zum Begriff des Sakramentes.* Eichstätter Hochschulreden 15. Munich: Minerva, 1979.

————. "Zur Frage der bleibenden Gültigkeit dogmatischer Formeln: These X-XII. Kommentar von Joseph Ratzinger." In *Die Einheit des Glaubens und der Theologische Pluralismus: Internationale Theologenkommission,* 36-42. Einsiedeln: Johannes, 1973.

————. *Zur Gemeinschaft gerufen: Kirche heute verstehen.* Freiburg: Herder, 1991.

"Re-envisioning Baptist Identity: A Manifesto for Baptist Communities in America." *Baptist Today* 15 (October 1997): 8-10.

Reid, J. K. S. "The Ratzinger Report." *Scottish Journal of Theology* 40 (1987): 125-33.

Ridderbos, Hermann. *Paul: An Outline of His Theology.* Grand Rapids: Eerdmans, 1975.

Robinson, H. Wheeler. *The Christian Doctrine of Man.* 3rd ed. Edinburgh: Clark, 1952.

————. *Corporate Personality in Ancient Israel.* Rev. ed. Philadelphia: Fortress, 1980.

Robinson, John. A. T. *Body: A Study in Pauline Theology.* Studies in Biblical Theology 1/5. London: SCM, 1952.

Rogerson, J. W. "The Hebrew Conception of Corporate Personality: A Re-examination." *Journal of Theological Studies* 21 (1970): 1-16.

Rollet, Jacques. *Le cardinal Ratzinger et la théologie contemporaine.* Paris: Cerf, 1987.

Roloff, Jürgen. "ἐχχλησία." *Exegetical Dictionary of the New Testament,* 1.410-15. Grand Rapids: Eerdmans, 1990-93.

Roof, Wade Clark, and William McKinney. *American Mainline Religion: Its Changing Shape and Future.* New Brunswick, N.J.: Rutgers University Press, 1987.

Russell, Letty M. *Church in the Round: Feminist Interpretation of the Church.* Louisville: Westminster/John Knox, 1993.

Schäfer, Klaus. *Gemeinde als "Bruderschaft": Ein Beitrag zum Kirchenverständnis des Paulus.* Europäische Hochschulschriften. Theologie 23/333. Frankfurt: Lang, 1989.

Schegler, Albert. *Die Metaphysik des Aristoteles: Grundtext, Übersetzung und Kommentar.* 3 vols. Frankfurt: Minerva, 1960.

Schillebeeckx, Edward C. *Christliche Identität und kirchliches Amt: Plädoyer für den Menschen in der Kirche.* Translated by H. Zulauf. Düsseldorf: Patmos, 1985.

————. *Menschen: Die Geschichte von Gott.* Translated by H. Zulauf. Freiburg: Herder, 1990.

Schleiermacher, Friedrich. *The Christian Faith*. Edinburgh: Clark, 1928.

Schlier, Heinrich. *Der Brief an die Galater*. Kritisch-exegetischer Kommentar über das Neue Testament. 5th ed. Göttingen: Vandenhoeck & Ruprecht, 1971.

―――. "Die Einheit der Kirche nach dem Neuen Testament." *Catholica* (Münster) 14 (1960): 161-77.

Schlink, Edmund. *Ökumenische Dogmatik: Grundzüge*. Göttingen: Vandenhoeck & Ruprecht, 1983.

Schmitz, Herman-Josef. *Frühkatholizismus bei Adolf von Harnack, Rudolph Sohm und Ernst Käsemann*. Themen und Thesen der Theologie. Düsseldorf: Patmos, 1977.

Schnackenburg, Rudolf. *Der Brief an die Epheser*. Evangelisch-katholischer Kommentar zum Neuen Testament 10. Zurich: Benziger, 1982.

Schoonenberg, Piet. "Trinität — der vollendete Bund: Thesen zur Lehre vom dreipersönlichen Gott." *Orientierung* 37 (1973): 115-17.

Schweizer, Eduard. "Konzeptionen von Charisma und Amt im Neuen Testament." In *Charisma und Institution*, edited by T. Rendtorff, 316-49. Gütersloh: Mohn, 1985.

―――. "σῶμα." *Exegetical Dictionary of the New Testament*, 3.321-25. Grand Rapids: Eerdmans, 1990-93.

Schwöbel, Christoph. "Particularity, Universality, and the Religions: Toward a Christian Theology of Religions." In *Christian Uniqueness Reconsidered: The Myth of a Pluralistic Theology of Religions*, edited by G. D'Costa, 30-46. Faith Meets Faith. Maryknoll, N.Y.: Orbis, 1990.

Scroggs, Robin. "The Earliest Christian Communities as Sectarian Movement." In *Christianity, Judaism and Other Greco-Roman Cults: Studies for Morton Smith at Sixty*, edited by J. Neusner, 1-23. Studies in Judaism in Late Antiquity 12. Leiden: Brill, 1975.

Shantz, Douglas. "The Place of the Resurrected Christ in the Writings of John Smyth." *Baptist Quarterly* 30 (1984): 199-203.

Siebel, Wiegand. *Der Heilige Geist als Relation: Eine soziale Trinitätslehre*. Münster: Aschendorff, 1986.

Smyth, John. *The Works of John Smyth*. Edited by W. T. Whitley. Cambridge: Cambridge University Press, 1915.

Sohm, Rudolph. *Kirchenrecht*. 2d ed. Systematisches Handbuch der Deutschen Rechtswissenschaft 8. Berlin: von Duncker & Humbolt, 1923.

―――. *Wesen und Ursprung des Katholizismus*. 2d ed. Leipzig: Teubner, 1912.

Stallsworth, Paul T. "The Story of an Encounter." In *Biblical Interpretation in Crisis: The Ratzinger Conference on Bible and Church*, edited by R. J. Neuhaus, 102-90. Encounter Series 9. Grand Rapids: Eerdmans, 1989.

Staniloae, Dumitru. *Orthodoxe Dogmatik*. Translated by H. Pitters. Ökumenische Theologie 12/15. Einsiedeln: Benziger, 1984-.

―――. "Trinitarian Relations and the Life of the Church." In *Theology and the Church*, 11-44. Translated by Robert Barringer. Crestwood, N.Y.: St. Vladimir's Seminary Press, 1980.

Steinacker, Peter. "Katholizität." In *Theologische Realenzyklopädie*, 18.72-80. Berlin: Walter de Gruyter, 1989.

―――. *Die Kennzeichen der Kirche: Eine Studie zu ihrer Einheit, Heiligkeit, Katholizität und Apostolizität*. Berlin: de Gruyter, 1982.

BIBLIOGRAPHY

Stoll, David. *Is Latin America Turning Protestant? The Politics of Evangelical Growth.* Berkeley: University of California Press, 1990.

Stormon, J. E., ed. and trans. *Towards the Healing of Schism: The Sees of Rome and Constantinople. Public Statements and Correspondence between the Holy See and the Ecumenical Patriarchate, 1958-1984.* Ecumenical Documents 3. New York: Paulist, 1987.

Strong, Augustus Hopkins. *Systematic Theology: A Compendium Designed for the Use of Theological Students.* Old Tappan, N.J.: Revell, 1907.

Studer, Basil. "Der Person-Begriff in der frühen kirchenamtlichen Trinitätslehre." *Theologie und Philosophie* 57 (1982): 161-77.

Stuhlmacher, Peter. *Der Brief an Philemon. Evangelisch-katholischer Kommentar zum Neuen Testament 18.* Zurich: Benziger, 1981.

————. *Gerechtigkeit Gottes bei Paulus.* 2d ed. Göttingen: Vandenhoeck & Ruprecht, 1966.

————. "Volkskirche — weiter so?" *Theologische Beiträge* 23 (1992): 151-70.

Suchocki, Marjorie Hewitt. *God, Christ, Church: A Practical Guide to Process Theology.* Rev. ed. New York: Crossroad, 1993.

Sullivan, Francis A. *The Church We Believe In: One, Holy, Catholic and Apostolic.* New York: Paulist, 1988.

Thomas Aquinas: Summa Theologiae. Taurini: Marietti, 1952-56.

Thils, Gustave. *En dialogue avec l' "Entretien sur la foi."* Louvain-la-Neuve: Peeters, 1986.

Thurian, M., ed. *Churches Respond to BEM: Official Responses to the "Baptism, Eucharist and Ministry" Text.* Faith and Order Papers 132. Geneva: World Council of Churches, 1986.

Tillich, Paul. *Systematic Theology.* Chicago: University of Chicago Press, 1967.

Tönnies, Ferdinand. *Community and Society.* New York, 1963.

————. *Gemeinschaft und Gesellschaft: Grundbegriffe der reinen Soziologie.* 2d ed. Berlin: Curtius, 1912.

Troeltsch, Ernst. *Die Soziallehren der christlichen Kirchen.* Tübingen: Mohr, 1912.

Turner, Max. "The Ecclesiologies of the Major 'Apostolic' Restorationist Churches in the United Kingdom." Unpublished.

Unitatis redintegratio. In *Das Zweite Vatikanische Konzil: Dokumente und Kommentare. Lexikon für Theologie und Kirche,* 13.11-126. Freiburg: Herder, 1966-68.

Veenhof, Jan. "Charismata — Supernatural or Natural?" In *The Holy Spirit: Renewing and Empowering Presence,* edited by G. Vandervelde, 73-91. Winfield: Wood Lake, 1989.

Vischer, Lukas. "Schwierigkeiten bei der Befragung des Neuen Testaments." In *Sie aber hielten fest an der Gemeinschaft: Einheit der Kirche als Prozess im Neuen Testament und heute,* by Christian Link, Ulrich Luz, and Lukas Vischer, 17-40. Zurich: Benziger, 1988.

Volf, Miroslav. "Arbeit und Charisma: Zu einer Theologie der Arbeit." *Zeitschrift für evangelische Ethik* 31 (1987): 411-33.

————. "Christliche Identität und Differenz: Zur Eigenart der christlichen Präsenz in den modernen Gesellschaften." *Zeitschrift für Theologie und Kirche* 92/3 (1995): 356-374.

————. "The Church as a Prophetic Community and a Sign of Hope." *European Journal of Theology* 2 (1993): 9-30.

————. "Demokratie und Charisma: Reflexion über die Demokratisierung der Kirche." *Concilium* (Einsiedeln) 28 (1992): 430-34.

————. *Exclusion and Embrace: A Theological Exploration of Identity, Otherness, and Reconciliation.* Nashville: Abingdon, 1996.

————. "Die Herausforderung des protestantischen Fundamentalismus." *Concilium* (Einsiedeln) 18 (1992): 261-68.

————. "Justice, Exclusion, and Difference." *Synthesis Philosophica* 9 (1994): 455-76.

————. "Kirche als Gemeinschaft: Ekklesiologische Überlegungen aus freikirchlicher Perspektive." *Evangelische Theologie* 49 (1989): 52-76.

————. "O kognitivnoj dimenziji religijskog govora. Teoloske opaske uz Susnjicevu knjigu 'Znati i verovati.' " *Crkva u svijetu* 24 (1989): 314-20.

————. "Soft Difference: Theological Reflections on the Relation between Church and Culture in 1 Peter." *Ex Auditu* 10 (1994): 15-30.

————. " 'The Trinity Is Our Social Program': The Doctrine of the Trinity and the Shape of Social Engagement." *Modern Theology* 14 (1998): forthcoming.

————. "When Gospel and Culture Intersect: Notes on the Nature of Christian Difference." In *Pentecostalism in Context: Essays in Honor of William W. Menzies*, edited by Wonsuk Ma and Robert P. Menzies, 223-36. Sheffield: Sheffield Academic Press, 1997.

————. "When the Unclean Spirit Leaves: Tasks of the Eastern European Churches after the 1989 Revolution." *Cross Currents* 41 (1991): 78-92.

————. *Work in the Spirit: Toward a Theology of Work.* New York: Oxford University Press, 1991.

————. "Worship as Adoration and Action: Reflections on a Christian Way of Being-in-the-World." In *Worship: Adoration and Action*, edited by D. A. Carson, 203-11. Grand Rapids: Baker Book House, 1993.

————. *Zukunft der Arbeit — Arbeit der Zukunft: Das Marxsche Verständnis der Arbeit und seine theologische Wertung.* Fundamentaltheologische Studien 14. Munich: Kaiser, 1987.

Wainwright, Arthur W. *The Trinity in the New Testament.* London: S.P.C.K., 1962.

Walker, Andrew. *Restoring the Kingdom: The Radical Christianity of the House Church Movement.* London: Hodder and Stoughton, 1985.

Walls, Andrew F. *The Missionary Movement in Christian History: Studies in the Transmission of Faith.* Maryknoll, N.Y.: Orbis, 1996.

Walton, Robert G. *The Gathered Community.* London: Carey, 1946.

Warner, R. Stephen. "The Place of the Congregation in the Contemporary American Religious Configuration." In *American Congregations: New Perspectives in the Study of Congregations*, edited by J. P. Wind and J. W. Lewis, 2.502-24. 2 vols. Chicago: University of Chicago Press, 1994.

Weber, Max. "Die protestantischen Sekten und der Geist des Kapitalismus." In *Gesammelte Aufsätze zur Religionssoziologie*, 207-36. Tübingen: Mohr-Siebeck, 1947.

Weber, Otto. *Versammelte Gemeinde: Beiträge zum Gespräch über die Kirche und Gottesdienst.* Neukirchen: Buchhandlung des Erziehungsvereins, 1949.

Weir, Allison. *Sacrificial Logics: Feminist Theory and the Critique of Identity.* New York: Routledge, 1996.

Welker, Michael. *Gottes Geist: Theologie des Heiligen Geistes.* Neukirchen-Vluyn: Neukirchener Verlag, 1992. English translation, *God the Spirit.* Translated by John F. Hoffmeyer. Minneapolis: Fortress, 1994.

————. *Kirche im Pluralismus.* Kaiser Taschenbücher 136. Gütersloh: Kaiser, 1995.

————. *Kirche ohne Kurs? Aus Anlass der EKD-Studie "Christsein Gestalten."* Neukirchen-Vluyn: Neukirchener Verlag, 1987.

————. *Universalität Gottes und Relativität der Welt: Theologische Kosmologie im Dialog mit dem amerikanischen Prozeßdenken nach Whitehead.* Neukirchen-Vluyn: Neukirchener Verlag, 1981.

Wells, David F. *God in the Wasteland: The Reality of Truth in a World of Fading Dreams.* Grand Rapids: Eerdmans, 1994.

Wendebourg, Dorothea. "Person und Hypostase: Zur Trinitätslehre der neueren orthodoxen Theologie." In *Vernunft des Glaubens: Wissenschaftliche Theologie und kirchliche Lehre. Festschrift zum 60. Geburtstag von Wolfhart Pannenberg,* edited by J. Rohls and G. Wenz, 502-24. Göttingen: Vandenhoeck & Ruprecht, 1988.

Westermann, Claus. *Schöpfung.* Themen der Theologie 12. Stuttgart: Kreuz, 1971.

White, R. B. *The English Separatist Tradition: From the Marian Martyrs to the Pilgrim Fathers.* Oxford Theological Monographs. Oxford: Oxford University Press, 1971.

Whitehead, Alfred North. *Process and Reality: An Essay in Cosmology.* New York: Macmillan, 1929.

Whitehead, James D., and Evelyn Eaton Whitehead. *The Emerging Laity: Returning Leadership to the Community of Faith.* Garden City, N.Y.: Doubleday, 1986.

Wilckens, Ulrich. *Der Brief an die Römer.* Evangelisch-katholischer Kommentar zum Neuen Testament 6/1-3. Zurich: Benziger, 1979-82.

Williams, George Huntston. "Believers' Church and the Given Church." In *The People of God: Essays on the Believer's Church,* edited by Paul Basden and David S. Dockery, 325-32. Nashville: Broadman, 1991.

Williams, James. "Znacaj rukopolaganja za sluzbe u crkvi." *Bogoslovska smotra* 12 (1984): 55-72.

Williams, Rowan. Review of *Being as Communion: Studies in Personhood and the Church,* by John D. Zizioulas. *Scottish Journal of Theology* 42 (1989): 101-5.

————. "Trinity and Pluralism." In *Christian Uniqueness Reconsidered: The Myth of a Pluralistic Theology of Religions,* edited by G. D'Costa, 3-15. Faith Meets Faith. Maryknoll, N.Y.: Orbis, 1990.

Wilson, Everett A. "Evangelization and Culture: A Paradigm of Latin American Pentecostalism." Paper presented at the International Roman Catholic–Pentecostal Dialogue, Castel Gondolfo, June 1992.

Wind, James P. and James W. Lewis, eds. *American Congregations.* Chicago: The University of Chicago Press, 1994.

Wittgenstein, Ludwig. *Philosophische Untersuchungen.* 3rd ed. Frankfurt: Suhrkamp, 1975.

Wolf, Erik. *Rechtsgedanke und Biblische Weisung: Drei Vorträge.* Tübingen: Furche, 1948.

Wolff, Christian. *Der zweite Brief des Paulus an die Korinther.* Theologischer Handkommentar zum Neuen Testament 8. Berlin: Evangelische Verlagsanstalt, 1989.

Wolff, Hans Walter. "Prophet und Institution im Alten Testament." In *Charisma und Institution,* edited by T. Rendtorff, 87-101. Gütersloh: Mohn, 1985.

Wolterstorff, Nicholas. *Until Justice and Peace Embrace: The Kuyper Lectures for 1981.* Grand Rapids: Eerdmans, 1983.

————. "Christianity and Social Justice." *Christian Scholar's Review* 16 (1987): 211-28.

Wuthnow, Robert. *The Restructuring of the American Religion: Society and Faith since World War II.* Princeton: Princeton University Press, 1988.

Yorke, Gosnell L. O. R. *The Church as the Body of Christ in the Pauline Corpus: A Re-examination.* Lanham, Md.: University Press of America, 1991.

Zaret, David. *Heavenly Contract: Ideology and Organization in Pre-revolutionary Puritanism.* Chicago: University of Chicago Press, 1985.

Zizioulas, John D. *Being as Communion: Studies in Personhood and the Church.* Crestwood, N.Y.: St. Vladimir's Seminary Press, 1985.

————. "The Bishop in the Theological Doctrine of the Orthodox Church." *Kanon* 7 (1985): 23-35.

————. "Christologie et existence: La dialectique créé-incréé et la dogme de Chalcédoine." *Contacts* 36 (1984): 154-72.

————. "Les conférences épiscopales comme institution causa nostra agitur?" In *Les conférences épiscopales: Theologie, Statut cononique, avenir,* edited by H. Legrand, J. Manzanares, and A. García y García, 499-508. Cogitatio fidei 149. Paris: Cerf, 1988.

————. "The Contribution of Cappadocia to Christian Thought." In *Sinasos in Cappadocia,* 23-37. London: Ekdoseis Agra, 1985.

————. "Déplacement de la perspective eschatologique." In *La chrétienté en débat: Histoire, formes et problèmes actuels,* 89-100. Paris: Cerf, 1984.

————. "The Early Christian Community." In *Christian Spirituality: Origins to the Twelfth Century,* edited by B. McGinn and J. Meyendorff, 23-43. World Spirituality 16. New York: Crossroad, 1985.

————. "The Ecclesiological Presuppositions of the Holy Eucharist." *Nicolaus* 10 (1982): 333-49.

————. Ἡ ἑνότης τῆς Ἐκκλησίας ἐν τῇ Θεία Εὐχαριστία καὶ τῷ Ἐπισκόπῳ κατὰ τοὺς τρεῖς πρώτους αἰῶνας. Athens, 1965.

————. "Die Entwicklung Konziliarer Strukturen bis zur Zeit des ersten ökumenischen Konzils." In *Konzile und die ökumenische Bewegung,* 34-52. Studien des Ökumenischen Rates 5. Geneva: ÖRK, 1968.

————. "Episkope and Episkopos in the Early Church: A Brief Survey of the Evidence." In *Episcopé and Episcopate in Ecumenical Perspective.* Faith and Order Papers 102. Geneva: World Council of Churches, 1980.

————. *L'être ecclésial.* Perspective orthodoxe 3. Geneva: Labor et fides, 1981.

————. "Die Eucharistie in der neuzeitlichen orthodoxen Theologie." In *Die Anrufung des Heiligen Geistes im Abendmahl,* 163-79. Ökumenische Rundschau Beiheft 31. Frankfurt: Limbeck, 1977.

————. "L'eucharistie: quelques aspects bibliques." In *L'eucharistie,* by J. Zizioulas, J. M. R. Tillard, and J. J. von Allmen, 11-74. Églises en Dialogue 12. Paris: Mame, 1970.

————. "Die eucharistische Grundlage des Amtes." In *Philoxenia,* edited by R. Thöle and I. Friedeberg, 2.66-78. Fürth: Flacius, 1986.

————. "Les groupes informels dans l'Église: Un point de vue orthodoxe." In *Les groupes informels dans l'Église,* edited by R. Metz and J. Schlick, 251-72. Hommes et église 2. Strasbourg: Cerdic, 1971.

————. "Human Capacity and Human Incapacity: A Theological Exploration of Personhood." *Scottish Journal of Theology* 28 (1975): 401-47.

————. "Implications ecclésiologiques de deux types de pneumatologie." In *Communio Sanctorum: Mélanges offerts à Jean-Jacques von Allmen*, 141-54. Geneva: Labor et fides, 1982.

————. "La Mystère de l'Église dans la tradition orthodoxe." *Irénikon* 60 (1987): 321-35.

————. "The Nature of the Unity We Seek: Response of the Orthodox Observer." *One in Christ* 24 (1988): 342-48.

————. "On Being a Person: Towards an Ontology of Personhood." In *Persons, Divine and Human: King's College Essays in Theological Anthropology*, edited by C. Schwö-bel and C. E. Gunton, 33-46. Edinburgh: Clark, 1991.

————. "L'ordination est-elle un sacrement?" *Concilium* (Paris) 74 (1972): 41-47.

————. "Ordination et communion." *Istina* 16 (1971): 5-12.

————. "Die pneumatologische Dimension der Kirche." *Internationale Katholische Zeit-schrift "Communio"* 2 (1973): 133-47.

————. "La relation de l'hellenisme et du christianisme et le problème de la mort — La réponse de Jean Zizioulas." *Contacts* 37 (1985): 60-72.

————. "Some Reflections on Baptism, Confirmation and Eucharist." *Sobornost* 5 (1969): 644-62.

————. "The Teaching of the Second Ecumenical Council on the Holy Spirit in Historical and Ecumenical Perspective." In *Credo in Spiritum Sanctum: Atti del congresso teologico internationale di pneumatologia*, 29-54. Vatican: Libreria Editrice Vaticana, 1983.

————. "The Theological Problem of 'Reception.'" *Bulletin of the Centro pro Unione* 26 (Fall 1984): 3-6.

————. "Wahrheit und Gemeinschaft in der Sicht der griechischen Kirchenväter." *Kerygma und Dogma* 26 (1980): 2-49.

————. "Die Welt in eucharistischer Schau und der Mensch von heute." *Una Sancta* 25 (1970): 342-49.

Index

Afanassieff, Nicolas, 73
Ainsworth, Henry, 10
"already" and "not yet," 100-101
Althaus, Paul, 147n.81
Anabaptists, 132n.19
analogy, 198-200
Anglican-Catholic Consensus Documents, 45n.94
anima ecclesiastica, 37, 53, 66, 281
anthropology, 198
anticipation, 140-41, 267-69
apostolic succession, 117, 119, 122, 133, 260
apostolic tradition, 275-76
Aristotle, 193, 212n.94, 261, 277
assensus, 170
Assmann, Jan, 133n.25
association, church as, 15, 179-81
Augustine, 29n.4, 30, 31, 48, 57, 62, 71, 99n.148, 141, 186, 205, 208, 214n.100, 237
authoritarianism, 3

Baillargeon, Gaëtan, 23n.60, 91n.99, 102n.161, 116n.230
Balthasar, Hans Urs von, 279
baptism, 42, 152-54, 177, 185, 199
  infant, 180n.107
  as ordination, 113-14

and priesthood of believers, 246
  as Trinitarian event, 195
  Zizioulas on, 88-91
Baptism, Eucharist, and Ministry (BEM), 20, 221-22, 228n.28, 247
Baptists, 16-17, 225
Barrett, C. K., 167
Barth, Hans-Martin, 221n.1, 225n.13
Barth, Karl, 19, 261
Baumert, Norbert, 226n.18
Beinert, Wolfgang, 269
Bentham, Jeremy, 178
Berger, Peter L., 5, 234
Bible:
  and catholicity, 266
  and church, 50-52
  infallibility, 52
  and tradition, 165n.38
Biedermann, Hermenegild, 201, 202n.52
Bilezikian, Gilbert, 6
bipolarity, 217, 224, 231
bishop(s), 55-58, 60, 107, 109-13, 132, 133, 156, 215, 217, 219, 224, 240, 250
  as *alter Christus*, 117
  collegiality of, 122
  equality of, 118
  and laity, 114-16
  office of, 117-22, 130-31
bishop of Rome. *See* Pope

307

INDEX

Bobrinskoy, Boris, 195n.23
body of Christ, 47, 99, 103n.164, 142-44
Boff, Leonardo, 193n.14
Bonhoeffer, Dietrich, 174, 178n.97, 180
Brachlow, Stephen, 133n.26
Brockhaus, Ulrich, 229n.31, 233n.53
Brunner, Emil, 174

calling, 226, 233
Calvin, John, 164n.29, 172
Calvinism, 153
Campenhausen, Hans von, 149n.87
Cappadocians, 75, 76
Catholic Church, 4, 130-31, 159
    catholicity, 260
    congregationalization, 12
catholicity:
    and eschatology, 266-69
    external marks, 274-76
    as fullness of salvation, 266
    and Holy Spirit, 281-82
    of persons, 278-82
    quantitative understanding, 265-66
    and universal openness, 106, 278
charismata, 63n.182, 115, 223, 225-26,
    228-33, 236, 243
    as institutions, 240-41
    interactive bestowal, 233
    interdependence, 231
    and law, 240-45
    and office, 232, 246, 248, 251
    universal distribution, 229-30
charismatic groups, 12
Chemnitz, Martin, 265
Christus totus, 34, 46, 51, 59-61, 62,
    99n.148, 141, 144n.68, 164, 223, 281
church:
    apostolicity, 122
    as assembly, 137-38, 145
    as association, 179-81
    and Bible, 50-52
    bipolar understanding, 225n.11
    catholicity, 103-4, 118, 122
    as commodity, 14, 18
    conciliarity, 122
    enculturation, 4, 239, 254
    eschatological character, 128, 138-41,

156-57, 181, 195, 199, 203, 238, 240,
    257
    and Eucharist, 99
    formalization, 238
    identification with Christ, 100-101
    as institution, 234-38
    locality, 103-4
    as means of grace, 174-75
    and mediation of faith, 36-38, 160-68
    monistic structure, 71
    as mother, 91, 162-68, 175, 180
    openness toward other churches, 155-57
    and presence of Christ and Spirit, 129-
    30
    relationship to Trinity, 196-97
    sacramentality, 164n.29
    and salvation, 172-75
    as sibling fellowship, 175, 180-81
    as social organism, 179-81
    as subject, 223
    as tradition bearer, 49
    as voluntary association, 175-76
    and world, 158
    See also local church, universal church
Church Growth movement, 277
church law, 238-39, 240-45
church members, 172
    and election of officers, 255-56
Church of South India, 227n.24
clericalism, 194
cognition, 92
cohesion, 236
collectivism, 159
commitment, 147-48
commodity, church as, 14, 18
communion, 35, 44, 145, 147, 163, 172,
    176-77
    and catholicity, 212
    and personhood, 77-80, 106
communion (sacrament). *See* Eucharist
communism, 237n.73
community, 11, 179
    and individual, 37
    and sacraments, 39-41
    and truth, 52-53, 54-55
confederation, of local churches, 107
confession of faith, 148-54, 163, 166, 248

308

INDEX